RETAIL BUYING

Retail Buying

From Basics to Fashion
Third Edition

Richard Clodfelter
University of South Carolina

Fairchild Books, Inc.
New York

Director of Sales and Acquisitions: Dana Meltzer-Berkowitz
Executive Editor: Olga T. Kontzias
Acquisitions Editor: Jaclyn Bergeron
Senior Development Editor: Jennifer Crane
Art Director: Adam B. Bohannon
Production Director: Ginger Hillman
Associate Art Director: Erin Fitzsimmons
Senior Production Editor: Elizabeth Marotta
Project Manager: Patricia Shogren
Copyeditor: GEX Publishing Services
Cover Design: Adam B. Bohannon
Text Design: Charles B. Hames
Layout: Jack Donner

Second Printing, 2008

Library of Congress Catalog Card Number: 2007940933

ISBN: 978-1-56367-703-8

GST R 133004424

Printed in the United States of America

TP08

Contents

Extended Contents vii
Preface xxiii
Acknowledgments xxvii

PART I Understanding the Retail Environment Where
        Buying Occurs 1

Chapter 1 Today's Buying Environment 3
Chapter 2 The Buying Function in Retailing 37
Chapter 3 Buying for Different Types of Stores 67

PART II Getting Ready to Make Buying Decisions 93

Chapter 4 Obtaining Assistance for Making Buying
           Decisions 95
Chapter 5 Understanding Your Customers 127
Chapter 6 Understanding Product Trends: What Customers
           Buy 155

Part III Planning and Controlling Merchandise
          Purchases 189

Chapter 7 Forecasting 191
Chapter 8 Preparing Buying Plans 221
Chapter 9 Developing Assortment Plans 249
Chapter 10 Controlling Inventories 277

PART IV   Purchasing Merchandise   305

Chapter 11   Selecting Vendors and Building Partnerships   307
Chapter 12   Locating Sources in Foreign Markets   333
Chapter 13   Making Market Visits and Negotiating with
             Vendors   361
Chapter 14   Making the Purchase   393

PART V   Motivating Customers to Buy   419

Chapter 15   Pricing the Merchandise   421
Chapter 16   Promoting the Merchandise   445

             Appendix A   471
             Appendix B   473
             Glossary   477
             Index   491
             Credits   513

Extended Contents

Preface   xxiii
Acknowledgments   xxvii

**PART I   Understanding the Retail Environment
Where Buying Occurs   1**

Chapter 1   Today's Buying Environment   3

Introduction   4

A Marketing Orientation   5
  Developing a Consumer Orientation   5
  Positioning a Retail Store   6
  Targeting Consumers   6
  Types of Target Marketing   9

Emerging and Growing Retail Formats: Where Will
  Consumers Make Purchases?   10
  Direct Marketing   11
  Electronic Retailing   13
  Superstore Retailing   18

Trends and Challenges Facing Retailers   20
  Too Many Stores   21
  *Increasing Consolidation and Shakeouts in
     Retailing*   21
  Marketing to Smaller Niches   22

Rapid Globalization 23
*Increased Customer Demand for Value and
    Service* 23
Customers Are Changing, Too 25
Growing Use of Database-Driven Marketing 26
Spreading Use of Technology 27
Other Trends and Challenges 27

Summary Points 28

Review Activities 29
Developing Your Retail Buying Vocabulary 29
Understanding What You Read 29
Analyzing and Applying What You Read 30
Internet Connection 30

SNAPSHOT: LandsEnd.com: From Catalog to Online
    Sales 31

SNAPSHOT: Lowe's Continues to Grow 32

TRENDWATCH: Targeting Current Customers 34

Chapter 2 The Buying Function in Retailing 37

The Buyer's Job 38
*Factors Affecting the Scope of the Buyer's
    Job* 39
The Buyer's Job: Duties and Responsibilities 41
Role of Assistant Buyers 42
Changing Role of the Buyer 43

Managing the Buying Function 45
Role of the Merchandise Manager 45
Evaluating Buyers' Performance 46

Planning for a Buying Career 47
Qualifications Needed 47
Career Paths 51
Employment Forecasts 56
Getting a Job As a Buyer 57

Summary Points 59

Review Activities   60
  Developing Your Retail Buying Vocabulary   60
  Understanding What You Read   60
  Analyzing and Applying What You Read   61
  Spreadsheet Skills   61
  Internet Connection   61

SNAPSHOT: The Macy's Internship Program: Starting
        Your Career   62

SNAPSHOT: AllRetailJobs.com: Using the Internet to
        Locate Merchandising Positions   63

TRENDWATCH: Today's Buyer   65

Chapter 3 Buying for Different Types of Stores   67

Buying Different Types of Products   68

Buying at Different Retail Formats   70
  Department Stores   71
  Discount Department Stores   72
  Outlet Stores   73
  Specialty Stores   74
  Supermarkets   74

Buying for Chain Stores   75
  Centralized Buying   76
  Types of Centralized Buying   76
  Drawbacks of Centralized Buying   78

Organizational Structure and the Buying
    Function   79
  Types of Departmentalization   79
  *Relationship of Merchandising to Other
      Departments*   82

Buying for Your Own Store   83

Summary Points   85

Review Activities   86
  Developing Your Retail Buying Vocabulary   86
  Understanding What You Read   86

Analyzing and Applying What You Read 87
Internet Connection 87

SNAPSHOT: Kohl's: A Department Store with a
Discount-Store Strategy 87

SNAPSHOT: The Future of the Department Store
89

TRENDWATCH: Is Bigger Really Better? Will the
Small Independent Retailer
Survive? 90

PART II   Getting Ready to Make Buying Decisions   93

Chapter 4   Obtaining Assistance for Making Buying
Decisions   95

Marketing Research   96
Using Marketing Research   96
Collecting Data   98
Analyzing and Interpreting Data   99

Internal Sources   100
Store Records   100
Management   101
Sales Associates   102

External Sources   103
Customers   103
Magazines and Trade Publications   105
Vendors   106
Trade Associations   106
Comparison Shoppers   106
Fashion Forecasters   107
Reporting Services   108
The Internet   108
Buying Offices   109

Buying Offices   109
Purpose and Importance   109
Services Provided by Buying Offices   111
Types of Buying Offices   113

Selecting a Buying Office 114
Trends Influencing Buying Offices 116

Summary Points 117

Review Activities 118
Developing Your Retail Buying Vocabulary 118
Understanding What You Read 118
Analyzing and Applying What You Read 119
Internet Connection 120

SNAPSHOT: Talbots: Committed to Marketing
Research 120

TRENDWATCH: Loyalty Cards: How Can They
Benefit Retail Buyers? 122

TRENDWATCH: Using Different Retail Formats to
Appeal to Diverse Customers in the
Same Market 124

Chapter 5 Understanding Your Customers 127

Introduction 128

Identifying Changes in Consumer Markets 130
*Demographic and Consumer Behavior
Trends* 131
Lifestyle Trends 134

Understanding Why Consumers Buy 136
Rational Buying Motives 137
Emotional Buying Motives 138
Patronage Buying Motives 138

Learning About Your Current Customers 139
Data Warehousing 139
Data Mining 141
Database Marketing 143

Summary Points 147

Review Activities 148
Developing Your Retail Buying Vocabulary 148
Understanding What You Read 148

Analyzing and Applying What You Read 149
Internet Connection 149

SNAPSHOT: Trends and Countertrends: Can Buyers
Predict What Customers Want? 150

TRENDWATCH: Hispanic Teens: The Largest Ethnic
Youth Group 151

TRENDWATCH: Baby Boomers: Reaching Them
After 60 153

Chapter 6 Understanding Product Trends: What Customers
Buy 155

Product Selection Decisions 156

Types of Products Customers Purchase 158
Purchases Bases on Availability 159
Purchases Based on Durability and Quality 160
Purchases Based on Fashion Appeal 161
Purchasing "New" Products 164
Purchasing Fads 166

Product Life Cycles and Fashion Adoption Theories 169
Product Life Cycle 169
Fashion Adoption Theories 171
*Using Product Life Cycles and Adoption
Theories* 173

Creating Product Differences 174
Brand Names 174
Licensed Products 175
Mass Customization 178

Summary Points 178

Review Activities 179
Developing Your Retail Buying Vocabulary 179
Understanding What You Read 180
Analyzing and Applying What You Read 180
Internet Connection 181

SNAPSHOT: Customizing Purchases Online 181

SNAPSHOT: Smart Cars: Will They Succeed in the
United States? 183

TRENDWATCH: Fads: What Is the Next Big Thing?
184

TRENDWATCH: Casual Fridays: Is the Pendulum
Swinging the Other Way?   186

PART III   **Planning and Controlling Merchandise
Purchases   189**

Chapter 7   Forecasting   191

Scope of Forecasting   192

Developing Sales Forecasts   195
Examining Internal Forces   195
Examining External Forces   195
Acquiring Needed Data   197
Making Sales Forecasts   199
Making Adjustments   202

Forecasting Decisions   202
Forecasting Sales   202
Planning Inventory Levels   207
Determining Stock Turnover   208

Future Direction of Sales Forecasting   211

Summary Points   211

Review Activities   212
Developing Your Retail Buying Vocabulary   212
Understanding What You Read   212
Analyzing and Applying What You Read   213
Application Exercises   213
Spreadsheet Skills   214
Internet Connection   214

SNAPSHOT: Family Dollar: Fine-Tuning Its Retail
Strategy   215

TRENDWATCH: Using Weather Forecasts to Improve
Retail Forecasts   217

TRENDWATCH: Market-Basket Analysis: How Do
Customers Shop a Store?   219

Chapter 8 Preparing Buying Plans 221

Merchandising Management 222

Six-Month Merchandise Plan 224
Purposes of the Plan 224
Components of the Plan 225

Preparation of a Six-Month Merchandise Plan 228
Planned Sales 228
Planned BOM Inventory 230
Planned EOM Inventory 232
Planned Reductions 232
Planned Purchases at Retail 233
Planned Purchases at Cost 234

Basic Stock Planning 235

Open-to-Buy Planning 239
Definition of Open-to-Buy 239
Open-to-Buy Calculations 239
Benefits and Uses of Open-to-Buy 240

Summary Points 241

Review Activities 242
Developing Your Retail Buying Vocabulary 242
Understanding What You Read 243
Analyzing and Applying What You Read 243
Application Exercises 243
Spreadsheet Skills 244
Internet Connection 245

SNAPSHOT: RMSA: Retail Merchandising Service
Automation 245

TRENDWATCH: Merchandise Planning: Taking the
Holiday Pulse 247

Chapter 9 Developing Assortment Plans 249

Planning Merchandise Assortments 251

Factors Affecting Merchandise Assortments 252
Type of Merchandise 253

Store Policies 255
Variety of Merchandise Available 256

Merchandise Classifications 258
Classifications and Subclassifications 258
Selection Factors 261

Preparing an Assortment Plan 264

Summary Points 268

Review Activities 269
Developing Your Retail Buying Vocabulary 269
Understanding What You Read 270
Analyzing and Applying What You Read 270
Application Exercises 271
Spreadsheet Skills 272
Internet Connection 272

SNAPSHOT: Fashion Forecasting: Doneger Creative
Services 273

TRENDWATCH: All Shapes and Sizes: The Plus-Size
Market Continues to Grow 274

Chapter 10 Controlling Inventories 277

Inventory Control Systems 278
Perpetual Control 279
Periodic Control 281

Establishing and Using Inventory Control
Systems 282
Information Required 282
Using Inventory Control Information 285

Inventory Calculations 287
Dollar Control Systems 287
GMROI—Measuring Profitability of Sales 289

Inventory Management: Quick Response 290
Requirements for Quick Response 291
Implementing Quick Response 293
Measuring the Impact of Quick Response 294

Summary Points 295

Review Activities   296
    Developing Your Retail Buying Vocabulary   296
    Understanding What You Read   296
    Analyzing and Applying What You Read   297
    Application Exercises   297
    Internet Connection   298

SNAPSHOT: VF Brands: Implementing Quick
       Response   298

TRENDWATCH: Scanners: How Accurate Are
       They?   300

TRENDWATCH: RFID: Can It Improve Retail
       Logistics?   301

PART IV   Purchasing Merchandise   305

Chapter 11   Selecting Vendors and Building Partnerships   307

Types of Vendors   308
    Manufacturers   309
    Wholesalers   309
    Manufacturers' Representatives/Brokers   310
    Rack Jobbers   311

Making Contact with Potential Vendors   311
    Buyer-Initiated Contacts   311
    Vendor-Initiated Contacts   312

Criteria for Selecting Vendors   314
    Merchandise and Prices Offered   314
    Vendors' Distribution Policies   315
    Vendors' Reputation and Reliability   316
    Terms Offered   316
    Services Provided   316

Analyzing Vendor Performance   318

Developing Strong Buyer–Vendor Partnerships   321
    Basis for Strong Partnerships with Vendors   321
    Buyers' Expectations of Vendors   322
    Future Trends   323

Summary Points   325

Review Activities   326
    Developing Your Retail Buying Vocabulary   326
    Understanding What You Read   326
    Analyzing and Applying What You Read   327
    Internet Connection   327

SNAPSHOT: IKEA: Building a Global Empire   328

TRENDWATCH: Manufacturers' Factory Outlet
    Stores   330

Chapter 12 Locating Sources in Foreign Markets   333

Foreign Markets   334

Purchasing from Foreign Sources   335
    Reasons to Buy from Foreign Sources   337
    Drawbacks to Buying from Foreign Sources   338
    Making the Decision to Buy from Foreign
       Sources   340

Locating Foreign Sources   342
    Making Personal Buying Trips   343
    Using Intermediaries   345

Globalization of Retailing   345

"Buy American" Campaigns   348

Summary Points   351

Review Activities   351
    Developing Your Retail Buying Vocabulary   351
    Understanding What You Read   352
    Analyzing and Applying What You Read   352
    Internet Connection   353

SNAPSHOT: Zara: Providing Style and Rapid
    Response   353

SNAPSHOT: Wal-Mart Exits Germany: What Are the
    Challenges of Global Expansion?   355

TRENDWATCH: Recalled Products: What Went Wrong? 356

TRENDWATCH: "Buy American" Campaigns 358

Chapter 13 Making Market Visits and Negotiating with Vendors 361

Preparing for a Market Visit 362
    Types of Markets 363
    Purposes of Buying Trips 365
    Frequency of Market Trips 365
    Planning the Market Trip 367

Visiting the Market 368
    Working with a Buying Office 368
    Visiting Vendors 371
    Visiting Factories 373
    Other Market Activities 373
    Visiting Online Showrooms 374

Preparing to Negotiate 374
    Analyze Your Position 376
    Determine the Vendor's Position 376
    Develop Negotiation Skills 376
    Determine Objectives of Negotiations 377

Setting the Stage for Negotiating 378
    Build Rapport 378
    Ask Questions 378
    Listen and Watch for Nonverbal Clues 379

Developing a Negotiating Strategy 379
    Personality Styles in Negotiations 380
    Negotiation Tactics 380
    Bargaining 382
    Negotiation Checklist 383
    Outcomes of Negotiation 383

Summary Points 384

Review Activities 385
    Developing Your Retail Buying Vocabulary 385

Understanding What You Read 385
Analyzing and Applying What You Read 386
Internet Connection 387

SNAPSHOT: The American International Toy Fair 387

TRENDWATCH: Which Furniture Market Will
Dominate? 389

SNAPSHOT: Springs Industries: The Loss of Another
U.S. Textile Manufacturer 391

Chapter 14 Making the Purchase 393

Negotiating Terms of the Sale 394
Price 394
Discounts 396
Transportation 398
Allowances 399
Return Privileges 399

Negotiating Special Buying Situations 400
Private Brands 400
Specification Buying 404
Promotional Buying 404
Job Lots 405
Off-Price 405
Seconds and Irregulars 406

Placing the Order 406
Types of Orders 407
Parts of the Purchase Order 407
Follow Up of Orders 409

Summary Points 410

Review Activities 410
Developing Your Retail Buying Vocabulary 410
Understanding What You Read 411
Analyzing and Applying What You Read 412
Spreadsheet Skills 412
Internet Connection 413

SNAPSHOT: Liz Claiborne 413

TRENDWATCH: Source Tagging: Bargaining for
Floor-Ready Merchandise 415

TRENDWATCH: Private Labels Spell Profits 416

PART V Motivating Customers to Buy 419

Chapter 15 Pricing the Merchandise 421

Establishing Retail Prices 422
  Elements of Retail Price 423
  Determining Markup Percentage 423
  Planning Initial Markup Percentage 424

Factors Affecting Retail Price 428
  Target Market 428
  Store Policies 429
  Competition 431
  Economic Conditions 432

Adjustments to Retail Price 433
  Markdowns 433
  Markdown Cancellations 435
  Additional Markups 436

Evaluating Pricing Decisions 437
  Market Share 437
  Profit 437
  Markup Achieved 437

Summary Points 437

Review Activities 438
  Developing Your Retail Buying Vocabulary 438
  Understanding What You Read 439
  Application Exercises 439
  Spreadsheet Skills 441
  Internet Connection 441

SNAPSHOT: Dollar Tree: Successfully Pricing Items
for a Dollar 441

TRENDWATCH: Outlet Centers: Do They Deliver
Lower Prices? 443

Chapter 16 Promoting the Merchandise 445

Retail Promotional Activities 447
Advertising 447
Visual Merchandising 448
Personal Selling 450
Publicity 451
Special Events 452
Other Sales Promotion Activities 453

Developing a Promotional Plan 454
Establish Objectives 454
Prepare the Budget 456
Select Merchandise for Promotion 458
Establish the Schedule 459
Prepare the Promotional Message 460
Evaluate Promotional Activities 460

Coordination of Promotional Activities 461

Summary Points 463

Review Activities 464
Developing Your Retail Buying Vocabulary 464
Understanding What You Read 464
Analyzing and Applying What You Read 465
Internet Connection 465

SNAPSHOT: Lillian Vernon: Promoting an Image
Through Catalogs 466

TRENDWATCH: Victoria's Secret: Using the Web as a
Promotion Tool 468

Appendix A: Basic Retail Math Formulas 471

Appendix B: Decision Making 473

Glossary 477

Index 491

Credits 513

PREFACE

The purpose of *Retail Buying* is to prepare students for merchandising careers in retailing. Throughout the text, students are introduced to basic concepts, principles, and techniques used by retail buyers as they complete their day-to-day duties and responsibilities. References to a wide range of merchandising careers are also found in the text. Not only are traditional retail stores examined, but also various examples relate to nontraditional types of retailing, such as mail order, online, and direct.

The use of technology in retail buying is presented throughout the text, and basic mathematical calculations performed by buyers are also presented to review and reinforce students' math skills. The overall goal is for students to use the information presented in the text to learn how to develop an effective buying strategy.

Many special features are used in *Retail Buying* to explain buying concepts in a challenging and practical manner. The author made every effort to ensure that the material is written clearly and concisely to enhance student understanding.

Snapshots are included in each chapter to present up-to-date highlights of current merchandising concepts, strategies, and techniques being used by actual retail businesses. Each **Snapshot** is related to material presented in the chapter, making it more interesting and relevant to students. Instructors may find it appropriate to assign students the task of conducting research to update material found in each **Snapshot** or to apply it to other retail businesses with which they may be more familiar.

At least one **Trendwatch,** which presents information about a trend is included in each chapter. Highlighted trends focus on the general direction that topics in the chapter have taken. In some chapters, students will be examining trends that have occurred in the past; most chapters, however, deal with recent trend changes. By their very nature, new trends were developing as this text was being written and published. Instructors and students will want to continually monitor the marketplace to discover new trends as they begin to appear. Constantly being aware of changes in the market is a task buyers use throughout their careers.

Material is included that gives students the opportunity to develop merchandising skills rather than simply reading about the types of activities that are performed by buyers. For example, step-by-step approaches are presented for buying tasks such as these: identifying and understanding potential customers, developing sales forecasts, preparing a 6-month merchandise plan, planning merchandise assortments, preparing an assortment plan, identifying criteria for selecting vendors, preparing for a market visit, negotiating with vendors, placing an order, and coordinating promotional activities.

Up-to-date information about current buying practices and techniques can be found throughout the text. Students will learn more about: trends and challenges facing retailers, such as consolidation, shakeouts, online retailing, and globalization; the increasing use of technology and the Internet by retail buyers; employment forecasts for merchandising careers; the growing emphasis on centralized buying; targeting current customers through more effective forecasting; understanding customers through techniques such as data warehousing, data mining, and database marketing; controlling inventories more effectively through Quick Response; and techniques for more effective negotiations with vendors.

Various viewpoints on key issues are also presented and can be adapted for classroom discussion or debate. For example, different views are highlighted on the future of specific types of retail stores, the use of centralized buying, the future of buying offices, and the use of domestic sourcing and "Buy American" campaigns.

References are presented throughout the text that can serve as a list of suggested readings for further study and research. The references present students with sources that are important to buyers as they study trends and make buying decisions.

Each chapter begins with a list of performance objectives and ends with a summary of key points presented in the chapter. Vocabulary terms related to retail buying are also highlighted in the text and listed at the end of each chapter.

A variety of questions are included. *Understanding What You Read* questions can be used to generate class discussion and review information presented in the chapter. *Analyzing and Applying What You Read* questions provide students with the opportunity to analyze buying principles presented in the chapter. A section titled *Internet Connection*, is included in each chapter. Suggested activities that utilize the Internet are presented to reinforce material found in the chapter. Chapters that emphasize mathematical calculations include a section on *Spreadsheet Skills*. Activities are suggested for developing and using spreadsheets. Additional spreadsheet activities that are also listed can be found in *Making Buying Decisions: Using the Computer as a Tool*, a companion text.

Throughout the text, charts present current data that affects many aspects of the retail buyer's job. Photographs used show examples of current retail practices in actual stores and showrooms. Sample forms used by buyers are presented to illustrate the kinds of records that buyers may encounter.

In **Part I: Understanding the Retail Environment Where Buying Occurs,** we learn that to be successful, buyers must understand the retail environment in which buying occurs. The first three chapters introduce buying practices and procedures of various types of retail businesses. In Chapter 1, students are introduced to buying and are presented a marketing orientation to factors that will influence many of the decisions that buyers make. Emerging and growing retail formats are described with a discussion of trends and challenges facing retailers. In Chapter 2, students examine merchandising careers in retailing. Detailed job descriptions for a buyer, assistant buyer, and merchandise manager are presented. Information is also presented on how to plan for a career in retail buying. In Chapter 3, students learn how the buyer's job differs in various types of retail formats. Retail organizational structures are presented, and the relationship of merchandising to other departments is highlighted.

Part II: Getting Ready to Make Buying Decisions discusses how once buyers understand the marketplace in which they work, they need to develop an understanding of customers and trends affecting future sales. In Chapter 4, students examine sources of information that would be available to them when making buying decisions. Internal and external sources are described with emphasis on the role of buying offices. In Chapter 5, information is presented to help buyers better understand their customers. Recent changes in the consumer markets are described, and reasons why customers buy are discussed. Targeting customers by using technology, such as database marketing, data mining, and data warehousing, is emphasized. In Chapter 6, students gain an understanding of what types of products customers purchase. New product trends, especially products with fashion appeal, are emphasized. Product life cycles and fashion adoption theories are explained.

Part III: Planning and Controlling Merchandise Purchases deals with how buyers now understand their customers and the environment in which they will be operating and are ready to make purchasing plans. In Chapter 7, the scope of forecasting is described, and students examine the steps for developing effective sales forecasts. In addition, material is presented about forecasting decisions to predict inventory needs. In Chapter 8, students learn how to develop merchandise plans for fashion and basic merchandise. In Chapter 9, students plan merchandise assortments and develop an assortment plan. In Chapter 10, different inventory control plans are presented, and the mathematical calculations needed by buyers are explained. Quick Response is described in relation to purchase planning and merchandise control.

Part IV: Purchasing Merchandise concerns how buyers having prepared their merchandise plans and are now ready to select vendors from whom to make purchases. In Chapter 11, students examine various types of vendors and learn how to identify criteria for selecting them. The development of partnerships between retailers and vendors is emphasized. In Chapter 12, students examine foreign sourcing for their planned purchases. Benefits and drawbacks are presented. In Chapter 13, steps for planning a market trip are explained in detail. Negotiation practices frequently used by buyers are presented. Emphasis is placed on developing a negotiation strategy that results in a win-win outcome. In Chapter 14, terms of the sale and special buying situations are described. Procedures for placing the final order are presented.

Part V: Motivating Customers to Buy concerns how once merchandise has been purchased for the store, buyers may be responsible for other retailing activities to motivate customers to buy. In Chapter 15, students examine the mathematical calculations needed to price incoming merchandise and make price adjustments on in-stock merchandise. In Chapter 16, students examine promotional activities that can be used to promote merchandise purchased by the buyers. Students learn how to develop and coordinate promotional activities.

Appendix A: Basic Retail Math Formulas is presented as a handy reference to review the basic math used in merchandising. **Appendix B: Decision Making** is presented as a step-by-step process of approaching individual and group decision making in classroom activities, as well as in retail buying careers. A **Glossary** of over 250 terms related to retail buying is included for students to use as a quick reference of key terms found in the text. An instructor's manual is available with the text, which presents suggested teaching ideas, a key to chapter review activities, and a test bank of questions for each chapter.

ACKNOWLEDGMENTS

Many retail professionals provided me with information on current buying practices that are included in this text. Representatives of Parisian, Bloomingdale's, Rich's, Lowe's, Hartmarx Corporation, Wal-Mart, Carolinas-Virginia Fashion Exhibitors, Belk, and Belk Store Services provided the answers to many questions while this edition was being written. In addition, many other individuals provided me with a wealth of materials and sources that have been incorporated in this text. Special thanks to the following JCPenney associates who conducted workshops and answered numerous questions when I completed a two-week professor internship with the company at their store in Columbia, South Carolina, and at corporate headquarters in Dallas, Texas: Debbie Herd (College Relations Manager); Haley Peoples (College Relations Manager); Derrick Flowers (Buyer, Young Men's Collection); Rosie Salinas (Assistant Buyer, Bedding); Susan Hardy (Brand Manager, Arizona Brand); Steve Larson (Inventory Planning Manager, Men's Shoes); David Kopach (Human Resources Manager, Outlet Stores); Denis Miller (Project Analyst, Catalog Marketing); Laura Owens (Project Analyst, Catalog Marketing); George Stasick (Director of Internet Commerce); Stephanie Gwin (Divisional Trend Manager); John Thomas (Director of Creative Services); Ira Silver (Assistant Director, Business Planning and Analysis); Carol Snyder (International Merchandise Manager); Mark Mears (Director of Sales Planning and Promotions); and Mark Anderson (Assistant Store Manager, JCPenney at Stone Briar Mall, Dallas).

Special thanks to the following individuals who conducted workshops and answered numerous questions when I participated in a three-day Advanced institute in Direct/Interactive Marketing for Professors in College Park, Maryland: Laurie Spar, Martin Baier, Dan Dale, Hal Malchow, Pat Faley, Ward Thomas, Scott Tilden, and Mark Heller. The Institute was sponsored by the Direct Marketing Educational Foundation of the Direct Marketing Association. Appreciation is also extended to David C. Hochberg, Vice President of Public Affairs for Lillian Vernon Corporation for the detailed information that he provided.

I also appreciate the many helpful suggestions made by the reviewers of the original manuscript for the text. These experienced and creative instructors included: Michele Granger, Rose Bednarz, June Fischer, Tana Stuttlebean, Luann Gaskil, Li Zhang, Glenda Lowry, Harvey Shoemach, and Cynthia Jasper.

I remain grateful to Mary McGarry and Joann Muscolo, former editors at Fairchild, for their guidance and encouragement in the second edition.

Finally, I appreciate the assistance of my graduate research assistant, and I am especially grateful to Jaclyn Bergeron, Fairchild editor of this revision.

RETAIL BUYING

Understanding the Retail Environment Where Buying Occurs

Today's Buying Environment

PERFORMANCE OBJECTIVES

Upon completion of this chapter, you should be able to:

- Recognize the importance of the marketing concept in retailing.
- Use positioning and targeting to develop retail strategies.
- Identify methods used to target retail customers.
- List and describe emerging retailing formats.
- Identify trends affecting retailing and buying.

Welcome to the exciting world of buying, one of many functions occurring every day in all retail businesses. By its very nature, retailing is dynamic and continuously changing. Within a single season, the merchandise assortment and market position of a retailer can be altered; and virtually overnight, pricing, promotions, and inventory levels can be changed. Within this fast-changing environment, buyers are making merchandising decisions daily.

INTRODUCTION

Retailing consists of all the business activities involved in the selling of goods and services to ultimate consumers. Retailing, however, does not always require a store. Catalog sales, vending machines, Internet sales, and door-to-door sales all fit within the scope of retailing. No matter where retailing occurs, however, someone must perform the buying function. *Buying* is the business activity that involves selecting and purchasing products to satisfy the wants and needs of consumers. Buying involves complex decision making in areas such as:

- Forecasting the wants and needs of consumers.
- Planning merchandise assortments to satisfy consumer wants and needs.
- Selecting vendors from whom to purchase merchandise.
- Negotiating contracts with vendors.

- Pricing merchandise.
- Keeping sales and inventory records.
- Reordering merchandise.

Over the next several weeks, you will learn more about buying as well as develop skills necessary to perform these primary buying tasks. But first, the retailing environment in which buying occurs will be described, and trends that will be affecting both retailing and buying will be examined.

A MARKETING ORIENTATION

A retailer's success is directly dependent on consumer satisfaction; therefore, as a buyer you must be responsive to the wants and needs of consumers. Let's review some key marketing concepts that affect all retailers today.

Developing a Consumer Orientation

In recent years, retailing has become more consumer oriented. In fact, a philosophy about the way in which retailers want to conduct business has developed. Fundamentally, this philosophy is based on the *marketing concept*, the belief that all business activities should be geared toward satisfying the wants and needs of consumers. As a buyer, you must identify what consumers want and then offer merchandise that will satisfy their wants and needs at a price they are willing to pay.

The marketing concept cannot be implemented and consumer satisfaction cannot be obtained without planning. A *retail strategy* is an overall framework or plan of action that guides a retailer. Usually, the store's owner or management team outlines the philosophy, objectives, target customer, tactics, and control activities that will guide the store's employees for a period of time, typically one year or more. Customer-driven stores, employing the marketing concept, have consistently better stocks of merchandise, more customer satisfaction, and broader and deeper assortments of styles and sizes than do stores that are concerned primarily with the profitability of each item sold.

A successful strategy helps retailers distinguish themselves from competitors and develop a merchandise assortment that appeals to a specific group of consumers. Making the effort to design a strategy also allows the retailer's total efforts to be coordinated. Management must develop an integrated strategy that coordinates factors such as store location, merchandise assortments, pricing, and promotion. Buyers, for example, may select the best products available that customers want, but a poor store location could mean few sales.

Positioning a Retail Store

Retailers must go beyond developing strategies; they must also determine how consumers perceive the store's *image*. For example, consumers may view your store as innovative, conservative, exclusive, budget, high priced, or a fashion leader. Their perception may or may not agree with your planned strategies.

Virtually all retailers are concerned with how they are perceived by consumers. A key part of developing a retail strategy will be how to create and maintain an image that you want consumers to have of you. Every retailer positions itself in the market with activities such as selecting merchandise assortments, pricing policies, and promotion activities. *Positioning* involves identifying a group of consumers and developing retail activities to meet their needs. For example, a mens wear store could be positioned as upscale, midpriced, or discount. Neiman Marcus positions itself toward upper-class, status-conscious consumers. It offers exclusive brands of high-quality merchandise, charges relatively high prices, and uses very distinctive print ads. In contrast, Wal-Mart targets middle-class, value-conscious consumers by utilizing discount prices and advertising that features a wide assortment of merchandise.

Targeting Consumers

The first step in positioning is to identify possible markets for your products. A *market* is a group of people with the ability, desire, and willingness to buy—in other words, your potential customers. Markets come in all shapes and sizes—some are large while others are small. Regardless, markets are the target of your retail strategy.

Few retailers can serve every consumer because consumer needs and wants are so varied. Today, rather than trying to please everyone, successful retailers attempt to serve a *market segment*, a group of potential customers who have similar needs or other important characteristics (Figure 1.1). Dividing the total market into segments is known as

Figure 1.1   Can you identify market segments that would purchase these products?

market segmentation. When retailers segment the market, they are attempting to identify and serve a particular group of customers with common characteristics. By identifying and understanding these groups of possible customers, buyers can tailor their merchandise assortments to meet the exact needs of those groups. Four types of data are typically used to segment markets. They include: (1) demographic data, (2) geographic data, (3) behavioristic data, and (4) psychographic data.

Demographic Data. Consumer characteristics, such as age, sex, family size, income, education, occupation, and race are known as *demographic data*. Retailers identify their potential customers in terms of those characteristics that would have an impact on purchasing products they have for sale. For example, consumers of all ages may purchase a specific product, but most of those consumers have incomes of more than $30,000 per year. In this instance, a retailer would want to make sure there were a sufficient number of individuals in the area earning more than $30,000 before purchasing the product.

Geographic Data. Information on where consumers live, such as ZIP codes, neighborhoods, cities, counties, states, or regions is known as *geographic data*. As a buyer, you must determine if there are enough potential consumers in your geographic area who will purchase products you are buying. For example, a product may have high sales in an urban setting but not be purchased by customers living in a small town.

Behavioristic Data. Information about customers' buying activities comprises *behavioristic data*. For example, most retailers attempt to determine information such as the time that most customers make purchases or the average amount of their purchases. Knowing this information can help buyers ensure they have adequate amounts of merchandise when and where customers want to purchase it.

Psychographic Data. Information on the lifestyle, interests, and opinions of consumers is termed *psychographic data*. In some cases customers' personality characteristics influence what and where they make purchases. For example, shoppers who make purchases regularly at Wal-Mart may be motivated by savings.

Most retailers use one or more of these data sources to segment their customers into groups or market segments. Retailers try to develop a profile of the consumers they will attempt to serve in order to buy the right merchandise and to present and promote it in the most effective manner. Read the Trendwatch titled "Targeting Current Customers" to learn more about one method some retailers are using to target their existing customers in order to build customer retention.

Because market segments have different consumption patterns, products that are satisfactory for one group may not be appropriate for another group. For example, an urban professional has dissimilar needs from a retiree in Florida. These differences require you to segment your total market into more manageable pieces.

Types of Target Marketing

Mass marketing is no longer the norm; the U.S. market is composed of many smaller segments, or *niches*. Retailers must create a competitive advantage by matching their strategies to specific market segments. After you have identified the characteristics of your market and divided the market into segments, you will want to identify your *target market*, the specific group or groups of consumers on which your store will focus. Typically, retailers use one of the following approaches to target their customers: (1) undifferentiated, (2) concentrated, or (3) multisegment.

Undifferentiated Target Marketing. An attempt by retailers to please all consumers is known as *undifferentiated target marketing*. Conventional supermarkets and drugstores are examples of retailers that use undifferentiated target marketing; they broadly define their potential customers. In the past, most department stores also used undifferentiated target marketing; however, many of them have changed this focus today. For example, JCPenney has narrowed its target market in recent years by eliminating many product categories, such as toys and appliances.

Concentrated Target Marketing. Focusing on one segment of the market involves *concentrated target marketing*. A women's shoe store or an upscale deli are examples of retailers that have selected a well-defined consumer group that they wish to target. A retailer focusing on one market segment does not attempt to appeal to every consumer.

Multisegment Target Marketing. Retailers who focus on more than one consumer segment are using ***multisegment target marketing***. They offer distinct merchandise aimed at several different groups of consumers. These groups, however, could have some similar characteristics. For example, big-and-tall mens wear stores appeal to two distinct but similar groups. In some situations, appeals may be directed toward quite different market segments. For example, supermarkets may stock microwave dinners for both working mothers and singles. In such instances, different advertising strategies and product assortments will be needed to reach both groups.

Today, most retailers have taken steps to distinguish themselves by identifying and appealing to specific target markets. Targeting is a technique that catalog retailers use extensively. L.L.Bean is only one of many catalogers that have made effective use of target market concepts. In addition to one general catalog, it now has over 12 other catalogs aimed at very different retail niches. Separate catalogs are focused on a plus-size collection and men, women, children, travelers, fishermen, and hunters.[1] Data on who shops from catalogs are shown in Figure 1.2.

As a buyer, developing and implementing your plans will be directly linked to your store's retail strategy. Management must clearly define the store, identify target customers, identify an image, and position the store in the marketplace. If management has successfully completed these tasks and the store is perceived as offering customer satisfaction, your job as a buyer will be much easier.

EMERGING AND GROWING RETAIL FORMATS: WHERE WILL CONSUMERS MAKE PURCHASES?

Retailing may look quite different tomorrow from the way it looks today. Because retailing is changing, the buying function is also changing. If you are to be a successful buyer, you need to understand where customers currently make purchases and where they are likely to make them in the future.

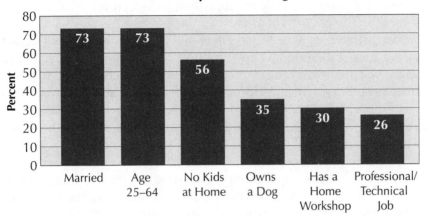

Figure 1.2   Catalog sales for consumer markets.

Retailing seems to be in a state of flux because customers are constantly looking for something new. Retailers must be continually aware of new market directions and react to those changes if they are to be successful. In this section, some emerging retailing formats will be described. Key elements of the buying process in each of these formats will also be examined.

Direct Marketing

Direct marketing consists of direct connection with carefully targeted individual customers to both obtain immediate response and cultivate lasting customer relationships. Direct marketers often communicate on a one-to-one, interactive basis. They tailor their marketing offers and communications to the needs of narrowly defined segments or even individual buyers.

For many companies today, direct marketing is much more than just a supplementary channel or medium. For these companies, direct marketing, especially Internet retailing, may constitute the ony format in which business is conducted. Some companies, such as Dell Computers and Amazon.com, began only as direct marketers.

Others, such as Egghead Software, began with traditional storefronts, but have recently relinquished those stores in favor of a presence only on the Internet.

Many strategists have hailed direct marketing as the retailing format of the new millennium. They envision a day when all buying and selling will involve only direct connections between companies and their customers, thus changing customers' expectations about convenience, speed, price, and service. They suggest these new expectations will reverberate throughout the economy, eventually affecting every business, whether business to business or business to consumer.

Direct marketing benefits customers in many ways. Primarily, it is convenient. Customers do not have to battle traffic, find parking spaces, and trek through stores and aisles to find and examine products. They can do comparative shopping by browsing through catalogs or surfing Internet sites. Most direct marketers never close their doors; customers can make purchases 24 hours a day, 7 days a week. Direct marketing often provides shoppers with a larger product selection and assortment than can be provided in stores. For example, the store at the mall may be limited in the colors and sizes it can carry; direct marketers can offer nearly all colors and sizes because they typically are all housed at one location.

Direct marketing also yields many benefits to sellers. Direct marketing is a powerful tool for building customer relationships. With today's technology, direct marketers can select small groups or even individual consumers, personalize offers to their special needs and wants, and promote those offers through individualized communications. Because of its one-on-one, interactive nature, the Internet is an especially potent direct marketing tool.

Catalog Marketing. Catalog marketing is another area that has grown explosively during the past 25 years. Many traditional mail-order catalogers have added Web-based catalogs to their marketing mixes, and a variety of new Web-only catalogers have emerged. Annual catalog sales (both print and electronic) are expected to reach $120 billion in 2007. General merchandise retailer JCPenney sells a full line of merchandise through its catalogs and offers many specialty catalogs that serve highly specialized market niches.

Are there any problems for catalogers? Catalog retailers promise no-hassle customer service, but do they deliver? *Money* magazine tested 20 of the leading direct-mail retailers to see if they lived up to this promise. Items were purchased and then returned. Eddie Bauer, Lands' End, L.L.Bean, and Patagonia were companies that the magazine rated as having attractive and accurate catalogs, accommodating and informed telephone operators, and prompt refunds. In addition to poor customer service, another problem for some catalog customers is inconsistent sizing in apparel. Because customers cannot try on clothing, return rates are as high as 40 percent for some women's items.

In reaction to increased customer sales through catalogs, many department stores have established mail-order purchasing for specific merchandise categories such as fragrances. Like other catalogers, they have even established toll-free (800) numbers to make ordering easy. Retailers such as JCPenney and Talbots operate separate retail store and catalog divisions. One opportunity for expansion of catalog retailing is the international market; however, it does not currently represent a significant percentage of catalog business for U.S. companies.

The Internet has had a tremendous impact on catalog selling. In the face of increasing competition from Internet retailing, many analysts predict the demise of mail-order catalogs as we know them today. In fact, more than three-quarters of all catalog companies now present merchandise and take orders over the Internet. Lands' End, for example, now gets more queries from its Web site than from its print catalog. Proponents of catalogs, however, stress that customers cannot curl up in a chair and thumb through a computer at the end of the day, dreaming about what they want to purchase.

Electronic Retailing

Electronic retailing, which has arrived in many forms, will affect all retailers in the future. Electronic retailing falls into three categories: TV shopping channels, kiosks, and the Internet. Electronic retailing provides consumers with the convenience of at-home shopping through shopping mediums that can be constantly updated and made more current than typical catalogs.

TV Shopping Channels. Shop-at-home convenience has increased with the growth of TV shopping channels such as HSN, the television shopping network, and QVC. In addition to assisting consumers make purchases, shopping channels also inform and entertain. Such shopping convenience particularly appeals to working women and the elderly.

TV shopping channels are one of the fastest-growing segments of the retail market today. On many of these shopping channels, celebrities, such as the one shown in Figure 1.3, frequently sell products they are endorsing.

Kiosks. Many retailers and shopping malls across the country are also using another type of electronic retailing; they are using touch-activated computer terminals housed in *kiosks*, which resemble video arcade games. At some of these kiosks, consumers view video ads of different products and collect coupons for products being displayed. Kiosks communicate with consumers and entice them to make a purchase.

These computer terminals are one form of electronic retailing that seems to be quite effective in stores where there is a high turnover of sales personnel. They can provide customers with product information and may actually help them make a purchase. Eyeworks, Clarion Cosmetics, and Elizabeth Arden are among the retailers who are successfully using the technology in this way. At Clarion computer stations, customers

Figure 1.3 Today, many celebrities are selling their own product lines using TV shopping channels.

answer specific questions about themselves, such as questions relating to skin tone and facial features, and then receive recommendations from the computer about the best Clarion products for them.

The technology probably has applications for most retailing areas. For example, some carpeting stores have computer terminals in place that require customers to answer questions such as: Kind of room? Children? Animals? Price range? Based on responses to these questions, products that best meet customers' needs are identified. The merchandise recommended does not have to be in the store—allowing the retailer to increase sales without having to increase inventory. Special orders can be made for customers who otherwise might not have made a purchase in the store because they did not see any products of interest to them. Also, sales may be increased where kiosks are used. Market studies have shown that customers are more trusting of retail advice given by a computer terminal than by a salesperson. These computer terminals also provide a tremendous market research tool for retailers because detailed information about the people who have interacted with the system is collected.

Internet Retailing. *Online retailing* continues to grow. Total U.S. purchasing on the Internet is expected to skyrocket to $205 billion by 2009.

Online marketing offers great promise for the future. Many market watchers envision a time when the Internet will replace magazines, newspapers, and even stores as sources of information and buying. For others, these claims are only hype. To be sure, online marketing will become the sole business outlet for some firms. But, for most companies, online marketing will remain just one important approach to the marketplace that works alongside other approaches in a fully integrated marketing mix. What is emerging today is that many of the traditional *bricks-and-mortar* retailers—those firms who, in the past, had storefronts on Main Street or in the mall—are now developing a *clicks-and-mortar* approach. In other words, these retailers have developed an online presence in addition to their traditional storefronts.

Direct marketing via the Internet yields additional advantages for the retailer, such as reducing costs and increasing speed and efficiency. Online retailers avoid the expense of maintaining a storefront and the accompanying costs of rent, insurance, and utilities. Online retailers, such as Amazon.com, also reap the benefit of an advantageous cash flow. For example, Amazon receives cash from credit card companies just a day after customers place an order. Then, the retailer can hold onto the money for nearly 45 days until it pays suppliers.

Another advantage that online retailers have is the savings generated from not having to pay for print advertisements. Communicating electronically costs a lot less than communicating on paper through the mail. For instance, a company can produce digital catalogs for much less than the cost of printing and mailing paper ones. Online promotion also offers greater flexibility, allowing the retailer to make ongoing adjustments to its offers and product mix. An online catalog can be adjusted daily or even hourly, adapting product assortments, prices, and promotions to match changing market conditions. To acquire new customers, however, most online retailers also run print ads, such as the one shown in Figure 1.4.

The Internet is truly a global medium that allows buyers and sellers to click from one country to another in seconds. Even small online marketers find they have access to global markets; however, the Internet offers some challenges. Although expanding rapidly, online marketing still reaches only a limited percentage of the market, and only about 25 percent of customers with access to the Internet have ever purchased products online. Although the Web audience is becoming more mainstream, online users still tend to be more upscale and technically oriented than the general population. The Internet offers millions of Web sites and a staggering volume of information. Thus, navigating the Internet can be frustrating, confusing, and time-consuming for customers.

Online shoppers still worry that unscrupulous snoopers will eavesdrop on their online transactions or intercept their credit card numbers and make unauthorized purchases. Privacy is also a primary concern of many online customers. Marketers can easily track Web site visitors, and many customers who participate in Web site activities provide extensive personal information. This may leave them open to information abuse if unauthorized use is made.

Despite these challenges, companies large and small are quickly integrating online retailing into their marketing mixes. Read the Snapshot titled "LandsEnd.com: From Catalog to Online Sales" to learn more about how one company has integrated catalog and Internet sales.

It's the same store, just a **different address.**

At our Web site, you can create your own Personal Model,™ then "try on" different outfits – without leaving home

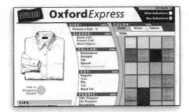

In just a few clicks, quickly find your way among our dizzying array of men's dress shirts

Find the perfect swimsuit to flatter your figure... mix and match coverups. We make it easy!

Big savings on products we ordered too much of. The deals change often – and they're *e-mazing!*

From catalog to the Web, the store is yours™

www.landsend.com
1-800-303-4486

© 1999 Lands' End, Inc

Figure 1.4 Most online retailers still must rely on traditional advertising to attract customers.

Superstore Retailing

The term *superstore* first appeared in the supermarket industry as grocery stores expanded in size to include a wide selection of general merchandise. Today, however, the term is interpreted much more broadly and can refer to just about any store that is bigger than what one would normally expect to find selling a particular category of merchandise. These stores tend to be the largest stores of their type in a geographic area and include warehouse clubs, supercenters, and specialized superstores.

Supercenters. *Supercenters* are megasupermarkets and general merchandise stores that stock everything from food to appliances under one roof. In Europe the concept has developed as *hypermarkets*, but the sheer size of those superstores (from 300,000 to 500,000 square feet) has never been well accepted in the United States. In this country discounters have built similar supercenters across the country, but these stores may cover only 225,000 square feet, and some are even smaller, at 150,000 square feet. Examples include Wal-Mart supercenters, Big Kmarts, and SuperTargets.

The strategy behind supercenters is to have on hand the products that represent 80 percent of customers' regular needs and to avoid specialty or slow-moving merchandise. The brand-name merchandise assortment is tailored to middle-income consumers; however, supercenters avoid being too fashionable because inventory requirements and risks are so large.

Response from other retailers has also been to increase the size of their stores. The Kroger grocery chain now has a standard for new stores of 69,000 square feet compared to 44,000 square feet in the 1980s. The new stores have become profitable in about half the time it took for earlier stores.

Warehouse Clubs. *Warehouse clubs* are indeed huge warehouses that sell just about everything, typically in commercial-sized quantities. They offer no frills, little sales assistance, no special decor, and no deliveries. Customers may even have to dodge forklifts as they shop.

Most warehouse clubs operate as members-only stores where customers pay an annual fee. Typically, warehouse clubs will not accept just anyone who wants to become a member; individuals would have to belong to a credit union or work for the government or another approved organization. Warehouse club managers feel that such members are less likely to write bad checks; however, some warehouse clubs are eliminating these restrictions.

Many warehouse club members are not individual shoppers. Nearly one-third of them are business owners who are buying in bulk for their businesses during special hours set aside for them to shop.

Common characteristics of the majority of warehouse clubs, like the one shown in Figure 1.5, include:

- Facilities that average 100,000 square feet or more,
- limited selection of items available, averaging 5,000 **SKUs** (*stockkeeping units*), and
- prices typically discounted 20 to 40 percent below those of other retail outlets.

Consolidation has hit the warehouse clubs, too. Three firms now account for about 90 percent of the market: Sam's Club, B.J.'s Wholesale Club, and Costco.

Figure 1.5   Costco is one of the top three warehouse clubs in the United States.

Specialized Superstores. *Specialized superstores* typically offer one to three categories of merchandise in tremendously large assortments at discount prices that are unmatched by any other retailer in the area. They are also known as "category killers" because of the way in which they totally dominate the market for a specific product category. Specialized superstores tend to be from 10,000 to 30,000 square feet in size but are easy to shop because of well-placed signs throughout the store.

Toys "R" Us was the first retailer to prove this type of store could work. Since then, superstores have come onto the retail scene in many different product categories such as videos, books, music, home and garden, and even crafts. Some of the newest superstores are in the office supplies category. Office Depot and Staples are the largest players in this product category.

To be successful as a specialized superstore, analysts predict that several conditions must be present: (1) total market sales must be at least $1 billion a year, (2) market share must still be dominated by small retailers, and (3) proliferation of product *SKUs* (stockkeeping units) has occurred so rapidly that traditional retailers cannot offer a complete selection. When these conditions exist, there is an opportunity for a specialized superstore in the field. Identifying areas where specialized superstores could work, however, may be easier than making the concept work.

The specialized superstore concept has also affected traditional retailers. Read the Snapshot titled "Lowe's: Continues to Grow" to learn how one company successfully moved from a small store format to become a specialized superstore on the national level.

TRENDS AND CHALLENGES FACING RETAILERS

In today's fast-changing market, retailers need to identify and quickly respond to trends and challenges. A *trend* involves change or movement in a general direction. The ability to predict trends and deal with them before they fully influence the market is critical in retailing. The only way retailers can plan for the future is to anticipate the forces that will have an impact on retailing in the decades ahead. Then, they must develop strategies in response to those changes if they are to survive.

Retailing is being revolutionized. Success in retailing will require strong decision makers who have a clear vision of what they want to do. All retailers must position themselves as shopping destinations rather than places into which consumers wander. Buyers, through their merchandise selections and other merchandising decisions, will play a key role in making their stores a shopping destination for consumers.

Retailers are also faced with other trends, challenges, and market forces that will have direct impact on retail buying. Some of them are described in the section that follows.

Too Many Stores

Most retail analysts agree that there are too many retail stores in the United States today. In recent decades, growth of retail space has consistently outstripped both population growth and consumer spending—resulting in more stores than are needed to serve the population profitably. Yet, the number of new stores still swells. One reason for this expansion is that the newest stores are often top performers; they are key in attracting new customers. These new stores also tend to be the big moneymakers because they have the latest innovations.

Because of the intense competition that results from being overretailed, retail mangers have tended to rely on price promotions as their primary marketing tool. Today, constant price promotions have almost destroyed the meaning of the word "sale." Consumers are confused about the real price of products. Why should they purchase a product at its "regular price" if there will be deep markdowns later? Unfortunately, the "perpetual sale" strategy has also significantly reduced profit margins for retailers.

Retail strategy for many firms may need to move from opening new stores to making existing stores more profitable. Above all, retailers must differentiate themselves to shoppers. There is little reason for a customer to go across town to a store when it is a foregone conclusion that she will find the same merchandise in Store C that she has already seen in Stores A and B. Differentiation can work. Target has seen dramatic growth recently by positioning itself as an upscale alternative to Wal-Mart.

Increasing Consolidation and Shakeouts in Retailing

Retail consolidation continues at an alarming rate. Instead of just consolidating and reorganizing, experts predict that many stores will simply disappear. Industry consolidation has brought many retailers under the same management team, and that move has created similar retail strategies.

Too many retailing formats result in sameness in merchandise assortments, store layout, merchandise presentation, and customer service. In some retail stores, this sameness can be attributed to a tendency to "copy the leader." In an attempt to imitate successful strategies, some retailers are simply copying the approach of industry leaders. Sameness of merchandise strategies also emanates from buyers who have been taught to play it safe by avoiding risky fashions, to play it cautiously by buying from a limited number of standard vendors who sell the same products to all their clients, and to play it safe by promoting only those products supported by manufacturers' advertising allowances.

A retail shakeout is also occurring with small retailers—those firms employing fewer than ten employees. There has also been a steady decline in the number of small retailers during the past decade, and that trend is expected to continue. Smaller retailers lack the flexibility of their bigger competitors in lean times. They often cannot renegotiate payment schedules with suppliers, nor can they close a few underperforming locations to improve profit.

Marketing to Smaller Niches

The mass market has fast become an anachronism. The consumer market has splintered into hundreds of different geographic, ethnic, economic, and age segments, as well as thousands of specialized niches within and across these segments. A greater emphasis on specialized shopping alternatives has developed.

Many analysts are already tolling the death of department stores as the consumer market becomes more fragmented. When Sears lost its position as the largest U.S. retailer, analysts said that the retailer did not respond adequately to changes in the marketplace. These changes included attacks from discount retailers such as Kmart and Wal-Mart, from specialty retailers including Circuit City and The Limited, and from catalogers such as L.L.Bean and Eddie Bauer. A clear example of the role that niche marketing plays in the catalog industry can be found in the demise of the Sears catalog. While competitors narrowed their focus and targeted specific customer bases, Sears' executives could not seem to move beyond the something-for-everyone vision of their founders.

Forward-looking retailers are becoming differentiated retailers–deciding what they want to stand for in the marketplace and staking out that role. Consider the following retailers–Target, Neiman Marcus, The Gap, Wal-Mart, and IKEA. Each of them can be characterized as filling a very specific role or marketplace niche–each has an identity, a personality. In other words, their stores are differentiated from similar retailers.

The key for retailers, then, is to view, define, and position themselves as ***destination stores***–shopping destinations for customers. That is, retailers must strive to become focused, presenting a clear picture of merchandise and service to a distinct audience, so that they become stores for customers to consciously seek, rather than places for customers to wander into. Stores, such as IKEA, use store layout and displays to position themselves as shopping destinations (Figure 1.6).

Everyone in the retail firm, particularly buyers, must have a clear vision of the store–what it is and is not; what makes it special to customers. Outstanding retailers have a clarity of purpose that is demonstrated throughout the organization. Retailers cannot be all things to all people, but they need to be the right things to their customers.

Rapid Globalization

Another major shift is occurring in the marketplace itself. There is a globalization of the world economy and a resulting interdependence of those economies. More global markets are being opened to American business. In fact, many of the top U.S. marketers are enjoying more share growth in foreign markets than they do domestically. The disappearance of trade barriers and the emergence of new markets are adding fuel to the trend toward globalization.

Success stories of retailers abroad include Wal-Mart, now the largest retailer in Mexico and Canada. In addition to Wal-Mart, The Gap already has 15 stores in Japan, and Toys "R" Us is now the largest toy retailer in that country.

Increased Customer Demand for Value and Service

In an attempt to focus on technology and cost savings, many retailers have moved away from their emphasis on customer service. Management must realize that the success of all retailing decisions will depend

Figure 1.6 Furniture stores use layouts and displays to position themselves as destination stores.

on how they are implemented by store employees. Providing a high level of service that generates customer satisfaction offers all retailers a way in which to distinguish their retail operations from competitors.

Retailers and, in particular, buyers must never lose sight of the fact that their primary goal is to serve the customer. If they cannot serve the customer well, another retailer will! Consumers are growing more discerning. They demand value not only in the products and services they want, but also in the quality of life they enjoy. No longer will brand-name items fly off store shelves unless retailers can clearly demonstrate a product's superiority to similar, lower-priced items.

The demand for value goes beyond price and quality. Today's consumers also want to make their purchasing dollars work for them with value-added programs such as credit cards that earn points toward a General Motors (GM) car, frequent flyer miles, or video rentals.

Today, the customer is in control. The twenty-first century customer is "informationally empowered," is actively engaged in the marketing process, demands instant gratification, and seeks only world-class quality. Retailers will have to get closer to their customers; they will have to innovate if they are to succeed. They must be absolutely obsessed with their customers and exceed their expectations.

One problem for retailers will be to determine which services their customers want. At Nordstrom's, customer service may mean trained sales associates who coddle shoppers. At Wal-Mart, it may mean having enough low-priced merchandise in stock and keeping checkout lines short so customers do not leave frustrated. No matter what service means at each retailer, keeping shoppers happy will be ever more important.

Finally, the high-performing retailers will compete on the basis of value rather than price. Low price may be an important element of their retail strategy, but never the only element. The top performers give customers what they want—in other words, they give them their money's worth. For example, Home Depot's success is not just a function of good prices and selection; it is also a function of staffing the stores with personnel who can teach consumers how to be "do-it-yourselfers." IKEA's success is not just a function of low-priced furniture; it a function of low-priced furniture that is well constructed and sleekly styled.

Customers Are Changing, Too

For a majority of customers, shopping has become an event necessary for purchasing only what they need. In fact, shoppers have stopped going to stores in record numbers, and retailers must cater to these time-challenged shoppers.

The demographics of the average customer have also changed. Today, there are clear distinctions among demographic groups that must be recognized, and smart retailers are paying attention to the differences and more directly addressing the needs of their target market. The United States is a multicultural society with nearly 30 percent of the population made up of African Americans, Latinos, and Asian-Americans. Women and gays are also speaking with a louder voice in today's society, and the nontraditional family is now the norm, not the exception to the rule.

The entire baby-boom population—those 75 million Americans born between 1946 and 1964—is now middle-aged. This fundamental shift requires that all retailers reassess their entire positioning strategies. Baby boomers who would not let anything come between them and their Calvins in the 1980s are pushing 60 now and finding that they need a roomier, more forgiving fit in their jeans.

Growing Use of Database-Driven Marketing

Technological advances allow retailers not only to more narrowly target consumers, but also to develop ongoing dialogues with them. *Database marketing* lets retailers develop programs that provide ongoing intelligence based on tracking and analyzing customer behavior. The more retailers learn about their target market's behavior, the more sophisticated the segmentation becomes, leading to highly targeted communications.

A *customer database* is an organized collection of comprehensive data about individual customers or prospects—including demographic, geographic, behavioristic, and psychographic data. Companies use databases to identify prospects, decide which customers should receive a particular offer, deepen customer loyalty, and reactivate customer purchasing. Although vast customer databases were once the preserve of big retail chains with deep pockets, today the falling cost of computing power allows almost any retailer to move into this area.

Database-driven marketing, and the computer technology that makes it possible, will enable savvy retailers to develop a much deeper understanding of their customers and their trading areas. The amount and specificity of the consumer data now available are extraordinary, but it is only the beginning. Just having lots of information about customers stored away somewhere is not enough; strategies based on that information must be developed.

Spreading Use of Technology

Computer technology is no longer enough; to stay ahead, retailers must use computers to innovate. Technology is relatively inexpensive, and it is available to everyone. The competitive edge will go to the retailer who can use that technology most effectively and who can best bridge the gap between high tech and high touch. With technology, the savviest retailers can give every customer—not just the big spenders—all the benefits of a personal shopper. With technology, a customer's local department store will know his or her tastes and preferences, sizes, and even household decor.

Technology will also influence the shopping experience. In the future, customers will not have to spend hours in front of a mirror in the retail store trying on apparel. They will be able to step into a holographic imaging device that takes their measurements and lets them "see" themselves in the clothing of their choice.

At some stores, customers have already accepted in-store, interactive technology as a tool to make their shopping experience more convenient and exciting. For example, when customers go to buy golf clubs at one store, they are taken to an electronic in-store theater where their swing is analyzed with different clubs as they practice on their favorite hole, projected on a screen.

Other Trends and Challenges

In the new millennium, retailing has become a more highly competitive battleground that will be fought on the basis of providing value to the customer. The retailers who survive will be multichannel retailers—those capable of operating storefronts, catalogs, and online businesses simultaneously and seamlessly.

The competition in retailing has never been as fierce as it will be in the current decade. The climate for small retailers is threatened, but even small stores can compete with big stores when they are able to motivate their employees to learn about their products and provide superior customer service. Smart retailers will keep the focus on the real reason they come to work every day–the customer. Retailers, and especially buyers, must probe, poke, reach, and search for new and exciting ways to satisfy their ever-changing customers.

Predicting all future trends and challenges is impossible, but retailers must anticipate trends and then prepare and execute strategies that will allow them to adapt to the fast-changing marketplace. Change presents opportunities; and for many retailers, how well they adapt to change will determine their survival.

Finally, keep in mind that better merchandising begins with buyers who understand the products they stock and the customers to whom they sell. Better merchandising will require buyers who understand the value of computers, but who recognize them only as tools to facilitate customer satisfaction. Better merchandising will require buyers who understand that taking risks is part of successful retailing. Are you ready to become that retail buyer?

SUMMARY POINTS

- Retailing operates in an ever-changing environment; therefore, buying, a key function of retailing, must deal with the continuous changes in the marketplace.
- All retailing and buying activities should be geared toward the marketing concept that is based on customer satisfaction.
- Retail stores cannot please everyone, so they target specific market segments based on demographic, geographic, behavioristic, and psychographic data.
- Positioning and targeting are key marketing tools that retailers use to develop their image and retail strategies.
- Retailers typically identify market segments they wish to serve using undifferentiated, concentrated, or multisegment target marketing.
- Emerging retail formats that are effectively challenging traditional retailers include direct marketing (particularly the Internet) and superstores.
- Superstores continue to grow, especially among the two largest discounters–Target and Wal-Mart.
- Buyers must recognize and anticipate trends that are currently developing in retailing. They must develop the vision that will allow their stores to become destination stores for customers.

REVIEW ACTIVITIES

Developing Your Retail Buying Vocabulary

Consult the Glossary if you did not add the following terms to your vocabulary.

Behavioristic data	Marketing concept
Bricks-and-mortar	Multisegment target marketing
Buying	Niches
Clicks-and-mortar	Online retailing
Concentrated target marketing	Positioning
Customer database	Psychographic data
Database marketing	Retail strategy
Demographic data	Retailing
Destination store	SKU
Direct marketing	Specialized superstore
Geographic data	Supercenter
Hypermarkets	Superstore
Image	Target market
Kiosk	Trend
Market	Undifferentiated target marketing
Market segment	Warehouse club
Market segmentation	

Understanding What You Read

1. Cite examples of retailing that do not require stores.
2. Identify the immediate goal of a retailer using the marketing concept.
3. Identify components of a retail strategy.
4. Distinguish between how Neiman Marcus and Wal-Mart position themselves in the marketplace.
5. List four types of data retailers use to segment consumer markets.
6. List and describe three types of target marketing.
7. Which retailing format was the first to develop superstores?
8. List three reasons that could explain the recent slowdown in the growth of catalog sales.
9. Identify reasons that TV shopping networks have become so successful.

10. List and describe the characteristics that must be present for a superstore to be successful.
11. Where have hypermarkets already been proven successful?
12. Describe how warehouse clubs compete with supermarkets.
13. Describe the buyer's role in the development of destination stores.
14. Describe new uses of technology being made in retailing today.
15. What challenges do online retailers face?
16. With the country being overretailed, why do existing retailers continue to open new stores?
17. What is meant by "informationally enpowered" customers?
18. How does database-driven marketing benefit retail buyers?
19. Describe how interactive technology can be used as a sales tool.

Analyzing and Applying What You Read

1. Choose a retail store in your community. Describe how its management has used positioning and targeting to develop a retail strategy. Evaluate the effectiveness of that strategy.
2. The number of department stores is declining. Develop retail strategies that you would implement to turn around this decline. Specifically, describe the positioning strategy that would be required.
3. Two market conditions facing retailers in this decade will be "too many stores" and "sameness." Develop specific strategies that a store buyer could implement to offset these conditions.

Internet Connection

1. Locate an online site for a retailer with whom you are familiar—one that also has a bricks-and-mortar presence. Develop a chart that compares the similarities and differences between the two, comparing such dimensions as assortments offered, prices, image, and so on.
2. Locate the mission statement for an online retailer (hint: This is usually found under company information). Explain how the mission statement is used to position the retailer in the marketplace and establish a target market.

SNAPSHOT

LandsEnd.com: From Catalog to Online Sales

When most consumers think about shopping on the Internet, the "dot coms" that come quickly to mind are probably sites like eBay, eToys, and Amazon.com. But very quietly, a catalog company, Lands' End, has become a major player in cyberspace. In fact, this e-tailer is one of the top sellers of apparel on the Web today and has received much recognition for superb online service. Started in 1963 as a mail-order operation catering to sailing enthusiasts, Lands' End Inc. (Dodgeville, Wisconsin) is today a successful catalog retailer of upscale apparel, luggage, and related items.

Some experts believe the firm has one of the best developed e-commerce sites today. A significant portion of Lands' End sales already occurs online.

A key strategy the firm has followed is to scale back the number of catalogs sent to customers and reduce the number of pages of each catalog. While making these cuts, management increased the store's presence on the Internet. In 2007, online sales were predicted to hit $145 million, a 27 percent climb from the previous year. However, the catalog is not yet dead. Even with its Internet success, Lands' End still receives about 2,200 orders a day through the mail compared to a decade ago when it received approximately 8,400 mail orders a day. Internet selling is now an essential sales avenue for its customer base.

Much of the credit for the ease with which Lands' End made the transition to the Internet can be attributed to the solid order-and-distribution system the firm already had in place for selling products through its catalogs. Lands' End already knew how to process an order, operate a warehouse, and ship goods quickly—things many new Web startups are still struggling to build. Almost all the new e-commerce retailers had to set up this infrastructure from the ground up.

While the company is embracing the technology of the Internet, the traditional product mix remains intact—khaki pants, colored T-shirts, and all the other standards on which the company has built its reputation. The Web site looks much like the Lands' End catalog, but online customers are provided shopping experiences they cannot get by reading a catalog. For example, women can use interactive three-dimensional tools to "try on" apparel using their exact measurements. Customers also receive recommendations on the best figure-flattering clothes for them. The Web site also uses interactive software that connects a customer service representative to a shopper by way of on-screen "chat" screens, allowing customers to get direct answers to their questions.

Retail analysts say that the Web site is the company's best shot at growth in the future. One reason is that the site is attracting lots of new customers, many of them in international markets. What management must do is capitalize on the firm's customer recognition and maintain the head start it already has against most of the competition. Competition, however, can catch up quickly.

BASED ON:

Grant, Lorrie. (2004, December 3). Lands' End is an ultimate online model. *USA Today*, B1–B2.

Internet Retailing. (2000, May 27). *The Economist*, 64.

Means to an end. (1999, December 25). *Winston-Salem Journal*, B8.

Tedeschi, Bob. (2000, May 15). Catalog companies show the upstarts that they know a thing or two about Internet retailing. *The New York Times*, C16.

SNAPSHOT

Lowe's Continues to Grow

The home improvement industry–the business of retailing building materials and home improvement products–has shown rapid growth in recent years. Two chains–Lowe's and Home Depot–dominate the market, but of the two, Lowe's has recently shown much more growth.

Home improvement retailing has changed dramatically in the past two decades. Lowe's and other home improvement centers have expanded product assortments, moving from the basics of hardware, tools, and building materials to plumbing materials, electrical supplies, and home décor items, such as carpeting, wallpaper, ready-to-assemble furniture, and even appliances. In recent years, Lowe's has also expanded its installation services and has made a concerted effort to attract women consumers.

In 1989, Lowe's had 295 stores, all less than 40,000 square feet. In fact, 60 stores were less than 20,000 square feet. Lowe's certainly was not a "Top 10" retailer at the time. Home Depot had been opening

80,000- and 100,000-square-feet stores and dominating the market. In the 1990s, Lowe's changed strategies by building bigger stores, concentrating on support systems, and strengthening its infrastructure.

When Lowe's began building and opening bigger stores, it switched to an "everyday low-price" marketing strategy. To do that profitably, Lowe's had to change the way it did business. In fewer than seven years, systems were improved, policies were modified, operating procedures were changed, training programs were enhanced, assortments were augmented, commitment to service was intensified, and an integrated logistics system and distribution network moved from a chain of small stores to a chain of warehouse stores. Heavy emphasis was also placed on customer satisfaction.

Today, Lowe's continues to lure customers away from its bigger rival, Home Depot, which is attributed to the great reputation Lowe's has been developing with consumers. The firm consistently wins consumer praise for a more appealing store design—especially with women shoppers. And, according to the 2005 American Customer Satisfaction Index, Home Depot ranked worst among specialty retailers, while Lowe's satisfaction rating was second only to Costco.

Even with the challenges of the slow housing market today, Lowe's is forging ahead with ambitious growth plans that call for opening up to 160 stores in 2008. Moreover, the retailer most recently posted an 8.5 percent increase in sales of $46.9 billion and a 12.5 percent increase in earnings of $3.1 billion.

Both Lowe's and Home Depot are in a good position for the long term. They are the two dominant retailers and have been able to keep other large retailers out of the home improvement arena. Strategies introduced by Lowe's seem to be having a dramatic impact. In 2006 Lowe's was the eighth largest retailer in the United States while Home Depot remained second. But, Lowe's is gaining—the firm now has 1,375 stores compared to 2,147 Home Depot stores. Moreover, the number of Lowe's stores is growing at a rate of 12.2 percent, while Home Depot's growth has slowed to 5.1 percent.

BASED ON:

Bell, Nichole Monroe. (2007, January 28). Home Depot dives as Lowe's thrives. *The Charlotte Observer*, D1.

Desjardins, Doug. (2006, September 11). Home merchants expect slower sales. *Retailing Today*, 1–2.

Desjardins, Doug. (2007, July 16). Downturn makes upscale harder to sell at Lowe's. *Retailing Today*, 26.

Hindo, Brian and Byrnes, Nanette. (2007, January 15). A sharper edge at Lowe's. *Business Week*.

Lowe's builds a case for optimism. (2007, February 26). *Business Week Online*.

Matthews, Steve. (2003, November 16). Lowe's winning over women. *The Charlotte Observer*, E1.

Painting a bright future with premium lines. (2007, July 16). *Retailing Today*, 29.

Steverman, Ben. (2007, August 20). *Business Week*.

TRENDWATCH

Targeting Current Customers

Against the backdrop of today's highly competitive retail environment and low single-digit sales growth, the importance of managing all customers–from the most loyal to the most indifferent–is critical. Too often, retailers fail to use targeting techniques with their existing customers. One technique is to classify current customers based on the list that follows. Then retailers can determine which customers need to be rewarded for their loyalty, but more importantly which customers might be ready to start shopping at the competition.

One framework for classifying existing customers is as follows:

- *Disciples*. Shoppers do most of their shopping at your store. They frequent multiple departments regularly.
- *Secure*. Shoppers do most of their shopping at your store and consider it "OK." These shoppers also frequent multiple departments.
- *Susceptible*. Customers shop regularly with you but do not really like it compared to the competition. These shoppers do it because it is convenient or close, or no other store has made the right appeal.
- *Vulnerable*. Customers shop your store regularly at more than one department. But, they really do not like it; in fact, a large percentage of this group is actively looking for a better alternative.
- *Disgruntled*. Shoppers patronize one department in your store, but do most of their shopping elsewhere. They do not really like the other store where they usually shop, but prefer it to your store. Many times, these shoppers are actively looking for a more acceptable alternative.

Placing customers into groups can be based on information from the store's database from credit card purchases. For example, parameters can be set in the database to trigger if a decline in a customer's shopping and spending is detected over a predetermined period. For example, you may find that a customer who had been spending $150 a month with your store is now making purchases only totaling $25.

Once these customers are identified, the next step would be to implement strategies that could help retain shoppers who may be straying and use that information to enhance the customer's relationship with the store.

More extensive surveying may also be needed. You need to determine why these shoppers are vulnerable, where they are spending their money now, and where they would shop if they defected. Once all the data are available for analysis, you can explore what can be done to ensure that a store's vulnerable shoppers do not defect.

The greatest opportunity targets are customers who are on the verge of leaving your store—susceptible, vulnerable, and disgruntled. If you focus on these groups with appeals that hit their hot buttons, your store can do a better job of retaining them as loyal shoppers.

The fundamental challenge of implementing such a plan will be having data available about your customers' shopping patterns. Remember that it takes about five times as much effort to get a new customer as it does to retain an existing one. Such targeting efforts may be worth the time and expense.

BASED ON:

Murphy, Patricia. (1998, March). Focus on existing customers seen driving revenue growth. *Stores*, 32–34.

Reda, Susan. (1999, May). 8 basic shopper groups. *RMS Magazine*, 15.

Reda, Susan. (1999, May). Turning customer infidelity into a worthy affair. *RMS Magazine*, 14–19.

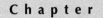

Chapter 2

The Buying Function in Retailing

PERFORMANCE OBJECTIVES

Upon completion of this chapter, you should be able to:

- Recognize factors that will affect the scope of the buyer's job.
- Describe the duties and responsibilities of the buyer.
- Describe the duties and responsibilities of the assistant buyer.
- Describe the duties and responsibilities of the merchandise manager.
- Explain how a buyer's performance is evaluated.
- Identify the qualifications needed to become a buyer.
- Outline career paths related to buying careers.
- Identify trends that will affect buying careers in the future.

As you read in the last chapter, retailing is an ever-changing environment. Because of those constant changes, working in the field is both exciting and challenging. One of the most challenging functions of retailing is buying. As the name implies, purchasing merchandise is a key task performed by buyers, but they also must spend time analyzing market data and reading the latest trade journals to keep abreast of what is happening in the market. Purchasing merchandise occurs only after buyers thoroughly understand their customers, the market, their products, and their competition—and that takes careful study and analysis.

As you read this chapter, you will have the opportunity to closely examine what buyers do and the qualifications you will need to be successful in the field. Possible career paths and current employment forecasts are presented to assist you with career planning. If you choose a buying career, you will find it demanding, but you probably will not mind so long as you are doing something you really enjoy.

THE BUYER'S JOB

Often, buying appeals to college students because they see the glamour associated with frequent travel to exciting places, such as New York City or Los Angeles, and buying trips where they get to spend thousands of dollars on the newest styles and fashions. Travel may be exciting, but often all that a buyer may see of a city is the view from a taxi on the way to a hotel or a merchandise mart. Nor does the hectic pace of a market week allow much time for sightseeing. Deciding what merchandise to buy with those thousands of dollars can be stressful. Because of this financial responsibility, the buyer's job is pressure packed. Many people, however, thrive on the pressure that comes from having the responsibility to make decisions. If you like such challenges, consider buying as a career option. However, if you like quiet contemplation, little stress, and routine activities, buying is probably not for you.

It is difficult to generalize about what a buying career will involve because of the diversity of the types of retailers that exist. The trends and changes that you read about in the previous chapter also have an impact on the activities buyers perform.

Factors Affecting the Scope of the Buyer's Job

Individuals in the retail organization whose primary job is to purchase merchandise are *buyers*. As you will learn in this chapter, their job is much more complex than purchasing merchandise. Three factors affect the scope of the buyer's job: (1) merchandise carried, (2) organizational structure, and (3) size of the retail organization.

Merchandise Carried. The merchandise carried by the retailer determines the responsibilities of a buyer. Buying *basic merchandise* will be much different from buying *fashion merchandise*. Basics are those products with which a business always wants to be in stock. Basics tend to have stable consumer demand so sales vary little from year to year. An analysis of last year's sales records and the current year's sales trends and marketing plans will determine the amount of basic merchandise that a buyer needs to purchase. That is not true for fashion merchandise. A fashion that sold extremely well last year may not sell at all this year. Buying fashion requires much greater reliance on forecasting consumer demand and market trends.

Today, there are fewer and fewer basic items in most retail stores; fashion is affecting almost all merchandise assortments. For example, kitchen appliances come in a multitude of colors and styles, there are various designer sheets and sunglasses, and automobile styles change yearly.

As shown in Figure 2.1, fashion buyers spend plenty of time in the market scouting for just the right merchandise that will provide their

Figure 2.1 Buyers must spend time in the market to locate unique products for their customers.

stores with unique items or fashion looks that the competition does not carry. They also seek items that their stores can receive before the competition. Fashion buyers may even have to seek out resources that will produce private brands just for their stores.

Buyers for discount stores may only be concerned with finding merchandise at the best possible price. Uniqueness is not a key factor; they are more interested in buying merchandise with proven sales records.

Organizational Structure. The type of organizational structure that a retailer uses also determines the duties and responsibilities of buyers. Many retailers today have centralized the firm's buyers at corporate headquarters. In these situations, buyers have little or no direct contact with the stores. Activities, such as management of sales associates and inventory control, are performed by managers at the store level. Large chain stores, such as JCPenney, Sears, and The Gap, conduct buying in this manner.

At some department and specialty stores, not only do buyers make purchases, but they are also responsible for supervising the sales floor.

They may be responsible for varied activities such as scheduling and evaluating sales associates and keeping them motivated.

In small independent stores, the owner usually performs all the buying duties, in addition to all the other responsibilities required in operating a retail business. In addition, he or she must buy for all product categories carried by the store.

Size of the Retail Organization. The size of the retail organization is another factor affecting the scope of a buyer's job. In small retail stores, the buyer may be responsible for buying all the merchandise for several departments. For example, a buyer may purchase all men's and boy's apparel. In large retail stores, however, buyers become more specialized; they are responsible for buying product categories–such as boy's jeans–rather than every product for a department.

The Buyer's Job: Duties and Responsibilities

Even though a buyer's duties and responsibilities vary at different retail firms, there are basic duties and responsibilities that most buyers will perform. They include the following tasks:

- Develop merchandising strategies for a product line, department, store, or the entire retail organization.
- Keep abreast of current market trends and economic conditions.
- Develop an awareness of fashion trends.
- Understand and identify needs and wants of consumers.
- Analyze and interpret reports.
- Make regular market trips.
- Plan and select merchandise assortments.
- Represent the store or retail organization to vendors.
- Negotiate with vendors for favorable terms and services.
- Plan and develop private brands (sold only by that retailer) or import programs for the store or retail organization.
- Price merchandise to generate desired profits.
- Experiment with new merchandising trends and vendors.
- Identify fast-selling and slow-selling products.
- Maintain well-balanced stocks and assortments.
- Control planned purchases, stock levels, and deliveries to stay within merchandise plans.

- Review and periodically revise basic stock programs.
- Contact or visit stores regularly; consult with sales associates and store managers.
- Coordinate promotion activities; develop a point of view for presentation of merchandise.
- Shop and analyze competing stores in the trading area to evaluate their merchandise assortments, prices, and merchandise presentation.
- Achieve goals in sales, markups, markdowns, gross margin, and turnover.

Most retail organizations will develop a job description for buyers that would probably include most of these tasks.

Role of Assistant Buyers

In large retail organizations, buyers may have one or more assistants to help perform these duties. *Assistant buyers* may be considered buyers in training. College graduates pursuing a buying career will usually hold this job after completing a management training program.

Assistants can be assigned much of the clerical and routine parts of the job. By turning over such time-consuming activities to assistants, buyers are better able to complete tasks that take them out into the market.

Duties that are typically assigned to assistant buyers include the following:

- Prepare daily reports to identify best-sellers and slow sellers.
- Replenish basic stock.
- Complete markdown records and reports.
- Review inventory records.
- Follow up with vendors on merchandise orders to ensure prompt delivery.
- Supervise returns to vendors.
- Analyze daily sales reports.
- Supervise price marking.
- Write purchase orders with information provided by the buyer.

Part of your job as a buyer will be to develop capable assistants. Make assistant buyers a part of your team; do not treat them as competitors for your job. You can develop an atmosphere of teamwork by allowing them to review merchandise lines with you in the store or on trips to market showrooms. When you return from market trips, review with them current trends you found. Let them provide input for the merchandise selection process, and keep your assistant buyers informed on how the department or product category is performing.

You and your assistant buyers have a common goal—the success of your department or product category. As a team you will be able to accomplish more, and at the same time, you will be contributing to the development of a future retail buyer or manager.

Changing Role of the Buyer

Technological advances are rapidly changing the buyer's role in many retail stores. Computerized Quick Response systems have been adopted by many retailers. The use of computers has allowed many stores to implement *automatic reordering systems*. Currently being used for basic merchandise, automatic reordering generates weekly orders based on sales in relation to model stock plans. These plans, in turn, have been developed based on past sales and current trends.

Implementation of computer technology and the use of automatic reordering have caused several trends in buying patterns to develop:

- Stronger partnerships are developing between retailers and vendors.
- More frequent orders in smaller quantities are being placed.
- Orders are being made closer to the selling season.
- Replenishment of basic merchandise is based on actual sales, forecasts, and trends.

Automatic reordering systems give the buyer more time to concentrate on other buying activities such as the selection of merchandise and the development of merchandising programs. Some retail organizations are even removing control for the replenishment of basic merchandise from buyers' responsibilities. Automatic reordering allows retailers to turn basics into a replenishment operation as opposed to a buying operation. Buyers can focus more attention on understanding customers and planning purchases more carefully. For example, at Dillard's Department Stores, buyers do not have to deal with writing orders for basic merchandise because automatic reordering systems have been implemented. At these stores, inventory management is being shifted to the store level.

Computers also are having a major effect on many other aspects of buyers' jobs. Computers are handling most of the routine tasks—enabling buyers to concentrate mainly on the analytical aspects of the job. Computers are used to obtain instant and accurate product and price listings, to track inventory levels, process routine orders, and help determine when to make purchases. Computers also record the history of vendor performance and issue purchase orders. Computerized systems have dramatically simplified many of the routine acquisition functions and improved the efficiency of determining which products are selling. For example, cash registers connected to computers, known as point-of-sale terminals, allow retail organizations to maintain centralized, up-to-date sales and inventory levels. This information can then be used to produce weekly sales reports that reflect the types of products in demand.

Buyers also use computers to gain instant access to the specifications for thousands of commodities, inventory records, and their customers' purchase records. Some firms are linked with manufacturers or wholesalers by electronic purchasing systems. These systems improve the speed of selection and ordering and provide information on availability and shipment, allowing buyers to better concentrate on the selection of goods and suppliers.

At many department stores, basic merchandise stocks are currently handled by a planner/distributor who weekly reviews computer-generated reports and suggests orders, makes any needed modifications, and transmits the order electronically. Mervyn's, a California-based retailer, also uses a similar approach by splitting the buying function and the inventory management function between a buyer and a unit control analyst. Most of the buyer's time is spent identifying the right products and market trends.

In each of these retail organizations, buyers have more time to get into the market and do better planning. As more retailers have implemented automatic reordering, these firms have been used as a model for what the buyer's job will look like tomorrow.

Changing business practices have also altered the traditional roles of buyers in many areas, particularly in developing private brands. For example, many apparel buyers are involved at most stages of new product development because of their ability to forecast a material's cost, availability, and suitability for its intended purpose. Furthermore, potential problems with the supply of materials may be avoided by consulting with buyers in the early stages of product design. Private brand merchandise requires buyers to work closely with vendors to develop and obtain the desired product.

The downsizing and consolidation of buying departments is also increasing the demands placed on buyers. Although the amount of work remains unchanged, there are fewer people to accomplish it. The result is an increase in workloads and levels of responsibility.

MANAGING THE BUYING FUNCTION

The manager of the buying function in most retail organizations is the *merchandise manager*–the buyer's direct superior. Merchandise managers set the direction of styles, product lines, and image for their area and oversee its budget, but their major duty is to supervise buyers and allocate resources among them.

Role of the Merchandise Manager

Usually, the duties of merchandise managers can be divided into four areas: (1) planning, (2) directing, (3) coordinating, and (4) controlling.

Planning. Even though merchandise managers are not directly involved in the actual purchase of merchandise, they formulate policies and set standards related to the merchandise areas for which they are responsible. The merchandise that buyers purchase must meet requirements established by merchandise managers, as well as fit the store's image that management has developed.

Another key planning task for merchandise managers is budget development. Buyers must make purchases within financial guidelines developed by merchandise managers, and they must also have merchandising plans approved by them. Merchandise managers are also involved with developing standards (such as sales goals, stock levels, or markups) against which a buyer's performance is measured. When developing these standards, merchandise managers should make every effort to seek involvement from buyers in the planning process. Resentment is likely to develop when performance standards are simply imposed from above; most employees want to have input into such decisions. In addition, input from buyers is vital in the budget-preparation process.

Directing. Supervision of buyers also involves training new buyers. Many times new buyers require counsel from someone with a broad perspective. New buyers are often timid about taking markdowns; others, if left unrestrained, may want to overbuy. Merchandise managers may need to prod buyers into taking markdowns to move merchandise out of the store and help them maintain a sense of balance as they make purchases. Merchandise managers, however, must remember that their function is to advise. In most situations, the buyer is probably more of an expert on buying specific categories of merchandise than is the manager.

Merchandise managers will also want to keep buyers up-to-date on business and economic trends. Many buyers are knowledgeable about product and fashion trends but are less aware of overall economic and market conditions.

Coordinating. Because merchandise managers usually supervise a number of buyers, much of their time is spent in coordinating all the buyers. They must unify their efforts to achieve the image and sales that management desires. Purchases for which different buyers are responsible must also be coordinated. For example, color and design of a new purchase of scarves must complement apparel purchases made by another buyer. Many times, merchandise managers are involved with coordinating promotional campaigns that involve merchandise from several departments, and there are times when they must coordinate merchandising plans with other divisions such as finance and operations.

Controlling. Merchandise managers are directly involved in reviewing the performance of merchandise areas under their control. They must also evaluate each buyer's performance. If a buyer is not meeting performance standards, merchandise managers must take corrective action that could mean working with a buyer on a problem area, such as too many markdowns, or removing a buyer from a job he or she is incapable of performing.

Evaluating Buyers' Performance

Buying is a retailing job for which *quantitative performance standards* can easily be developed. Standards can be established in numerical terms, such as having a certain sales level while maintaining a specific markup percent. How effectively buyers meet these standards will determine how fast they advance in the firm, or, possibly, whether they will keep their jobs. A buyer's goal, for example, may be "To secure a maintained markup of 45.2 percent with sales of $56,000 and markdowns of $2,000" for a department or product category. Precise goals make it easier to evaluate buyers' performances and reward buyers who achieve their goals.

Quantitative considerations may vary with different retailers but are likely to measure such factors as

- Net sales,
- maintained markup percentages,
- markdown percentages,
- gross margin percentages, and
- stock turn.

In addition, a buyer's performance may be measured by how well he or she handles relationships with assistants, other management personnel, vendors, and store managers. A key part of the buyer's job is to create a team atmosphere.

At most retail stores, performance appraisals are formal processes based on documentation. Because buyers plan and set goals for their merchandise areas, their performance can easily be measured.

PLANNING FOR A BUYING CAREER

Now that you know what buyers do, you may have more firmly decided on buying as your career choice. As with any job that you are considering, you need to compare your qualifications with those of people who already have the job. Successful buyers share very definite traits and skills. Decide which qualifications you possess, and then make an effort to sharpen the ones you already possess and develop those you lack. Read the Trendwatch titled, "Today's Buyer," to learn more about how the buyer's job is changing.

Qualifications Needed

Qualifications needed to become a buyer include: (1) appropriate personality traits, (2) human relations skills, and (3) merchandising knowledge and skills. Each area is vital to your future success as a buyer.

Personality Traits. Most retail managers will select new buyers based on whether or not they possess the following personality traits:

Enthusiasm. You must be enthusiastic about the merchandise you are purchasing, your job, and the company. When you make market visits, you must be able to feel the thrill of discovery when you find just the right merchandise for your customers. Enthusiasm is infectious; it will rub off on everyone with whom you come in contact. That enthusiasm will eventually find its way to your store's customers.

Drive. Ambition and hard work are usually prerequisites for success in any retailing career. Buying requires perseverance—the ability to stay with a job until it is completed. Often, long hours may be required.

Vision. As a buyer, you will always be looking ahead—to next season or to next year. Doing just what you did last year may guarantee failure. Consumer demand, fashions, and market trends are constantly changing. As a buyer, you must be alert to these changes and anticipate them before they occur. In business, the most profit is usually made by the firm that has the merchandise first.

Goal-setting ability. Management will be looking for individuals who have set a path to a goal and reach it. Completing college is such a goal. A large part of a buyer's job involves planning, so management will want individuals who can prioritize their time to attain high but realistic expectations.

Ability to work under pressure. Management will be looking for individuals who work well under pressure. In buying, as soon as you have completed one task, others will be waiting. You will probably be juggling multiple tasks at the same time.

Creativity. Even though much of the job is numerical and analytical, buyers must also be creative; they must be innovative. In other words, they must give direction to merchandising decisions that are made to distinguish their merchandise areas from competitors who may be selling similar products. Merchandise selection also allows buyers a certain degree of self-expression as they choose products to meet consumers' wants and needs. Buyers must also use creativity in solving many of the day-to-day problems they face.

Curiosity and imagination are the source of all innovation. Buyers must exploit those traits in themselves and employees with whom they work. They should be willing to consider new ideas from wherever they come. Even customers often have great ideas for changing and showcasing products. The secret to real innovation lies not in doing things just to be different but in doing things to be better.

Human Relations Skills. Another fundamental qualification for a buyer is having the capacity for teamwork. Working with a variety of people is an essential part of the buyer's job. Buyers must be able to work well with superiors (merchandise managers), subordinates (assistant buyers), vendors, department managers and sales associates, and other managers in the organization with whom they coordinate buying activities. Buyers have to value people and demonstrate that they care. Often, just by listening, buyers can show that they recognize colleagues' importance to the company. Working with each of these audiences requires a unique set of skills.

Communications. Communication is essential for buyers because they have constant contact with people. Communication is vital as they channel product information, trends, and enthusiasm from the market to the selling floor and the customer. Communications may also involve oral presentations on product information or written product reports and bulletins sent to store personnel. Advertising may be created based on your reports and bulletins, so it is important that you be clear and concise. You will also need to develop a technical vocabulary that can be used clearly in your communications.

Because stores and vendors are scattered worldwide today, clear and concise written communications are crucial. You must learn to effectively present information in faxes, memos, and e-mails.

Leadership. As a buyer, you head a team. You must be able to provide leadership for your merchandising area. Management wants individuals who can innovate and motivate. Another crucial task is to ensure that other staff members follow through on directives. Many times you will have to use your leadership skills to enlist the help and support of others to plan and implement merchandising decisions.

Leadership demands flexibility—the ability to handle the many changes that are certain to occur every day. For effective buyers, it means keeping their fingers on the pulse of the competitive landscape, monitoring changing consumer trends, being aware of what is happening in the economy, and most importantly, anticipating how all these changes will affect them and their stores. Buyers must have the leadership skills to be able to move quickly to modify their strategy and correct their course when conditions warrant. Buyers cannot rest on past accomplishments because what worked yesterday may not work today, and it almost certainly will not work tomorrow.

Merchandising Knowledge and Skills. In addition to personality traits and human relation skills, buyers will usually be selected based on the merchandising knowledge and skills they already possess. Buyers have to develop an understanding of customers' wants and needs and be prepared to satisfy them. Even though training and internship programs are conducted by most retailers to train buyers, management usually looks for the following qualifications:

Education. A college education is more the rule than the exception for hiring buyers today. Many retailers prefer a four-year degree, but outstanding two-year graduates may be given consideration. Generally, retailers seek buyers who have majors in retail management, fashion merchandising, marketing, or closely related business programs. Courses in marketing, economics, sales, computer applications, personnel management, retailing, and merchandising are essential.

Some liberal arts majors are considered because of their strong background in psychology or sociology. Both of these areas give graduates extensive insight into what motivates customers. Even though they may not have the merchandising skills, their education has developed their self-discipline and sharpened their intellectual abilities.

In addition, rapid technological developments require that buyers be able to adapt to change. Training and retraining are likely to be an ongoing part of the job.

Analytical ability. Buyers must be decision makers. Pricing, merchandise selection, and vendor selection are just three of the decisions they make daily. A strong math background is a prerequisite, with a solid understanding of retail math calculations. Your performance as a buyer will be measured in numerical terms, so you need skill with numbers. Strong analytical skills give buyers the confidence to act decisively. In these days of instantaneous communication overload, buyers have to be able to cut through the clutter using all the tools at their disposal, combined with their own judgment and intelligence, to make informed decisions. Above all, they have to balance decisiveness and analytical skills to avoid "paralysis by analysis." Long response times are a luxury retail buyers seldom have. To meet customers' needs and exceed their expectations, buyers must make decisions frequently and quickly.

You will frequently need to work with budgets and make merchandise plans. Both tasks require that you be able to analyze and present information in numerical terms. You will also have to translate numerical reports into merchandising strategies.

Computer literacy. Computers have made the buyer's job even more numerical and statistical than they used to be. Familiarity with computers is essential for most buyers today. In addition to computer operation, buyers must be able to read and interpret computer output.

Experience. When selecting new buyers, management will desire some actual retail experience. Sales experience is preferred because it provides you with firsthand knowledge of consumers' wants and needs; however, if you do not have extensive retail experience, emphasize any experience you have had. For example, instead of simply describing your duties on a résumé, emphasize performance that is measurable in numbers and percentages. Buyers are always being evaluated against such performance standards.

Qualifications may vary from one retail organization to another, so it will be important to investigate specific firms with which you are interested in working. Several want ads stressing buyer qualifications are illustrated in Figure 2.2. Examine those ads to determine what skills you may already possess.

If you take a job as a buyer, you will need to be observant, beginning with the first day on the job. Nothing is wrong with showing eagerness as you assume new responsibilities; be a good observer, and ask the right questions. Pay attention to the dress codes and the style in which others interact to get work done. All these factors will also play a part in how successful you will be as a buyer.

Career Paths

Rarely do college graduates enter retailing as buyers. Most buyers begin their careers in a ***management training program*** or as assistant buyers. In either situation, the emphasis of your training will probably be on selling. Buyers must know the products they are purchasing as well as understand customers' wants and needs. Time spent in such training programs will vary from one company to another. Read the Snapshot titled "The Macy's Internship Program: Starting Your Career" to learn more about internships offered by Macy's. Similar programs are offered by many retailers. Internships are a great way to enter management training programs.

Most retailers believe strongly that working in the aisles and waiting on customers extends the knowledge base of management or buyer trainees. You really need the store experience to fully know and appreciate the scope of the retail store. Customers can be great educators, and employees are probably the best source of ideas to improve the way things are done.

The main reason that college graduates need to start their careers in retail stores is that working directly for the customer is essential to

Buyer

Energized.
And Growing

Aeropostale is a rapidly expanding retailer with a fresh approach to fashion. We currently have the following opportunities available:

Women's Buyer
&
Assistant Buyer

These challenging buying opportunities will expose individuals to the design and production process. To qualify for the Women's Buyer position, you will need a minimum 3 years of apparel buying experience. For the Assistant Buyer position, a minimum of 2 years apparel buying experience is required. To qualify for both positions, candidates need to possess initiative and a keen fashion sense. Prior junior knit experience a plus.

We offer a competitive salary and comprehensive benefits package that includes a generous merchandise discount, bonus opportunities, a casual work environment and growth potential. Please forward your resume, indicating position of interest, to:

We are an equal opportunity employer M/F

Aeropostale

Ladies Buyer

Forman Mills, the high growth, aggressive, entrepreneurial off-price casualwear apparel chain located in the Philadelphia area is looking for dynamic individuals with strong off price buying experience.

The successful candidate will have:
- 5+ years solid off-price buying exp in Missy &/or Plus
- Strong negotiation skills
- Current branded contacts in LADIES /MISSEY and or PLUS SPORTSWEAR, INTIMATE APPAREL AND FASHION ACCESSORIES.
- Product Development
- Strong Work Ethics
- PC Literate

This is an exceptional career opportunity for individuals looking for a growth opportunity who have entrepreneurial spirit and are creative thinkers. We offer excellent salary, and comprehensive benefits. Forward or fax resumes with salary requirements to:

FORMAN MILLS
Designer Fashions For The Family

BUYER
WOMEN'S CASUAL APPAREL
Must have previous retail buying experience. Previous product development experience a must. Maintain optimal inventory levels. Regional buying skills required. Negotiate marketing funds. Must be willing to relocate to Indianapolis. EOE.

BUYER
Ladies' Shoe Buyer
FOX'S
Designer Clothes at Off-Prices. Long Island based retailer w/ 13 locations seeks exp. Shoe Buyer to develop a new shoe division. Comp. sal./wkly. bonus/401K.

BUYER
Women's Sportswear
Established Midwest retail chain looking for Women's sportswear buyer. Travel required. Please send resume with salary expectations to:

Figure 2.2 Do you possess the skills needed to apply for these buying jobs?

a retailing orientation. The experience develops empathy toward the customer and sensitivity to store personnel. When buyers move to the corporate office, they are better prepared to deal with the needs and requirements of store employees and customers—they are more emotionally attuned to both of these groups.

As a buyer, job promotions can mean that you will be given additional product classifications or departments for which to buy, or you may take on major departments with corresponding increases in pay and pressure. Other promotions could lead to your becoming a merchan-

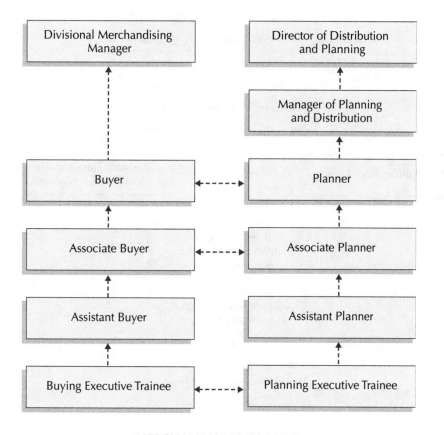

MERCHANDISING/BUYING

Figure 2.3   Sample career path in merchandising.

dise manager or head of the merchandising division for an entire retail organization.

In some retail organizations, jobs in buying may lead you to a management career. Many retail buyers make career changes by moving into the store as department managers. From there, future promotions may take them to management positions in personnel, merchandising, or operations. Some successful buyers could eventually become store managers. Typical career paths found in many department stores are illustrated in Figures 2.3 and 2.4. These job progressions are called *career ladders* or *paths*. Realize that there is nothing carved in stone about suggested career paths; they merely represent how individuals might advance in a career area.

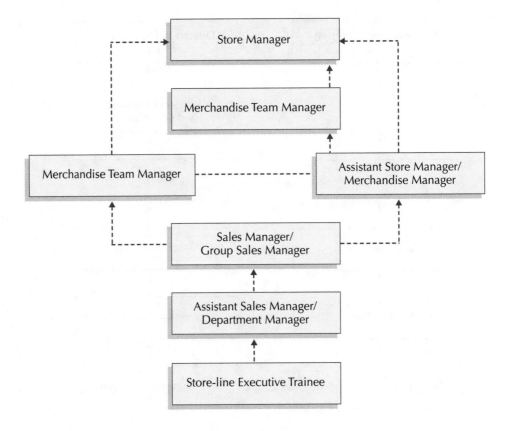

STORE MANAGMENT

Figure 2.4   Merchandising career paths can also lead to store management positions.

Buying provides excellent training and background for other fields too. You could enter a job as a fashion coordinator, comparison shopper, product tester, or product designer. You may even have a strong entrepreneurial inclination and decide to open a retail business of your own. Jobs at businesses associated with buying, such as buying offices and apparel manufacturing plants, may also present opportunities for career advancement. Many of the skills that retail buyers possess could also be used to seek employment as purchasing agents for industrial products. Many of these types of jobs are listed and briefly described in Table 2.1.

Many career paths and options are open to you. Select one that interests you and sharpen and develop the skills you will need to succeed in that area.

Table 2.1: Other Jobs in Retailing

Job Title	Description
Assistant Buyer	Works under the direction of a buyer, usually in a specific product category. Assists in sales analysis, handling reorders, and purchasing some merchandise.
Assistant Department Manager	Works under the supervision of a department manager. Assists in managing personnel, controlling inventory, and other store operations.
Assistant Store Manager	Helps in implementing merchandising strategy and policies. Works with personnel and overall store operations.
Catalog Manager	Selects merchandise for inclusion in catalogs. Works with vendors, places orders, and monitors order fulfillment.
Department Manager	Responsible for a department's merchandise displays, analyzing merchandise flow, and the training and direction of sales associates.
District Manager	Responsible for management personnel, sales generation, merchandise presentation, expense control, and customer service at all stores in the district.
Fashion Coordinator	Directs buyers in evaluating fashion trends.
Fashion Director	Responsible for developing and maintaining a retailer's overall fashion perspective.
Management Trainee	First position for most college graduates entering retailing. Involves company orientation, classroom and on-the-job training, and contact with all facets of the store.
Marketing Research Director	Acquires and analyzes relevant and timely information that assists executives in making important decisions. Heavily involved in research methodology and data collection.

(*continued*)

Job Title	Description
(Table 2.1 continued)	
Merchandise Analyst	Plans and evaluates merchandise allocation to stores to ensure merchandise is delivered at the right time and in proper assortments. Develops assortment plans based on trends and past performance histories.
Merchandise Manager	Plans, manages, and integrates buying for an entire merchandise division composed of several departments or product categories.
Sales Promotion Manager	Plans and enacts special sales, themes, and sales promotion tools, such as contests.
Store Manager	Oversees all store personnel and operations in a particular store. Coordinates activities with other units of a chain. Responsible for customer service, merchandising, and human resource policies.
Vice President for Merchandising	Responsible for developing and evaluating the performance of all product categories. Has responsibility for growth and profit.

Employment Forecasts

The 2006–2007 edition of the *Occupational Outlook Handbook* reports that in 2004 approximately 520,000 individuals in the United States were employed as purchasing managers, buyers, and purchasing agents. They worked in retail, wholesale, and manufacturing and for the government. A small number were self-employed. Employment in these occupations is expected to grow more slowly than average through the year 2010. Demand for these workers will not keep up with the rising level of economic activity because the increasing use of computers has allowed much of the paperwork typically involved in purchasing to be eliminated, reducing the demand for lower-level buyers who perform these duties. Also, limited sourcing and long-term contracting have allowed companies to negotiate with fewer suppliers less frequently. Consequently, most job openings will result from the need to replace workers who transfer to other occupations or leave the labor force.

In retailing, particularly, mergers and acquisitions have forced the consolidation of buying departments, thus eliminating many jobs. In addition, larger retail stores are removing their buyers from stores or district offices and centralizing them at their headquarters. In 2004, the median annual earnings for wholesale and retail buyers was $43,720, with the middle 50 percent earning between $31,550 and $57,010 a year. The highest 10 percent earned more than $79,340 a year.

Getting a Job As a Buyer

Because buying jobs vary, you may need to investigate specific retail firms to determine how buying is conducted there. In addition, there may be differences from one geographic region to another. A key step in career planning involves research. Discover as much as you can about jobs in which you are interested. The best way to do that is not by reading, but by talking with individuals who work as buyers. When you talk with them, ask questions that will reveal what it takes to be a buyer in that retail organization. Questions you could ask may be similar to the following:

- "How do you spend your time during a typical work week?"
- "What skills or talents are most essential to being effective in your job?"
- "What are the toughest problems you face?"
- "What is most rewarding about the work itself, apart from salary or fringe benefits?"
- "If you decided to leave your job, what would drive you away?"

Questions such as these give you insight into both the positive and negative aspects of the job. Realize, however, that changes in retailing will change the buyer's job in the future. Information is presented in Table 2.2 about some of the key reasons why applicants lose out on a job in retail buying. Identify your weaknesses and develop plans to begin eliminating them today.

Staying in touch—with colleagues, friends, neighbors, customers, suppliers, and just about anybody else—will be one of the keys to your getting a job as a buyer. In other words, networking will be critical to identifying job leads. *Networking* involves identifying and communicating with individuals who can be helpful in your job search.

Once you have identified a job opening that looks promising, realize that your résumé and job interviews cannot be approached haphazardly.

Table 2.2: Why Applicants Lose Out on Jobs in Retail Buying

- Poor scholastic record—low grades and/or low level of accomplishments.
- Personality problems—poor attitude, lack of poise and self-confidence, timid, too introverted.
- Lack of goals or objectives—poorly motivated, indecisive, no specific career plans.
- Lack of enthusiasm—lacking drive, little evidence of initiative.
- Inability to express ideas verbally.
- Failure to get information about the company—lack of preparation for the interview.
- Unrealistic salary demands—more interest in salary than opportunity, unrealistic expectations.
- Poor personal appearance.
- Lack of maturity—no evidence of leadership potential.
- Objections to travel—unwilling to relocate.
- Inadequate preparation for a buying career—inappropriate background.

For example, instead of just describing your past or current job duties, describe what you have accomplished on the job, especially performance that is measurable in numbers and percentages. If you instituted a safety program, stress the reduction in on-the-job injuries. There are many online services today where college graduates can post their résumés. Read the Snapshot titled, "AllRetailJobs.com: Using the Internet to Locate Merchandising Positions," to learn about one of the sites devoted entirely to retailing careers.

Retailing management or buying careers will place enormous responsibilities into your hands. A single department in a large department store generates revenue of about $2 million a year and requires supervision of a staff of ten or more employees. Buyers may be responsible for purchasing millions of dollars worth of merchandise. There is stress, but there are also rewards. Can you handle the pressure?

SUMMARY POINTS

- The key function of the buyer is purchasing merchandise, but that requires analysis and interpretation of data and trends. Buyers must thoroughly understand their customers, the market, their products, and the competition before decisions can be made.
- Buying offers an attractive and challenging career for individuals who like being responsible for making decisions. Buyers must also like working with products, as well as people.
- The buyer's job will vary in different types of retail stores. The merchandise carried, the organizational structure of the store, and its size will all have an impact on the buyer's job.
- Buyers perform many activities in and out of their offices. Many buyers have assistant buyers on their staff to perform many of their routine activities.
- The buyer's job is changing at many retail stores. Computerization has allowed buyers to implement automatic reordering systems for many basic merchandise items.
- Merchandise managers are the immediate superiors of buyers in most retail stores. Their duties can be grouped into planning, coordinating, and controlling.
- Buyers are evaluated against quantitative performance standards.
- There are specific personality traits, human relations skills, and merchandising knowledge that potential buyers should possess. A college education is usually a prerequisite.
- Buyers can advance along career paths in both merchandising and management tracks in many stores. Buyers can also advance into occupations related to their field such as fashion coordination and product testing.
- Forecasts for buying occupations indicate slowed employment growth.

REVIEW ACTIVITIES

Developing Your Retail Buying Vocabulary

Consult the Glossary if you did not add the following terms to your vocabulary.

Assistant buyer	Fashion merchandise
Automatic reordering system	Management training program
Basic merchandise	Merchandise manager
Buyer	Networking
Career path/ladder	Quantitative performance standard

Understanding What You Read

1. List and categorize positive and negative characteristics of the buyer's job.
2. Identify reasons why college students may initially be attracted to a job as a buyer.
3. List the factors that affect the scope of a buyer's job in retail organizations.
4. Distinguish how buying basic merchandise differs from buying fashion merchandise.
5. Summarize how buying may be different in large and small retail stores.
6. Identify activities that a buyer can do to ensure that an assistant buyer feels part of the merchandising team.
7. How have automatic reordering systems changed the buyer's job?
8. List the benefits that automatic reordering systems provide the retailer and the buyer.
9. Summarize the planning duties of a merchandise manager.
10. What is the key reason that many buyers lose their jobs?
11. List quantitative performance standards that can be used to evaluate a buyer's performance.
12. Describe how "vision" is an important trait needed by all buyers.
13. List the different groups with whom the buyer must communicate.
14. Explain how buyers use written communications on the job.
15. Describe why a college degree is required of prospective buyers by many retailers.

16. Identify how college graduates would probably spend their first weeks of employment in a management training program to become a buyer.
17. Outline one career path that a buyer could pursue.

Analyzing and Applying What You Read

1. Should extensive travel opportunities be viewed as a positive or negative feature of the buyer's job? Explain.
2. Predict how the buyer's job will change with increased use of computer technology by retail organizations.
3. Will there be a need for buyers in retailing 30 years from now? Explain.
4. Develop a job description for a merchandise manager.
5. Assume that you are applying for a job as a buyer. Describe how you would ensure that the interviewer knew you possessed the following personality traits: enthusiasm, vision, and goal-setting ability.
6. Interview an individual at a local retail store who is responsible for buying merchandise. Ask questions similar to the ones presented in the text to determine traits and qualifications needed for the job as well as the person's duties. In class, compare and contrast your findings with those of other students.

Spreadsheet Skills

1. One of the critical computer skills that all buyers must have is the ability to work with spreadsheets. In *Making Buying Decisions: Using the Computer As a Tool*, complete the problems related to Merchandising Concept 1–1 (Input Data and Interpret Computer Output).
2. One of the first calculations that all retailers must make is determining whether or not their decisions have been profitable. In *Making Buying Decisions: Using the Computer As a Tool*, complete the problems related to Merchandising Concept 12–1 (Calculate Profit and Loss).

Internet Connection

1. Go to http://www.macys.com and locate specific procedures for applying for one of the available internship programs offered by the company. Locate one other online retailer offering an internship

program. Describe the features of that internship (eligibility, length of internship, pay, etc.).

2. On the Internet, go to http://www.AllRetailJobs.com and use the search function on the site to identify retail opportunities that are listed for your area.

SNAPSHOT

The Macy's Internship Program: Starting Your Career

For a number of years, Macy's has offered a ten-week, paid buying/planning internship during the summer months. The internship is available at any of the division headquarters across the country—Atlanta, Miami, Minneapolis, New York, San Francisco, Seattle, and St. Louis—and provides an overview of the buying and planning functions and why specific merchandise is purchased by Macy's. Interns gain experience in financial analysis, advertising, professional development, and communication skills. Above all, the internship provides the foundation for more rapid advancement for those who join the company's Executive Development Program upon graduation from college.

Interns participate in core classes in functional areas of business such as financial analysis, purchase processing, and merchandise tracking. In addition, they receive exposure to stock analysis and competitive shopping. Above all, interns participate in a hands-on experiential learning environment as they improve their professional development skills. Participants work with systems and store planners to help analyze consumer trends in order to identify potential hot sellers and key items. Interns also have the opportunity to visit wholesale markets and meet with vendors.

The following skills and qualifications are required for internship participants:

• Solid academic achievement and the ability to use analytical and quantitative concepts.
• Strong communication, interpersonal, and time-management skills.

• Visionary approach to prioritizing projects and multiple tasks to achieve business goals.
• Strong business acumen and appreciation of professional business ethics.
• Ability to promote teamwork environments.
• Proficiency in MS Word and MS Excel.

In addition to the Buying/Planning internship, Macy's also offers specialized internships in management, product development, and design. An internship with this company is well worth exploring. Check with the career services office at your school or visit with Macy's recruiters when they visit your campus. Internships are usually filled by early March of each year, so start your planning early.

BASED ON
Information from http://www.macysjobs.com

SNAPSHOT

AllRetailJobs.com: Using the Internet to Locate Merchandising Positions

As you continue your study of retail buying, you will probably start asking questions such as:

• "What types of merchandising/buying jobs are available?"
• "Where are these jobs located?"
• "What compensation is available?"

Today, there are many sites on the Internet that can help answer questions like these. One of these sites is AllRetailJobs.com, which was launched in March 2001. This site has emerged as the number one job board dedicated to the retail industry. With nearly 50,000 retail jobs listed across the United States, AllRetailJobs.com offers more retail career opportunities than any other source. In fact, the site lists more than twice as many retail jobs as Monster.com and fourteen times more than Careerbuilder.com. Sixteen hundred retailers have registered with AllRetailJobs.com, including more than half of the top 100 retailers.

Faced with tight budgets and disappointing results from larger generalist job boards, many recruiters have turned to niche sites, such as this one, that focus on a specific industry. For many retailers, career-specific sites help them find candidates more quickly and efficiently than through general sites. Career-specific sites are not overwhelmed by as many poor-quality résumés as the general sites.

Job seekers on AllRetailJobs.com can conduct a free search for career opportunities by job category, location, salary range, and keywords. Moreover, when potential job candidates apply for these jobs online, their résumés are automatically e-mailed to the appropriate companies. Candidates can also receive weekly e-mails that alert them to all new jobs that meet their specifications. In addition, recruiters can maintain an electronic log of all candidates who apply for jobs.

AllRetailJobs.com divides retail job opportunities into two sections: management and hourly positions. Management positions include store and assistant store managers, district managers, buyers, merchandisers, and corporate positions. Hourly positions include sales associates, cashiers, customer service representatives, and stock clerks. Pay for the jobs listed range from standard hourly wages to six-figure annual salaries as high as $300,000. Listed positions cover the entire retail industry, including apparel/fashion, automotive, big box, catalog, department, discount, drug, electronics, hardware/home improvement, home products, jewelry, music/video/books, office products, specialty, sporting goods, supermarkets, and toys/hobbies.

AllRetailJobs.com also markets their services in retail magazines, through Internet sources and in newsletters distributed to customers and potential clients. They are listed prominently on search engines, with more than one thousand retail-related keywords. Job listings are also cross-posted on TopUSAJobs.com.

Internet job-search sites like AllRetailJobs.com provide you with one way to start your career planning. Be proactive; start the hunt for that perfect job today!

BASED ON:
Information from http://www.AllRetailJobs.com

TRENDWATCH

Today's Buyer

The world of today's buyer is more of a numbers game than ever before! Technology is providing buyers with *access to increasing quantities of data*, making buyers' jobs more scientific than they were years ago. Today, buyers must do much more than scour the market for the most appropriate merchandise and negotiate the best deals. Buyers must analyze numbers, in real time and historical formats, and then make purchasing decisions based on trends and past product performance.

Buyers can no longer rely solely on the right "hunch" about which products might sell the best. Successful buyers must become competent researchers and forecasters. Because the job has changed, some retail analysts believe that the term *buyer* may be obsolete. In some retail organizations, buyers are now referred to as "category managers," while other firms view the buyer as the "purchasing agent" for a store's customers.

There are positives and negatives as to how the buyer's job has changed. Although an abundance of data can assist buyers in making more appropriate decisions about quantities to order and inventory levels, buyers can also become inundated with too much data. In fact, many buyers feel overwhelmed with the enormous amount of information that can be easily generated; they receive more data than they can ever actually use or implement.

Much of the data generation is being fueled by consolidation in the retail environment. Fewer, but larger, retail corporations means each corporation is under constant pressure to increase profits. Today, a large part of a buyer's evaluation is not based solely on number of sales, but on the profitability of those sales.

Buyers must also know how to bring new products into their stores with minimal risk. This has made product testing and evaluation a growing part of the buyer's role. They must possess a keen eye for fashion—even if they are not buying fashion per se. Products like cell phones and computers also have a fashion element because they come in many colors and models.

Buyers today must be knowledgeable about logistics. They need to understand the cost of moving merchandise, including delivery costs and delivery times—across town or across the globe. There is an increasing emphasis on developing partnerships between vendors and retail buyers and making these relationships far more collaborative than in the past—which takes effort and time.

Buyers must have the skills to utilize an ever-growing list of available technologies. That list includes everything from complex, mathematical computer programs to weather forecasts and the Internet. E-mail allows buyers "24/7" communications with resources around the world. However, e-mail has some drawbacks. Because it is easy and inexpensive to use, buyers can quickly become overwhelmed with the mass of communications received each day. They must spend a great deal of time filtering through their e-mails, a task not required years ago.

Does all of this data analysis make buyers today more mechanical and less creative? Some in the industry feel that is indeed the case. Buyers, however, will be required to look beyond the data provided to them by computers. Their best "hunch" still may be needed after they have assimilated and analyzed all the data at hand. The buyer who succeeds gets the product first, turns it around fastest, and replenishes it quickest, all the while keeping costs down and providing customers with retail prices they are willing to pay.

Chapter 3

Buying for Different Types of Stores

PERFORMANCE OBJECTIVES

Upon completion of this chapter, you should be able to:

- Describe the differences between buying hard lines and soft lines.
- Describe the differences between buying fashion merchandise and basic merchandise.
- List and describe retail formats for which buyers make purchases.
- Describe centralized buying.
- Identify advantages and drawbacks of centralized buying.
- Identify types of centralized buying.
- Describe how buying is conducted for a single independent retailer.
- Explain the rationale for departmentalization at retail organizations.
- List and explain the types of departmentalization.
- Recognize the need for buyers to coordinate activities with other departments in a retail organization.

As you learned in the previous chapter, the key duty of the buyer is to purchase merchandise for the store that will meet customer needs. This is true of all retail stores, regardless of their size or organizational structure or what products they sell. As you also learned, a key measurement of the buyer's performance is sales volume; however, in most retail stores today, the individuals who buy merchandise are separate from the individuals who sell the merchandise. As you will learn, separation of buying and selling has both advantages and drawbacks for the buyer. This chapter focuses on how the buying function is performed in different types of retail stores. Departmentalization is also described, along with a discussion of the coordination that must occur between the buyer and other departments.

BUYING DIFFERENT TYPES OF PRODUCTS

Almost all the duties that are described in the last chapter are performed by a buyer at any type of retail store—no matter what products are sold. As you start to plan your career in retail buying, one of your first decisions should be to determine the types of merchandise that would interest you the most. Are you more interested in soft lines or hard lines? *Soft lines* are typically the apparel and accessory product categories and fashions for the home such as linens, curtains, and bathroom items. In most stores the remainder of the merchandise would be classified as *hard lines* and would include such product categories as hardware, sporting goods, appliances, furniture, toys, and lawn and garden products. Each of those areas could be further subdivided, depending on the size of the store. Soft lines could include women's, men's, and children's clothing. Even these categories could be further broken down—for example, men's jeans or men's dress pants. At large retail chains, some buyers may be responsible for only one product type—boy's jeans, for example.

Another way of further subdividing these two broad categories would be to classify merchandise as fashions or basics. Basic merchandise includes items that customers buy year in and year out; they expect the store to have these items in stock at all times. For example, socks, hosiery, and blue blazers would be considered basics in soft lines. In hard lines, basics would include products such as Barbie dolls, notebooks, or votive candles. Fashion merchandise, however, includes products that have high demand over a relatively short period of time—usually one selling season. Fashion merchandise includes most apparel items but also many hard lines. The newest aroma candles, the "hottest" color of notebooks, or a "special edition" Barbie doll would all be considered fashion merchandise. These items will be in the store for only a few months before being replaced by the next trend or newest model.

New buyers will find that forecasting for basic merchandise is much easier than for fashion merchandise. Sales for basics tend to vary little from year to year; that is not true with fashion merchandise. Fashions come on the market quickly and are gone just as quickly. Fashion buyers must be able to *predict* what their customers will buy this year without having last year's sales figures available because the merchandise is entirely new to the store. Even looking at similar products from last year may not provide valuable information. A trend that sold well last year may not sell at all this year.

Fashion buyers must always be seeking out new and innovative products to buy. Their buying decisions will involve many more risks than decisions of buyers who handle only basics. For many fashion buyers, these are the reasons that make buying fashion merchandise exciting and challenging. In addition, because of the pressure of taking these risks, fashion buyers are paid more than buyers who purchase only basics. Having the "right" fashion products in a store can be very profitable.

As you enter a career in retail buying, your first job will probably be buying basic merchandise. As you make purchasing decisions for that product category, you will be able to develop and hone your buying skills before having to deal with the risks and uncertainties of buying fashion merchandise. Which types of products interest you the most as you start your buying career?

BUYING AT DIFFERENT RETAIL FORMATS

After you decide which types of products interest you the most, you need to make a choice about the type of retail store for which you would like to be a buyer. By looking around your community, you can identify many types of retailers for whom you could work. Some of those stores may be located in malls or in downtown areas. Others may be stand-alone stores or located in strip shopping centers. These stores probably range from small independents to large stores that may be a part of a chain found in communities across the country. Examine the types of stores that interest you. Who performs the buying duties? Do they have buyers at the local store? Are all buying duties performed by individuals at corporate headquarters? The answers to these questions may narrow your list of potential employers.

Do your career interests lie more with large retailers or small independents? Or are you interested in one day owning your own retail store? Before making your choice, you need to carefully examine the various kinds of retailers–their similarities as well as differences. On the one hand, you may want to examine the largest retailers in the country. These firms probably offer many employment opportunities due to their size and expansion plans. Review Table 3.1 to identify the top ten retailers in the United States. You are also provided with information on how fast these retailers are growing.

On the other hand, you may be more interested in starting your buying career at a local independent store that is not part of a chain. Such a decision certainly offers benefits. You will probably face less pressure and be better able to know your customers' wants and needs. But, you will probably have to make purchases for the entire store or an entire department. You will be dealing with many different products, and that requires broad product knowledge. Also, at small independent retail stores, opportunities for advancement probably will come more slowly. No matter where you work, however, retail buying will provide you with an exciting and rewarding career.

As you make your decision about where to start your buying career, you need to examine the different types of retail formats that exist. Stores

Company	2006 Revenues	Y/Y Change	Number of Stores	Y/Y Change
Wal-Mart	$348,650,000	11.7%	6,779	10.6%
Home Depot	$90,837,000	11.4%	2,147	5.1%
Kroger	$66,111,200	9.2%	3,659	(1.8%)
Costco	$60,151,227	13.6%	488	5.9%
Target	$59,490,000	13.1%	1,487	6.4%
Sears Holdings	$53,012,000	7.9%	3,835	(0.6%)
Walgreens	$47,409,000	12.3%	5,461	10.3%
Lowe's	$46,927,000	8.5%	1,375	12.2%
CVS	$43,813,000	18.4%	6,202	13.4%
Safeway	$40,185,000	4.6%	1,761	(0.8%)

Table 3.1: Top 10 Retailers in the United States

Source: *Stores* (July 2007).

today are quite different from the way they were only a few years ago, and retailing tomorrow will look much different from the way it does today. One of the biggest changes has been in classifications of retail stores themselves. Already the lines between many retailers have blurred. Sears decided to compete with discounters by offering "everyday low prices." Kmart has gone upscale by offering designer merchandise. Discounters and some department stores have added food lines to their product assortments, and Macy's basement offers customers a full-service deli. SuperTargets now sell groceries, and grocery stores sell hosiery. In the new millennium, new retail formats are likely to emerge to compete with traditional retailers for the customer's shopping dollar. What formats do you see appearing?

As you will learn, old formats are changing, but general retail formats exist, many times in an altered state. They include department stores, discount department stores, outlets, specialty stores, and supermarkets.

Department Stores

Department stores are businesses that sell all kinds of merchandise for the individual and the home. These stores typically offer a wide assortment of merchandise and services organized into departments based on product categories. One-stop shopping for the entire family has been the lure of the department stores.

For years, the dominant retailers in the United States have been large department stores such as Sears, JCPenney, and Macy's. This dominance, however, has been threatened by other retail formats such as specialized department stores that have eliminated less-profitable product categories. Many specialized department stores, for example, Parisian, sell only apparel and home fashions. Kohl's is another specialized department store, but it also has many features of a discount store. Read the Snapshot entitled, "Kohl's: A Department Store with a Discount-Store Strategy" to learn more about how this store blurs the classification between department and discount store.

The future of department stores will probably depend on how well management defines the market segments the company wants to reach. Some department stores have already narrowed their product assortment as well as their customer base; they no longer try to offer something for everyone. For example, JCPenney has expanded its apparel lines, attempted to offer more national brands, and eliminated other product categories such as appliances and hardware. Sears added many national brands to its product mix, eliminated its "big book" catalog, and for many years was stressing "the softer side of Sears." Department stores have realized that they must change with the times if they are to survive. Read the Trendwatch titled "The Future of the Department Store" to learn more about future trends affecting department stores. Figure 3.1 illustrates the percentage of total retail sales represented by department stores.

Discount Department Stores

Discount department stores, like department stores, emphasize one-stop shopping to meet the needs of all family members and appeal to consumers who value savings over service. Discounters typically offer an extensive selection of national brands in a modest setting with few salespeople on hand to offer service to consumers. Emphasis is on selling nationally advertised brands at low prices. Typically, they do not carry the same broad categories found in department stores but tend to concentrate on the fastest-moving merchandise. In addition to these differences, department stores usually offer more customer services, whereas merchandise in discount department stores is organized to encourage self-selection by the customer. Giants in the field include Wal-Mart, Kmart, and Target.

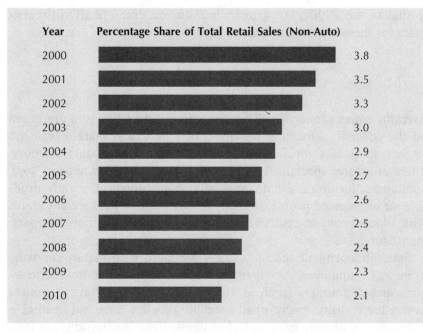

Year	Percentage Share of Total Retail Sales (Non-Auto)
2000	3.8
2001	3.5
2002	3.3
2003	3.0
2004	2.9
2005	2.7
2006	2.6
2007	2.5
2008	2.4
2009	2.3
2010	2.1

Figure 3.1 Projected decline in department store sales.

Outlet Stores

Many traditional retail stores have established *outlet stores* across the country where they sell slow movers and out-of-date merchandise. JCPenney and Nordstrom Rack are two examples of retailers that have entered this retailing format. Many manufacturers also have established outlet stores to sell factory overruns, usually at deep discounts. Buyers at outlet stores often have the responsibility of developing specifications for products that will be sold only at the outlets—new merchandise not offered in traditional stores. The buyers must work in tandem with other buyers so that the two lines are complementary.

Some outlets may even sell the same merchandise being offered at traditional retail stores near the end of the selling season. Other outlet stores are also used as test markets for new styles or models coming into the market. Polo, Bose, Eddie Bauer, Bassett Furniture, and Tommy Hilfiger are just a few of the manufacturers that have been selling merchandise through this retail format. Outlet stores were a fast-growing format in the 1990s, but growth has slowed dramatically in recent years for these types of stores.

Specialty Stores

Specialty stores primarily sell one specific product line and are based on the concept of meeting the needs of a particular market segment. In fact, there is a specialty store for almost every product category. There are stores specializing in women's apparel, men's apparel, toys, appliances, furniture, plants, and gifts; some stores offer only products for left-handed people. In many product categories, specialty stores with much broader assortments are challenging traditional department stores.

Small independent specialty stores are faced with merely surviving in many communities. As superstores, specializing in one product category, and discounters (such as Target and Wal-Mart) have expanded across the country, many small specialty retailers have not been able to compete and have gone out of business. Read the Trendwatch entitled, "Is Bigger Really Better? Will the Small Independent Retailer Survive?" to learn more about how these small retailers will have to compete in the future.

Supermarkets

The *supermarket* is also a departmentalized store, which sells groceries, dairy products, meats, and produce along with some nonfood items. To meet the "one-stop-shopping" demands of consumers, most supermarkets have broadened their product lines to include nonfood items such as hardware, health and beauty aids, housewares, stationery, or clothing.

Supermarkets were the first retailers to develop a "superstore" concept by offering both food and general merchandise in large settings. Today, however, discount supercenters and warehouse clubs have expanded the superstore concept and are luring customers away from local supermarkets.

Consolidation and retrenchment have also marked supermarket retailing in this country. At one time, Food Lion was the fastest-growing supermarket chain in the country, but in recent years it has had to retrench from its expansion into Texas. The giants of the industry include Kroger, Safeway, and Albertson's.

BUYING FOR CHAIN STORES

With mergers and expansion of many independent retail stores, there has been a tremendous growth in the number of chain stores. A *chain store* is two or more stores under single ownership. Typically, a chain store has a central headquarters that manages and buys merchandise for all stores in the chain. It is hard to generalize about chain store organizations because they are so complex. Some have two or three stores, whereas others have hundreds. Chains can be located in one city, one state, one region, or nationwide. Some chains own all their units, whereas others franchise part of their operations.

As retail stores grow and expand, management looks for ways to increase control as well as profitability of their stores. Standardizing merchandise assortments and store operations in all stores of the chain has become an approach that is frequently used. Buyers are removed from individual stores and placed at the chain's headquarters. By purchasing the same merchandise for many different stores, the chain also has the advantage of mass buying power, providing the opportunity for increased profits. In fact, some of the largest national chains purchase the complete output of certain manufacturers.

There are chains that carry varied assortments of merchandise such as grocery, department, discount, and drugs; but some chains specialize in a single line of merchandise such as shoes, men's clothing, candy, jewelry, toys, tires, or sporting goods. Buyers for such specialty stores may have responsibility for only one line or brand of merchandise.

Buyers for a chain store plan sales goals, seek out sources of merchandise, and purchase merchandise to be sold in all the chain's stores. In most chain stores, selling is separate from the buying function. Buyers have very little responsibility for sales personnel and practically no personal contact with them. Removal of selling responsibility enables them to devote their entire time to product and market knowledge; therefore, they become product specialists. Due to the separation of buying and selling, buyers must keep in contact with stores and sales associates through bulletins and other communications because the buyer's performance is still measured by the amount of merchandise sold in the stores.

Centralized Buying

Centralized buying occurs when all buying activities are performed from the store's central headquarters. Buyers there have the authority and responsibility for the selection and purchase of merchandise for all stores. The primary advantages of central buying include the following:

- A steady flow of merchandise is provided to the store because buyers are able to spend more time in the market. They are able to make frequent small shipments to keep store assortments complete and balanced.
- Sales forecasts for all stores in a chain are more reliable than forecasts for each separate store. Centralized data allow buyers to be more accurate in predicting consumer trends because examining a small number of sales in each individual store may not to be enough to detect trends.
- A specialist is making the buying decisions. Centralized buyers make merchandise decisions for only a few products rather than a multitude of items, allowing them to be more knowledgeable about that merchandise.
- Expenses are reduced because each store does not need individual buyers. Travel expenses to markets are also reduced.
- Purchasing power is consolidated at headquarters, and this leads to lower merchandise costs because the chain will be in a better position to take advantage of quantity discounts.

Types of Centralized Buying

Central buying usually occurs in one of three forms: (1) central merchandising plan, (2) warehouse requisition plan, or (3) price agreement plan.

Central Merchandising Plan. Under the ***central merchandising plan***, a central office representing a group of stores has complete responsibility for the selection and purchase of merchandise for all the stores. Stores using this plan include major department stores such as JCPenney and Sears, as well as national specialty store chains such as The Limited, Lane Bryant, Old Navy, and The Gap. Each store receives whatever the corporate office considers appropriate; however, these decisions are not made haphazardly. Buying decisions for each store are based on factors such as sales history and average ticket sale. Centralized buyers spend a great deal of time collecting and analyzing sales and inventory data collected from each store. Because of a dependence on reports, there is a tremendous reliance on computer output.

The chief disadvantage of this approach is that individual store needs may not be met. Managers may be less enthusiastic about selling merchandise that they had no choice in selecting and may even be critical of the merchandise received. Some store managers may even blame the buyers for slow-selling merchandise.

Warehouse Requisition Plan. The *warehouse requisition plan* attempts to overcome some of the limitations of the central merchandising plan; however, it is typically used only by stores carrying basic merchandise. Regional distribution centers are established to serve a number of stores in the area. The buyer at headquarters still determines the assortment of merchandise carried in the warehouse; however, each store manager is allowed to requisition the assortment that he or she wishes for the individual store. This plan allows managers to eliminate items they feel are unnecessary for their store, or items that will not sell well in their locality. Requests for merchandise are sent directly to the warehouse, which many times is located less than 24 hours from the store. Chain stores that decide to use this plan must have a sufficient number of stores in one area to make the establishment of a distribution center cost-effective.

The plan provides several advantages. Usually, shipping distances from the distribution center to each store are short so that orders can be filled quickly. Using the warehouse requisition plan also reduces the amount of inventory that must be carried by each store. Because stores can obtain quicker reorders, less merchandise has to be kept in stockrooms, freeing additional space for sales.

This plan is used extensively by food, drug, and discount chains. Department stores such as Sears and JCPenney have also established warehouses for many of their lines; however, this plan is *not* usually effective for fashion items. Fashion items change so quickly that they need to come directly from the manufacturer. Fashion goods have too short a selling life to permit storing them for a time in a warehouse.

Price Agreement Plan. In the *price agreement plan*, centralized buyers still select the merchandise assortment, and they also select the vendors from which each store will make purchases. After examining past sales records and current trends, centralized buyers decide what merchandise the stores will be carrying. They then make agreements with various vendors, and a list of approved merchandise is sent to each store. The buyers have already negotiated prices and terms when the list is sent. Some buyers even develop a catalog that illustrates and describes every item available.

Individual store managers then order directly from the manufacturers listed. The manager chooses what the store will carry from these selections, and manufacturers ship goods directly to the store in drop shipments. This plan retains the mass purchasing advantage of the central merchandising plan, and it also allows store managers to make choices that they feel are best for their store.

Drawbacks of Centralized Buying

As you have read, buying and selling have become separated in most retail stores. Advantages are gained with increased profitability, standardized operations, and improved control, but there are drawbacks to central buying.

The most evident challenge is that adjusting merchandise selection for local conditions may be difficult. Larger sizes and different colors may sell at various rates in particular areas depending on characteristics of the population. Timing of seasonal goods also varies from one part of the country to another. Winter comes earlier to some sections of the country than others. However, this may not be as serious as it sounds. Except for weather variations, demand in all parts of the United States today is remarkably uniform, no doubt due to mass media advertising and the large amount of consumer travel. Centralized buyers also have a wealth of store data to analyze, even though they are not in the area where an individual store is located.

Centralized buying can lead to a lack of cooperation between buyers and store managers. There is a difficulty in fixing responsibility when merchandise does not sell well. In fact, some managers may be apathetic or prejudiced against the merchandise sent by buyers at headquarters because they did not have a choice in its selection.

Sometimes, centralized buying makes it difficult to maintain enthusiastic and knowledgeable sales associates. The merchandising division and the buyers are still judged by the amount of goods sold, but the use of centralized buying has removed control of sales associates from the buyer. In fact, except for an occasional visit to a nearby store, many buyers may never have been in the vast majority of a chain's stores.

Buyers have the responsibility for informing the stores of the manner in which the merchandise is to be sold. Because this cannot be done orally, a constant flow of written communication is required. Written bulletins, however, are a poor substitute for the enthusiasm built up by actual involvement in the selection of goods.

To overcome these drawbacks, some chains have moved toward decentralization. Some duties that once were performed at headquarters are delegated to the stores. For example, both the warehouse requisition plan and the price agreement plan give each store manager more choice in merchandise selection.

Almost all national chains use centralized buying today. Since it has become so dominant in the retail industry, fewer complaints are heard at the store level. Most store-level associates have never known buying to occur any other way. In fact, JCPenney has been one of the last holdouts. Until summer 2000, department managers in the individual stores were still making buying decisions for the store. Today, all buying functions are performed by buyers located at the corporate headquarters in Dallas.

ORGANIZATIONAL STRUCTURE AND THE BUYING FUNCTION

At large retail operations, job functions are assigned to different sets of employees–they are departmentalized. **_Departmentalization_**, organizing different store activities into departments or divisions, results in managers who are directly responsible to the store or chain's manager.

Types of Departmentalization

Usually, departmentalization is based on job function, but it may occur based on product line or geographic location. The size of the firm usually determines which approach is used.

Functional departmentalization is one of the most commonly used methods by which work is organized in retail stores. With **_functional departmentalization_**, activities of a similar nature are grouped together into a major area of responsibility and headed by an individual who reports to the owner or chief executive of the firm.

A basic four-function plan of store organization known as the "Mazur Plan" has been used by most retailers since 1927, when Paul M. Mazur recommended it to what is now the National Retail Federation. The four functions he presented occur in every retail store organization, regardless of size or number of people employed. They are:

- *Control*. This department would be responsible for safeguarding the firm's assets and is usually divided into accounting, credit, and financial control.
- *Promotion*. Responsibilities of this department would usually include advertising, visual merchandising, public relations, special events, and fashion coordination.
- *Operations*. This department would typically be responsible for the stockroom, maintenance, delivery, receiving, and customer services.
- *Merchandising*. Duties of this department would be to forecast the type, quality, and price of merchandise that will be wanted by the store's customers, and then to purchase these goods as economically as possible.

Today, the organizational structure of many retail stores also includes the function of personnel or human resource management. This department is responsible for interviewing, placing, and terminating employees as well as maintaining employee records and conducting training programs.

Product-line departmentalization occurs at some retail stores that have a varied product offering. Stores using **product-line departmentaliza- tion** group merchandise by categories such as furniture, appliances, children's wear, or jewelry. Large food stores are all departmentalized this way, with departments such as grocery, meats, produce, deli- bakeries, and health and beauty aids. An individual is responsible for all business operations affecting a particular product line, including buying and selling.

Using product-line departmentalization, a buyer could be in charge of a single product category or several. Other store functions can also be departmentalized this way. For example, control can be divided into accounts receivable and accounts payable; however, the focus of this chapter is on the merchandising function.

Stores could also decide to departmentalize based on both function and product line. An independent department store, for example, may establish a merchandising division for the store, with buyers directly responsible to this division manager. Each buyer would be making purchases for specific product lines.

Geographic departmentalization can be found at many retail chains that have expanded nationally. *Geographic departmentalization* breaks the organization down by region of the country. For example, some national firms may have a north, south, east, and west division, each headed by an executive. Under this executive would be various other managers, each with a different area of responsibility. Usually, these areas are the functional areas presented previously.

Some retail firms are so large they may use all three types of departmentalization–functional, product line, and geographic departmentalization. This type of combined organizational structure is presented in Figure 3.2.

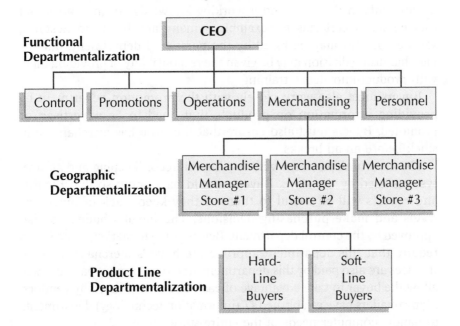

Figure 3.2 The organizational structure for some retail stores combine several types of departmentalization.

Relationship of Merchandising to Other Departments

To be successful as a buyer, you must understand the relationship of your job duties to other jobs in the organizational structure of your firm. In particular, you must understand the relationship of the buying and selling functions within your store. Many firms design an *organizational chart* of their internal structure that indicates all the employees and their relationship to one another. Seldom are any two retail stores organized in exactly the same manner; however, there are many common elements in every retail organization as well as differences.

There must be communication and cooperation between departments of any business if it is to operate efficiently. Each department's functions must be clearly defined and understood by every employee. This section, however, focuses on the relationship of the merchandising division to the other store functions. As a buyer, you must be ready to coordinate your efforts with those of others in the firm.

Buyers should know the relationship of the merchandising division to all the other departments that make up the store's organizational structure. As a buyer, you should have specific knowledge of other departments in the store and a working knowledge of the duties that each employee performs. For example, in many large independent stores, sales associates may be hired by the personnel department, but the merchandising division may be given the responsibility of providing them with product-knowledge training.

Buyers must also work closely with the promotion department by providing information on products that need to be advertised or promoted. Buyers must also ensure that the store has merchandise in stock before an ad breaks.

The control department will develop the recordkeeping and control systems used by the store. Buyers should have input so that records and reports will be useful to them as they keep track of inventory levels and make purchasing decisions. The buyer's budget is also approved by the control department. Before going to market, some stores require that this department approve the buyer's merchandise plan. Invoices are also paid by this department, and their prompt payment will allow the buyer to take advantage of cash discounts offered by vendors. Many retailers have established *IT* (information technology) departments to handle computer needs of the entire store.

Operations are another key partner for the buyer. The department is responsible for receiving and marking merchandise and getting merchandise to the selling floor promptly and correctly marked. It also has responsibility for merchandise in the stockroom. The merchandise purchased by buyers cannot be sold if it is not on the sales floor.

As the organizational structure for retail stores becomes larger and more complex, buyers must understand the internal store environment in which they are working. Buyers cannot perform their jobs in isolation. There must be cooperation and coordination with all departments if the buyer is to succeed and the store is to satisfy the needs of its customers.

BUYING FOR YOUR OWN STORE

Your community probably has many independent firms such as a neighborhood grocery store, hardware store, furniture store, clothing store, or shoe store. Single, small, independent stores are a vital part of our economy. In fact, almost half the businesses in the United States are operated entirely by one or two people, usually the owner and a spouse, partner, or employee.

In small independent stores, the owner is responsible for all aspects of the business operations, including all buying duties; therefore, he or she must have a thorough understanding of the buying process. Store owners not only decide what to purchase for the store, but also they will probably receive, check, and mark the merchandise when it is delivered and will probably be responsible for selling it.

Because buying and selling activities are both performed by the store owner, selecting merchandise that customers want and need is probably easier than at most national chains because of the owner's direct day-to-day contact with customers. Moreover, because store owners purchased the products being sold, they are probably very knowledgeable about the merchandise and enthusiastic about selling it.

The combination of a changing consumer and aggressive big retailers has been very tough on small independent retailers. Do they have a future? The answer is yes, but not without some dramatic changes in behavior. Blocking the big boxes, such as Wal-Mart, is only delaying the inevitable. Keeping out big retailers is not the answer; small retailers must differentiate themselves in such a way as to reduce or quite possibly eliminate comparisons with their big competitors.

Independent retailers must examine their market segments carefully. They need to find out where else their customers shop—small, as well as large, stores. Then, they need to learn as much as they can about those stores. A toy retailer should understand Toys "R" Us. Apparel retailers must frequently visit the malls and understand why customers are shopping there. They must put themselves in the customers' shoes. The more that independent retailers learn about their "big" competition, the better they will be able to compete. Most small independents will not be able to compete on price and depth of assortment. If customers want the lowest price or a large assortment, the big stores win. Small independents cannot look and act like big stores; these retailers must act differently.

One of the critical success factors for small retailers is expertise in, and enthusiasm for, the merchandise being offered the customer. Sales expertise is not dead at large chain stores, but it is rarely outstanding. This void creates a perfect opportunity for small independent retailers who really know their product. An example is Record-Rama Sound Archives. To the owner, music is not just a business; it is a passion. Turning a passion into a business is what made the owner successful. Today, this small store claims one of the largest collections of sound recordings in the world—valued at some $50 million. Another example is Alcala's Western Wear, which specializes in western apparel and boots. Product expertise is a large part of the company's success. At the store, sales associates go through several days of training before moving to the sales floor. One special requirement of the job is that they have to love boots and wear them. By some estimates, Alcala is responsible for nine out of every ten pairs of boots sold in Chicago.

Unique merchandise is another critical success factor for small retailers. Most chains are not able to implement merchandise plans that are wildly unique. Their size tends to make them conservative, even though they first rose to success due to a unique approach to business. One of the most unique merchandising ideas does not belong to a chain but can be found at Stew Leonard's supermarket in Connecticut. Stew offers a "Disneyland" of activities for the store's customers—from a petting zoo to mechanical singing animals. It is an approach that is working—parking lots are filled to near capacity most days.

Probably the most important critical success factor for a small business is dedication to customers. Many retailers give "lip service" to the customer being king; few are able to implement the idea really well. Magnolia Hi-Fi has done just that. Outstanding customer service is the reason Magnolia has been able to thrive in the face of formidable competition from much larger chains. The store is designed so that customers can easily compare the features of comparable equipment, and every product is backed with a nearly fanatical dedication to complete customer satisfaction.

Not all independent businesses are small; they range in size from the small enterprise described above to large stores owned by corporations. Key differences between small and large independent retail stores are related to the store's size and organizational structure. Because of their size, large independents have many more employees, and different duties will probably be delegated to different employees. Large independent stores also have greater buying power and carry larger merchandise assortments. In these stores, the buying function will usually be assigned to other employees—not management.

SUMMARY POINTS

- The way in which individual stores are organized contributes to their uniqueness. A store's organizational structure will also influence how buying is conducted in that store.
- In many small independent stores, the owner typically is responsible for both the buying and selling functions; however, as a store grows and expands, there is a need to departmentalize.
- Three types of departmentalization can be found in retail stores—functional, product-line, and geographic. A retail store can use a combination of any of these types of departmentalization in its organizational structure.
- As stores expand, owners start to identify ways to make their operations more profitable. Many chains use centralized buying, where all buying activities are handled from the store's headquarters.
- Centralized buying usually occurs in one of three forms—central merchandising plan, warehouse requisition plan, or price agreement plan.
- Few retail stores are organized in exactly the same manner. As a buyer, you must understand how the store you work for is organized, as well as obtaining a general understanding of how each department operates.
- Buyers must coordinate their activities with other departments if they are to be successful.

REVIEW ACTIVITIES

Developing Your Retail Buying Vocabulary

Consult the Glossary if you did not add the following terms to your vocabulary.

Central merchandising plan	IT
Centralized buying	Organizational chart
Chain store	Outlet store
Department store	Price agreement plan
Departmentalization	Product-line departmentalization
Discount department store	Soft lines
Functional departmentalization	Specialty store
Geographic departmentalization	Supermarket
Hard lines	Warehouse requisition plan

Understanding What You Read

1. Identify reasons that might cause buying to be easier for the owner of a small independent retail store than for a centralized buyer.
2. Compare and contrast the three types of departmentalization.
3. Identify specific areas of coordination between the merchandising division and other departments.
4. Identify the key disadvantages of centralized buying.
5. List and discuss the major advantages of centralized buying.
6. Compare and contrast the three types of centralized buying.
7. Which centralized buying plan gives the most freedom to store managers? Explain.
8. Describe how centralized buying can improve a store's merchandise offerings.
9. Describe the importance of written communications to buyers at headquarters.
10. Identify the differences between department stores and discount department stores.

Analyzing and Applying What You Read

1. Are the disadvantages of centralized buying serious enough to prevent retail chains from growing and expanding in the future? Explain.
2. Describe how buyers, removed from direct customer contact, can make better merchandise selections than store or department managers.
3. Outline the steps you would take as a buyer located at your firm's headquarters to build enthusiasm among managers and sales associates for merchandise you have purchased.
4. Develop a plan that you could implement as a buyer located at headquarters that could involve managers in the merchandise selection process.

Internet Connection

1. For one of the top ten retailers listed in Table 3.1, use the Internet to locate current sales and number of stores for that retailer. Describe any rationale given for increases or decreases in either of these areas.
2. Use the Internet to locate an organizational chart for a major retailer. Describe the type of departmentalization the firm is using.

SNAPSHOT

Kohl's: A Department Store with a Discount-Store Strategy

Kohl's is rapidly expanding beyond its Midwest roots and taking market share away from national retailers in the process. Based in Wisconsin, Kohl's sells moderately priced apparel, shoes, accessories, and home products. It has thrived in a market niche between mall department stores, such as Macy's and JCPenney, and discount retailers, such as Wal-Mart and Target. And, the chain has been outperforming some of its bigger competitors.

Kohl's builds stores in densely populated markets with household incomes of at least $48,900. The stores mainly anchor strip centers that have other high-profile retailers. Strip centers have parking readily available and consumers who want to avoid the crowds at the mall.

Analysts attribute Kohl's success to a low-cost structure based on having relatively small stores and few sales associates. That enables Kohl's to offer brand-name products at competitive prices. The stores combine department store national brands with the convenience of discount shopping and centralized checkouts.

Kohl's stores have a department store ambiance, complete with enticing layouts, fixtures, and signage, but the similarities end there. Without high rents associated with regional malls, operating costs stay controlled. Kohl's also tends to move into empty existing buildings.

The stores are typically one level and approximately 86,500 square feet. They are laid out in racetrack format with merchandise placed along the periphery and in the center. The merchandise mix is composed of 25 percent home goods (domestics, housewares, decorative home items) and 75 percent apparel. National brands—from Bugle Boy clothes for kids to Oneida flatware to Norton McNaughton apparel—make up 80 percent of the store's inventory. Cash registers are centralized and not interspersed in various departments, keeping staff at a minimum as well as keeping overhead low. Some critics say this strategy has its flaws—mainly slow customer service. For example, in the shoe department, customers are left to serve themselves, unlike a typical department store where sales associates pull the desired size and styles from a stockroom.

Brands and pricing seem to be what keep customers coming back. Retail analysts attribute Kohl's growth to a low-cost structure, superb automated control systems, strong relationships with key vendors, and superior execution. Along with aggressive merchandising, strong vendor relationships, and a keenly focused management team, Kohl's also benefits from its advanced merchandising systems. These systems have allowed store management to improve inventory tracking and interpretation of sales data.

Based on past performance, this retail hybrid is certainly a competitor that more department stores and discount stores will have to deal with in the future!

BASED ON:

Grant, Lorrie. (2004, April 8). Kohl's works to refill consumers' bags. *USA Today*, B1.

Kohl's Department Stores. (2001, September). *Chain Store Age*, 80.

Sales improve for 3 retailers, pushing profits higher. (2007, August 17). *The New York Times*, C7.

Sloan, Carole. (2007, July 16). Top 50 retailing giants. *Home Textiles Today*, 1.

Zaczkiewicz, Arthur. (2001, May 7). Why Kohl's is on a roll. *HFN The Weekly Newspaper for the Home Furnishing Network*, 1.

SNAPSHOT

The Future of the Department Store

At the beginning of the century, there were dire predictions about the future of department stores. Would they continue to exist? Statistics show that the number of traditional department stores in the United States declined from 4,264 in 1992 to 3,938 in 2002. That is, 326 department stores closed during that ten-year period. Since then, May Department Stores acquired Marshall Field's from Target, which was next acquired by Federated, which became Macy's. The Mercantile chain of department stores was purchased by Dillard's, and Kmart acquired Sears. As department stores continue to merge, the pace of closings will likely accelerate, especially where the merged entity has two or more branches in the same mall or in close proximity. Moreover, between 1992–2002, department stores achieved only 3 percent sales growth while sales for all retail sectors grew by 67 percent.

The department store now has to adjust to new realities in the marketplace and to the changing preferences of shoppers. For example, many department stores lost their one-stop-shopping appeal as product categories were eliminated from their mix. Many department stores retreated to selling clothing, accessories, and home products, and these areas are now under assault from companies like Bed Bath & Beyond and Kohl's. Some department stores have shown an overdependence on nonexclusive brands that can now be found in other stores. Moreover, many department stores are located at inconvenient locations in traffic-bound regional malls. This problem is a key reason for the move of many Sears stores away from malls and into converted Kmart locations.

Today, more Americans are wealthy, which explains why the high-end department stores, such as Neiman-Marcus and Nordstrom's, have continued to do well. At the same time, however, a greater number of Americans are becoming much less wealthy and cannot even afford to shop at the mid-tier department stores such as Macy's and Dillard's. Wal-Mart is where many of these consumers shop, along with Dollar General, Family Dollar, and similar retailers.

Can a new department store model be created? Years ago, each department store chain had a different point of view, with fashion trends set by many of them. Today, most department stores are virtually interchangeable–looking nearly identical with the same product assortments.

Department stores need to make fashion a top priority again by partnering with designers who develop product lines specifically for their shelves. Department stores need to feel new and cutting-edge, and marketing efforts need to reinforce this excitement.

Private label will and should be an increasing part of the product mix at department stores, but hot national brands will also be critical. Department stores cannot afford to be out of step with the latest brand names. Department stores must seek products ahead of the curve and in tune with changing consumer tastes, and they must be able to respond to consumer trends with lightning speed. Above all, department stores must promise customers a high level of service, and then deliver on that promise.

Some retail analysts have suggested that department stores should become known for product categories in which they are strong. This would cause the department store image to gradually change to that of a multi-specialty power retailer with less, but stronger-focused, merchandise offerings.

The next ten years will be critical for department stores. They must find ways to differentiate themselves from other retail establishments by creating stores that will attract and retain customers whose shopping behavior continues to change.

BASED ON:

Atmore, Michael. (2005, March 14). Revival time; all eyes are on the Federated team as they attempt to reinvent the troubled department-store chain. *Footwear News*, 8.

The department store of the future: three leading design firms tackle the issues facing department stores of today. (2003, June). *Display & Design Ideas*, 26–30.

Rogers, David. (2005, Spring). Department store consolidation: causes and consequences. *European Retail Digest*, 57–60.

TRENDWATCH

Is Bigger Really Better? Will the Small Independent Retailer Survive?

Are the big retail mergers, which are seemingly good for stockholders, constraining and injurious to the retail industry? If the big entities keep eating the little ones, will we be faced one day with one big retailer, one big airline, and one big telecommunications company?

Category killers, discounters, superstores, and outlets are spreading like wildfire. Perpetual "sales" have become a daily routine for many retailers. How do independent small stores compete? Stores such as Wal-Mart and Home Depot seem to be taking customers from these small independent stores faster and faster.

- What happens to the neighborhood office supply store when Staples comes to town?
- Can the local computer retailer survive against a new Comp USA?
- How does the small, family-run hardware store compete in the shadow of Home Depot?
- How do local men's and women's apparel stores stand up to the large department store chains?

Today's customers are practiced shoppers who know a great deal about quality and value, and their wealth of product knowledge plays a big part in their purchase decisions. They expect more from retailers. With these higher expectations, consumers in even smaller markets have more choices from ever-expanding chains such as Wal-Mart and Lowe's. These chains feature low prices, speed, and convenience, and have used technology to control expenses. While these changes occurred, most small store independents were slow to change; some analysts have said extremely slow. Many of these stores still offer unchanged product mixes and services. For many, their physical stores have remained unchanged, too.

Small independent retailers must know where they can win and where they cannot. They cannot buy merchandise at the same price paid by big retailers. They cannot consistently sell at low prices. They cannot obtain the concessions from vendors and suppliers that big stores can. They cannot instantly replenish inventory. Nor can they operate their business as inexpensively as the big stores can. There are, however, some strategies they can implement.

Most big stores carry merchandise that is not fashion forward; it is safe but boring. Independents must seek out and buy from fresh, new, innovative vendors. They must avoid carrying too much basic merchandise. Even though it is dependable, it does little for the merchandise mix and their profitability. The products they select should add personality to the store and set it apart—not be the same brands carried by the big stores.

Most big stores offer little or no customer service. This is the real opportunity for independent retailers to distance themselves from their big competitors. They need to provide real customer service to their shoppers. Sales associates must be available who know the products they are selling.

Most big stores are technology-dependent. Small retailers need to take advantage of existing technology, but not become its slave. Contact with sales associates at small stores should be an inspiring experience for customers. These associates should be able to make the sale, even if the computer crashes!

Many big retailers present a "low price" image to their customers. Small independents should use price as a weapon *as little as possible*. Clearance sales should be really special events with aggressive price-cutting and promotions. The goal is to sell out the old merchandise fast and get new products in as quickly as possible.

Once small retailers know what they want to be, marketing and advertising will become much easier; they will more easily identify new product opportunities for the store. More importantly, customers will be satisfied and keep returning. They will have been given reasons to shop there rather than at the big retailer a few miles away.

Getting Ready to Make Buying Decisions

Obtaining Assistance for Making Buying Decisions

PERFORMANCE OBJECTIVES

Upon completion of this chapter, you should be able to:

- Describe how retail buyers use marketing research.
- Identify the differences between primary and secondary data.
- Identify the sources of the assistance available to buyers.
- Identify internal sources of information for making buying decisions.
- Identify external sources of information for making buying decisions.
- Explain the importance of buying offices to buyers.
- Differentiate between the different types of buying offices.
- List and describe services performed by buying offices.
- Outline the process for selecting a buying office.

As a buyer, you will not want to make decisions alone in your office. Buyers typically use some form of marketing research before they make decisions. Various internal and external sources of information will be available to help you in predicting consumer demand and making purchases, and you will want to seek out and use information from as many sources as possible. It is doubtful, however, that any one source alone will be sufficient to provide all the information you need.

MARKETING RESEARCH

Marketing research is a systematic process of gathering, recording, and analyzing information about problems related to marketing. Good marketing research must be conducted in a comprehensive, step-by-step process; it cannot be haphazard. Marketing research involves using information, or *data*, from many different sources. As a buyer you must be able to do more than locate information, you must be able to analyze and use the information that you collect.

Using Marketing Research

One of the most frequent uses of marketing research is to locate information that describes current economic and market conditions that would help you better understand the environment in which your store operates. In addition, many stores want to develop a profile of their customers with respect to characteristics such as age, income, education level, and spending patterns. Developing a customer profile will help you make day-to-day business decisions, such as selecting products to purchase and choosing which types of promotion to use. You will also be interested in information about the size of a potential market and where those customers are located. Marketing research can also be used to determine an area's unemployment rate, new housing starts, or similar economic data that can be used to make forecasts about future sales. Examples of economic data that buyers could use are shown in Table 4.1. As you can see, many times buyers are faced with conflicting data when making a decision.

Marketing research is essential for all businesses if they are to remain competitive in the marketplace and satisfy customer wants and needs. Your key to success will be to know your customers better than your competitors do. Good marketing research allows you to anticipate and capitalize on changes occurring with customers; failure to adequately monitor what is going on with them may lead to some

Table 4.1 Types of Economic Data That Buyers Can Use to Make Forecasts.

Building Permits Monthly total building permits issued.	↓	−0.15%
Unfilled Orders for Durables Changes in manufacturer's unfilled orders for durable goods.	↑	+0.23%
Commodity Prices Change in sensitive materials' prices.	↓	−0.04%
Stock Prices Average for 500 common stocks.	↑	+0.13%
Consumer Confidence Consumer expectations of economy's health.	↑	+0.03%
New Plants, Equipment Contracts and orders, plant and equipment.	↓	−0.22%
Unemployment Claims Weekly claims on unemployment insurance.	↑	+0.15

bad decisions. Above all, marketing research should help take the guesswork out of your decision making.

The size of your store will affect how marketing research is conducted and used. Most small retailers cannot afford the money or the time to conduct and analyze hundreds of customer surveys. They typically rely on general findings reported in newspapers or magazines. Some retailers use *informal* surveying extensively—they observe their customers or have sales associates ask them simple questions as they are completing their purchases. Many large retailers have their own marketing research departments and are continuously monitoring their customers and the marketplace. As you will learn in this chapter, there are also many private firms that specialize in marketing research activities, and many retailers purchase these services.

Marketing research does not have to be time-consuming and expensive. Simply comparing sales figures from this year with sales at the same time last year is marketing research. Observing the colors teens in the mall are most often wearing is marketing research. Keeping a file of newspaper and magazine articles about product trends is marketing research. Marketing research activities will be vital to your success as a retail buyer.

Collecting Data

To help you make decisions, your marketing research may involve primary data, secondary data, or both. Your first step should be to locate all relevant secondary sources. **Secondary data** consist of data that already exist—someone else has done the work for you. Government agencies are an excellent source of secondary data, as are trade journals, newspapers, and trade associations. In addition to being able to obtain most secondary data quickly, you will be able to obtain a wealth of information at little or no cost. Some secondary data, however, may not be suitable for your purposes—they are too general or incomplete. Other secondary data may be dated or obsolete. Census data, for example, are only collected every ten years. In many situations, secondary data cannot provide all the information you need to make a decision; you may then need to collect primary data.

Primary data consist of information collected for the specific purpose at hand. The key advantage of using primary data is that this information specifically relates to the problem being researched. As the photo in Figure 4.1 illustrates, primary data are usually collected by interviewing consumers, either individually or in small groups. Obtaining primary data, however, may be time-consuming and expensive for your store. Read the Trendwatch titled, "Using Different Retail Formats to Appeal to Diverse Customers in the Same Market," to learn how retailers are experimenting with different formats based on marketing research findings.

Analyzing and Interpreting Data

When you conduct marketing research, you are looking for answers, not just information. Your job is to study the data that you have collected and determine their meaning. For example, if several sources of secondary data were obtained, you must compile and summarize the relevant information. If you conducted a customer survey, you will need to analyze the data once all responses are tabulated.

By themselves, data that you have collected usually will not lead to an immediate solution to your questions. You must draw conclusions and make recommendations based on your interpretation of the data collected. In other words, you must make a decision: How many will

Figure 4.1   Primary data are usually collected by interviewing consumers.

you buy? What styles and colors will you buy? From which vendors will you make your purchases? What models will be stocked at which stores? What merchandise should be eliminated from stock? What new products should be added? The list of questions you will face as a buyer will be endless, but with good marketing research and assistance from other sources, you will be able to answer them.

In your search for information, there will be various internal and external sources available to you. Use as many as you can, and do not be afraid to ask for help. Read the Snapshot titled, "Talbots: Committed to Marketing Research," to learn how one retailer has successfully used marketing research for decision making.

INTERNAL SOURCES

Key sources of internal information include (1) store records, (2) management, and (3) sales associates. Each of these sources can provide you with valuable information as you make buying decisions.

Store Records

In most buying situations, past sales and inventory records may be your most important source of information. Analysis of store records is essential for all buyers, but especially for buyers who are located at the headquarters of a retail chain. These buyers may not have easy access to managers and sales associates at the store level. Increasingly, retailers are tracking much more information about customers than just total sales. For example, information recorded in store records may indicate types of products that customers generally purchase together. Data may reveal characteristics of customers who purchase a particular product. These situations involve data warehousing and data mining and are examined in Chapter 5.

The key limitation to relying on sales and inventory records to predict consumer demand is that they reveal only what your customers have purchased or not purchased in the past. What happens when customers visit your store or department and do not make a purchase? Sales and inventory records do not reflect what the customer would have purchased if the merchandise had been in stock. Such sales data cannot reveal what sales might have been made to customers who were seeking items that were temporarily out of stock or were not carried by your store.

Some stores operate a formal ***want slip system*** in which a form is completed each time a customer requests a product not in stock. If you use such a system, you will need to impress upon sales associates the importance of keeping accurate records and taking the time to complete the form when customers ask for an out-of-stock item or one not carried by your store. You cannot, however, meet every customer request. Analysis of want slips could help plan future merchandise assortments if a large number of your customers are making similar requests.

Sales and inventory records should be made to work for you. If you carefully analyze these records, your planned merchandise purchases could be more in line with customers' demand. Moreover, store records are the only means of checking the accuracy of your forecasts against sales that actually occur. Read the Trendwatch titled, "Loyalty Cards: How Can They Benefit Retail Buyers?" to learn more about the information available to buyers from customer transactions involving loyalty cards.

Even though store records are likely to be your most important source of information, they are not sufficient by themselves. You need to use other internal sources, as well as external sources, before making your final buying decisions.

Management

In large stores, you probably need to consult with your merchandise manager as you plan your purchasing decisions. Before approving your merchandise plan, your merchandise manager may suggest changes. He or she should also be able to offer you valuable assistance in predicting future economic and market trends. The controller or finance officer will also need to be consulted for approval of the budget for your buying plan.

Buyers located at corporate headquarters will want to seek input from store managers. Short phone calls to these managers can make them feel more involved in the buying process and probably more enthusiastic about selling the merchandise you will order. Important information about consumer demand that may not be readily detected from store records can possibly be found. Small store owners probably have no other management personnel from whom they can get advice; therefore, it will be critical that they use external sources.

Sales Associates

Whenever possible you should obtain input from the store's sales associates. Records may reveal what merchandise is selling or not selling, but only sales associates may be able to tell you *why* it is selling or not selling.

Sales associates are in constant contact with customers and can be aware of their wants and needs, which may not be reflected in sales records. In fact, because they are typical customers, sales associates are probably good judges of the sales potential for new products being considered. Some sales associates, however, may *not* be able to distinguish their personal likes and dislikes from those of their customers.

Sales associates are the store's personal representatives to its customers, and in such a role, they are in a position to conduct primary research for you. If your store does not use want slips, consulting with sales associates may reveal if they have been asked for merchandise that the store does not sell. Also, sales associates can quickly and easily ask questions that will be important to you. For example, they can ask about a customer's satisfaction with past purchases, or they can get requests for items not carried by the store.

During telephone conversations or at store meetings, you should be able to determine which sales associates are the most insightful and can offer you genuine feedback. Discuss with these sales associates what should be in stock, and allow them to inspect new product samples and give their opinion as to whether they should be purchased. Their opinions may support what you have already learned from other sources or give you an entirely different perspective that could cause you to alter your plans.

If possible, visit the sales floor. Buyers located at a store's headquarters should regularly visit stores nearby to observe customers in action. While visiting the sales floor, observe cues about the kinds of styles, colors, and fabrics that are popular with your customers. The problem with making personal contacts is that you may be so completely absorbed with merchandising activities that visits are difficult. Store visits, however, are likely to provide benefits to you in the form of more enthusiastic sales associates and more specific knowledge for you to consider when making your buying plans. If you solicit opinions and suggestions from sales associates, take the time to extend a personal word of thanks to them describing how their suggestions were acted on.

Once you have exhausted sources inside your store, seek assistance from external sources. Remember, however, that information from these sources could reflect national or industry trends rather than local trends.

EXTERNAL SOURCES

Many sources outside your store will be available to help you when making purchasing decisions. They include (1) customers (2) magazines and trade publications, (3) vendors, (4) trade associations, (5) comparison shoppers, (6) fashion forecasters, (7) reporting services, (8) the Internet, and (9) buying offices. The type of merchandise that you are selling and the time you have available will determine how many and which sources you will use.

Customers

Some large retailers are able to conduct formal marketing research involving questionnaires to determine consumer wants and needs; however, consumer research can be quite informal. You or other employees of the store may simply talk with customers on the selling floor, or just observe them while they are in the store. Both activities involve informal marketing research.

Are your customers quick to experiment with new fashion trends? Or do their tastes tend toward the classic or traditional? Are they price conscious when they shop? Or are they more interested in quality and fashion? Extensive customer questionnaires will probably be needed to adequately answer these questions. Some simple questions, however, may reveal a lot about your customers. An example of a survey that customers may be asked to complete is shown in Table 4.2, "Style Assessment." Take a minute to complete and score the survey to determine your own attitude toward fashion. Do you think the results described you correctly? For the survey results to have meaning to a retail buyer, hundreds of customer responses will probably need to be completed and tabulated.

Some stores organize consumer advisory groups. Teen boards are an advisory group that many department stores use. They are established by selecting student representatives from local high schools or colleges to serve as advisers for the store. Teen board members may also serve as fashion show models and provide assistance with special promotions. Some members even wear new merchandise from the store on their school campus.

Other stores may establish **consumer advisory panels** consisting of typical customers who make suggestions about store policies, services,

---

Table 4.2: Style Assessment

Sections 1 and 2: Rate yourself on a scale of 0 to 10 for each of the following questions. Assign higher numbers to the statements that strongly represent your feeling.

SECTION 1   **Score (Assign 0 to 10)**

1. I keep up-to-date on the latest styles and fashions.   _____

2. I like to buy top designer brands of clothes.   _____

3. I am an individualist and like my clothes to project attitude.   _____

SECTION 2   **Score (Assign 0 to 10)**

4. When I shop, I look at the price tag first.   _____

5. I like a store where I can shop for the whole family.   _____

6. I try only to buy things that are on sale.   _____

SECTION 3   **Circle Your Response**

7. I like to indulge myself.   Agree / Disagree

8. I usually talk things over with other people.   Agree / Disagree

9. Women should offer to split the cost when they go out with men.   Agree / Disagree

10. I would choose to do my own housework, even if I could afford help.   Agree / Disagree

11. Success at school or work is important to me.   Agree / Disagree

12. I am a fun-loving person.   Agree / Disagree

How to Score

1. _____ Add up your points from Section 1.

2. _____ Add up your points from Section 2.

3. _____ In Section 3:

                If you agreed with statements 7, 11, and 12, add one point for each "agree" to your total score in Section 1.

                If you agreed with statements 8, 9, and 10, add one point for each "agree" to your total score in Section 2.

4. _____ Subtract the total score in Section 2 from the total in Section 1 (Score may be a minus.)

5. _____ If your score is

                +10 to +30 you are an Updated (Fashion Forward) Shopper

                +9 to –15 you are a Classic or Traditional Shopper

                –16 to –30 you are a Conservative Shopper

and merchandise assortments. The panels usually meet weekly for a few hours to provide their input by offering opinions and suggestions about store activities and merchandise assortments.

Magazines and Trade Publications

As a buyer, you have to stay ahead of what is selling on the floor. You must be aware of changes in styling, new materials, new models, and other innovations long before they are available to customers. You will need to read several publications to update your knowledge of current trends in new product developments, resource information, economic conditions, and other market news that will enhance your understanding of customers. You will also want to subscribe to the local newspaper as well as an out-of-town paper from a large metropolitan area. If you are in a small town, examining retail ads appearing in these out-of-town papers will alert you to trends and styles that may eventually be accepted by your customers.

Fashion news is reported in many consumer magazines. *Vogue, Harper's Bazaar, Jane, Elle, Glamour, Mademoiselle,* and *GQ* are several magazines you can pick up at your local newsstand to keep abreast of changes in fashion. Other publications such as *The Wall Street Journal, USA Today, Business Week, Fortune,* and *Forbes* are excellent sources of information about economic and market trends. Several of these publications also feature columns on new product innovations. Reports on trends, technological developments, marketing plans of various companies, and the impact of economic developments on business areas are frequently reported.

You should also subscribe to trade magazines directly related to product categories for which you are buying. In fact, almost every retail activity has some trade publication associated with it. Some of these include: *Women's Wear Daily, Stores, Chain Store Age, Furniture Age, Footwear News, Progressive Grocer, Hardware Age,* and *Home Furnishings Daily*. These publications can provide you with valuable information about the products that you are buying. For example, most of these publications conduct national surveys and report information about typical customers for specific products.

Vendors

Your merchandise suppliers, *vendors*, will be able to inform you about what merchandise is being heavily ordered by other retailers. Also, the information they have about merchandise reorders will give you an excellent indication of customer acceptance of specific products. Vendors are usually eager to pass on useful information because they have a stake in the success of your store, too; however, there is a distinct difference between accepting advice and letting the vendor make your decisions. As a partnership develops between you and the vendor, you will be able to put more confidence in these suggestions.

Trade Associations

You or someone from store management will want to join and actively participate in a *trade association* related to your area of retailing. These organizations of businesses with similar characteristics usually publish newsletters updating members on current trends and market conditions. They also provide the opportunity for you to make important personal contracts and discuss matters relevant to a particular retailing area. The National Retail Federation is the largest and most important trade association to which most retailers belong. The organization covers areas of interest for both large and small retailers, providing them with publications, videos, and periodicals. You should also consider joining the merchants' associations at your state and local levels. Another positive feature of trade associations is that they typically sponsor trade shows as part of conferences where vendors exhibit new products.

Comparison Shoppers

You should also study the promotion campaigns of competing stores. Study both their print and broadcast ads to obtain information on price and quality. If possible, you will want to visit competing stores to see what is being stocked, what is featured in displays, as well as what appears to be selling. Observe prices, assortments, services, and customer response to the merchandise stocked. Comparison shopping reports also give you information about products not carried by your store.

If you do not have the time to conduct comparison-shopping activities yourself, you may need to assign this task to assistant buyers or department managers or hire *comparison shoppers*. These firms shop competing stores to provide information on the merchandise assortments, prices, and promotion policies of other retailers in the area. They are located in many large cities and charge their clients based on the services provided.

Do not spend so much time watching competitors that you forget the work to be done at your own store. Few retailers are successful if they merely copy someone else with their prices and merchandise assortments. Some stores have found that it is not necessary to make adjustments each time a competitor makes a price change. They build their reputation on the services they provide to their customers. However, many retailers stress in their advertising that they will "meet or beat" the competition's prices. For these stores, comparison shopping is extremely important.

If possible, obtain information on stores similar to yours in other geographic areas. At trade association meetings, you can network with buyers from noncompeting stores in other locations. They are frequently happy to exchange information because it will help them make better buying decisions, too.

Fashion Forecasters

Fashion forecasters are business consultants that you or your firm can hire to help predict fashion trends months in advance. Fashion items change frequently, and buyers must be aware of trends so the store has the right products to meet the wants and needs of its customers. On a weekly or monthly basis, fashion forecasters provide their clients with a report on predicted consumer trends. These services are most helpful with long-range planning.

Youth Intelligence, a company that forecasts fashion and other trends involving young consumers, advises Levi's, Calvin Klein's CK line, and Benetton. Reporters for the firm find trends by following fashion-forward designers; scoping out the streets of London, Los Angeles, and New York; and monitoring eclectic boutique wares. Many retailers often consult more than one forecasting firm. For example, Saks Fifth Avenue uses a forecaster with its buying office as well as the firm Here & There. Forecasting services may be expensive, but most major retailers agree that they cannot afford *not* to use them.

Reporting Services

Reporting services are organizations that report on constantly changing market trends that will have an impact on the products you purchase. Changes occur most frequently and most rapidly for fashion merchandise, so it is extremely important that fashion buyers keep current. Several reporting services conduct market research valuable to buyers and mail their analyses to clients on a weekly or monthly basis. Today, the Internet has made the *immediate* delivery of information possible; breaking news no longer has to wait for the next issue of a newsletter. Articles describe topics such as the latest fashions from Europe, economic indicators, or the newest colors and fabrics for the new season. Several independent firms provide reporting services to retail buyers, including the following:

- *The Public Pulse* is a monthly newsletter produced by the Roper Organization that reports on what "Americans are thinking, doing, and buying."
- *Inside Retailing* is a biweekly report on retailing strategies published by Lebhar-Friedman Inc.
- *Retailing Today* is a 24 hours a day, 7 days a week source for news coverage of the retail industry.

The Internet

The Internet is the newest research tool that buyers can use. Millions of pages of information are archived and available at the click of a computer mouse. More importantly, buyers are able to obtain *up-to-the-minute* news and information about their industry or products they are buying. At no time in the past have buyers had such a wealth of information at their fingertips.

For example, at apparelsearch.com, buyers can find information on customers, conversion charts, trade shows, apparel news, and designers—all at the click of a mouse. At fashion.net, they can find daily fashion news, view runway videos, or read fashion profiles. And, at apparelresources.com, buyers can find a directory of apparel exporters from India. Information that once took weeks and months to collect can now be located in minutes. The Internet has proved a very powerful tool for buyers.

Buying Offices

Buying offices are organizations that provide consulting services to retailers. Because they are so widely used by both small and large retailers, they are described in depth in the next section.

BUYING OFFICES

A buying office is an organization located in a major market center for the purpose of providing buying advice and other market-related services to client stores. Essentially, they serve as researchers and advisers to save the store buyer time and money. Few stores can afford to have a permanent staff in central markets. For that reason, many retailers use the services of buying offices.

Purpose and Importance

By using a buying office, you are able to "feel the pulse" of the market without being there, and you will no longer have to rely on just an occasional visit to the market to make your purchasing plans.

Buying offices vary in size from a one-person operation to giant offices employing hundreds of people. The largest number of buying offices are located in New York City, the major fashion market in the United States. Many also have branch offices in other major market centers in the United States as well as worldwide. Mergers and acquisitions have made the Doneger Group one of the strongest buying offices in the country. The firm has been able to broaden its client base as well as develop many specialized services. Table 4.3 shows the various divisions of the Doneger Group and provides a brief description of the services performed.

A buying office is employed by a retail store to act as a buying specialist and adviser. They become your "eyes and ears" when you are not in the market by constantly scouting the market for new merchandise, new resources, and the best prices.

Buying offices are important to retailers for the following reasons:

• Many retailers are placing an increasing importance on fashion products, and the rapidity with which fashion changes requires that a buyer have constant contact with the market.

Table 4.3: Divisions of the Doneger Group, a New York Buying Office

MERCHANDISING

Henry Doneger Associates	The foundation block of the company's merchandising division offers retail buyers extensive consulting services, current business and market analysis, and special merchandise programs for womenswear, menswear, and childrenswear. In 2005, the firm opened a West Coast office in the California Market Center in Los Angeles that concentrates on market trends in the contemporary, accessories, junior's, men's contemporary, and surf/skate lifestyle markets.
HDA International	This division provides information, sourcing, and product development opportunities to international retailers from a wide range of U.S.-based manufacturers and importers.
Carol Hoffman	Started in 2001, this division provides extensive market coverage in all classifications of sportswear, dresses, outerwear, suits, accessories, and lingerie.
Price Point Buying	Price Point Buying locates off-price deals in women's sportswear and outerwear, childrenswear, and menswear. Its goal is to provide retailers with outstanding opportunistic buys.

TREND SERVICES

Doneger Creative Services	This is the trend and color forecasting division of the Doneger Group. It addresses the creative needs of retailers, manufacturers, and other style-related businesses.
Here & There	This division has 30 years of experience in trend forecasting and reporting and provides retail clients with color, lifestyle, fabric, and print forecasts.
Margit Publications	Since 2003, this division has provided style-related trend services and fashion publications to the retail industry.
Tobe	The Tobe division offers international retail consulting services and is best known for *The Tobe Report*, a fashion publication distributed for more than 75 years. This division provides in-depth trend and business analyses to many of the nation's top retailers.

RELATED SERVICES

Doneger Consulting	This division offers customized projects tailored to clients' individual needs. Projects can be geared to the needs of style-related businesses, ranging from apparel to consumer products for the financial community.
Online Services	Launched in 1998, this online division provides members with resources, information, and services. The site provides up-to-the-minute fashion and merchandising information.

Adapted from www.doneger.com

- Many buying offices are able to make group purchases for their client stores so that merchandise costs are reduced.
- Retail stores represented by buying offices can have their buyers make fewer and shorter trips to market, thereby reducing expenses.
- Many times, buying offices will be able to obtain exclusive merchandise for client stores. Most stores want to carry some products that are unique to their trading area.
- Finally, being a member of a buying office brings retail stores together to pool their information and knowledge. Information can be shared freely, because a buying office will not represent competing stores in a trading area.

Reasons to use a buying office will probably vary from one retailer to the next.

Services Provided by Buying Offices

Buying offices communicate vital market information to client stores through bulletins and reports and give much-needed assistance to buyers when they visit the market. While the buyer is at his or her store, representatives of the buying office can:

- Answer requests for information on such topics as market conditions, prices and styles available, and location of new resources.
- Place orders on request of the store's buyer. The buyer specifies the type, price, and quantity of merchandise desired and leaves the selection of the vendor and specific styles to the representative of the buying office. Store buyers still have the primary responsibility for purchasing.
- Keep on the lookout for merchandise a buyer may find of interest, such as new products and new styles. Calls are frequently made to store buyers about new merchandise offerings.
- Follow up and check on deliveries. Manufacturers may be more motivated to ship quickly if pressured by a buying office because of its size and location in the market.
- Handle adjustments and complaints. Again, a buying office may be able to apply more pressure than retailers can by themselves.
- Save the retailer money by pooling orders from several member stores to make purchases at one time for a lower cost.

- Locate new resources. Most buyers are constantly seeking fresh merchandise to satisfy the needs of their customers. It may not be possible for the store buyer to thoroughly scout the market to seek out new resources. Representatives of a buying office are more capable of performing this function. In fact, many manufacturers seek out buying offices because of the number of stores they represent.
- Recommend hot items. A *hot item* is a product that the buyer cannot keep in stock because of great demand by customers. All buyers are interested in products that will provide a quick return on the store's investment.
- Secure private brands for the retail store. Many buying offices have developed private branding programs to assist their member stores to meet the competition and provide store individuality.
- Provide fashion forecasts on style, color, and fabric trends and new market offerings.
- Prepare promotional activities. Most small retailers have neither the specialized talent nor the capital to develop promotional campaigns. Many buying offices supply their member stores with promotional materials such as ideas for window displays, interior display hints, or sample ad layouts. Even canned fashion show commentary may be provided.
- Provide research findings to client stores. Information may be from informal studies, which might involve conversations with representatives of key stores to find out what is selling or from more formal market research activities involving questionnaires and interviews. Market and economic trend analyses are also provided by most buying offices.
- Maintain foreign connections so that they can offer expertise to the retailer who is interested in importing merchandise.

Once the store buyer is in the market, the buying office helps by carefully planning the market trip so that the visit is productive. Representatives of the buying office can locate merchandise and resources in advance of the buyer's market trip and schedule his or her time so it is used most productively. Most buying offices provide office space and sample rooms for buyers of their member stores. These offices will usually collect samples from vendors so they are easily accessible to buyers while they are in the market. Having samples readily available saves buyers time during the rush of market week because they do not have to visit manufacturers whose samples are inappropriate for their needs.

Representatives of buying offices may even accompany store buyers to market showrooms on request. Such a service, however, may not always be available if a large percentage of the buyers from member stores are in the market at the same time. Many buying offices also make hotel and transportation reservations for store buyers. These services may be provided at reduced prices because the buying office is representing a large number of stores and probably qualifies for a group discount. Finally, buying offices can vouch for the credit standing of member stores when buyers are in the market.

Types of Buying Offices

Buying offices can be grouped into two broad categories: (1) independent buying offices and (2) store-owned buying offices. Buying offices in both categories essentially provide the same type of services.

Independent Offices. Most buying offices are *independent buying offices*– they are privately owned and operated. Store buyers use independent offices just as they would any other business consultant. Two variations of this type of buying office are (1) the salaried (fixed-fee) office and (2) the commission (merchandise-broker) office.

The *salaried* or *fixed-fee office* is paid directly by the retail stores the firm represents. The retailer signs a contract with the buying office and agrees to pay a fee based on a percentage of the store's annual sales volume. This fee typically ranges from 1/2 to 1 percent of sales and is paid monthly. Smaller stores, with low sales volume, may pay a flat fee each month.

The salaried office is mainly used by store owners and buyers who do not have the time to spend away from their stores to make frequent market visits. Some stores may be so far removed geographically from the market that it would be too costly for the owner to make regular market trips.

The *commission* or *merchandise-broker office* provides similar advice and services to retailers, but it is paid by the manufacturers represented by the firm. From 2 to 4 percent of the client store's purchases are paid to the buying office by the manufacturer. Many brokers represent several noncompeting manufacturers.

Merchandise brokers offer another avenue for manufacturers to broaden their contact with small stores because representatives are able to visit store owners in the field who seldom come to market. Merchandise brokers are extremely important to retailers who cannot afford the services of salaried buying offices. You must realize, however, that conflict of interest may be present. Brokers are interested in selling the lines they represent, even though they may not be the best ones for your store. Most merchandise brokers, however, will give good service because they are interested in keeping your continued patronage.

Store-Owned Offices. Some buying offices are owned by the store or stores they represent. Large department and specialty stores generally use this type of service.

Private buying offices are maintained in market centers by some large retailers. For example, Neiman Marcus is among the small number of stores that operate such an office. These offices require a large financial investment, which is warranted if the retailer's sales volume would require an extremely high fee to be paid to a salaried buying office. Therefore, establishing their own buying office is more economical for these stores. These buying offices perform the same functions as independent buying offices except there are no other stores with whom to exchange information.

Selecting a Buying Office

How will you go about selecting a buying office? First, you need to determine if your store needs the services provided. Then, you will need to screen the possible choices from which you have to select. Make a thorough search, and do not be afraid to ask questions. Ask for references and speak to some of the buying office's clients. Following are some of the typical questions you will want to ask.

- What kind of merchandise lines are represented by the buying office? Does its merchandising approaches fit your store's image?
- Is the buying office too small or too large for your needs?
- Do you feel an atmosphere of compatibility when communicating with representatives of the buying office? Are they the kind of people with whom you feel you can do business?

- Is the staff of sufficient size to give adequate service?
- Does the buying office provide references?
- Who are the buying office's current members? You want to be associated with stores that are similar to yours because information exchange is beneficial. For that reason, you may not be able to be represented by a buying office already representing your competitor. Exchange of information might divulge company secrets.
- Which manufacturers does the buying office deal with regularly?
- What is the scope of services provided?
- What standard, regular services can you expect that will help save time, avoid needless market trips, and provide professional buying assistance?
- What will joining the buying office cost?
- How is the fee determined? What kind of contract arrangement is required?
- Can you afford the costs?
- Will the buying office treat you as an individual?
- How will your store benefit?

Once you have selected a buying office, make use of the services it provides. Read the bulletins and reports that are sent to you. This will be the buying office's primary means of communicating with you. You can learn about products with which other stores have had success and also obtain information on new resources.

Get to know the various representatives at the buying office who will be assigned to your store. Develop a close working relationship with them. Communicate your ideas and problems on a regular basis through phone calls or letters. By knowing you and your situation better, the buying office will be more effective in working for you.

Let your representatives at the buying office know well in advance of any market trips that you are planning. Communicate to them your particular needs and the merchandise categories that you will be purchasing. Advance notification will allow someone at the buying office to block out time to devote to you.

Participate in group activities that have been organized for you by the buying office. Much of the strength of a buying office is based on member stores sharing their experiences with one another. These activities provide an opportunity for you to gain insight into general market conditions and trends as well as specific information on vendors and merchandise availability. Share information about successful and unsuccessful merchandise in your store.

Communicate with representatives of the buying office when you are not in the market. Work toward developing a long-term partnership that will be mutually beneficial for both you and the buying office.

Trends Influencing Buying Offices

In the past, retailers were small and scattered throughout the country, so manufacturers and vendors found it difficult to contact stores directly; therefore, buying offices developed to serve as a link between retailers and the market. Today, however, the major retail stores have grown so large that it is possible for manufacturers to contact all their major customers and prospective customers directly. Also, retail mergers have eliminated many buying office accounts. One day the buying office is doing business with a retailer, and the next day that retailer is part of a chain that has its own buying office or an account with a competing buying office. For these retailers, there has been *less* reliance on buying offices.

Buying offices, however, offer much-needed assistance for any retailer that cannot easily perform the services offered. As many retailers become larger, there will be a very strong need by smaller retailers to band together to compete. They may need the services of buying offices just to remain competitive.

What does the future hold for buying offices? Will their role change? Some retail analysts feel that buying offices should begin performing some new functions with which most have never dealt—services related to the use of technology, store planning, site selection, and human resource management. Such services, however, may be beyond the realm of expertise for most buying offices. Some retail analysts are already starting to question whether or not buying offices really own the talent to make a difference, and this may be one of the main reasons why retailers are using them less often.

The most recent trend has been the use of the Internet to maintain constant contact between a buying office and member stores. New developments can be relayed instantly, as can information on a manufacturer's price break that retailers must take advantage of quickly. Most buying offices now maintain online sites that members can access with passwords.

Buying offices have consolidated, and many have gone out of business, but those that remain seem to have a strong position in the marketplace. Most fashion retailers need a buying office so they have someone to cover the market for them on a day-to-day basis, to tell them what is hot and what is not. Using buying offices is especially important today because it is so costly to send buyers to markets in metropolitan areas. Above all, buying offices help small retailers compete with industry giants.

SUMMARY POINTS

- Buyers do not make decisions alone. They seek out and use as much information as possible before making purchasing decisions.
- Retail buyers use some form of marketing research to help them make decisions, even if it is very informal. They seek out secondary data first before trying to obtain primary data on their own.
- Store records, such as sales and inventory, are key sources of information for buyers; however, such information shows a buyer only what sold or did not sell. Buyers should contact sales associates and store managers for assistance in determining *why* customers purchased or did not purchase merchandise in the store.
- Buyers can seek information from customers through formal surveys or advisory groups.
- Buyers need to read to keep up-to-date. Consumer magazines and newspapers are required reading, as are trade magazines directed toward their specific retailing area.
- Vendors are sources of information and assistance but should not make decisions for the buyer.
- Buyers must continually monitor the competition through comparison-shopping trips or through similar information provided by comparison-shopping bureaus.
- Buyers can use the services of fashion forecasters and reporting services to monitor trends and changes in the retail market. Such services are especially useful for recognizing long-range tends.
- Buying offices serve as consultants and advisers to buyers and provide many market-related services to their member stores. Buying offices provide assistance to buyers while they are in their store and when visiting the market.
- Buying offices are either independent or store-owned. They all offer similar services to stores, but vary in how they are paid and who becomes a member.

- Buying offices are changing as retailing changes. Consolidation has occurred; many buying offices are no longer in business. Today, the Internet provides an immediate connection between buying offices and their members.

REVIEW ACTIVITIES

Developing Your Retail Buying Vocabulary

Consult the Glossary if you did not add the following terms to your vocabulary.

Buying office	Marketing research
Commission (merchandise-broker) buying office	Primary data
	Private buying office
Comparison shopper	Reporting service
Consumer advisory panel	Salaried (fixed-fee) buying office
Data	Secondary data
Fashion forecaster	Trade association
Hot item	Vendor
Independent buying office	Want slip system

Understanding What You Read

1. Describe some simple approaches to marketing research that buyers can use to answer questions and make decisions.
2. What are the advantages that secondary data provide the buyer?
3. For the buyer, what are the problems with using primary data?
4. What is probably a buyer's most important source of information when making purchasing decisions?
5. Describe why contact with store managers and salespeople is critical for a buyer.
6. What is the limitation of using only sales records to make purchasing decisions?
7. Identify the two individuals who will likely need to approve a buyer's purchasing plans in large retail stores.
8. Describe how centralized buyers receive feedback from store managers and salespeople.

9. Describe why visits to the sales floor are vital to buyers.
10. Identify the purpose(s) of teen boards.
11. What is a buyer's purpose in subscribing to an out-of-town newspaper from a metropolitan area?
12. What information should a buyer obtain from comparison shopping that will assist in making purchasing decisions?
13. List two reporting services, and describe the information they provide to clients.
14. Describe why buying offices are important to retailers.
15. Describe specific services that buying offices can provide to buyers when they are in the market.
16. Describe the difference between fixed-fee buying offices and merchandise brokers.
17. When might retailers choose a merchandise broker over a fixed-fee buying office to represent them?
18. Describe how being a member of a buying office can save the store money.
19. Identify general trends that are affecting the operation of buying offices today.

Analyzing and Applying What You Read

1. What reasons could explain why most retailers do not collect want slips?
2. You are a centralized buyer for a large specialty store chain. Outline a plan that you would implement to encourage involvement in the buying process from store managers and sales associates.
3. You are a new buyer at a local hardware store. Briefly describe the specific steps you would take to seek external information to aid in making purchasing decisions.
4. The owner of the small menswear store that you manage is considering using a buying office. Categorize the pros and cons of hiring a buying office.
5. Do you feel that buying offices should offer services related to the use of technology, store planning, site selection, and human resource management? Explain.
6. A buying office that specializes in menswear has experienced declines in billings each of the past three years. What changes would you recommend that this buying office consider?

Internet Connection

1. Visit the Doneger Group buying office online at *http://www.doneger.com*.
   a. Record information about any market trends they are providing visitors to the site.
   b. Describe the process that a retail store would use to join the buying office.
   c. Use an Internet search engine to locate the home page of another online buying office. Read and analyze the information provided at the site.
   d. Describe the similarities and differences of the two sites.
2. As a buyer you must constantly be aware of retail prices being charged for products in stores as well as online. Use the comparison-shopping site found at http://www.mysimon.com to locate the prices of one specific product for which you already know the retail price being charged in a bricks-and-mortar store.
   a. Record the names and Web addresses of the sites offering the product for sale.
   b. Record the retail price at each site.
   c. Provide information on delivery charges.
   d. Discuss the price differences or similarities that you found.

SNAPSHOT

Talbots: Committed to Marketing Research

Talbot's is one retailer that is committed to making decisions through the use of intensive marketing research. The chain, most noted for classic women's clothing, has a clearly articulated vision that it builds through various research strategies. Most importantly, the company takes advantage of the synergy between its retail and catalog operations, which are run as an integrated business. Utilizing the customer information and demographic data that have already been gathered in the catalog database, management at Talbot's has moved to increase the efficiency of the entire firm.

It has been able to reduce out-of-stock positions and lessen the risk associated with brand extensions and new store locations. Using the catalog database has taken most of the risk out of selecting a site for a new store. Talbot's method, which has worked with almost complete success, places stores in clusters of ZIP codes where shoppers have already spent $150,000 on apparel from the catalog. Management knows exactly where its customers are located. In fact, analysis of the database information led to Talbot's opening several very highly profitable stores in markets that might otherwise have been ignored. Moreover, 95 percent of Talbot's new stores have become profitable in their first year of operation.

Talbot's is a very focused company—it has become synonymous with classic women's apparel. Management feels that women today do not want to empty their closets every other year for new styles and fashions. Talbot's customers want "exceptional quality at reasonable prices, a comfortable shopping experience, and knowledgeable service that they value." The company briefly went into fast-changing fashion in 1990, but that move caused operating profits to slump 40 percent and led to a $7 million loss. Store management quickly shifted gears.

Management's watchwords ever since that move have been to build and maintain close relationships with shoppers. In fact, the company's credo, which originated in 1947, is "Do what's right for the customer." How does the firm build these relationships? Again, it relies on marketing research. Consumer focus groups are held throughout the year, and an annual benchmarking survey is conducted with customers, allowing them to voice their likes and dislikes. The results of that survey are required reading for all executives at Talbot's.

Dialogues with customers have led to changes and new avenues of growth for the company. The decisions to increase the proportion of private label brands in the store and to make stores more comfortable, with amenities such as larger dressing rooms, have proven to be successful moves. Both changes were fueled by customer feedback. Management says that it has "constantly got our ears to the ground to find out what our shoppers want. They've been very loyal to us, and we're willing to do whatever we can to keep it that way."

In addition to building its future on the use of marketing research, a number of other factors point to continued success for the firm. It has superior customer service that is very knowledgeable, and it has found out how to update classic items with enough fashion to keep them interesting without alienating customers who are not really fashion forward. Growth is also occurring in international markets where Talbot's has opened stores–Canada, Great Britain, and Japan.

Most retail analysts believe the chain will continue to prosper. One key to that success is using marketing research to take the guesswork out of decision making.

BASED ON:

Grant, Lorrie. (2000, December 11). Talbots dresses for success on three fronts. *USA Today*, 1B.

Grant, Lorrie. (2002, July 5). Talbots to market menswear. *USA Today*, 7B.

Seamless shopping. (2000, November 20). *Business Week*, EB 18.

Sliwa, Carol. (2000, September 18). A classic makeover. *Computerworld*, 42.

Talbots. (2000, June 26). *Advertising Age*, 534.

Talbots heats up by cooling down. (2000, December 18). *Business Week*, 98.

Talbots plans to add 300 plus stores. (2000, June 5). *Providence Business News*, 10.

TRENDWATCH

Loyalty Cards: How Can They Benefit Retail Buyers?

Today, most shoppers have a number of loyalty cards in their wallets and pocketbooks. Each time they go to the grocery store and swipe their card, they save money on certain products, but they are also providing information about themselves to the retailer.

Consumers may use a loyalty card when they rent movies. Some pet supply stores offer customers "free stuff" when using their loyalty cards. And, most air travelers have at least one or two frequent flyer loyalty cards on which they collect points for free travel. Loyalty cards are proliferating in all areas of retailing, with the greatest usage at grocery store chains. In fact, today over 50 percent of major grocery stores in the United States incorporate a loyalty card program as part of their promotional efforts.

Participation in loyalty card programs is important to retailers because it is estimated that 20 percent of shoppers account for 80 percent of store sales, so finding out what their best customers want is essential. Customers who use loyalty cards tend to be the most frequent shoppers.

Who uses loyalty cards, and how do they view these cards? In 2006, only 3 percent of consumers said they did not like loyalty cards–reflecting a growing trend that shoppers are more accepting of these programs. Women are significantly more likely to have loyalty cards than men, a difference that should not be suprising because mothers living with children under the age of 18 tend to be the primary purchaser in most households. Over 70 percent of consumers 25 to 34 years old belong to loyalty programs, and shoppers older than 55 comprise the highest percentage of nonprogram members. The Northeast has the highest concentration of loyalty program participants while consumers in the South are significantly more likely *not* to belong to any type of loyalty program.

Loyalty cards not only allow stores to track what products are selling, but also they can obtain specific information about who is buying those products. With such a massive amount of data on shoppers being collected through loyalty cards–from the types of cola bought to whether they shop late at night–retailers are getting smarter at tracking consumer trends. By knowing who joins loyalty programs, buyers can adjust their merchandise offerings, store layouts, product adjacencies, and advertising efforts. Theoretically, through loyalty card programs, retailers can gather information about consumer purchases and target individuals with communications offering them something that is directly relevant to them.

CVS Drug Stores launched its loyalty card program in 2001 and discovered that cosmetic buyers were the company's best customers. Beauty products were moved to the front aisles of most stores instead of being relegated to the back counters. Winn-Dixie grocery stores rolled out its loyalty card program in March 2002. The company now knows the 25 items that attract the most loyal shoppers to the store.

While retailers insist that loyalty cards only keep loyal customers satisfied by offering the right products at the right prices, some privacy advocates contend there can be a dark side. Every time a customer uses their card, they give up some privacy. Some insist the cards are nothing more than data collection devices. There are even some advocacy groups that have devoted entire Web sites to the elimination of loyalty cards, and they may be having some impact. Albertson's grocery stores in the Southwest discontinued the use of loyalty cards in 2007.

BASED ON:

Are there really hidden dangers to data collection? (2007, April 6). *Precision Marketing*, 12.

Croft, Martin. (2006, December 21). Are loyalty cards missing the point? *Marketing Week*, 6.

D'Innocenzio, Anne. (2003, March 22). Loyalty cards help stores track what shoppers want. *Charlotte Observer*, D1–D2.

Gruehn, David. (2006, April). Counting cards: emerging technologies trim the "fat" out of loyalty retailing. *Chain Store Age*, 54.

Hamstra, Mark. (2007, July 2). Albertsons LLC eliminates loyalty cards in Southwest market. *Supermarket News*.

Johannes, Amy. (2006, April 5). Value tops customers loyalty preference. *Promo (Online Exclusive)*.

Loyalty cards run hard to stand still. (2006, March 12). *Nilewide Marketing Review*.

Retail loyalty cards receive mixed consumer response. (2007, April 9). *The Food Institute Report*, 1.

Who has loyalty cards in their pockets? (2006, August 9). *Promo (Online Exclusive)*.

TRENDWATCH

Using Different Retail Formats to Appeal to Diverse Customers in the Same Market

Grocery stores, being pressured by competition, have responded by developing very focused formats that address specific customer segments. One prominent example of this trend is the approach being undertaken by Food Lion supermarkets.

Food Lion, a regional grocery store chain in the Southeast, is expanding by introducing two new store formats—Bloom and Bottom Dollar. Before expanding into new markets, the company conducts market analyses to determine which of its three banners—Food Lion, Bloom, or Bottom Dollar—best meets the needs of consumers in that market.

Food Lion has 1,151 stores in 11 states, and many of the stores are currently undergoing a redesign to widen aisles and lower shelves while upgrading the produce and wine departments. Stores offer a smaller selection of specialty foods, such as international and organic foods. Seafood is fresh but prepackaged, and shoppers with the store's MVP loyalty card receive discounts on select items.

The Bloom banner, which was introduced in 2004, presents innovative store designs that aim to make it easier for customers to shop and provides services geared toward their needs, such as take-home meals that are located near the front of the store. Based on customer feedback from test stores, Bloom stores now offer a greater variety of fresh fruits and vegetables, more cuts of fresh meat, new fresh seafood counters, more fresh-baked breads, a wider selection of wines, and greater variety throughout the grocery aisles. Overall, Bloom has a broader selection than Food Lion stores, including more than 40 organic items in addition to exotic offerings such as sugar cane and red baby bananas. Fast-movers like milk, eggs, and perishables are located near the front of the store, allowing customers to do all of their perishable shopping in mere minutes. Shopping carts even have cup holders, include a place to put a handheld scanner for easy checkout, and come equipped with a store map for easy navigation.

Stores operating under the Bottom Dollar banner have a deep discount concept combining highly competitive prices with a limited assortment of about 6,500 products. Bottom Dollar's no-frills approach allows the retailer to offer lower prices than the competition.

Other grocery store chains are also rolling out their own version of Bottom Dollar. For example, Albertson's has developed a Super Saver format, a deep-discount operation that complements the company's traditional supermarkets. In addition, on the upscale side, Albertson's operates Bristol Farms—a gourmet grocery chain.

These new formats remain a test, but they are an aggressive effort to move away from the cookie-cutter, one-size-fits-all approach in the supermarket industry that has prevailed for decades. The next growth stage for retailers may be all about segmenting their business.

BASED ON:

Bell, Nichole Monroe. (2007, March 18). Trying to survive in a competitive market. *The Charlotte Observer*, D1.

Feigner, Brent. (2007, May 21). One-size retailing not in our future. *Home Textiles Today*, 2.

Food Lion continues rollout of new concepts. (2006, January 23). *The Food Institute Report*, 1.

Grant, Lorrie. (2005, August 10). Supermarkets try to defend turf. *USA Today*, 3B.

Merrefield, David. (2005, March 7). Localized marketing will be the future of food retailing. *Supermarket News*, 12.

Retailers change face with formats. (2006, January 9). *MMR*, 38.

Turcsik, Richard. (2006, October). Exploring the extraordinary: fun and shopper-friendly, Food Lion's new Bloom store is a far cry from a run-of-the-mill supermarket. *Grocery Headquarters*, 31–35.

Zwiebach, Elliot. (2005, December 12). Food Lion to expand Bloom, Bottom Dollar to new markets. *Supermarket News*, 8.

Understanding Your Customers

PERFORMANCE OBJECTIVES

Upon completion of this chapter, you should be able to:

- Cite recent demographic and behavior changes in the consumer market.
- Cite recent psychographic changes in the consumer market.
- Identify the different types of buying motives.
- Describe data warehousing.
- Describe data mining.
- Identify how buyers can use the information maintained in data warehouses.
- Describe database marketing.
- Identify goals of database marketing.
- Recognize methods buyers can use to learn more about their customers.

As you learned in the last chapter, marketing research can be used to help buyers make decisions. In this chapter, you will concentrate on learning more about consumers. Knowing and understanding consumers will be vital to your success as a buyer. A wealth of information from secondary sources will be available as you identify and track changes in the consumer market. More importantly, retailers today are using technology that allows them to know more information than ever about their current customers. This information is invaluable to buyers as they make purchase decisions. And, it will be critical that you understand why your customers are buying—what motivates them to purchase a specific product or shop at your store.

In this chapter, you will learn about some of the changes occurring with consumers; demographic, geographic, behavioristic, and psychographic trends are explored. You will examine the basic reasons why customers make purchases as you learn about data warehousing and data mining techniques. Finally, database marketing is examined to illustrate how retailers can make use of all the customer data they collect.

INTRODUCTION

Consumers in the United States are changing, and they will continue to change. Current population numbers are known; future population trends can be forecasted. The number of people who will be over 65 and the number of teenagers ten years from now can be accurately predicted. Those customers are already born, and because forecasters have a good idea of mortality rates, these predictions are more than guesses. Retailers can safely use population and other demographic forecasts as they make future plans. Buyers can accurately use the numbers when forecasting the size of potential markets. What cannot be forecast with as much certainty are the tastes and attitudes of consumers. How will consumers in the future want to live? What products will they want to purchase?

Forecasts can be made in these areas, too, although with much less accuracy. By looking at the numbers that can be accurately forecast, buyers can ask questions about what these groups will want from retail stores in the future. There is no mystery to collecting the data; this information is available from a wide range of sources. Such statistics are reported every day by government reporting agencies, private market research firms, business magazines, and daily newspapers. The difficulty is putting the data together to develop plans. For example, knowing that the over-55 market is growing at a rapid rate does not mean that retailers should drop their juniors' and young men's departments and concentrate on merchandise assortments for the older consumer. Consumer demographic data are illustrated in Table 5.1. Buyers will want to closely examine growth rates for specific age groups.

Demographic trends related to consumer characteristics change very slowly, and retailers cannot look at such trends and make immediate changes in their strategies. The most successful stores are the ones that are consumer-driven and adjust their focus season to season by listening to their customers.

Most retailers have been adept at targeting a consumer segment and providing merchandise assortments to meet the wants and needs of those individuals. Too many retailers, however, have not been adept at forecasting changes in their customers. They must respond to events such as:

• Changes in the tastes and attitudes of customers,
• Declines in the size of their target market, and
• Changes in spending patterns of customers.

Market size, consumer attitudes, and future spending patterns of consumers depend on many factors that can be forecast based on an analysis of major demographic trends. Read the Snapshot titled "Trends

Table 5.1: U.S. Population Projections by Age Range, 2005–2010					
Age Group	2005	% of Total	2010	% of Total	% Change 2005–2010
0–4	21,166,000	7.1	21,885,000	6.9	7.2
5–9	20,727,000	6.9	21,457,000	6.8	1.8
10–14	21,747,000	7.2	21,360,000	6.8	3.2
15–19	21,638,000	7.2	22,656,000	7.2	12.6
20–24	21,020,000	7.0	22,502,000	7.1	17.7
25–29	19,979,000	6.7	21,834,000	6.9	11.9
30–34	20,145,000	6.7	20,566,000	6.5	(0.9)
35–39	20,946,000	7.0	20,331,000	6.5	(10.9)
40–44	22,753,000	7.6	20,898,000	6.6	(8.1)
45–49	22,529,000	7.5	22,555,000	7.2	10.2
50–54	20,179,000	6.7	22,224,000	7.1	22.9
55–59	17,232,000	5.7	19,723,000	6.3	44.0
60–64	13,127,000	4.4	16,555,000	5.3	51.5
65–69	10,193,000	3.4	12,304,000	3.9	28.7
70–74	8,561,000	2.9	9,196,000	2.9	3.4
75–79	7,457,000	2.5	7,251,000	2.3	(2.8)
80+	10,638,000	3.5	11,627,000	3.7	28.1
TOTAL	300,037,000	100.0	314,924,000	100.0	10.5

Source: The U.S. Census, 2001.

and Countertrends: Can Buyers Predict What Customers Want?" to learn more about the difficulty of detecting customer trends in the marketplace.

When analyzing trends, however, buyers must realize that a general trend for the country may not be valid for a particular city or region. These trends are useful only as guidelines when preparing forecasts of what customers at a specific store will want in the future.

IDENTIFYING CHANGES IN CONSUMER MARKETS

As a retail buyer, you must have a thorough knowledge and understanding of who your customer is, as well as general trends occurring in the marketplace. A discussion of some of the most prevalent trends that will affect the decisions you make as a buyer follows. These trends are designed as a starting point; as a retail buyer you will need to identify and examine specific trends related to your store's target customers. Buyers will need to analyze each trend and ask themselves, "What are the implications for my store, department, or product category?" Let's examine some of the more important consumer trends that will be affecting future purchases.

Demographic and Consumer Behavior Trends

As buyers begin to learn more about consumers, they usually begin by identifying trends related to their characteristics and lifestyles. Once they identify relevant information, buyers must then be able to use that information in making purchasing decisions.

Marital Status and Birthrates. Single-person households are showing the greatest increase in numbers, and that trend is projected to continue. According to the Census Bureau, a 26 percent increase in single-person households is projected between 1995 and 2010, contrasted to overall household growth at 18 percent. Women are in the majority (58 percent) of those who live alone, and half of those are 65 years old and over. Of the men who live alone, almost half (47 percent) are 25 to 44 years old. Projections to the year 2020 also show a dramatic increase in the number of middle-aged singles.

The number of marriages is increasing. Although they comprise only 3 percent of the total population, young marrieds purchase a disproportionate number of products such as furniture, appliances, tableware, cookware, home entertainment products, and linens.

The birthrate has remained relatively stable since 1994. The decline in births has been steady since a peak of 4,158,000 births in 1990, as women of the baby-boom generation moved out of their childbearing years and were replaced by a smaller generation of women who apparently had no intention of starting another baby boom. Overall, population growth in the United States will continue to slow, with five states—Arizona, California, Florida, Georgia, and Texas—accounting for the largest percentage of growth.

Households. Education level correlates with the percentage of women returning to work. Of women aged 30 to 40 with a college education,

77 percent returned to the workforce before their child reached one year of age. The percentage of back-to-work mothers decreased, however, with the birth of a second child. The growing percentage of working women means that department and specialty stores will need to offer more career clothing, while grocery stores will need to offer more convenience foods—prepared foods from in-store delis and microwavable foods. Work also puts time constraints on customers, limiting when and where it is convenient for them to shop.

Increasingly, today's homemaker has a "five o'clock shadow." Mediamark Research shows that the percentage of male "homemakers" (defined as the person in the household who does most of the shopping) continues to increase. Women, however, will continue to make the majority of purchasing decisions—from big-ticket items to small items, from clothing to food.

Age Groups and Spending Patterns. The U.S. Census Bureau reports the age group of 5- to 11-year-olds numbers more than 27 million and is expected to continue to climb. Estimates of their future spending range from $17 billion of direct purchases to over $23 billion. Kids already directly influence the purchase of all goods and services. And, kids are smart shoppers. As more responsibility is placed on younger children due to latch-key lifestyles, they are learning savvy shopping skills, along with gaining confidence in their role as shoppers. Figure 5.1 illustrates the impact teens have on the purchase of home computers.

As mentioned earlier, the baby-boom generation is reaching 60. By 2020, that cohort will number 115 to 120 million people. Research indicates that this group of "seniors" will be much healthier than previous generations, and marketers are finding that as the boomers age, these older consumers are still big spenders. Older households, with their higher incomes, are spending more. Retailers have found, however, that baby boomers vary markedly in their attitudes and values, and thus cannot be looked at as a single market segment. Because they are typically well educated, this group tends to spend lavishly on their children, buying millions of dollars worth of educational toys, video games, and children's books. Read the Trendwatch titled, "Baby Boomers: Reaching Them After 60," to learn more about the baby-boom generation.

As the population ages, retail buyers will have to carefully select products for this older market segment. Products appealing to older customers

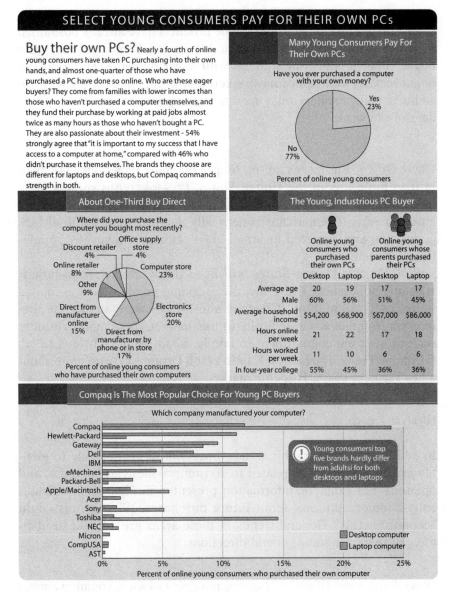

Figure 5.1 Teens influence PC buying.

will probably need to focus on comfort, security, convenience, sociability, and old-fashioned values. Some products have already positioned themselves for this market. Levi's Action Slacks are cut for fuller bodies, Bulova is offering watches with larger numerals, and a host of home-security companies have taken aim at this market segment. In addition, many retailers today are offering discounts to seniors on special days of the week.

Ethnic Origin. Europeans are no longer the most numerous ingredient in the ethnic mix of the United States. Present trends show a large influx of people from the Middle East and Caribbean areas. The population of African Americans is generally younger than the total U.S. population and centered in urban areas, although suburban populations are increasing.

By 2025 the United States will have the world's second-largest Hispanic population. Currently, the Hispanic population is estimated to be nearly 38 million. JCPenney and Macy's were among the first retailers to target ads specifically to this market, focusing on attitudes such as a strong commitment to family. Read the Trendwatch titled, "Hispanic Teens: The Largest Ethnic Youth Group," to learn more about a key segment of the Hispanic market.

Lifestyle Trends

In addition to demographic trends, buyers must also be able to identify *psychographic trends* related to consumers' lifestyles, attitudes, and opinions. For example, information presented in Figure 5.2 indicates baby-boomer opinions about future purchases. What trends could account for this? General trends in these areas are difficult to identify, but there are some general directions.

"Busy, Busy, Busy" Lifestyles. Juggling multiple tasks was common among harried Americans in the 1990s, but it took its toll on their physical and mental well-being. Many individuals are reevaluating their lives and restructuring them to find more personal time. Most people feel a "time crunch," even when there is none. They seem to always be under pressure and feel they do not have enough time to do all the tasks they need to accomplish. For many consumers, shopping has become

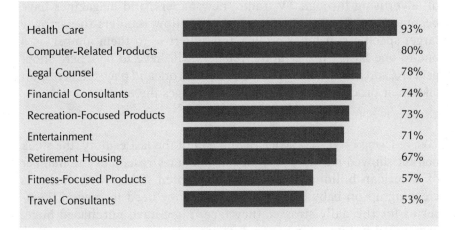

Health Care	93%
Computer-Related Products	80%
Legal Counsel	78%
Financial Consultants	74%
Recreation-Focused Products	73%
Entertainment	71%
Retirement Housing	67%
Fitness-Focused Products	57%
Travel Consultants	53%

Figure 5.2 What Baby Boomers say they will be purchasing when they reach 65.

a chore—an activity that many hate. In fact, most consumers are spending less time shopping at retail stores.

Retail buyers are reacting to this trend with the products they purchase. Many are stocking and promoting items directed at calming and relaxing customers. Aromatic candles, relaxing teas, crystal jewelry, bath soaps, and small home-size water fountains are just some of the products being promoted to relieve the stress that consumers are feeling.

Computer Junkies. The younger generation has grown up with computers, just as the baby boomers grew up with television. Although in-home computers have developed the technological skills of this generation, there may have been some negative impact.

For retailers, increased computer usage can have a positive impact. Primarily, the Internet has the potential to enlarge their markets. No longer are retailers limited to consumers within a certain trading area. Now, shoppers worldwide are potential customers. Retailers have answered this trend by establishing online sites, but one of the most significant effects will probably be with advertising. As the mass market evaporates into smaller and smaller niches, traditional forms of advertising through TV, radio, newspapers, and magazines have become less effective. The Internet will allow retailers to narrowly target specific consumer groups and advertise to them almost on a one-to-one basis. In the future, retailers will have to be where shoppers are, and as consumers move online for work and play, retailers must take their products and promotional messages there too.

"We're Living Large" Lifestyle. By the end of the last century, the stock market showed steady gains, median incomes rose, and the number of American billionaires more than doubled. Today, retirement is creeping up on baby boomers, who feel they need to reward themselves for the daily stresses they face. They have purchased huge, overstuffed furniture for houses that are three rooms bigger than they were two decades ago, with an "urban assault" vehicle in the garage. Americans are bigger too, with one-third of the U.S. population tipping the scales as obese. Big, comfortable clothes are available, as are big meals—72-ounce drinks, 2-foot pizzas, tubs of popcorn, and huge servings at most restaurants.

The "good life" according to Roper Starch Worldwide has seen changes in the past 20 years. Happy marriages, a steady job, a home, and college for their kids were on the wish list of Americans in the twentieth century. Today, the list of material desires is considerable, including a second car, travel, a swimming pool, and a pile of money. Americans seem to want it all.

These trends affect individual retailers and specific products differently. Even different geographic locations of the same store within a chain could be influenced differently. Retailers must interpret the national trends based on a complete knowledge of their local customers. State and local forecasts need to be obtained, and if necessary, direct customer surveys may be required to determine what your customers want and the reasons why they buy.

UNDERSTANDING WHY CONSUMERS BUY

Once buyers have an understanding of how consumer markets are changing, they must determine why consumers buy. What causes targeted consumers to make purchases? In other words, what are their buying motives, their reasons for making purchases? As a buyer making purchasing decisions, you will need to determine the reasons why customers would buy each product you have purchased for your store. Such knowledge will be critical when planning promotional campaigns and providing product knowledge to sales associates. Typically, buying motives can be grouped into three categories: (1) rational, (2) emotional, and (3) patronage.

Rational Buying Motives

Rational buying motives are concerned with basic human needs such as food, clothing, and shelter. Such needs would correspond to the physiological needs on Maslow's Hierarchy, which include hunger, sex, and thirst. Consumers tend to satisfy these needs first, but once they

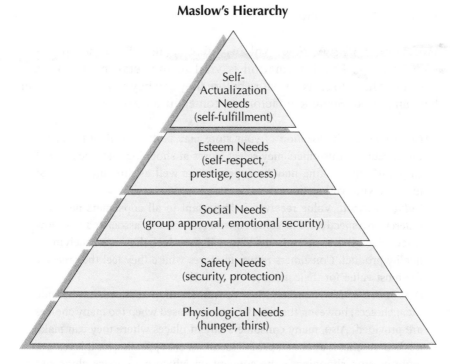

Maslow's Hierarchy

Self-
Actualization
Needs
(self-fulfillment)

Esteem Needs
(self-respect,
prestige, success)

Social Needs
(group approval, emotional security)

Safety Needs
(security, protection)

Physiological Needs
(hunger, thirst)

Figure 5.3   Can you identify products that would satisfy consumers at each level of Maslow's Hierarchy?

are met, they will seek to satisfy needs on the other levels. An illustration of Maslow's Hierarchy is presented in Figure 5.3.

Rational buying motives are based on a customer's ability to reason in logical terms. Typical motives of customers that fit into this category could include economy, savings, durability, dependability, reliability, and gain.

Emotional Buying Motives

Customers may purchase food, clothing, and shelter to satisfy rational needs, but those needs can be satisfied with minimum purchases. What causes consumers to purchase several sweaters or two coats? These purchases can be explained by *emotional buying motives*, which involve customers' feelings rather than logical thought. Examples of emotional buying motives could include social acceptance, curiosity, change, sex appeal, self-esteem, and group approval.

Patronage Buying Motives

Patronage buying motives explain why consumers choose one store over another. This information is vital to the retail buyer because customers have to enter the store before they can buy products the buyer has purchased. Some key factors customers use include:

- *Convenience.* The location of your store may be the deciding factor for the consumer. Customers may select stores at shopping malls because of easy parking. Parking may be expensive as well as difficult to find at many downtown locations.
- *Value Received.* Value received is important to all consumers but from different perspectives. For some consumers, value is associated with low price. For others, price is no object if they feel they are receiving a quality product. Consumers return to stores where they feel they receive the most value for their money.
- *Assortment of Merchandise.* Most consumers shop at stores that provide them choices; however, they can become confused when too many choices are provided. Also, many consumers buy in places where they can make all their purchases at one stop. Mall locations are appealing for this reason, and one-stop shopping is the concept on which warehouse clubs and hypermarkets are based.

- *Services Offered*. Many consumers may decide to make purchases at a particular store because of the services offered, such as credit, delivery, gift wrapping, or alterations. For example, a consumer could buy a recliner anywhere but may choose the store that offers free delivery. Providing services is a key method retailers can use in distinguishing themselves from competitors.
- *Experienced and Courteous Sales Associates*. Consumers will usually return to stores where they find friendly, courteous, and experienced salespeople who are crucial to the image that a retailer is attempting to develop. Many customers return time after time to their favorite salesperson. Nordstrom's has built an industry reputation on the high level of service provided to customers by its sales associates.

LEARNING ABOUT YOUR CURRENT CUSTOMERS

In addition to identifying and examining trends related to the general population, most retail decision makers, and specifically buyers, are now using techniques that allow them to identify, analyze, and take advantage of trends prevalent among their own customers. These techniques include data warehousing, data mining, and database marketing.

Data Warehousing

Retailers have searched for ways to efficiently collect the wealth of information they gain from customers every day and to use that information to develop better retail strategies. **Data warehousing** involves electronically storing all this information. Retailers have generally used the data for financial and accounting purposes only and ignored the value of the data for marketing purposes. Typically, this data had been kept in many different computer systems. With data warehousing, there is only a single source of data. Data warehousing acts as a comprehensive single source for sales, margin, inventory, and other key merchandising performance measures.

The process of building a data warehouse requires retailers to transfer significant amounts of data from operational computer systems to analysis systems. This data transfer makes vital sales data more readily accessible to decision makers and buyers in the store as well as its vendors. Data warehousing provides them all with access to the vast amount of information that is stored on the computer system. The result is usually strengthened partnerships with vendors, improved selection of merchandise in the store, and more effective promotional campaigns. Using data warehousing can also effectively boost the retailer's potential to offer the right merchandise at the right time. Additionally, decision makers have a unified understanding of the company as a whole.

Benefits and Uses of Data Warehousing. Storing and using data are more important than ever for most retailers as they seek ways to improve their businesses through technology. Rather than using a broad brush stroke to market all products to all customers, retailers want to maximize purchase decisions and promotion efforts by directing them to consumers who are most likely to buy. Data warehousing allows retailers access to detailed customer, inventory, and financial data on a perpetual, real-time basis. With a data warehouse system in place, retailers can perform very specific analyses, such as how a particular product is doing in a particular store, as well as conduct merchandise replenishment and make customer analysis-related decisions based on facts rather than intuition. Data warehousing provides all retail decision makers with the tool to understand their business *in detail*, not just in summary.

For example, each week, information from Lands' End order processing and customer mailing systems is added to the company's data warehouse. Detailed information is kept on approximately 20 million customers, enabling management to find and analyze data by customer, product, and transaction. The system can also track what customers ordered that was not in stock. Williams-Sonoma, another cataloguer, uses its data warehousing system to improve its bottom line by better targeting customers who generate sales and eliminating from its mailing list individuals who seem unlikely ever to order anything.

Data warehousing has a strong foothold in large retail firms but is also rapidly gaining popularity among midsized and even small chains. Some firms have seen a payoff of 10 to 70 times their initial data warehouse investments through more effective decision making. Wal-Mart, for example, currently operates the world's largest commercial data warehousing system. The decision support system now has more than five terabytes of online storage. The chain's system is used to store 65 weeks of sales data by item, store, and day. A similar system is also in operation at Sears.

The surge of data warehousing is due to a growing recognition that it is a tool that provides retailers with the best means of understanding and satisfying the needs of their ever-more-demanding customers. Data warehouses, running on ultrafast computers with specialized software, are the basis on which companies hope to operate in real time—instantly adjusting such factors as product mix, inventory levels, cash reserves, and marketing programs.

Data Mining

Technology is not the difficult aspect of implementing data warehousing. The hard part is deriving meaning from the data. Significance must be extracted from the blizzard of numbers, facts, and statistics. ***Data mining*—**searching through warehoused data to find trends and patterns that might otherwise have gone unnoticed—is a cutting-edge technology that uses the information already maintained in the firm's data warehouse. Data mining can also be used to identify real and perceived threats to the company. Data-mining software has enough built-in "intelligence" to detect meaningful patterns and relationships on its own. These trends might otherwise take many years to detect.

Typically, buyers and other retail decision makers have used a firm's database to supply answers to such simple questions as, "What was the sales volume for stores in the Southeast region last month?" Data mining reaches much deeper into databases. Electronic processes dig through and analyze information as well as extract its meaning; computer tools find patterns in the data and make inferences from them. Those findings can then be used to guide decision making and better forecast the effect of actions being considered.

Using Data-Mining Techniques. Most analysts agree that past behavior is more predictive than age, sex, and income; but, with hundreds of behavioristic variables to choose from, the difficult questions when using data-mining techniques become which ones will help retailers understand the customer better. Effective data mining almost requires an explorer's mentality—retailers never know what they are going to find and what changes may result. Data mining, however, produces some general types of data. They include:

- *Associations*. The system links occurrences to a single event. For example, data-mining analysis may reveal that customers buy cola 65 percent of the time when chips are regularly priced, but 85 percent of the time when chips are on sale. Having mined this information, retailers can evaluate the profitability of various promotional strategies.

• *Sequences*. The system links events over time. For example, 50 percent of customers who purchase a suit may then purchase shoes within 30 days. This information lets the retailer formulate more informed buying, merchandising, and promotional decisions.

• *Clustering*. Data-mining tools can discover groups within the data. For example, decision makers may be better able to pinpoint customer groups most likely to obtain the store's proprietary credit card.

• *Forecasting*. Tools can be used to analyze data to predict whether a customer will continue to shop at the store, and even forecast future purchases based on patterns within warehoused data.

Clustering customers into segments is one of the top objectives of data mining for management at Fingerhut catalog. At that firm, data mining has led to the creation of new catalogs. In one analysis using data mining, decision makers found that customers who changed their residence tripled their purchasing in the three months after their move. The company developed a new "mover's catalog" filled with targeted products for this consumer segment. At the same time, it saved money by not mailing other catalogs to these customers right after they moved.

Data mining allows retailers to understand what customers buy and when they buy it; therefore, retailers are able to do a better job of marketing to those customers. For example, a new mother goes to her local pharmacy to fill a prescription for postnatal vitamins. After her profile has been collected at the store, management can then send a steady stream of coupons for products that she will need at each stage of the baby's development. Such product selections can easily be based on results of data mining that have shown what products similar customers have purchased over time.

Generally, data mining can be used by management, buyers, and other retail decision makers for a number of purposes. They include the following:

• *Competitive Price Analysis*. Data warehousing and mining allows for a better interpretation of competitive price data collected by comparison price shoppers. The system can use mathematical algorithms to identify overpriced and underpriced items and product categories on a store-by-store basis.

- *Markup/Markdown Opportunity Identification.* Mathematical algorithms in data-mining techniques allow retailers to single out SKUs that have rapidly accelerating or decelerating sales volumes, compare the prices of these items with prices charged by competitors, and recommend new price points.
- *Promotional Price Analysis.* Data warehouses and data-mining techniques can be used to compare average prices in local markets with the buyer's or manager's suggested promotional price. The system then reviews promotional sales history to understand item movement at various price points. Finally, a recommended promotional price is generated.
- *Private Brand Analysis.* Data warehouses and data mining can be enlisted to calculate the price points at which consumers will switch from a national brand to a competing private label product.
- *Promotional Performance Analysis.* Data warehousing allows retailers to scrutinize their promotions at an item level to isolate products that yield the greatest promotional sales increase or that customers buy without making any other purchase in the store or department. Insight into individual items and product categories that are more likely to be cannibalized by promoted items can also be gleaned.
- *Affinity Analysis.* Data warehousing can identify products and merchandise classifications most commonly purchased together, such as those shown in Figure 5.4. The result can be better in-store product adjacencies, improved promotional display effectiveness, and more effective advertising campaigns.

Effective use of data-warehousing and data-mining techniques results in a sharper competitive edge, a selling and merchandising approach based on real data, a marketing plan that correlates with customers' needs, and reduced operational costs. But above all, retailers must remember that the computer does not provide all the answers. Decision makers who implement data mining must be people with a solid knowledge of the marketplace.

Database Marketing

Today, more and more retailers are using data-warehousing and data-mining techniques to market to their customers. Even very small business owners are developing their own customer databases to learn more about their customers so they can build a lasting relationship. The technique

Figure 5.4   Display of products commonly sold together.

they are using is *database marketing*, which is based on analyzing and understanding customers and their behaviors through an analysis of information. This concept has several names—database marketing, relationship marketing, one-to-one marketing—but in all cases it involves collecting mountains of information about customers, analyzing it to predict how likely customers are to buy a product, and using that knowledge to develop a marketing message designed to best match customers' wants and needs.

Database marketing has evolved over time, but computerization has dramatically expanded its implementation by retailers. First, there was the mass market—the vast, undifferentiated group of consumers who received identical, mass-produced products and promotional messages. Then, retailers starting using market segmentation, which divided consumers into smaller groups with common characteristics. Today, more powerful computers are enabling retailers to zero in on ever smaller niches of the population. They are taking aim at the smallest consumer segment of all—the individual.

Retailers increasingly are recognizing that past customer behavior, as recorded in actual business transactions, is by far the best indicator of future buying patterns. For example, knowing customers' ZIP codes or income levels yields less insight and opportunity than knowing that they just purchased a new house. Such a move signals the need for lots of new purchases, such as window treatments, carpets, and furniture, and retailers can better stock their stores and design promotional messages based on that information.

The fundamental principle that should guide retailers who use database marketing is that a retailer's most important asset is a satisfied customer. Satisfied customers stay with the store, and it is much less expensive to keep existing customers than to find new ones. Examples of database marketing are varied. For example, one men's specialty retailer may find itself with too many suits in size 42-regular. After electronically sorting through its database, previous customers who have purchased that size are sent promotion offers to buy a suit at a reduced price. The retailer is able to clear excess inventory while also building customer loyalty among its customer base. Many national chains track credit card holders who spend more than a predetermined dollar amount at the store each year. Those customers who meet or exceed the required purchasing are sent special offers, advance notice of sales, and discount coupons. Some firms have found that loyal customers are not always motivated by the most expensive rewards. One of the most popular benefits at Neiman Marcus is a chance to have lunch with the store manager and attend a private fashion show.

Database marketing starts with information about the customers from databases stored on in-store personal computers or on mainframe data warehouses. The initial building block of information is data on each sale. Items from credit or debit card purchases can provide even more information. The retailer can then mix in data from other sources. Research houses such as Donnelley, Metromail, and R. L. Polk glean vast amounts of data from public records—auto registrations, drivers' licenses, and tax records. Even income can be estimated based on mortgages and automobile registrations. Retailers must be aware, however, that such information is not cheap.

Consumers, wittingly or unwittingly, also offer retailers plenty of information about themselves. Most product warranty cards ask a gamut of questions such as age, income, occupation, education, and marital status. But, many go on to ask many psychographic questions, such as what sports the purchaser plays or whether he or she participates in other specific activities.

Challenges Facing Database Marketing. Analysts point to problems and challenges facing the spread of database marketing. Too many retailers have jumped into the field without a complete understanding of the basic concepts of database marketing. Some retailers are uncertain of its benefits, while others lack a strategy for coordinating database marketing with other traditional approaches. Stores are also faced with the resistance of consumers and consumer groups that feel having stores collect and use information on their shopping habits constitutes an invasion of privacy.

Goals of Database Marketing. Clearly, any retailer implementing database marketing programs must have specific purposes for using the technique. Survey research conducted by the Direct Marketing Association revealed the following nine basic goals that most retailers have for database marketing programs:

1. Targeting promotional offerings to specific customers
2. Gaining a better understanding of customers
3. Strengthening the store-customer relationship
4. Gaining a more detailed understanding of the best customers
5. Tailoring merchandise offers to specific customer segments
6. Reducing the cost of new customer acquisition
7. Improving customer service
8. Assisting in the merchandise selection process
9. Preventing customer defections

More retailers are learning that customer databases can be developed, organized, and used successfully to encourage customer loyalty. Such programs are likely to continue to grow. Fueling the move toward database marketing is a paradigm shift away from the idea that consumers can be marketed to as one huge market and toward the idea that consumers want customization. In other words, they "want it their way." Above all, these programs help build store traffic, improve customer service and merchandise strategies, and, for multichannel retailers, develop synergies among store, catalog, and online sales.

SUMMARY POINTS

- The most successful retailers are consumer-driven. They know who their customers are and listen to them.
- Retailers must monitor changes in the consumer market, particularly demographic and lifestyle changes.
- Buyers must do more than identify consumer trends; they must understand the implications for their store or department. Identifying consumer trends will help buyers make better decisions.
- Buyers must identify local and regional trends that have a direct impact on their customers. These trends may be very different from national trends.
- Reasons that customers make purchases can be grouped into three categories: (1) rational, (2) emotional, and (3) patronage buying motives.
- Many retailers are using data-warehousing techniques to store a wealth of information about their customers.
- Retailers and buyers are implementing data-mining technology to extract meaning from the information stored in data warehouses.
- Many retailers use database-marketing techniques to target specific customer groups. Such efforts have the potential to strengthen store–customer relationships.
- Technology is playing a critical role in enabling buyers to learn more about their customers.

REVIEW ACTIVITIES

Developing Your Retail Buying Vocabulary

Consult the Glossary if you did not add the following terms to your vocabulary.

Data mining	Emotional buying motive
Data warehousing	Patronage buying motive
Database marketing	Psychographic trend
Demographic trend	Rational buying motive

Understanding What You Read

1. Identify demographic trends that are occurring in the United States related to (a) number of single-person households, (b) median age for marriage, (c) birthrate, (d) U.S. population growth, and (e) number of male homemakers.
2. Identify behavioristic trends that are occurring in the United States related to spending patterns of (a) children, (b) baby boomers, and (c) teen Hispanics.
3. Describe lifestyle changes that are occurring in the consumer market.
4. Describe the differences between rational and emotional buying motives.
5. How do customers select one store over another when making a purchase?
6. List types of data maintained by retailers in data warehouses.
7. Describe how retailers use data mining.
8. Describe how associations are using data mining to learn more about customers.
9. How is data mining used for affinity analysis?
10. List some of the challenges retailers face when using database marketing.
11. List the basic goals of using database marketing.

Analyzing and Applying What You Read

1. You are the buyer for a grocery store. Describe the implications related to your purchase decisions of knowing that there are (a) more single-person households and (b) more women working than you projected.
2. You are the owner of a used-car dealership and have just purchased 100 small cars. Your advertising agency is preparing your next promotional campaign. Because you purchased the cars, the agency has requested that you supply reasons that customers would purchase them. Provide rational, emotional, and patronage buying motives that prospective customers could have.
3. Locate an example of database marketing. Examples might include a direct-mail piece that used your name in the copy or an e-mail reminder you have received from an e-commerce site.
4. After reading the Snapshot titled, "Trends and Countertrends: Can Buyers Predict What Customers Want?" identify a trend and a countertrend for an area of retailing in which you are interested.

Internet Connection

1. Go to www.census.gov on the Internet. Locate the following information about consumers in your state and community: (a) population of your state and (b) population of your city or community. Then, locate data related to the number of individuals in different age categories.
2. Use a search engine of your choice on the Internet to locate new information about one specific consumer group–generation Y, generation X, baby boomers, Asian Americans, male homemakers, and so on. Identify major trends that are occurring with the group you research.

SNAPSHOT

Trends and Countertrends: Can Buyers Predict What Customers Want?

Healthier and microwavable products top consumers' lists of what they consider to be the most important developments in packaged food products over the past several years, followed closely by vitamin-fortified foods. Consumers were also asked to identify grocery trends they perceived to be on the rise—seven in ten shoppers said purchasing bottled water is the biggest current trend, while shoppers in higher income ranges identified the upswing in "meal solutions"—meals that are prepared and ready to go. What do these trends tell retailers? How much faith can they put in what customers say?

Decision makers should be wary of attempts to identify megatrends. Consumers are extremely complex and notoriously difficult to categorize and can be frustrating even to professional trend watchers. Although today's consumers continue to shop for low-fat foods, at the same time there has been a return to self-indulgence, and that often means foods with more fat and taste. The average consumer may eat fat-free pretzels for a midafternoon snack, salad and mineral water for dinner, and top it off with a bowl of chocolate ice cream.

Consumers' attitudes about foods, family, and entertainment are reflected in a tendency to buy and build bigger homes—but the dining rooms in these homes are getting smaller. In food retailing, experts predict that we will see more meatless meals; however, meat seems to be back in vogue. Many consumers "go vegetarian" two or three nights a week, but high-end steak houses are among the fastest growing restaurant segments. In most restaurants, "bigger is better" when it comes to portion size, as nouvelle cuisine is a distant memory. At Hardee's, for instance, the fastest growing item is a monster burger (900 calories with more than 70 grams of fat). These same consumers probably nibble on Snackwell cookies two hours later.

When it comes to cooking, some surveys suggest that cooking from scratch is dead, that kitchens have become museum pieces, and that people only venture there to use a microwave. But on the countertrend side, TV cooking shows are growing in popularity, and cookbooks have burgeoning sales. Kitchen-remodeling trends include induction-heat cooktops, professional stoves, and restaurant-style refrigerators. What is more, as the size of the formal dining room shrinks, big kitchens remain more popular than ever.

Although lite beers continue to sell successfully, it is the hot new microbrews that are stealing the spotlight with their richer, darker, and more calorie-filled taste. And, when reduced-fat Oreos were introduced, consumers flocked to double-stuff Oreos at the same time. Along the same vein, Healthy Choice pasta sauce has done extremely well in a category traditionally viewed as low-fat. Yet, Five Brothers markets a line of ten sauces, and their best-seller is Alfredo—which has an extremely high fat content.

Buyers and other retail decision makers must constantly try to detect and monitor trends in the marketplace. They should, however, also attempt to detect any countertrends that may also be arising.

BASED ON:

Horovitz, Bruce. (2001, October 15). Low fat loses out as consumers favor flavor. *USA Today*, B1.

Hudson, Kris. (2005, November 21). Upscale experience, downscale prices. *The Wall Street Journal*, R3.

Hyde, Linda. (2003, April). *Twenty Trends for 2010: Retailing in an Age of Uncertainty*. Columbus, OH: Retail Forward.

Loeb, Walter F. (2005, December). Flexibility—a priority for growth. *Stores*, 97.

Reda, Susan. (2005, December). What fortune holds: six fearless predictions for 2006. *Stores*, 30–36.

TRENDWATCH

Hispanic Teens: The Largest Ethnic Youth Group

The Hispanic market is growing rapidly in the United States; it now outnumbers African Americans as the largest minority group. Currently, there are 38.8 million Hispanics in this country, which represents a 9.8 percent increase since the U.S. Census was taken in 2000. During that same time, the total U.S. population grew only 2.5 percent. Moreover, Hispanics accounted for half of the national increase. Until recently, Hispanics were overwhelmingly concentrated in five states—California, Florida, Illinois, New York, and Texas. This geographical dispersal had made it difficult to treat Hispanics as one mass market; however, their gradual movement to additional geographic areas has occurred. Another reason that the Hispanic market cannot be viewed as one market is that it is composed of several distinct subgroups, including Mexicans, Puerto Ricans, Cubans, and other Latino cultures.

Hispanics can also be categorized by various demographic characteristics. One of the most attractive groups for marketers is Hispanic teens.

Based on the 2000 U.S. Census, there are currently 4.3 million Hispanic teens (ages 12–19) living in this country. Census projections estimate that this market will grow by 62 percent by the year 2020. Most importantly, Hispanic teens spend money, and they represent the largest ethnic youth population in the United States.

The population gains by Hispanics reflect a U.S. society that is changing—from the food on grocery shelves to movies and to the rosters of professional sports teams. The impact of Hispanics on the marketplace has been dramatic. Food was the first product category that was readily accepted by the general population. Now, the crossover appeal of music is being felt across the country. In fact, Latin music, is one of the hottest trends in music stores today. Yet, even within Latin music there is a variety of styles that retailers must monitor. In southern California, mariachi, banda, and norteño music rule. Cumbia sounds, such as tejano, are hot in Texas, but in Miami, Caribbean salsa is big. Latin radio stations account for 7 to 8 percent of the radio audience, up from 5 percent just five years ago. Hispanics are also having a dramatic impact on other areas. They represent 15 percent of movie-ticket sales, which is higher than their share of the total U.S. population. Today, the top-selling Spanish-language magazine in the United States is *People en Español* from Time Inc.

Following on the heels of Latin music is Latin-influenced fashion. Tighter-fitting, Jennifer Lopez-inspired dresses and pants are a big fashion statement. Strong eye makeup, darker lined lips, and liquid eyeliner are other trends that have continued to grow. In fact, Hispanic girls spend more money on makeup than girls in other demographic categories, and they spend more than twice as much on hair products. These are shopping patterns that interest a lot of retailers.

Hispanics also tend to demonstrate greater brand loyalty than other groups. When retailers solidify the purchasing habits of Hispanic youth, they often have their support for life. Yet for advertisers and marketers, Hispanic teens are a difficult group to reach; they are culturally different from other teen groups.

As with other segments of the population, retailers will need to target specific segments of the Hispanic population to effectively meet their wants and needs. Hispanic teens will certainly continue to be an appealing market.

BASED ON:

Consumers to watch: knowing your customers one demographic at a time. (2004, February). *Dealerscope*, 20.

Courting Hispanic teens. (2000, January). *Food Processing*, 14.

El Nasser, Haya. (2003, June 19). 39 million make Hispanics largest minority group. *USA Today*, A1.

Gonzalez-McPherson, Jennifer (2001, September). Targeting teens. *Hispanic*, 32.

Hispanic teens: a generation of new customers with special concerns and conditions. (2005, February). *Souvenirs, Gifts and Novelties*, 124.

Teens are different from everyone else. (2005, May 9). *MMR*, 96.

Wells, Melanie. (1999, September 7). Teens and online shopping don't click. *USA Today*, 3B.

TRENDWATCH

Baby Boomers: Reaching Them After 60

As the first of the 79 million baby boomers reached their 60th birthdays in recent years, most retailers agreed that the marketing and merchandising strategies that worked with their parents as senior citizens probably would be ineffective with this group. As this market segment continues to age, the retail landscape will change as well. Most retailers, however, are betting that this generation will continue spending.

With purchasing power of $2.1 trillion and numbering 79 million, baby boomers (born between 1946 and 1964) are significantly shaping all areas of retailing. For example, boomers comprise the largest food-buying demographic, collectively spending $22.8 million per week. However, because boomers make up a 19-year span, this demographic segment is not a homogenous group. Therefore, developing new products and marketing to baby boomers will take patience and skill.

Boomers will go kicking and screaming into old age; most are not ready to accept growing old. The task for retailers wanting to attract this group is to find ways to market products and services without giving the connotation of "mature" or "graying" customers. Although, items that appeal to their age-defying lifestyle will sell, there clearly is no one-size-fits-all approach to targeting aging baby boomers. Merchandising methods must be in sync with their lifestyles, needs, interests, and opinions.

Andersen Consulting's Retail Place encourages retailers to retool their marketing and merchandising strategies toward understanding boomers' shifting priorities and changing definition of value. In their twenties and early thirties, boomers spent a disproportionate amount of money on clothes. By the time they were in their 40s, boomers shifted their attention to more luxury items and financial investments. The hard task for retailers will be to predict how they will spend in the future. Some analysts see vitamins, travel, home improvement products, and nostalgia as safe bets. Retailers such as GNC, Restoration Hardware, and Crate & Barrel are well positioned to capture this market.

Aging boomers are also shopping differently today. They are shopping less often in department stores, malls, and specialty clothing stores, and more frequently in grocery stores, drug stores, and nonclothing specialty stores. For example, the percentage of adults taking vitamins increased by 35 percent in one year during the late 1990s. Auto makers believe that boomers, who boosted sales of sport utility vehicles, will soon upgrade to more prestigious models.

Research has also shown that boomers gravitate toward retail stores that sell solutions. Prepared meals at the grocery store are one such solution. Many analysts expect that boomers will also be leaving their "do-it-yourself" years behind, focusing instead on finding retailers that offer repair and maintenance services.

The message that boomer's have for retailers in the future may indeed be, "Make it easy for me."

BASED ON:

Baby boomers, a $43 billion retail opportunity. (2006, August 28). *The Food Institute Report*, 4.

Carpenter, Dave. (2001, January 26). Poised for new boomer tide. *The Charlotte Observer*, D1.

Elias, Marilyn. (2001, February 28). A generation rewrites the rules. *USA Today*, 1D.

Elias, Marilyn. (2001, February 28). Boomers generate new business. *USA Today*, 6D.

Marketing to boomers requires focus on lifestyles/stages. (2007, July 30). *The Food Institute Report*, 4.

McCarthy, Michael. (2002, November 19). Some consumers want ads for a mature audience. *USA Today*, B1–B2.

U.S. baby boomers shown to be big food spenders. (2006, February 10). *Just-food.com*.

Chapter 6

Understanding Product Trends: What Customers Buy

PERFORMANCE OBJECTIVES

Upon completion of this chapter, you should be able to:

- Recognize that the merchandise mix offered must be geared to satisfying customer wants and needs.
- Identify product categories based on availability and durability.
- Recognize that fashion is a powerful force in almost all retail stores.
- Describe how retailers establish a fashion image.
- Distinguish between fads and trends.
- Identify stages of the product life cycle.
- Describe merchandising decisions occurring at each stage of the product life cycle.
- Identify theories of fashion adoption.
- List ways buyers use to differentiate products they purchase from those sold by competitors.

Once buyers have an understanding of customer behavior, they must decide which products to purchase that will best satisfy the wants and needs of their customers. The store image that management has established will greatly influence these purchases.

In this chapter you will learn more about how customers decide which products they will purchase. You will also gain an understanding of product life cycles and fashion adoption theories and how they help buyers make merchandising decisions. And, you will identify techniques that buyers use to differentiate the products they purchase from those competitors are offering.

PRODUCT SELECTION DECISIONS

As a buyer you must plan and control the kinds of products that will be offered in your store or department. In other words, you must be concerned with the *merchandise mix*–the types or mix of products that are available for customers to purchase. The merchandise mix that you select should meet the specific needs of your customers. It must be frequently monitored because an appropriate mix today might not contain the right products tomorrow.

After you determine the types of products that will be offered, you must determine the product lines that you will be carrying. A *product line* is a group of products that are closely related because they function in a similar manner. For example, New Balance has several lines of athletic shoes, and RCA offers several lines of televisions. Buyers typically want to provide a variety of products for their customers. You may also have to think in terms of which products customers associate with other products. If they purchase New Balance shoes, will they also purchase New Balance caps and jackets?

The image that your store is attempting to project will also have a direct impact on the types of products that you will purchase. Decisions made by top management in the following areas will determine the image that the store projects to its customers:

- *Target Market.* The types of products that you purchase must be matched to the wants and needs of your store's identified target market.
- *Competition.* Management may decide to sell merchandise similar to the competition or carry entirely different products that appeal to a different market from that of your competitors.
- *Store Location and Layout.* Store location, layout, store design, fixtures, lighting, and display all will have an impact on the product assortment desired by management, as illustrated in Figure 6.1.

Figure 6.1 Store fixtures, lighting, and displays will all have an impact on the product assortment a store offers.

- *Merchandise Selection.* Brand names carried in the store will also influence the store image. For many customers, national brands denote higher quality than private brands; however, private brands create exclusivity—a goal of all stores. Merchandise selected can also create a fashion image. High-quality products tend to bring a higher profit per unit than low-quality goods, but they usually represent slower turnover.
- *Personnel.* Skilled, knowledgeable personnel are necessary when stores offer some products such as designer gowns, cameras, or computers.

Management's decisions in these areas will determine the image that is established. In addition, stores that wish to develop a fashion image must be known for offering new and unique products in the marketplace. Today, more and more stores are attempting to establish a fashion image. For example, mass merchants and discounters are promoting brands to develop a fashion image. JCPenney has added many national brand names, while Kmart has developed private brands such as Jaclyn Smith, to create a more fashionable image for the store.

As a buyer, you must make decisions about merchandise selection that require understanding your customers' desire to purchase new, innovative, or fashionable products. Generally, stores attempt to attract upscale customers by offering high-quality and fashionable merchandise that will also tend to be more expensive. Other stores use moderately priced items that have mass appeal to cater to middle-class customers, while inexpensive items are used to attract bargain-conscious customers.

As you select merchandise for your store, you must be aware of trends in the marketplace. Identifying trends will allow you to make the most appropriate product selections for your store or department. Customers continuously change. If you can capitalize on opportunities created by that change by quickly identifying emerging trends, you will provide your store with a competitive advantage.

TYPES OF PRODUCTS CUSTOMERS PURCHASE

As a buyer, you must thoroughly understand the trends that will have an impact on the products you are purchasing. You will also need to understand how your customers make their product purchases and be able to answer questions such as the following:

- What types of products do your customers most often purchase?
- How much time are customers willing to spend buying a particular product?

• What are customers' expectations about durability and product quality?
• Are your customers fashion forward?
• Do customers expect your store to have "new" and cutting-edge products?
• Will your customers purchase the latest fads and crazes?

Purchases Based on Availability

Availability refers to the amount of effort customers are willing to exert to obtain a particular product. Today, products offered at one retailer in the community can probably be found at several other retail outlets, too. If customers cannot find exactly what they are looking for at one store, will they accept a substitute? For some products, they will; for other products, they will *never* accept a different model or brand.

Products purchased by consumers can be grouped into four broad categories: (1) convenience products, (2) impulse products, (3) shopping products, and (4) specialty products. As a buyer, you need to categorize the products you purchase into one of these areas to have a better understanding of how customers view them.

Convenience products are those products that the customer is not willing to spend time, money, and effort in locating, evaluating, and purchasing. Easy and quick availability of these products are paramount to the customer. For convenience products, if a particular brand is not available, customers will easily switch brands as well as stores. Customers usually purchase convenience products frequently—with little planning and comparisons. Examples would include batteries, candy, toothpaste, fast food, and gasoline—to name but a few. Convenience products are usually low priced, and suppliers place them in many retail outlets to make them readily available when customers need to purchase them.

Impulse products are purchased by customers because of an often irresistible urge. Impulse purchases are sudden and spontaneous without much deliberation by customers. Many retailers have seen sales skyrocket of some items simply by the placement of the products in the store so that they create the impulse purchase. Batteries and candy at the cash registers of most grocery stores are prime examples. Stimuli, such as smell and touch, often trigger the purchase of these types of products. Seeing a product demonstrated in a department store stimulates impulse purchases of many products, such as the latest "kitchen gadget."

For *shopping products*, customers make price, quality, suitability, and style comparisons. They are willing to spend considerable amounts of time, money, and effort in obtaining shopping products. What constitutes a shopping product, however, varies from one customer to another. Customers purchase shopping products less frequently than and make careful comparisons to similar products based on suitability, price, and style. Examples of shopping goods include furniture, clothing, automobiles, and major appliances. Customers may be willing to accept a substitute product if their comparisons indicate it would better suit their purposes. Manufacturers usually distribute these types of products in few retail outlets.

Specialty products are those products for which customers' buying behavior is geared to obtaining a particular product without regard to time, effort, or expense; and, they will *not* accept a substitute. Again, which products fall into this category would vary among customers. Examples could be a particular brand of perfume customers always use or the newest Barbie doll for their collections.

Purchases Based on Durability and Quality

As a buyer, the quality level and durability of products that you purchase must support your store's positioning strategy in the marketplace as well as meet the needs of your target customers. Most retailers rarely try to offer the highest-quality products—few customers want or can afford the high levels of quality offered in products such as a Rolls Royce or Rolex watch.

Durability refers to how long a product will last. *Durables* are products (such as cars, furniture, and appliances) that are capable of surviving many uses and usually last for years. These products are relatively expensive, and customers purchase them infrequently. In fact, during difficult economic times, consumers tend to stretch the life of durables and hold onto them as long as possible. *Nondurables* are products that are used up in a few uses or simply become out-of-date as styles change. Consumers tend to make frequent and regular purchases of these products if they are fresh, new, unique, current, or fashionable. Food products represent the largest category of nondurables.

Quality and durability can also be related to the features that a product provides. Products can be offered with varying features—from a model with only a minimum number to one with all the extras. Product features offer retailers a competitive tool for differentiating products in their store from those of competitors. Buyers must identify which product features available are most desired by their customers. To learn about customer wants and needs, customers can simply be asked questions like these:

• "Which new features would improve the product?"
• "Which features do you like the most?"
• "Which other features would make this product more appealing to you?"

Purchases Based on Fashion Appeal

Another way to add value to a product is through distinctive product style and design—making it more "fashionable" or making it a better product. *Style* is a basic and distinctive mode of expression—the appearance of a product. Styles can be eye-catching, or they may never excite shoppers (Figure 6.2). A sensational style may generate attention, but such products may not perform better. A *fashion* is the currently accepted or popular style. Many people confuse fashion and style. Style is the characteristic or distinctive way a product looks: the combination of features that makes it different from other items. For example, a bow

Figure 6.2 What factors must buyers consider before offering new products like these?

tie is a style of tie, a four-door sedan is a style of car, and a turtleneck is a style of sweater.

Conversely, good design contributes to a product's usefulness as well as to its appearance. For example, men's shirts are available in "wrinkle-free" fabric. Appearance, as well the usefulness of the shirt, are improved for customers when this fabric is used by designers and manufacturers.

Almost every product sold today is influenced by fashion. In fact, almost all retailers are increasingly in the fashion business. Fashion occurs in all areas of retailing, not just apparel–automobile dealers offer new styles every year, appliances now come in a multitude of fashion colors, and many fashion designers have their own line of sheets and bedspreads. Therefore, all buyers should have a general understanding of what fashion is and how it works. As a buyer, you must realize that customers determine fashion. That is why building your forecasting skills is so important to your success, and being able to predict the future depends to a large extent on understanding what has happened in the past. Manufacturers and retailers cannot dictate what products will become fashion; customers make that decision when they make purchases. Many times, customers are wearing an entirely different look from what is being promoted by the retailers and manufacturers; or, they may not rush out to buy the newest style automobile that is being heavily promoted.

Fashion is a powerful force in our society because a desire to change is a part of us all. Fashion satisfies the desire for changes and gives customers the opportunity to identify with certain groups and be accepted by their peers. That is why customers reject many useful products when they are no longer fashionable. In fact, today's biggest sellers may be tomorrow's biggest flops because they are no longer "in fashion."

Fashions change because people's ideas and behaviors change. As a larger portion of women entered the workplace, their clothing changed. As more firms accepted "casual Fridays," clothing changed. Read the Trendwatch titled, "Casual Fridays: Is the Pendulum Swinging the Other Way?" to learn more about this fashion trend.

Political and leisure activities also influence fashion changes. New clothing or accessories worn by the First Lady show up in retail stores the next week. Designs worn by stars at award ceremonies make their way to the mass market within weeks. Products that customers see in movies or TV programs are on their "must have" list the next day. Fashions also change because of technology. New fibers have altered most apparel. And technology itself spreads the word on new fashions and trends—TV and the Internet have greatly increased the speed of new fashion awareness and acceptance by customers.

Change is inevitable in retailing and a vital component of the industry. Buyers must understand fashion by remaining up-to-date on current trends and make merchandising decisions based on an understanding of their customers. In previous chapters you learned about the importance of reading magazines, trade publications, newspapers, and other sources in order to forecast trends. Buyers need a firm grasp of the dynamics of fashion trends. They need to know what fashion involves, how it moves, and how to forecast the impact of fashion on a store or department.

Fashion encourages customers to buy new products and discard the old, but at varying speeds. Some fashions change every few months, whereas others change only after several years. While making purchasing decisions, you must be alert to **obsolescence**—the outmoding of a product due to a change in fashion before its usefulness has been exhausted. Fashion apparel, cameras, computers, and home electronics are examples of products that typically remain useful when customers decide to purchase replacements.

Carrying fashion items also gives your store or department a competitive advantage. A consumer may not replace some basic items until they are worn out. Because American consumers quickly tire of what they are wearing or using, purchasing new products makes them feel a sense of change and renewal. Purchasing new fashion items provides for this sense of change.

You must also realize that new fashions create "ripple effects" with new customer needs. When the length of skirts changes, women will probably purchase new slips, shoes, and hosiery. So, as you make new product purchases, you must determine the impact on other products that your store is selling.

Increased fashion importance also causes problems in reordering and timing of purchases, but most buyers welcome the addition of fashion items into their inventory because new products tend to stimulate sales and enhance the store's image. One area where fashion is having a tremendous impact on the type of merchandise available is products for the home. Many home items are being recast as décor merchandise—items that are high in fashion but low in function. Most notable are crafts and silk flowers; both are linked with the color themes of the home.

The broad fashion decisions for a store will probably have been made by top management as merchandising policies were established.

In fact, management may have already identified "looks" that are expected to be acceptable to your customers. Your job will then be to execute how these looks will be expressed in your merchandise selections.

Purchasing "New" Products

Buyers are constantly besieged with a barrage of "new" products and must evaluate each of them before making a decision about whether to purchase them for the store. Some factors that should be considered before adding new products include:

- The compatibility of the new product with existing products carried by the store,
- The potential profitability of the new product,
- The placement of existing products within the product life cycle,
- The appropriateness of the new product for your customers, and
- The ability of the competition to offer the same or similar products.

Today, new products arrive in the marketplace frequently. Most "new" products simply offer improvements over existing products. For example, the "newest" camera or computer has many more features that will probably make these products more useful to customers. Some "new" products, however, are really new—they have not been available before in any form. Wine coolers, when they were first introduced, were an example of one such product.

Buyers must be aware of the world around them and sensitive to the changes that are constantly occurring. They must be aware of trends. Even though product changes are constantly occurring, those changes tend to be evolutionary rather than revolutionary—most changes tend to be made slowly. For example, men's ties become narrower or wider slowly from year to year, sometimes almost imperceptibly. Occasionally, new products become revolutionary—a very quick change. In the 1970s during the oil crises, small cars moved into general acceptance almost overnight. Today, small hybrid automobiles are gaining quick acceptance as gas prices soar. However, such revolutionary changes are rare. If current products differ too dramatically from those in the past, they will not fit in with what customers already own.

Buyers have to create excitement on the sales floor, and they do that with newness. New products make customers want to buy; new and innovative products create store traffic. There are always customers who want something different, and there is always something new available in the market for buyers to purchase. Some buyers are reluctant to purchase new and untried products because they may not understand newness and hesitate to make such purchases—causing a lot of staleness on the sales floor. Every year there are many new products available in the market, but it is up to the buyer to want to take the chance on them. When the economy slows, buyers tend to become even more cautious in their purchasing.

As a buyer, you will face a tremendous selection of new products every time you enter the market. Knowing what consumers want—before they know themselves—can make a difference between your purchase decisions being a hit or flop. Consumers may not even be aware of the availability of new products before you purchase them and place them on the sales floor. Read the Snapshot titled, "Smart Cars: Will They Succeed in the United States?" to learn more about how automobile buyers forecast sales for new vehicles.

In fact, the pace of new products appearing in the market is speeding up because many companies are reducing the time involved in product development. Moreover, products survive in the market for a shorter time because competitors are introducing rival products at a more rapid pace as well. Stores that offer any new product today have only a three- to six-month head start on the competition.

One reason for all these new products is that stores can command a higher price for them than for standard items. Japanese consumer-electronics companies continually strive to make their existing products less expensive while at the same time adding new features so they can sell them at the same price. The result of incremental innovation is that many products are not totally new, but they are packaged differently and have a new idea added.

Buyers must also decide how innovative or fashionable their merchandise selections should be. Several factors should be examined before making this decision. They include:

- *Target Market*. You will need to evaluate whether your target market is conservative or progressive. Will the newest, most fashionable products on the market be accepted by your customers?
- *Store Image*. The kinds of products a retailer carries are influenced by its image, and the level of innovativeness should be consistent with this image. Consumers may look to your store as an innovator—the first in town with new products and styles. Or your store may wait to see which

products are accepted by the public before making the purchases. The more clear-cut your store is in establishing its image, the more confidently you can make purchases.

• *Competition.* You must also decide if you want to lead or follow the competition. You must decide to undertake fashion leadership or wait until a product is widely accepted.

• *Fashion Trends and Theories.* You will also need to understand the theories that apply to fashion adoption. A useful tool for assessing the potential for a new product is the product life cycle, a helpful planning tool used to develop buying strategy. Sales and inventory data must be analyzed to chart trends as they develop. Adequate store records reveal how fast or how slowly product classifications have sold, how frequently they had to be reordered, or whether they had to be marked down. Examining all the best-sellers may reveal characteristics that each of the products has in common. For example, popular colors with your customers may be determined using past sales data. You will also want to become a shrewd observer of people. Your own observations will substantiate trends you have already detected or may reveal entirely new trends.

Buyers must also be aware that some products are **classics**–styles that are in demand continuously even though minor changes may be made in the product. Cardigans, button-down collars, and jeans are examples of classics. Classics appeal to a great number of people for a long period of time.

Purchasing Fads

One of the most challenging tasks facing a buyer is being able to distinguish between fads and trends. **Fads** are products that enter the marketplace quickly, are purchased with zeal, and then have sales that decline quickly. Fads have invaded every area of retailing and present several merchandising problems to buyers. There is the problem of obtaining enough supply while the fad is strong, and then there is the problem of disposing of the leftover stock when the fad quickly dies. Fads require that buyers carefully watch for trends. For example, when goods are offered in all types of stores at constantly lower prices, the end is near for the fad. Wise buyers forgo profits late in the selling season and cut the fad from stock early. If your store serves a fad-prone group, such as teenagers, you will need to keep in the closest possible touch with them.

The consumer marketplace is characterized by rapid changes that provide opportunities for buyers if they anticipate those changes and use them to create a competitive advantage for their stores or departments. However, early identification of trends requires sound judgment and the ability to analyze data. If you miss the emergence of a trend by thinking it as a fad, you will play catch-up with the competition. For many years, the U.S. auto industry paid the price for missing or ignoring changes in U.S. consumers. In contrast, many firms have been able to capitalize on trends by identifying them early. For example, having identified the growing health and fitness trend in the marketplace, Nike exhibited fantastic growth with athletic shoes, and Lean Cuisine redefined the market for single-serving, healthy frozen food.

There are also benefits to identifying a fad as a fad. Your store can make a lot of money quickly, but you must get out when the fad has reached its crest. If you think the fad will be a trend, you may keep purchasing merchandise and get caught with a lot of unsold inventory. Read the Trendwatch titled, "Fads: What Is the Next Big Thing?" to learn more about how buyers can distinguish between fads and trends.

In the toy market, fads come and go yearly. Is your favorite toy from childhood still on the market? Or, did it drop out of stores at the end of its first Christmas season? Examine Figure 6.3 for some of the "hits" between 1986 and 2008. Which ones do you remember?

How do you identify a trend? Fads tend to be inflexible. There are few, if any, ways to alter the product. The "pet rock," for instance, was such a fad. Trends, however, tend to be more flexible with many ways of expression, but some products may appear to be a fad when they enter the marketplace. The first microwave, known as the "Radarange," came to market in 1947; weighing in at 750 pounds and standing $5\frac{1}{2}$ feet tall, it cost $3,000. In 1967, Amana introduced a countertop version for $495. But between high prices and anxiety about radiation, it took years for microwave sales to explode and the product to become more than a fad. Gradually, technology improved and prices came down; at the same time, consumers' hurried lifestyles demanded speed. These days a microwave can be found in 93 percent of American kitchens. Many households have two, and they come in a variety of fashion colors. In addition, the microwave has transformed the food industry. Popcorn, for example, is now a $750 million industry. Orville Redenbacher's Gourmet Popping Corn, launched in 1983, provides 90 percent of company profits.

Figure 6.3   Once popular-selling fad items.

PRODUCT LIFE CYCLES AND FASHION ADOPTION THEORIES

Through strategic planning and understanding the market and consumers, buyers can learn to develop effective retail strategies. Planning is especially crucial in dealing with inevitable product changes. An understanding of product life cycles and fashion adoption theories aid buyers in making many merchandising decisions.

Demand for and sales of all products move in cycles, and the lengths of these cycles vary. One product may have a very short sales cycle, while others remain on the market for years or even decades. When customers have rejected a product, however, stores must clear out the merchandise as quickly as possible.

Product Life Cycle

To improve their forecasting skills, buyers must understand the life cycle of each product they are purchasing—particularly its impact on sales. The **product life cycle** illustrates the expected behavior of a product over its lifetime. The traditional product life cycle has four stages: (1) introduction, (2) growth, (3) maturity, and (4) decline (Figure 6.4). Products move through this cycle at various rates. **Velocity**, or the

The Product Life Cycle

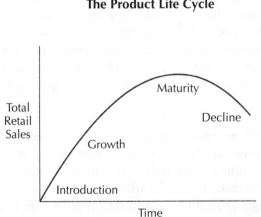

Figure 6.4   The product life cycle.

speed at which products move through the product life cycle, must be a concern of buyers. Some products, such as women's clothing, have a high velocity, completing the cycle in a few months; other items, such as luggage and furniture, move through the cycle much more slowly.

A buyer's chief concern is that risks are greater the faster a product moves through the cycle. Yet rewards are there for successful products with fast sales and higher-than-average profit margins—which is why there seems to be constant pressure to introduce fashion into traditionally basic items such as sheets, men's underwear, and appliances.

Products pass through several stages in their lifetime, and sales performance varies at each stage. Knowing which stage a product is in helps the buyer judge both its existing and future sales potential. Each stage of the product life cycle also suggests different retailing strategies.

Introduction Stage. In the *introduction stage*, products are characterized by low sales and losses, as well as high risk. Many products never make it out of the introduction stage. For example, new perfumes are introduced every year, but only about 10 percent are hits with customers. During the introduction stage, the risk is great because buyers are gambling on an unproven product. During this stage, buyers generally utilize a high-price strategy and develop promotion activities that are designed to tell the customer about the new product. For most retailers, new products are essential for their image.

During the introduction stage, products are usually accepted by a limited number of customers. Buyers should anticipate a limited target market composed of high-income or innovative customers. *Innovators* are those customers who are more likely to purchase a new style. In the past, new styles appeared first among the wealthy and slowly reached other groups; however, that is not as true today. Teenagers may be the first group to purchase a hot new product. As an increasing number of consumers accept a product, it moves into the growth stage.

Growth Stage. When innovative consumers purchase products and recommend them to friends, the product enters the *growth stage*. The most desirable products for retailers are those in this stage because they are characterized by accelerating sales and the highest-profit levels of any stage. Digital televisions and iPhones are two products currently in the growth stage.

In the growth stage, product variations begin to appear, and the number of retailers carrying the product expands. Usually, there is also an increased number of suppliers. In this stage, *early adopters* are those customers who purchase the products in its early-rise stage. The majority of customers finally make the purchase as it reaches the last rise and peak of the cycle.

Maturity Stage. In the *maturity stage*, sales increase at a slower rate and finally begin to level off. Characteristics of this stage are a highly competitive market, falling prices and profits, and more intensive advertising. Video sales and rentals are currently in this stage. No longer are video tapes available for sale only at retailers such as Blockbuster; the discounters, like Target and Wal-Mart, now sell videos at very low prices. In the maturity stage, sales reach maximum levels, and all types of retailers carry the product. This is the most competitive stage, and price is prominently mentioned in promotions. In this stage, *late adopters* accept the product when it is past its peak, while *laggards* adopt it during the decline stage.

Decline Stage. Buyers, as a rule, will not be purchasing products in the decline stage. During the *decline stage*, the target market shrinks, and price cutting minimizes profit margins. Normally, products reaching this stage are dropped, and heavy markdowns are taken on remaining inventory. These products are high-risk and low-reward items. At this stage, the target market is composed of price-conscious individuals and laggards. Most stores cut back on the variety of their offerings during this stage, while many retailers drop the product altogether before customers abandon it completely. The product life cycle can easily be applied to fashion apparel. Several different product life cycles are illustrated in Figure 6.5.

Fashion Adoption Theories

Buyers who purchase fashion merchandise must be familiar with theories of fashion adoption and how they affect products they are purchasing. There are three theories that attempt to explain how fashion is adopted.

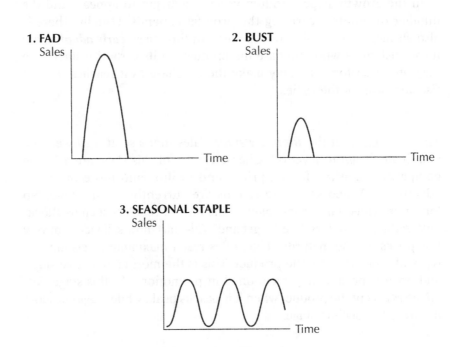

Figure 6.5   Variations of the product life cycle.

Downward Flow Theory. The downward flow theory maintains that fashion innovators are those people at the top of the social pyramid such as royalty, world leaders, and the wealthy. Over time, fashion that this group accepts moves to progressively lower social levels. For example, hats and jewelry worn by many First Ladies become a fashion statement for the masses. Fashion is passed from the upper to the lower social classes through three vertical stages: (1) distinctive—original, custom-made designs are worn by high society; (2) emulation—original designs are modified and carried by finer department stores, and they appeal to the middle class; and (3) economic emulation—the original design is mass-produced and mass-marketed.

Many fashions start their life cycle as *haute couture* from designers such as Yves Saint Laurent, Givenchy, and Christian Dior. Every year a few thousand women pay $30,000 and up for hand-made, one-of-a-kind creations. Although these gowns are glamorous, they are only marginal money-makers. These designers rely on related items, such as fragrances and accessories, to generate profits. In addition, many European couture houses and prestigious U.S. designers are developing "secondary lines," which are designed by couturiers but cost from $100 to $900—within reach of the middle class, although still expensive.

One problem designers will have to deal with is the possible damage that the less expensive lines could have on the haute couture image. Designers such as Halston lost much of their luster when they attached their names to too many products. Although some designers are shying away from secondary lines; many may have no choice if they expect to remain profitable.

Horizontal Flow Theory. The horizontal theory maintains that fashion adoption moves horizontally within groups. In each group, there are innovators who are willing to try the new product. When other members of the group see the fashion being worn, they are more likely to make a similar purchase. If fashion is adopted in this manner, it does not matter what the upper classes are wearing or purchasing. Within each social class there are innovative customers who act as opinion leaders. Once they accept a fashion, they convince other members in the same social class to accept it as well.

Upward Flow Theory. This theory is the opposite of downward flow and maintains that the fashion innovators are the young. For example, T-shirts, for a long time part of the teenager's basic wardrobe, are now a part of many designers' lines. Today, considerable fashion influence is exerted by young consumers.

Each of these theories is based on the concept that fashion innovators and fashion followers exist. Understanding each theory and determining which one is most appropriate for your customers and the products you are purchasing will enable you to predict future adoptions. Most buyers use all three theories to predict what styles are likely to become fashion successes.

Using Product Life Cycles and Adoption Theories

Understanding product life cycles and fashion adoption theories can assist buyers in making many merchandising decisions, including those of timing, forecasting, and product elimination.

Timing. Knowing your target market allows you to determine when new products, particularly fashion merchandise, should be introduced in the store at a time when your customers will be ready for them. Product selection must reinforce the store's reputation as either a leader or a follower. Stores attempting to establish a fashion image cannot continue to carry fashion merchandise after customers are tired of it without giving the feeling of staleness.

Forecasting. Understanding these theories also helps you predict the merchandise that will be desired by specific groups of consumers. You can obtain general forecasts from trade publications, reporting services, buying offices, or consumer publications. By knowing what the innovators are purchasing, you may be able to pick the next "hot" product for your customers.

Product Elimination. Knowing the stage of the product life cycle in which the product happens to be also allows you to determine when products should be eliminated from stock. You should begin considering substitutes as new products begin appearing on the market. Before eliminating products entirely; however, you may want to consider other strategies such as revisions in marketing strategies or price cutting.

Sharpening your product sense is a matter of increasing your sensitivity to your customers' readiness to accept new products. Combining that sensitivity with a knowledge of the marketplace will allow you to make the most intelligent buying decisions.

CREATING PRODUCT DIFFERENCES

As a buyer, you will want to purchase products that can be differentiated by your customers from what the competition is offering. Typical ways to do this are by adding private label merchandise, licensed products, and mass-customized products to your merchandise mix.

Brand Names

Customers rely on brand names to distinguish products among the massive number from which they have to choose. In essence, consumers use brand names to help them make a product choice. ***National brands*** are products that are sold almost everywhere—Ragu spaghetti sauce, Arrow shirts, Levi jeans, Ford Mustangs, and the list goes on. National brands dominate the product selections at most retail stores, creating a sameness at stores that all sell identical brands.

An increasing number of retailers are creating their own ***private brands*** (or ***store brands***). For example, Sears sells Craftsman tools, Kenmore appliances, and DieHard batteries—all are private brands that are available only at Sears. Private brands belong to the store and can be found on products sold exclusively at that store. At some retailers, such as Eddie Bauer and Lands' End, almost everything sold is a private brand. JCPenney has developed its Arizona jeans label, Kmart has Jaclyn Smith apparel, and Wal-Mart has Sam's Choice. Most grocery stores usually have at least one private brand. Private brands are also gaining prominence in home fashions. Some private labels on domestics have the added benefit of appearing on apparel and other merchandise so customers are already familiar with them. For example, Macy's uses its long-running Jennifer Moore apparel brand on sheets.

Some stores offer generic brand products. ***Generic brands*** attach no significant identity to the product through the name. Generic products are usually found at grocery and drug stores and are typically promoted to price-conscious customers. For example, the cost of a generic bottle of aspirin may be half that of the same size bottle of Bayer aspirin.

Consumers view brand as an important part of a product, and brand names add value. For example, most customers would perceive a Ralph Lauren Polo knit shirt as a high-quality product. But the same shirt without the logo and brand label would probably be viewed as lower in quality, even though it is identical. Brand names can even be found at product counters in grocery stores. Sunkist oranges, Dole pineapples, and Chiquita bananas are several products in an area that continues to be unbranded.

Branding helps buyers in several ways. Brands help customers identify products that might benefit them. Brands also indicate something about product quality to most customers. Shoppers who always buy the same brand know that they will get the same features, benefits, and quality each time they purchase the product.

Licensed Products

Another way buyers create differences in their merchandise mix is through purchasing ***licensed products*** that are designed and sold through identification with a celebrity or corporate name, logo, slogan, or fictional character (Figure 6.6). For an extra cost, buyers have an instant and proven brand name. Cartoon and story characters are the most popular among children, with Mickey Mouse being the leading character. Names of sports stars and teams have also been very popular on licensed products. As expected, sales vary by the region in which the team is located, but some teams, such as the Dallas Cowboys and the New York Yankees, have national appeal.

While licensed products run the gamut from trinkets to expensive collectibles, apparel products dominate the list. Licensed products also tend to be higher-quality today with a wider assortment of items being offered. In the past, quality was not always the chief concern with licensed products because a new, hot cartoon character or sports celebrity would hit the market within a few weeks. Today, licensed products adorn expensive jackets and denim shirts. Most licensed apparel is "fashion right." The shift to higher-quality merchandise has resulted in many licensees producing two lines—one that is sold to discounters

Figure 6.6 Cartoon and story-book characters are popular licensed products for children.

and the other to department and specialty stores. However, some licensees, such as Hello Kitty and Blue's Clues, want to keep an upscale image and are producing most of their products for upscale stores.

Licensed products for the bed and bath market continue to be a viable and growing area for sales. Throughout all areas there is an emphasis on classics such as Mickey Mouse, Bugs Bunny, and Superman. For both discounters and department stores, classics are "safer" purchases. On children's products there is an almost endless list of character names and images on toys, clothing, school supplies, cereals, lunch boxes, and many other items. In fact, almost half of all toy sales come from products based on TV shows and movies.

Buyers must evaluate licensed products as they would any other merchandise, looking for quality, design, price, and compatibility with the store image and customer wants and needs. The uncertainty of whether licensed names will catch on with customers makes choices difficult for buyers. Furthermore, in recent years, the novelty of these items has diminished.

Buyers must also be particularly alert to the timing and markdowns of licensed products. Disney items may be strong sellers for years, but other products typically have sales that peak and then fall precipitously. For example, sales of merchandise with the Olympics logo fall dramatically as soon as the games are over.

The biggest challenge for every retail buyer is selecting the right license. The anticipated release of a big summer movie will have all buyers guessing. Will the success of the new movie measure up to the hit of last summer? Will that appeal translate into customers wanting to purchase licensed products based on the new movie? Movies that do not meet their expectations mean heavy markdowns on licensed products promoting characters or symbols of the movie. For example, many retailers got stuck with lots of yellow raincoats when *Dick Tracy* was not the hit movie it was expected to be. Licensed products based on movies do not have the same staying power as those linked with TV shows that people see regularly for many years.

Buyers also have to be careful when making purchases of sports-licensed products. A bad season for the team will probably mean a bad season for sales. Yet being the first retailer in town with sports apparel featuring the local team that just made the playoffs can generate high-volume, as well as high-profit, sales.

Licensed products have broad appeal, particularly among younger consumers, women, and households with limited incomes. The appeal of licensed products wanes rapidly as customers grow older. People over 50 have little interest in purchasing such items for themselves.

Mass Customization

Many retailers are discarding the one-size-fits-all philosophy that has guided them for decades. They are beginning to experiment with ***mass customization***, which involves efficiently providing customers with unique products that give them "exactly what they want." Mass customization is based on harnessing technology to narrowly target products to the needs of the *individual* shopper. Customers choose their options, and the product is assembled according to their specifications. The challenge is to offer enough options for the customer to feel that the product is custom-made, without substantially increasing costs.

Making custom-made products can be efficient. Inventory is reduced, saving warehouse space and the expense of monitoring stock in order to maintain a wide assortment. And there is little leftover merchandise on which markdowns must be taken. Although mass-customized products are more expensive to make, their profit margins tend to be much higher. Read the Snapshot titled, "Customizing Purchases Online," to learn how online retailers are providing products to meet individual customer needs.

Mass customization is also occurring in other areas of retailing. General Nutrition Centers (GNC) is testing machines in some of its stores that custom-mix daily vitamins, shampoos, and lotions. The revolution has spread to the Internet, where greeting card retailers allow customers to customize their cards with personalized remarks. Many bricks-and-mortar retail stores have also begun offering this option with in-store kiosks.

Many retail analysts predict that mass customization may become as important to the twenty-first century as mass production was to the twentieth century. It provides one way for retailers to give customers exactly the products they want. Buyers must constantly be alert to techniques that will allow them to differentiate their product offerings.

SUMMARY POINTS

- A store's merchandise mix must meet the specific needs of its customers.
- Four broad categories of products based on availability include convenience, impulse, shopping, and specialty.
- Fashion occurs in all areas of retailing, not just apparel.
- Even though fashion presents problems in reordering and the timing of purchases, most buyers seek fashion additions to their lines because these products tend to stimulate sales and enhance the store's image.

- Stores attempt to establish a fashion image through such factors as merchandise selection, store location, visual merchandising, fixtures, and store personnel.
- To understand the impact of fashion on customers, buyers must be able to distinguish between fads and trends.
- The product life cycle includes the introduction, growth, maturity, and decline stages.
- All products are continuously moving through product life cycles at varying and individual rates. Fashion adopters during the cycle can be described as innovators, early adopters, late adopters, and laggards.
- Fashion adoption theories include downward flow, horizontal flow, and upward flow.
- Buyers differentiate the products they purchase from the competition by using private brands, licensing, and mass customization.

REVIEW ACTIVITIES

Developing Your Retail Buying Vocabulary

Consult the Glossary if you did not add the following terms to your vocabulary.

Availability	Late adopter
Classic	Licensed product
Convenience product	Mass customization
Decline stage	Maturity stage
Durability	Merchandise mix
Durables	National brand
Early adopter	Nondurables
Fad	Obsolescence
Fashion	Private brand
Generic brand	Product life cycle
Growth stage	Product line
Haute couture	Shopping product
Impulse product	Specialty product
Innovator	Store brand
Introduction stage	Style
Laggard	Velocity

Understanding What You Read

1. Why should buyers constantly monitor their merchandise mix?
2. Explain how products that buyers purchase influence personnel decisions for a store.
3. What have JCPenney and Kmart done to establish a fashion image?
4. List five examples of convenience products.
5. Describe how department stores can sell kitchen gadgets as impulse items.
6. Give two examples of specialty products.
7. When do customers tend to stretch the life of durable products?
8. What is the difference between a style and a fashion?
9. Explain why buyers cannot determine fashion.
10. Why do many buyers welcome the addition of fashion items into their inventory?
11. Provide examples of how fashions have changed because of technology.
12. Describe how new fashions may create a "ripple effect" with the sale of other products.
13. Provide examples of how movies have influenced "new" products on the market.
14. What problems do fads present for buyers?
15. How can buyers distinguish between a fad and a trend?
16. List the four stages of the product life cycle.
17. Describe differences in pricing strategy between the introduction and decline stages of the product life cycle.
18. Describe the downward flow theory of fashion adoption.
19. How can knowledge of the product life cycle help buyers decide which products to eliminate from their merchandise mix?
20. Why do buyers add private brands to their merchandise mix?
21. Why is the timing of markdowns on licensed products crucial for buyers?
22. What is the primary reason for the move to mass customization?

Analyzing and Applying What You Read

1. Why is it important for buyers to identify and capitalize on trends early?
2. Identify the stage of the product life cycle at which each of the following products is found: records, cassette tapes, compact discs, and DVDs.

3. Give reasons as to why new apparel fashions are not just first appearing among the wealthy as they did in the past.

4. How will you determine if an item is moving into the decline stage of the product life cycle? What could a buyer do to prolong the life of that product?

5. Which do you feel has more relevance in today's apparel market—downward or upward flow theory? Explain.

Internet Connection

1. On the Internet, use a search engine to locate current information on Smart cars. Record information on actual sales and sales trends for those new cars. Determine if sales have met original forecasts.

2. On the Internet, go to www.etoys.com, www.toysrus.com, or a similar site that sells toys. Identify the hottest trends in the toy market.

SNAPSHOT

Customizing Purchases Online

Today, when shoppers cannot find apparel that fits, many turn to Internet retail Web sites where customization and personalization of apparel and accessories are growing dramatically. Nike and Converse have allowed online shoppers to customize their purchases for several years. Now there are sites where customers can design their own high-fashion heels, handbags, jeans, and even bras.

Lands' End was one of the first online retailers to incorporate customization in 1998 when they launched the "My Virtual Model" component. The site allows users to enter their body shape, frame size, weight, height, and coloring. A three-dimensional model of the customer is then constructed, and lets the shopper virtually "try on" items of clothing.

Tools on the site also allow customers to take their own measurements and register them online, allowing for accurate sizing advice on more than 1,000 garments sold by Lands' End. The customer can tell if a garment will be a loose, snug, or optimal fit without physically trying it on. Better fit means more satisfied customers and fewer returns. "My Virtual Model" tool has become the site's most popular tool after the "search" function. In 18 months, the tool created more than 1.2 million personal models. Lands' End has found that there is a 34 percent higher sales conversion rate among customers who use "My Virtual Model," and those same customers place an average order that is 8 percent higher in dollar value than nonmodel users. Lands' End also found that shoppers who use the virtual model spend more time on the site. The assumption is that if a customer spends more time on a Web site, he or she is more likely to make a purchase. Moreover, by giving shoppers access to an interactive try-on session, Lands' End offers them greater confidence in their final purchase decision.

Customized jeans, chinos, blouses, and swimsuits for women and shirts and pants for men can also be customized for shoppers on the Lands' End site. For example, to customize chinos for women, the customer first picks among such details as low or high waists, flat or pleated fronts, belt loops and pockets or not, tapered or straight legs, plus the customer's measurements and a detailed body description including everything from shoe size to bra size to overall body shape. Customized women's chinos range from $70–$80 plus shipping, compared with $39.50 for noncustomized chinos.

Lands' End is not the only online retailer to adapt customization and personalization tools. At FreddyandMa.com, shoppers can design their own leather and fabric handbags. First, they click on "Design Your Handbag," pick among several shapes (e.g., clutch, tote, bowler), and then choose the fabric pattern, color of leather trim, and finally, the hardware color. Retail prices range from $85–$350, plus shipping. Retail prices are similar to mid-priced handbags in department stores.

At SteveMadden.com, shoppers can design their own high-fashion footwear. First, they click on "Design Your Own," pick among a half-dozen styles (e.g., ballet, flats, pumps, sandals), and then choose the heel height, leather shoe color, and the decorative details. Shoes retail from $89.95–$149.95 plus shipping, which is about 25 to 30 percent more than similar, noncustomized shoes on the site. Shipping is additional.

As usage of such Internet sites increases, retail buyers will need to monitor the impact on in-store sales. Online customization and personalization tools will probably necessitate reduced in-store inventories.

BASED ON:

Kemp, Ted. (2001, October 8). Virtual models equal real buyers. *InternetWeek*, 16.

Lands' End improves online profitability via my virtual model technology. (2001, June). *Direct Marketing*, 64–65.

Lands' End virtual model gives shoppers right fit. (2004, February 13). *Just-style.com*.

Puente, Maria. (2007, August 1). Online shopping: now it's personal. *USAToday*, 3D.

Young, Vicki M. (2004, February 11). Landsend.com updates "My Virtual Model" tool. *Women's Wear Daily*, 32.

SNAPSHOT

Smart Cars: Will They Succeed in the United States?

Smart cars, the mini-autos that are already a regular sight on European streets, will make their official U.S. debut in 2008. The modern two-seater car fits in half a parking space, can go 90 miles per hour, and drinks gasoline slowly. Drivers could wedge one into the bed of a pickup truck, or even drive down the aisles of some stores. They are less than 9-feet long and barely over 5-feet wide.

The car has been sold in Europe since 1998, and there are now more than 770,000 Smart cars in 36 countries. By the middle of 2007, over 20,000 U.S. residents had already paid the $99 required to reserve a car. Color seems important to some of these Smart car enthusiasts. Many of those paying the fee were upset that the car would not be sold in green. In the United States, Smart cars are expected to cost less than $12,000 for a basic model and up to $17,000 for a convertible.

There are already nearly 75 dealerships nationwide who have signed up to sell Smart cars. These car dealers are forecasting that with high gas prices, mounting concerns about global warning, and waning interest in sport utility vehicles, U.S. consumers will welcome a car that is no bigger than a large riding lawn mower.

In Europe, Smart cars maintain a hip image with their ability to easily navigate small winding streets and have even been featured in two movies–*The DaVinci Code* and *The Pink Panther* remake.

The biggest selling point of the vehicles will be their fuel efficiency. Some projections are for 46 miles per gallon in the city and 69 miles per gallon on the highway. Smart cars will be lighter than anything else on the road, but that weight brings safety concerns. Even with modern safety features like multiple air bags, people in small, light cars are always at a disadvantage in crashes. Smart cars have earned acceptable safety ratings in Europe based on their stiff frame and features such as extra air bags. American roads, however, have many large vehicles on them, so Smart cars in the United States are more likely to be involved in accidents with cars and trucks that are three or four times their size and weight.

One of the biggest questions surrounding Smart cars is whether consumers will actually purchase them. There are already concerns that U.S. sales will not be strong. Some predictions expect that the Smart car will only appeal to a small niche of American car owners, and J.D. Power projects that the Smart car will capture only 0.1 percent of new car sales during their first year in the United States.

Are Americans ready for Smart cars? As a retail buyer at an auto dealership in your community, how many sales would you forecast for the first year?

BASED ON:

Agha, Laith. (2007, July 6). A fit-anywhere car. *Monterey County Herald*.
Brinckman, Jonathan. (2007, March 9). Smart in the showroom. *Orian* (Portland, OR).
Daimler's Smart cars win early U.S. praise. (2007, May 2). *UPI NewsTrack*.
Kurylko, Diana T. (2007, January 22). Trailers take Smart cars on tour. *Automotive News*, 6.
Loerzel, Robert. (2007, July 30). Smart cars for U.S. debut. *Crain's Chicago Business*, 14.
Schoenberger, Robert. (2007, July 19). Tiny, efficient cars on the way to Cleveland. *The Plain Dealer*, C1.
Smart cars prove popular. (2007, May 10). *The Grand Rapids Press*, C1.

TRENDWATCH

Fads: What Is the Next Big Thing?

Fads are a key ingredient of the product mix for most retail buyers. They can hit fast and furiously, providing buyers with one shot at making quick profits. The danger is that buyers can overestimate a fad's long-term appeal and be left with lots of worthless inventory. But, overlooking or dismissing a product that develops strong consumer appeal can lead to a stodgy reputation for the retailer.

While fads are only a small blip in relation to the sales longevity of other products, they have a disproportional importance in terms of store image and customer appeal. Buyers cannot ignore the importance of fads. When new fads are really hot, consumers go searching for that product. For many retailers, this new business walks in the door and increases normal sales revenue. These new customers are also likely to find other products in the store that they purchase.

Fads help buyers keep their stores vital and attract new customers; however, the sales cycle for a fad is vastly different from that of regular products. Sales of fads generally show a meteoric rise, followed by an equally dramatic drop. Trends show gradual sales growth that eventually evolves into stable business. It is imperative that buyers identify fads and then closely monitor inventory levels and sales for those products. What is critical is the amount of inventory the store has left when the fad dies.

Impacting the longevity of fads is whether a retailer can maintain exclusivity. Several years ago, Razor scooters were hot, but too many knockoffs entered the market. The product was available everywhere from department stores to convenience stores so the scooters quickly lost their appeal, and retail prices plummeted as the fad quickly ended. When distributors can keep distribution tight, the "cool factor" stays high for a longer period of time. Moreover, if a fad can evolve and be updated, the product may remain "fresh" for several seasons and not die out as quickly as most fads.

All buyers face the challenge of determining "the next big thing." Today, almost all areas of retailing are being impacted by "green" products. For example, clothing purchasers are faced with recycled apparel and the use of more natural fibers like organic cotton, wool, hemp, bamboo, and coconut-based blends. Will green products be "the next big thing," or will they die the quick life of most fads? Only time will tell. Products have the best chance of becoming a trend, rather than a fad, if they are in sync with broad cultural and social shifts in the consumer marketplace. Some other factors that may help buyers distinguish between fads and trends follow.

Generally, fads tend to appeal to a limited demographic segment of the market. They are marked by a rapid rise in popularity, followed by a fast decline. Fads tend to appeal to early adapters, such as technology lovers and teens. Often, fads are tied to current events, such as the Olympics.

Trends, however, generally develop more slowly and are followed by a leveling of sales. They tend to mesh with broad cultural values and offer multiple benefits to the consumer. Moreover, trends tend to be adopted by key consumer groups such as young adults, working mothers, and baby boomers.

Retail buyers cannot ignore fads. Without them, buyers are positioning their stores in the vast sea of retail sameness. Buyers cannot jump on every trend, however. Their task is to filter and select the fads most appealing to their market. This may mean missing out on a successful fad. If that happens, buyers should skip it completely and move on. One of the worst mistakes a buyer can make is to jump on a fad band-wagon too late. The end result will probably be lots of unsold product.

In the final analysis, knowing the customer and market conditions are the most important factors as buyers select products that may become "the next big thing" for their stores.

BASED ON:

Bouchard, Nancy. (2007, May). The next big thing: retailers weigh the advantages of fast fads against steady trends. *Sporting Goods Business*, 6–7.

Kleinman, Rebecca. (2007, January 17). In and out: today's styles arc more swiftly than ever. How can retailers stay ahead of the curve? *Women's Wear Daily*, 28S.

This year's fads. (2006, December 25). *People Weekly*, 131.

TRENDWATCH

Casual Fridays: Is the Pendulum Swinging the Other Way?

During the 1990s, casual dress in the workplace bubbled up from California's technology companies and drifted throughout corporate America. In 1998, 97 percent of companies surveyed by the Society for Human Resource Management allowed casual dress every day or once a week. In 2000, that number dropped to 87 percent. In recent years, the pendulum has swung away from casual dress even more sharply. In 2005, 41 percent of U.S. companies allowed casual dress, down from 51 percent in 2001, according to research by the same organization. A separate survey by America's Research Group found that 28 percent of Fortune 500 companies allowed casual dress in 1999. Today, that figure is slightly under 10 percent. Few employers are requiring the formal attire commonplace at many companies during the 1980s and early 1990s. Instead, managers are attempting to ensure that "business casual" does not devolve into simply "casual."

Since its inception, appropriate dress for "Casual Fridays" has been a source of confusion among employees and management. Some employees have taken the term "casual" too literally and started wearing clothes that fit the beach rather than the workplace. For some employees, flip-flops qualified as dress shoes. The result has been that at many companies, "Casual Fridays" have been dropped or management has revised employee handbooks to better define casual dress codes.

What exactly is business casual? The definition varies from firm to firm, but one company has defined it as pants in cotton, wool, flannel, or synthetic fabrics; polo or golf shirts or shirts with a collar; sweaters, turtlenecks; casual dresses; and skirts. Appropriate footwear includes conservative athletic or walking shoes, loafers, clogs, boots, flats, dress heels, or leather deck-type shoes. What is not appropriate business casual wear at this company? Included are sweatshirts and sweat-pants, exercise pants, shorts, bib overalls, leggings, form-fitting pants, short and tight skirts, mini-skirts, skorts, sun dresses, beach dresses, spaghetti-strap dresses, tank tops, midriff tops, halter-tops, and T-shirts with potentially offensive words, terms, logos, pictures, cartoons, or slogans. Inappropriate footwear includes flip-flops, slippers, and flashy athletic shoes.

Not all companies are tightening up "Casual Friday" dress policies, however. Some simply deal with inappropriate attire when it occurs. Other companies, especially in the technology field, celebrate informality. Proponents of casual dress say that it is more than an act of goodwill by corporate America. Many analysts believe that casual dress improves morale. The competition for hiring good employees has also affected "Casual Fridays." Companies are using any lure possible to attract, retain, and motivate employees—even casual dress.

The pendulum shift can be felt in some retail sales. For example, the movement away from casual dress can be detected in sales of men's tailored clothing, which includes suits, suit separates, sport coats, and jackets. This product category generated $5.1 billion in sales during 2005, up 7.1 percent from $4.8 billion in 2004. Ties for men are also making a comeback. In the 1990s, tie sales dropped by

50 percent, but in recent years, tie sales have been well over $1 billion dollars–the highest ever! Casual dress trends are probably so entrenched, however, that they will not vanish anytime soon. As the pendulum swings in a less casual direction at many businesses, retail buyers will need to monitor this trend carefully and its impact on what apparel customers will be purchasing tomorrow.

BASED ON:

Carlson, Jill. (2007, July 20). Employers changing their attire. "Business casual" sent some businesses running to define its limits. *Wisconsin State Journal* (Madison, WI), C8.

Fit to be tied: Neckties show no sign of loosening their grip on men's fashion. (2006, September 12). *Pueblo Chieftain* (Pueblo, CO).

Men's ties making a comeback. (2006, July 24). *UPI News Track*.

Osterman, Rachel. (2006, March 20). Casual loses its cool in business: more employers are trying to tighten up workplace clothing standards. *Sacramento Bee* (Sacramento, CA).

Serious purpose dresses up casual Fridays at Investors Capital. (2007, March 8). *Business Wire*.

Smart casual not so clever as the tie makes a comeback. (2005, September). *Australasian Business Intelligence*.

Planning and Controlling Merchandise Purchases

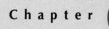

Chapter 7

Forecasting

PERFORMANCE OBJECTIVES

Upon completion of this chapter, you should be able to:

- Recognize the value of accurate forecasting to the buyer.
- Identify the benefits of developing sales forecasts.
- Describe internal forces affecting sales forecasts.
- Describe external forces affecting sales forecasts.
- Identify uses of primary and secondary data in developing sales forecasts.
- List the steps involved in developing a sales forecast.
- Describe methods used in forecasting inventory needs.
- Predict sales based on stock-to-sales ratios and stock turnover.
- Recognize that buyers need quantitative skills.

After collecting information from the sources described in the previous chapters, buyers must use the data to make forecasts about what will happen in the future. *Forecasting* involves predicting what consumers may do under a given set of conditions. Buyers most often make forecasts concerning consumer demand, sales, and required inventory levels. To make these forecasts, they must collect and analyze information from a number of sources, including forecasts that other people have made. Many forecasts concerning the entire retailing industry are described in Chapter 1.

In this chapter, you will learn more about forecasting. How buyers identify consumer trends and anticipate changes in market conditions will be described and the steps used to make a forecast examined. Then, you will learn how buyers use these skills for sales forecasting and stock planning.

SCOPE OF FORECASTING

Buyers typically develop forecasts to answer questions such as these:

- How much of each product will need to be purchased?
- Should new products be added to the merchandise assortment being offered?

• How much inventory is needed to support the planned sales?
• What price should be charged for each product?

Answers to these questions are based on predictions of what you believe the customer will do in the future. Just like a prediction about tomorrow's weather, your forecast will not always be correct, but steps can be taken to improve your forecasting ability. Read the Trendwatch titled, "Using Weather Forecasts to Improve Retail Forecasts," to learn more about how long-term weather forecasting is being used as a tool to improve retail forecasts.

First, you need to obtain past sales records. In making a forecast, most buyers start with information on past sales to predict future sales, but you cannot stop there. You must also consider other internal forces that are operating in your store such as expansion of sales space or reduction in the number of sales associates. Then you need to examine external forces such as competition and economic conditions. As you probably realize, no sales forecast will match actual sales exactly. You may purchase too much of some items and not enough of others, but if you keep accurate records, you have the opportunity to improve your future forecasts.

Once you have identified all the sources of assistance that are available to you, you are ready to collect and analyze information about market conditions and your target consumers to develop forecasts. The most important forecast you will make is the *sales forecast*, a prediction of future sales for a specified period under a proposed marketing plan. The sales forecast can be a prediction of total sales volume, or sales can be forecast for:

• Specific products or services (brands or models),
• Specific consumer groups (males, over 65),
• Time periods (weekly, monthly), or
• Specific store locations.

A sales forecast is made for a specified period of time that can cover a few weeks or even years. *Short-term forecasts* usually include a period of up to one year. Buying fashion merchandise usually requires developing a sales forecast for a six-month period. Grocery stores and drug stores that deal with more basic merchandise may have to forecast sales for only a few days or a week. *Long-term forecasts* extend for more than a year.

The time period for which the sales forecast is made will have a great impact on its accuracy. Forecasts that attempt to predict sales many years into the future may be much less accurate than a forecast for sales during the next two months. Existing market conditions may remain the same for a few weeks; however, these conditions could drastically change by the end of the season. Customers' tastes could also change rapidly. If the market is volatile and changes quickly, long-term forecasts may be meaningless.

Forecasting is a crucial planning tool for buyers. Preparing sales forecasts requires them to think in detailed terms about (1) target market groups the store is trying to serve, (2) existing and potential competitors, and (3) future trends occurring in the market and the economy. In other words, they must make a thorough examination of the store and its markets before preparing a sales forecast and developing merchandise buying plans. In addition, sales forecasts:

- *Stimulate Planning.* Without a sales forecast, buyers could not make other critical decisions such as inventory levels required and retail prices to charge customers.
- *Promote Coordination.* A sales forecast becomes a target for all members of the merchandising team. Buyers, store managers, and sales associates must all tailor their activities to reach the desired sales goal.
- *Support Control Activities.* The sales forecast becomes the basis for measuring success or failure of the buyer's efforts. It provides a quantitative measurement against which the buyer's performance can be measured for pay raises, promotion, or dismissal.

Because they play such an important role, sales forecasts need to be as accurate as possible, but since forecasting is an attempt to predict the future, they can be inaccurate. In the final analysis, accuracy of sales forecasting tends to improve as more data analysis and interpretation are applied.

Buyers must have confidence in forecasts they make, and that confidence increases with a thorough understanding of all the forces that can have an impact on sales. Forecasts should be based on facts, not guesswork! Before developing a sales forecast, buyers must first identify their target customers, understand why they buy, and gain an understanding of trends affecting these markets. Read the Snapshot titled, "Family Dollar: Fine-Tuning Its Retail Strategy," to learn more about one retailer's use of forecasting and planning.

DEVELOPING SALES FORECASTS

Forecasting sales requires that buyers identify and understand the internal and external forces that will have an impact on those sales.

Examining Internal Forces

All *internal forces* within the store that probably will affect sales should be carefully examined before developing a sales forecast. For example, future sales can be affected by increasing or decreasing advertising expenditures, liberalizing or tightening credit policies, and increasing or decreasing retail prices. Even changes in store hours or physical facilities will affect future sales. You must estimate the impact of such changes on projected sales before any sales forecast is developed.

Examining External Forces

Before making a sales forecast, you must also analyze *external forces* that may affect sales. You will need to examine changes in economic conditions, demographic trends, and competitive conditions.

Economic Conditions. Both the national and local economic climate should be analyzed, but you must realize that economic conditions will not affect all businesses in the same way. For example, during economic slowdowns, sales at some stores, such as do-it-yourself home stores, actually increase. Plant closings and employee layoffs are local economic conditions that will generally cause sales to decline. Headlines from the newspaper, such as those presented in Figure 7.1, provide information that should be considered when you are making a sales forecast. You must also realize that during inflationary periods, increases in dollar sales may occur without a corresponding increase in unit sales.

Demographic Trends. Demographic factors should also be analyzed before developing a sales forecast. The movement of people into or out of your store's trading area can have an impact on future sales. Sales forecasts should be adjusted downward if the store's trading area appears to be losing a large number of residents.

Stocks Slide as Rate Fears Grow
By REUTERS

Stocks End Day Slightly Higher

Tokyo, Hong Kong Shares Tumble

Dow Loses Ground in Mixed Market

By BLOOMBERG NEWS

Net Up at Two Retail Firms

EDITORIAL DESK |
Crawling Out of Recession

European Stock Markets Close Lower
By THE ASSOCIATED PRESS

Women's Wholesale Apparel Prices See 0.2 Percent Drop in February

Figure 7.1 How would each of these headlines affect buyers' decisions?

Changes in the composition of the population may also affect sales. A firm that relies on purchases by 18-to-35-year-olds may find that the most rapidly growing segment in its trading area is over 65, requiring forecasts to be adjusted downward.

Even lifestyle changes in your target market need to be examined. For example, your customers may become more conscious of environmental issues and start purchasing only products that are environmentally sound. You must be alert to all demographic trends and changes in your customer base before making your sales forecast.

Competitive Conditions. Competitors may enter or leave your market area at any time, and sales forecasts need to be adjusted accordingly. Your competitors' promotional strategies may also change. For example, a competitor may decide to increase advertising or introduce a new contest, and if they are effective, both could cause decreased sales for your store.

Acquiring Needed Data

To make sales forecasts, you need to locate and use information; therefore, you must be knowledgeable about the types of data available and how to obtain them. Many of these sources are described in Chapter 4. Your first decision is whether primary data collection will be needed. To make that decision, you must thoroughly examine secondary data sources because they can be the most cost-effective to use.

Primary data originate with the specific research being undertaken. In other words, you collect the information to solve the current problem at hand. Direct customer surveys are the chief means used to obtain information on your customers' attitudes and opinions. Secondary data are data that have been gathered for some other purpose but are applicable to solving your problem. Business records produced by other departments in your store and information that is obtained from books and magazines are examples of secondary data. Let's more closely examine these data sources and the uses that can be made of each one.

Primary Data Sources. Many retailers spend both time and money to collect information from their customers on a perpetual basis. Stew Leonard's, the famous Connecticut food store, attracts more than

100,000 shoppers a week to its flagship store. The company relies heavily on primary data collection to improve its service and product offerings to customers. Holding weekend focus group sessions, reading comments from the suggestions box (which customers actually use), and simply walking the aisles speaking with customers and employees are techniques the company has used since it opened its first store. Management is constantly on the lookout for ways to improve customers' shopping experience. They do not wait until sales decline before making changes; they know that without careful attention to the desires of the market, sales could change quickly.

Dillard's is another retailer that uses direct customer surveys extensively. In focus groups or in one-on-one interviews, customers are asked which products they would like more of in the stores. Creative Marketplace, a marketing consulting firm, reports that most women go into a store to buy something specific, yet 67 percent leave without having made the purchase. Dillard's realizes if it can reduce that number, it can increase sales. Dillard's is even experimenting with computer-aided designs to gauge customer opinions. For example, a store employee is able to show a skirt on a computer screen to a customer and ask in what color or length she would most likely purchase the item.

Retailers can also use customer surveys to forecast future consumer buying patterns. In a recent Harris poll, 54 percent of Americans said they did not have as much free time as they used to, and they are spending fewer of those leisure hours shopping. Currently, only 6 percent say shopping is their favorite thing to do, while nearly 63 percent say it is mostly or entirely drudgery. Even shopping time in the stores is decreasing; 47 percent reported they were spending less time shopping than a year ago. New strategies will be needed in the future to get consumers back to the stores, and once there, make that experience as pleasurable as possible. Read the Trendwatch titled, "Market-Basket Analysis: How Do Customers Shop a Store," to learn more about a data-mining technique that some retailers are beginning to use.

Secondary Sources. Searching for external data may be quick or extensive. For example, the only information that you may need is the average annual sales of men's suits by stores with less than 2,500 square feet. A single trade journal will be able to provide this information to you. Other questions that deal with consumer opinions may require obtaining as many sources as are available.

Business Publication Rates and Data is an index published by the Standard Rate and Data Service, Inc., which will be a great help to you in identifying trade sources. Every major industry has one or more magazine specifically aimed at its member firms.

Professional and trade associations are also good sources of forecasting data. *The Encyclopedia of Associations*, published by the Gale Research Company of Detroit, lists associations' names, addresses, number of members, and, most importantly, their publications.

General business publications and newspapers should not be overlooked when you need to locate information on market trends or economic conditions. There are even specific sources that report and forecast customer purchasing patterns. The *Survey of Buying Power*, published annually by *Sales and Marketing Management Magazine*, contains valuable information on markets by state, county, and MSA (metropolitan statistical area). Data are provided on population, household incomes, and retail sales. *Consumer Buying Indicators* is issued quarterly by the Bureau of the Census and contains 6-month and 12-month expected purchase estimates (in units) of automobiles, homes, furniture, carpets, major appliances, and home improvements.

If you use secondary data in making sales forecasts, you must realize there are several shortcomings of this information. Some of the data may be out-of-date. There is no rule as to when data are out-of-date, but in volatile times, data more than five years old are of questionable value. Also, you need to determine the bias of the source that collected the data; be aware of who collected the data and for what purpose. Numbers can usually be twisted to defend almost any side of an argument.

There is a huge amount of secondary data available to you. Seek out what you need and make use of it. However, you may be forced to collect primary data in situations where available information does not fit your specific needs.

Making Sales Forecasts

When developing a sales forecast, a step-by-step process should be followed that analyzes both internal and external forces that will affect sales. This process involves the following steps:

1. Review past sales.
2. Analyze changes in economic conditions.

3. Analyze changes in sales potential for specific products or markets.
4. Analyze changes in marketing strategies of your firm and the competition.
5. Forecast sales.

Let's more closely examine each of these steps.

Review Past Sales. A review of past sales records will determine if there are any patterns or trends in the sales figures. Sales will need to be compared with those of last month as well as last year during the same period. This information will give you an initial estimate of any change that might be expected during the coming year if everything else remains the same—which rarely happens. From this information you can answer the following questions:

• Have sales shown a pattern of increase or decrease over the past several years?
• If a pattern is present, what is the average percent?
• Do recent sales data support this trend?
• Can you identify a percentage figure that will reflect the sales trends you have observed?

Analyze Changes in Economic Conditions. You may need to adjust the trend percentage figure you have identified after reviewing economic trends and examining published national and local economic forecasts.

Analyze Changes in Sales Potential. Your next step will be to relate demographic changes in the market to your store or the products for which you are responsible. Such information may be difficult to obtain, but here are sources that you can use. The *Census of Population* (published every ten years) can supply some data, but it will be dated. One of the best sources is the *Survey of Buying Power* (published annually), which reports population data and sales by major lines of merchandise broken down by region, state, county, MSA, and by cities of more than 25,000 population; however, you may face problems using the data. Merchandise line categories may be too broad for your forecast, or sales data may not be current enough for short-term forecasting purposes. You may want to modify your sales trend percentage figure at this point to reflect changes in market conditions.

Analyze Changes in Marketing Strategies. Next, you need to consider any changes in marketing strategies planned by your store as well as by the competition. For example, a decision to remodel a store, the addition of new lines of merchandise, or a new promotional event will attract customers and can increase sales. There is little information that can be used to predict what the competition will do in the future; however, you can gain information through comparison shopping trips, studying competitor's ads, and listening to customers. Your trend percentage figure will need to be adjusted again based on any changes in marketing strategies by your store or the competition.

Forecast Sales. Now, it is time to make your sales forecast. Assume that after analyzing past sales records, you determined that there was an average 6 percent increase in sales for the previous six-month periods. You determine that economic growth will increase sales by 2 percent and the size of your market will grow by 5 percent. In addition, you have learned that a competitor will be opening a new store this year, causing an estimated 5 percent decrease in your sales. From this information, you decide to forecast an 8 percent (6 percent + 2 percent + 5 percent − 5 percent) increase in sales for the next period.

Sales forecasting is not a precise process, but ultimately it provides the best starting point available from which to plan future sales. The only other alternative–no planning–is not acceptable to professional buyers.

Because sales forecasts have such a critical impact on your store, they need to be simultaneously challenging and attainable. If they are not, it spells disaster. If your sales forecasts are dramatically increased over previous periods, the cost of doing business will also have to rise to accommodate the projected sales increase. For example, advertising expenditures may need to be increased or additional sales associates may be needed.

If your sales forecasts are set too high and cannot be attained, your resulting expenses-to-sales ratio will be too high, causing profits to fall below expectations. Or if you dramatically underestimate your sales forecast and purchase an inadequate amount of inventory, you will not be able to sufficiently meet consumer demand, which may translate into loss of loyal customers who turn to your competitors.

Once you have developed a sales forecast, your merchandise manager's approval will be needed. You will want to include a brief rationale that should summarize the assumptions that you made and the factors that you considered in developing the forecast. Input from your manager should also have been requested while you were gathering data to use in your sales forecast.

Once your forecast is approved, your next step will be to develop a merchandise buying plan. That process will be described in Chapter 8.

Making Adjustments

Actual sales should be periodically monitored to determine the accuracy of your sales forecasts; however, the forecast should not become a goal that must be met regardless of unforeseen competitive changes or changes in general economic or business conditions. That would cause inefficient use of store resources. During the selling season, you may uncover greater-than-expected sales. You may determine that your store does not have the capital to purchase the required inventory, greater competition than expected may occur, or consumer demand may be less than anticipated. Adjustments in your plan may be required.

For some products, reorders can be made quickly if you underestimated consumer demand; however, manufacturers may be out of stock, and customer dissatisfaction has already occurred. Overestimating sales will require changes in marketing strategies. First, examine activities that might be accomplished at little expense. Consider moving the merchandise location or retraining sales associates. Additional advertising expenditures may be required, or markdowns may be needed.

FORECASTING DECISIONS

Two of the most important forecasts that buyers make are of sales and stock levels. Let's examine how these two important calculations are made.

Forecasting Sales

Sales forecasting is a subjective part of the planning process, but it involves much more than guessing. Your forecasting abilities can be improved with practice and experience that will enable you to make more precise and reliable forecasts (Figure 7.2).

Most retailers will develop a sales forecast, then plan the amount of inventory required to generate that amount of sales. If basic merchan-

"I didn't see anything I liked."

Figure 7.2   Some stores wait too late before collecting information on what customers want.

dise is carried year-round, planning will be less complicated; however, where fashion changes are frequent, keeping inventories and sales balanced will be more difficult.

Past sales figures are important to a buyer when making sales forecasts, but they should be used only as a guide. In addition to past store records, your planning and forecasting activities must also consider other internal and external factors that are likely to affect sales. Some of these factors include:

- Storewide or departmental promotions and sales,
- holidays,
- current storewide and departmental sales trends,
- population shifts,
- shifts in demographic characteristics of the population,
- new competition moving into the area,
- economic conditions,
- changes in store hours, and
- changes in the amount of selling space.

Year 1

SEPTEMBER						
S	M	T	W	T	F	S
					1	2
3	4	5	6	7	8	9
10	11	12	13	14	15	16
17	18	19	20	21	22	23
24	25	26	27	28	29	30

Year 2

SEPTEMBER						
S	M	T	W	T	F	S
1	2	3	4	5	6	7
8	9	10	11	12	13	14
15	16	17	18	19	20	21
22	23	24	25	26	27	28
29	30					

Figure 7.3   Buyers must make adjustments for changes in the selling season that occur from one year to the next.

The accuracy of your forecasts will depend on the accuracy of your past records and your ability to interpret that information in relation to current trends and make projections about future possibilities. Forecasting also requires a certain amount of judgment and experience.

Buyers begin developing sales forecasts by reviewing past sales figures. Last year's sales figures are important, but you will also want to review the figures for the past two or three years. You will also want to determine the reasons for any sales increases or decreases.

By analyzing sales trends for several years, you get a more realistic picture of past sales to guide your forecasting efforts. Accurate forecasting also involves making adjustments for differences in the number of selling days in a month during different years. For instance, as shown in Figure 7.3, September may have five Saturdays one year but only four may appear in the following year's calendar. A month with five Saturdays would tend to generate more sales than a month with only four Saturdays. You must also realize that there may be a variation in monthly sales because holidays occur at different times in different years. When Easter is in March, for example, the possibility of cold weather tends to reduce spring clothing sales. Business conditions will also affect future sales. When business is good, sales may increase or remain at the usual level. Sales frequently decline, however, when business conditions become unfavorable.

Sales cannot be forecast with absolute accuracy; yet buyers must make educated guesses. One helpful guide is the average rate of increase or decrease in sales. Although a trend may be evident, you will need to study the reasons for the changes and the conditions that may affect future sales before making any adjustments in plans.

A buyer has the following sales data available and wants to forecast sales for July. The illustration below shows how a sales forecast is developed:

PROBLEM ILLUSTRATION

Month	Sales Last Year	Sales This Year
April	$50,000	$55,000
May	$55,000	$61,000
June	$59,000	$64,000
July	$60,000	?

First, you would need to determine the percentage of sales increase or decrease for the first three months from the previous year by using the following formula:

Percent Increase or Decrease in Sales =

Difference in Sales from Last Year to This Year / Previous Year's Sales

Your calculations for each month would be as follows:

April = ($55,000 − $50,000) / $50,000 = 10% increase

May = ($61,000 − $55,000) / $55,000 = 10.9% increase

June = ($64,000 − $59,000) / $59,000 = 8.5% increase

Although sales are currently ahead of last year for each month, the percentage decreased from May to June. You would then want to consider the direction of monthly sales during the current year. For example,

April to May = ($61,000 − $55,000) / $55,000 = 10.9%

May to June = ($64,000 − $61,000) / $61,000 = 4.9%

Sales growth has been declining. You would also want to consider the direction of sales growth last year during the same period by completing the following calculation:

June to July (Last Year) = ($60,000 − $59,000) /$59,000 = 1.7%

You could then conclude that the sales increase for July should be planned between 1.7 and 4.9 percent. At this point, you would want to consider other internal and external factors that might affect sales. If you feel that nothing drastically different will occur during the month, you might arbitrarily select a 3.3 percent increase because it is approximately midway between the two figures. Other conditions, such as more promotions from the competition or changes in your target market, could cause you to forecast the sales fluctuation at a higher or lower level.

Every effort should be made to ensure that your forecast is as accurate as possible because all other merchandising decisions are planned in relation to sales. Bad forecasts wreak havoc on any firm. If your sales forecast is in error, other decisions will be in error, too. Only by doing your homework, by researching your particular market segment, and by talking to customers will you improve the accuracy of your sales forecasts. Of course, you will never completely eliminate the uncertainty in forecasts, but you can reduce it to a manageable level. Once sales are forecast, you will need to plan inventory levels that will support the sales you have predicted.

Planning Inventory Levels

After you forecast sales for a specific period, you must then plan required inventory levels. Merchandise in stock must be sufficient to meet sales expectations while allowing for unanticipated demand. As a buyer, your goal will be to maintain an inventory assortment that will be sufficient to meet customer demand and yet be small enough to ensure a reasonable return on the store's investment in inventory.

There are several methods of inventory planning; however, the one most often used is the stock-to-sales ratio method. The stock-to-sales ratio method involves maintaining inventory at a specific ratio to sales. *Stock-to-sales ratios* are calculated by dividing the dollar value of stock on hand by actual sales in dollars. For example, if a department had merchandise valued at $40,000 to begin the month of April and sales amounted to $20,000, the resulting stock-to-sales ratio would be 2. The stock-to-sales ratio is calculated using the following formula:

Stock-to-Sales Ratio = Value of Stock / Actual Sales

For this example, the calculation would be made as follows:

Stock-to-Sales Ratio = $40,000 / $20,000 = 2

The stock-to-sales ratio indicates the relationship between planned sales and the amount of inventory required to support those sales and is used to calculate planned *BOM stock levels*–the amount of stock required to begin the month. By multiplying the stock-to-sales ratio for the month by the planned sales for that month, you can determine the inventory level needed at the beginning of the month (BOM). Planned BOM inventory can be calculated using the following formula:

Planned BOM inventory = Stock-to-Sales Ratio × Planned Sales

Industrywide stock-sales ratios are available from sources such as the National Retail Federation and Dun & Bradstreet. Buyers can also calculate stock-to-sales ratios for their store or department based on previous stock and sales levels.

PROBLEM ILLUSTRATION

Using the stock-to-sales ratio method, calculate planned BOM inventory for November given the following information:

Stock-to-Sales Ratio = 1.2
Planned Sales for November = $19,000

Planned BOM inventory = Stock-to-Sales Ratio × Planned Sales

Planned BOM Inventory = 1.2 × $19,000 = $22,800

Therefore, using the stock-to-sales method of planning inventory, you would want to start the month of November with $22,800 worth of inventory.

Determining Stock Turnover

Decisions you make in relation to sales forecasting and stock planning must yield a profit for your store. One measure of how accurately you balance sales to inventory levels is the ***stock turnover rate***. How fast merchandise is sold, replenished, and sold determines the stock turnover for a store or department. The stock turnover rate is the number of times the average stock is sold during a given period and is calculated using the following formula:

Stock Turnover Rate = Sales / Average Stock

The ***average stock*** for any period of time is the value of inventory at the beginning of the period, plus the value of inventory at predetermined periods during the period (such as end of the month), plus the value of inventory at the end of the period divided by the total number of stock listings.

Buyers and management can determine a great deal about how well a store, department, or product classification is doing by knowing stock turnover rates. Like stock-to-sales ratios, turnover rates of comparable retailers can be determined from trade journals. Buyers can also use past sales data for their stores to calculate turnover. Turnover may be determined for any period of time; however, it usually refers to a one-year period.

PROBLEM ILLUSTRATION

Calculate stock turnover given the following information:

Total sales = $60,000
Monthly inventory figures are listed below:

Month	Stock Level
Jan 31	$8,000
Feb 28	$12,000
Mar 31	$14,000
Apr 30	$12,000
May 31	$10,000
June 30	$8,000
July 31	$10,000
Aug 31	$16,000
Sept 30	$18,000
Oct 31	$20,000
Nov 30	$30,000
Dec 31	$16,000
Jan 31	$6,000
Total Inventory = $180,000	

First, determine the average monthly inventory by dividing the total inventory in dollars by the number of inventory listings. Average stock would be $13,846 ($180,000 / 13).

Next, calculate the stock turnover rate using the following formula:

Stock Turnover Rate = Sales / Average Stock

Stock Turnover Rate = $60,000 / $13,846

Stock Turnover Rate = 4.3

Therefore, the average stock for this department is sold and replenished 4.3 times during the year.

Stock turnover figures can also be used to plan both sales and stock levels using the following formula:

Sales = Stock Turnover Rate × Average Inventory

For example, if your goal is a 3.1 turnover rate and your average stock is $25,000, planned sales to reach this goal would be $77,500.

The type of merchandise carried and store policies have an impact on stock turnover; however, almost every decision a retailer makes affects turnover. Less frequently purchased items, such as furniture and jewelry, have much lower turnover rates than items found in a grocery store.

Store policies in regard to carrying wide assortments of merchandise in many sizes and colors will tend to cause low turnovers because some colors and sizes may not sell as well as others. For that reason, some stores carry only fast-selling colors and sizes to generate higher turnover rates.

Higher stock turnover rates are usually an advantage to the store or department because rapid turnover of stock reduces the number and amount of markdowns required to move dated merchandise. Merchandise that is being replaced frequently always looks fresh and has much greater appeal to the customer. However, when attempting to increase turnover, you must also be concerned with increased expenses, such as advertising or more salaries for additional salespeople. Both might be required to generate more sales. In these situations, increased turnover may not result in increased profits.

How can buyers improve stock turnover? You will need to examine sales and inventory information from your store or department. Slow-turning merchandise may be due to several reasons:

- You may be attempting to carry too wide an assortment of merchandise. Offering a wide selection of styles, colors, and sizes often causes slow turnover rates. Merchandise may be remaining on your shelves for long periods of time to satisfy a few customers.
- You may have selected the wrong merchandise. The goods that have been purchased may not be the ones that your customers want or need. Learn from such situations to improve your buying decisions the next time.
- The merchandise may have been placed into stock too late. Delayed deliveries or late purchases may cause merchandise to arrive at your store after your customers have purchased the goods elsewhere.
- The merchandise may be priced too high. Prices may have to be reduced to generate sales.
- The store may not be conducting an effective sales promotion campaign for the product.

There are other reasons for low turnover rates, but these five should be examined first. Once you have developed a sales forecast and determined required inventory levels for your store or department, you are ready to develop your buying plan, a step that is examined in detail in the next chapter.

FUTURE DIRECTION OF SALES FORECASTING

Quantitative skills of buyers must continue to improve. The increased use of computers will affect sales forecasting in the years ahead. Software packages will become easier to use and more versatile. Large amounts of internal and external data will become available and accessible quickly through computerized information systems, and better techniques should improve the overall accuracy of computer forecasts. But, more competitive conditions and more volatile markets will increase the difficulty of making accurate forecasts. The successful buyer will be the individual who can merge computer forecasts with his or her personal insights about the marketplace.

SUMMARY POINTS

- Forecasting involves predicting what customers are likely to do in the future.
- Buyers use forecasting to predict what products customers will buy and how much they will purchase.
- Buyers can make short- or long-term forecasts for specific products, customer groups, time periods, or store locations.
- Long-term forecasts in volatile market conditions may be meaningless.
- Developing forecasts stimulates planning by forcing the buyer to have a thorough understanding of market conditions and customers, promotes coordination with other members of the merchandising team, and provides a control mechanism by which to evaluate a buyer's performance.
- When developing sales forecasts, buyers must examine all internal and external forces that may affect sales. They collect both primary and secondary data.
- Two of the most important forecasts that buyers make are sales and inventory levels.

- The key component of most sales forecasting is past sales records.
- Buyers can also use stock-to-sales ratios and inventory turnover to estimate sales.
- All other merchandising decisions are planned in relation to sales forecasts; therefore, if a sales forecast is in error, other decisions will be inaccurate too.

REVIEW ACTIVITIES

Developing Your Retail Buying Vocabulary

Consult the Glossary if you did not add the following terms to your vocabulary.

Average stock	Market-basket analysis
BOM stock level	Sales forecast
External forces	Short-term forecast
Forecasting	Stock-to-sales ratio
Internal forces	Stock turnover rate
Long-term forecast	

Understanding What You Read

1. Identify the most important source of information when buyers develop sales forecasts.
2. Describe factors that will affect the accuracy of a sales forecast.
3. List and describe three benefits of forecasting sales.
4. Describe how buyers can increase their confidence in sales forecasting.
5. Identify economic conditions that would cause a buyer to project a decrease in sales.
6. Describe competitive conditions that would cause a buyer to project a decrease in sales.
7. Why do most buyers use secondary data before using primary data?
8. Describe the information provided in *Survey of Buying Power*.
9. List the steps needed to develop a sales forecast.
10. Describe the impact of a forecast that underestimates sales.
11. Describe the impact of a forecast that overestimates sales.

12. List several internal and external factors that should be considered along with past sales records when forecasting sales.
13. Upon what will the accuracy of a sales forecast depend?
14. How will holidays affect monthly sales forecasts from one year to the next?
15. What would be one source for industrywide of stock-to-sales ratios?
16. What are the advantages of forecasting an increase in stock turnover rates?
17. How can computers be used to make sales forecasts?

Analyzing and Applying What You Read

1. As a buyer you must constantly make forecasts about consumer demand. What factors would cause the sale of men's ties, cigarettes, disposable diapers, and American flags to increase or decrease?
2. You have developed a sales forecast for men's suits that predicts a 20 percent increase in sales. Identify marketing strategies that could be utilized to reach that goal.
3. Sales last year during June were $20,000. Sales this June were $21,500. What percentage increase or decrease in sales has occurred? If this trend continues, what sales should be forecast for next June?
4. A firm wants to maintain an average stock of $25,000 every year. Last year, the firm had a 4.3 stock turnover rate. This year, management forecasts that stock turnover should increase to 4.5. By what dollar volume must sales increase for this forecasted turnover to occur?

Application Exercises

1. A department has the following sales data available. Forecast sales for May.

	Sales Last Year	Sales This Year
February	$24,000	$26,000
March	$26,000	$27,000
April	$29,000	$29,000
May	$33,000	?

2. Use the following information to answer the questions below.

	Last Year Monthly Sales	BOM Stock
January	$10,000	$20,000
February	$12,000	$25,000
March	$14,000	$30,000
April	$18,000	$38,000
May	$19,000	$40,000
June	$18,000	$39,000
July	$19,000	$41,000
August	$21,000	$43,000
September	$23,000	$47,000
October	$26,000	$52,000
November	$31,000	$60,000
December	$30,000	$58,000
Ending Inventory December 31		$28,000

a. For the time period presented, what were total sales?

b. What was the average inventory for the period?

c. What was the annual stock turnover rate?

d. Calculate last year's stock-to-sales ratio for each of the months given.

e. Next December, the buyer wants to maintain the current stock-to-sales ratio but reduce the BOM stock to $55,000. What sales must occur next year for this to occur?

Spreadsheet Skills

1. Complete the spreadsheet application problems in Chapter 7 of *Making Buying Decisions: Using the Computer as a Tool* to develop your skills with manipulating spreadsheets related to stock planning.

2. Use a spreadsheet to complete the Application Exercises above.

Internet Connection

1. On the Internet, go to www.weather.com and record the weather forecast (highs, lows, and weather conditions) for the next three days for your town or nearest city. Each day record the actual conditions.

Also, locate weather forecasts appearing in your local newspaper, on TV, or on the radio. Compare the forecasts and discuss their accuracy. Which source made the most accurate forecasts? Compare weather forecasting to making a short-term sales forecast.

2. On the Internet, go to www.farmersalmanac.com and compare weather forecasts made for your area over a year ago. Discuss how such long-range forecasts are made. How accurate were these forecasts? Compare long-term weather forecasting to making a sales forecast.

SNAPSHOT

Family Dollar: Fine-Tuning Its Retail Strategy

Family Dollar Stores is a chain of general merchandise stores headquartered in Charlotte, North Carolina. The firm was started by Leon Levine, an iron-willed merchant who turned a single store into a national chain.

Even though the company is bigger and more professionally managed today, a close inspection reveals that it is essentially the same business that Leon started in 1959. Family Dollar stores are still little stores stocked with a jumble of everything from T-shirts and toothpaste to cheap plastic toys. But management has found a retail strategy that works for the company.

Management's approach has been relatively simple—build no-frills stores in low-income neighborhoods, sell a variety of carefully selected merchandise at reasonable prices, and keep expenses low. Management's goal is to ensure that the plan is executed properly.

Today, Family Dollar operates about 6,200 stores in 44 states and supports them with nine strategically located distribution centers. In fact, 17.2 percent of the U.S. population lives within a mile of a Family Dollar store compared to 12.4 percent who live within a mile of a Dollar General store. Recently, Family Dollar stores have struggled in some areas, but remain a formidable competitor in the extreme-value retail sector. Although posting a 9.8 percent increase in sales to $6.4 billion in 2006, Family Dollar saw customer count and gross margin, as a percentage of sales, decline. On the plus side, the average transaction amount increased by 4.8 percent to $9.66.

In the 1980s, Family Dollar kept growing, but performance turned erratic. Profits dropped, then rebounded again. And new challenges arose not only from Wal-Mart, but also from Dollar General Stores, which were almost the mirror image of Family Dollar stores—neighborhood discount stores.

In 1993, Family Dollar found its prices being undercut by big stores such as Wal-Mart and small stores such as Dollar General. Customer research found shoppers still liked the Family Dollar locations, merchandise, and convenience, but they did not like the prices. Customers were going to Family Dollar for sale-priced items and doing the rest of their shopping elsewhere. This was bad news for the company because it made little or no profit on these items.

Management decided that to survive, prices would have to be cut. Experiments with price-cutting were conducted in a few stores in 1994 before the strategy went companywide in 1995. All prices were cut 10 to 15 percent. To cover these cuts, advertising was reduced, which had consisted primarily of direct mail circulars. Instead of 22 circulars as had been released previously, only 15 were produced. This move reduced advertising costs by $15.4 million.

It was a risky strategy that depended on customers finding the stores on their own. Initial reports were not encouraging; same-store sales dropped 0.8 percent, and net income fell 8 percent. Consultants, however, said it would take 18 months for customers to catch on—which they did.

Family Dollar seems to have found the right strategy for the urban market. Following extensive company research, the firm launched its "urban initiative" in 2005, a $25 million effort to strengthen its 1,400 urban stores. The initiative focused on improving hiring practices and training for managers, while strong efforts were made to tailor merchandise offerings to customers in urban markets rather than stocking the same items in all of its stores. As a result, same-store sales gains of 3.7 percent were achieved.

Recent developments would indicate that the future is bright for Family Dollar. Today, two-thirds of U.S. households have shopped a dollar-store channel at least once this year.

BASED ON:

Dollar store markets: Family Dollar's recipe for urban success. (2007, April 23). *The Food Institute Report*, 3.

Family Dollar profits advance 6.1 percent. (2007, August 13). *MMR*, 5.

Family Dollar rebounds as it improves key metrics. (2007, May 28). *MMR*, 6.

Family Dollar works to increase relevance to customer base. (2007, April 23). *Chain Drug Review*, 72.

TRENDWATCH

Using Weather Forecasts to Improve Retail Forecasts

When retailers mention the weather, it is usually as a way to explain sales, particularly poor sales. All retailers know from experience that store traffic and sales are definitely related to weather, but very few retailers (estimated at less than 10 percent) keep any weather records at all. Although most retailers realize how dependent they are on weather, they also know how little they understand it. A check of weather forecasting services around the country reveals that few retailers are numbered among their clients. The idea that weather can be forecast early enough to affect buying plans and promotional calendars is a entirely new concept for many retailers. Yet, weather forecasting has tremendous implications for retailers, especially in climates where seasonal temperatures vary greatly. For instance, if buyers know that the weather is going to be unseasonably hot or cold, they can plan their purchases accordingly.

Most retailers, however, do not consciously factor future weather into their business decisions. Typically, their business decisions merely assume the weather's effect on their business will repeat from last year to the current year. In fact, weather is similar one year to the next only about one-third of the time–causing most retailers to have too much or too little seasonal merchandise on hand.

At one time, Sears employed two meteorologists to assist with long-range planning, but discontinued the practice in 1979 due to budget cuts. Although the meterologoists did alert buyers to expedite emergency shipments of merchandise such as pumps to areas to be affected by flooding, their main function was to examine historical sales figures and extract the impact of weather.

Today, one weather-forecasting service–Strategic Weather Services of Wayne, Pennsylvania–specializes in 12- and 15-month forecasts for retailers. And, according to audits by Ernst & Young, it has an accuracy rate of about 70 percent. The service also provides software that "deweatherizes" historic sales data, so that past effects of unusual weather are taken out of previous years' sales. The software also integrates a weather forecast that adjusts future sales up or down. In doing so, weather information is used proactively–as a way to spot opportunities or improve planning.

Strategic Weather Services has found many strong correlations between temperature and product sales, such as an increase in coat or space heater sales when temperatures drop below normal. The firm's research indicates that weather can affect 10 to 30 percent of the demand for weather-sensitive merchandise. For example, the service routinely identifies the best periods to run promotional events, resulting in sales increases of over 25 percent. It advised a national catalog showroom retailer that there would be unseasonably heavy rain in the company's West Coast markets. The retailer altered its mix of humidifiers and dehumidifiers and increased dehumidifier sales from 10,000 units to 30,000 units.

For retailers, the challenge of how to use the data still remains. Knowing that more snow is forecasted is great information. Determining how many additional pairs of skis to have in inventory is quite another matter. More understanding is needed on how to apply this information to various decision-making processes, including merchandise allocation and planning, merchandise delivery and markdown timing, and promotional scheduling.

Weather influences consumer behavior, affecting store traffic and demand for specific products. Weather determines the beginning and ending points of a merchandise season; yet weather is a huge unknown. Retailers cannot control the weather, but they can control how it affects their businesses. Better planning based on weather forecasts can increase revenues and profits on weather-sensitive products.

BASED ON:

Circumventing the whims of weather. (1997, April). *Stores*, 83.

Pasquallina, Marco. (1998, September). The weather as a business tool. *American Demographics*, 12–17.

Reda, Susan. (1997, September). Apparel merchants: arming for fall with weather forecasting. *Stores*, 66–68.

Rosenfeld, Jeff. (2001, January). Betting on the weather. *Weatherwise*, 1.

Steinhauer, Jennifer. (1997, June 6). Retailers' usual suspect is the weather. *The New York Times*, C3.

TRENDWATCH

Market-Basket Analysis: How Do Customers Shop a Store?

Sales data provide a view of what customers are purchasing but do not provide a view of how they are buying—in what combinations and in what quantities. One method that is being used to better determine *how* customers are buying is market-basket analysis.

What is a market-basket analysis, and how do retailers use it? ***Market-basket analysis*** is a term that describes data-mining solutions that identify the correlations among items in a customer's shopping basket. Buyers and merchandisers can apply these categorical findings and respond to customer demand more effectively. It also helps them to make strategic planning and diagramming decisions that consider the types of items consumers are most likely to purchase during any one shopping trip. Their first step is to associate the products in the customers' market basket with a product category. Through analysis, the percentage that each category represents is calculated. For example, if there are ten items in a market basket and five are cosmetic products, 50 percent of the basket is represented by the cosmetics category.

Management predetermines a percentage to represent a customer in a particular purchase profile. For example, a retailer may determine that having more than 25 percent of items in a product category places a customer into the profile. In the preceding example, the customer would be categorized as belonging to a "Beauty Conscious" shopper profile. A market basket with more than 25 percent of the items related to photographic equipment and supplies would be categorized as a "Photographer," and so on for each type of basket found. In essence, the analysis captures the key reason that the customer was in the store.

The category becomes more than a product grouping; it becomes a shopper profile. For example, makeup, cotton balls, hair dye, and cologne may be in different product categories and in different physical locations within a store; yet, they are all part of the "Beauty Conscious" purchase profile.

Customers' behavior is measured objectively by what they purchase. By using this analysis, retailers are not trying to pin labels on customers; they are attempting to categorize shopping experiences and analyze how customers collectively behave while shopping.

Once specific customer purchase profiles are identified, the next step is to provide information to decision makers, such as buyers, on which they can act. A gross margin figure is calculated for each profile. This figure can then be used to base decisions about key areas of the business. For example, the data can provide information to the retailer about how to spend advertising dollars. "Beauty Conscious" may generate $15.24 in profits per market basket, whereas the "Photographer" generates only $2.55. Obviously, advertising dollars should be spent on the products that generate the most profit, but further study may show that the store is spending money on product categories that bring in the least profit.

Another way in which market-basket analysis can be used is to make fact-based decisions about space allocation and product placement. Space allocation needs to be correlated with customers whose purchase profiles generate the most profit. Also, product placement decisions can be made by determining affinity purchases. This concept involves using market-basket analysis to determine what items are most frequently purchased with other items in the same market basket. For example, analysis may reveal that in the "Beauty Conscious" shopping basket, greeting cards were found 25 percent of the time and seasonal candy was found 16 percent of the time. Such data would indicate that sales of these two products would increase by moving them adjacent to a primary beauty care area. By using affinity analysis, a store can be moved from being a product-driven business to being a customer-driven business.

Decisions may not always be made using the results of market-basket analysis. For example, new fathers with no time to go out and socialize tend to pick up a six-pack of beer when buying disposable diapers. This is an exploitable relationship that is not obvious at first glance; however, it is doubtful that any retailer would stock diapers alongside beer. But, if acted on properly, effective market-basket analysis can bring increased sales, a stronger in-stock position, and increased customer satisfaction.

Knowing the customer better leads to a more personal relationship between a retailer and the customer. As a retail buyer, you should realize that every customer transaction tells a story. Implementing a market-basket analysis is one way to reveal the details of that story.

BASED ON:

Johnson, Walter E. and Tratensek, Dan M. (1999, October). Market-basket analysis: discover how customers shop your store. *Do-It-Yourself Retailing*, 48–54.

Koslowsky, Sam. (2006, October 15). Match 'em up. Utilizing market-basket analysis techniques in marketing. *Direct*, 1.

Market basket offers a new set of metrics. (2003, October 27). *Chain Drug Review*, 52.

Nishi, Dennis. (2005, May). Market-basket mystery: what do beer and diapers have in common? For retailers, the answer could be powerful. *Chain Store Age*, 12A–13A.

Preparing Buying Plans

PERFORMANCE OBJECTIVES

Upon completion of this chapter, you should be able to:

- Distinguish between top-down and bottom-up planning.
- Identify the purposes of merchandise plans.
- Outline a process to forecast sales.
- List and describe the components of a merchandise plan.
- Calculate planned BOM (beginning of the month) inventory levels.
- Identify the components of planned reductions.
- Calculate planned purchases at retail.
- Calculate planned purchases at cost.
- Prepare a six-month merchandise plan.
- Describe basic stock planning.
- Describe the importance of open-to-buy.
- Calculate open-to-buy.

Whether buyers are purchasing fashion or basic merchandise, they must plan and control merchandise purchases. Planning is essential to provide direction and serve as a basis of control for any store or department. As a buyer, you must provide the right merchandise, at the right place, at the right time, in the right quantities, and at the right price. To accomplish these goals, you must plan a deliberate course of action—planning merchandise budgets and merchandise assortments. As you will learn, the merchandise budget or merchandise plan is a forecast of specific merchandise purchases in dollars that typically covers a period of six months or a year. Assortment plans break down merchandise budgets into specific units of merchandise to be purchased, such as styles, colors, and sizes.

In this chapter, you will learn how to prepare a six-month merchandise plan. Inventory planning for basic merchandise and the concept of open-to-buy are also described. Chapter 9 explains how the merchandise plan is translated into an assortment plan for specific units of merchandise.

MERCHANDISING MANAGEMENT

Integrally related to planning is the necessity to control merchandising decisions. You must check your plans periodically to ensure they are being followed and are achieving the desired results. Your success as a buyer will be measured by how well you plan and control the amount of money spent for merchandise to yield the desired sales and profit.

Retailers need some type of planning and control device to guide their activities toward the achievement of their stated goals and objectives.

Most retailers develop merchandise plans for the entire store as well as specific departments and product classifications. These merchandise plans provide for an effective control over purchases and tend to prevent the department or store from becoming overstocked or understocked.

The *merchandise plan* is a projection in dollars of the sales goals of the store or department over a specified period of time–usually six months. With this information, a buyer can determine how much money can be used to purchase merchandise. In addition, information from the merchandise plan helps top management judge the effectiveness of merchandising decisions that were made.

Two methods of developing the merchandise plan are used today. They involve top-down and bottom-up planning. *Top-down planning* involves top-level management estimating total sales for the upcoming period (Figure 8.1). Then, expected sales are planned for each depart-

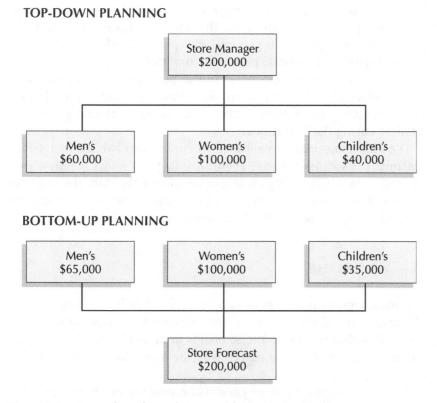

Figure 8.1   Examples of top-down and bottom-up planning.

ment according to its past contribution to the sales of the entire store. One advantage of top-down planning is that top management tends to have a better perspective of all economic and competitive conditions facing the business than would other employees.

The other method used to develop a merchandise plan is ***bottom-up planning***. The planned sales for the store are determined by adding together the planned sales figures that are developed by each department manager. Planned sales figures for all departments are then totaled to arrive at planned sales for the store. Many large retailers use both the top-down and bottom-up methods, then arrive at the final planned sales figure for the store and each department through a process of discussion and compromise.

SIX-MONTH MERCHANDISE PLAN

Most retailers will use a ***six-month merchandise plan*** to represent planning efforts. Key components of every plan include sales forecasts and stock planning. In addition, the amount of merchandise to be purchased each period to generate the planned sales is calculated. The six-month merchandise plan is the tool that translates profit objectives into a framework for merchandise planning and control. Read the Trendwatch titled, "Merchandise Planning: Taking the Holiday Pulse," to learn more about critical merchandise planning for most retailers during the fourth quarter.

The plan is normally established to conform to two distinct selling seasons: (1) spring–summer (February to July) and (2) fall–winter (August to January). Using these months allows the store the opportunity for clearance sales at the end of the summer and holiday seasons before making plans for additional purchases.

Purposes of the Plan

The merchandise plan regulates inventory levels in accordance with planned financial objectives. As with all merchandising activities, the essential goal of the merchandise plan is to minimize the use of capital and maximize profits. Key purposes of the merchandise plan are:

• To provide an estimate of the amount of capital required to be invested in inventory for a specific period.

• To provide an estimate of planned sales for the period that translates into cash-flow estimates for store management and accounting personnel.

If used successfully to plan and control inventories, the following outcomes should result from developing a merchandise plan:

• *Increased Turnover*. Merchandise that customers want should be more readily available at times when they want to make purchases.
• *Reduced Amount of Markdowns*. By planning merchandise purchases in relation to planned sales and stock levels, there is less likelihood of being in an overbought position and having to make markdowns.
• *Improved Ability to Maintain Markups*. Because fewer markdowns may have to be taken, an improved ability to maintain markups should result.
• *Maximized Profits*. A balanced assortment of merchandise leads to more sales and an increase in profits because items will not remain in stock too long and become shopworn and difficult to sell. Greater profits can result because the buyer is informed about both fast-selling items that should be reordered quickly and slow-selling items that should be dropped.
• *Minimized Inventory Investment*. A six-month merchandise plan helps determine how much money should be spent on merchandise. Ideally, a buyer makes the smallest investment possible in goods that will satisfy customer demands and sell well enough to build store profits.

Components of the Plan

Most retailers have different forms for developing a six-month merchandise plan, but generally they all contain the following components:

• *Initial Markup for the Period*. Goals will be indicated as to the desired markup that should be placed on merchandise when it enters the store.
• *Planned Net Sales*. Planned net sales represent gross sales minus customer returns and allowances. Last year's sales usually provide the basis for determining planned sales for the current year; however, you should also examine sales figures from previous years. Usually, you will be able to detect an upward or downward trend in sales, but what happens this year will depend on whether conditions are similar to past conditions.
• *Planned Beginning of Month Inventory*. There must be adequate stock to achieve planned sales. The relationship between the amount of stock in the store and planned sales is most frequently calculated using the stock-to-sales ratio method of stock planning.

• *Planned End of Month Inventory.* Planned **EOM inventory** represents the retail value of the ending inventory for each period. In merchandise plans, the **BOM inventory**, beginning inventory for a period (usually a month), must be the value of the ending inventory (EOM) for the preceding period.

• *Planned Reductions.* **Reductions** (the total of planned markdowns, shortages, and employee discounts) must also be entered into the merchandise plan. Dollar amounts for these items can be calculated using planned percentage-of-sales figures that are usually found in the seasonal data on the six-month merchandise plan.

• *Planned Purchases at Retail.* Planned purchases at retail represent the retail value of merchandise that is to be purchased during a given period. Planned purchases at retail are calculated by using the following formula:

Planned Purchases at Retail = Planned Sales + Planned Reductions
+ Planned EOM − Planned BOM

• *Planned Purchases at Cost.* Planned purchases at cost represent the amount of money that the buyer expects to spend on merchandise purchases during a given period. Planned purchases at cost are calculated using the following formula:

Planned Purchases at Cost = Planned Purchases at Retail × (100% − Initial Markup %)

With the exception of planned purchases at cost, all amounts on the six-month merchandise plan are entered as retail values. Examine Figure 8.2 to view a merchandise plan based on these components. As you can see, each of these components is further subdivided into the following four categories:

• *Last Year (Actual)*–represents the actual amount last year for the month. This information would be found on the previous six-month merchandise plan from actual figures recorded.

• *Plan (This Year)*–represents the amount planned for the current year.

• *Revised (This Year)*–represents any revisions made in the current plan owing to unanticipated events. After you make your plans, you will need to check them periodically to determine if they are progressing as you thought they would. Sometimes everything goes as expected, but at other times, you have to adjust your plans. When a store or department does not meet its planned sales or exceeds its planned sales for a given month, adjustments will be required in future months.

Dept Name_____ Dept No._____

	PLAN (This Year)	ACTUAL (Last Year)
Workroom cost		
Cash discount %		
Season stock turnover		
Shortage %		
Average stock		
Markdown %		

SIX MONTH MERCHANDISING PLAN

SPRING 20___ FALL 20___		FEB AUG	MAR SEP	APR OCT	MAY NOV	JUNE DEC	JULY JAN	SEASON TOTAL
SALES $	Last Year							
	Plan							
	% of Increase							
	Revised							
	Actual							
RETAIL STOCK (BOM)	Last Year							
	Plan							
	Revised							
	Actual							
RETAIL STOCK (EOM)	Last Year							
	Plan							
	Revised							
	Actual							
REDUCTIONS $	Last Year							
	Plan							
	Revised							
	Actual							
PURCHASES AT RETAIL	Last Year							
	Plan							
	Revised							
	Actual							
PURCHASES AT COST	Last Year							
	Plan							
	Revised							
	Actual							

Comments
_____
_____

Merchandise Manager _____ Buyer _____
Controller_____

Figure 8.2 Six-month merchandising plans involve making predictions about the components on this form.

• *Actual (This Year)*—represents the actual sales for the month. At the end of each month, you must record actual figures on the six-month merchandise plan form. A comparison of actual (this year) with planned (this year) sales determines whether you reached your goals.

The six-month merchandise plan is one of the buyer's most important planning and control tools. Because it shows the amount you should spend on new inventory purchases to achieve planned sales, the merchandise plan keeps you from overspending and not achieving planned profit for the store or department.

For a small store, the plan may be prepared for the entire store; however, for larger stores, the plan may be prepared on a departmental or product classification basis. Later, these individual plans are incorporated into a plan at the divisional or storewide level. Read the Snapshot titled, "RMSA: Retail Merchandising Service Automation," to learn more about one firm that assists independent retailers in preparing, implementing, and monitoring merchandise plans.

PREPARATION OF A SIX-MONTH MERCHANDISE PLAN

In this section, you will be taken step-by-step through the process of preparing a six-month merchandise plan. Calculations for each component of the plan are described in detail.

Planned Sales

The first and most important part of the six-month merchandise plan is forecasting sales. All other merchandising decisions are planned in relation to sales or stated as a percentage of sales. Therefore, if the sales forecast is inaccurate, all the other parts of the plan will be in error, possibly causing disastrous results for the retailer.

From the previous year's merchandise plan, the following sales data were obtained:

Sales	February	March	April	May	June	July	Totals
Last Year Planned	$10,000	$12,000	$23,000	$18,000	$12,000	$12,000	$87,000
Revised							
Actual							

First, you will need to calculate last year's monthly sales figures as a percentage of last year's total sales. For each month, the calculations would be:

	Sales Last Year		Total Sales Last Year		% of Sales Last Year
February	= $10,000	/	$87,000	=	11.5%
March	= $12,000	/	$87,000	=	13.8%
April	= $23,000	/	$87,000	=	26.4%
May	= $18,000	/	$87,000	=	20.7%
June	= $12,000	/	$87,000	=	13.8%
July	= $12,000	/	$87,000	=	13.8%

You may find that over several years, these percentage figures have remained stable. Therefore, you may forecast that a similar percentage of sales would occur each month of the current year. However, as previously explained, there may be both internal and external factors that would cause changes. For example, the Easter holiday occurs in either April or March, or your store may be planning on changes in marketing strategies during a specific month that did not occur in the past. In addition, most retailers track the busiest shopping days, particularly during holiday seasons. If you determine such factors will have an impact on the percentage of sales occurring each month, you must adjust the planned sales percentage for each month.

Let's assume that you detected no major changes during the current season. In addition, a sales analysis of previous years indicates that the percentage of total sales occurring during each month has remained fairly constant. Based on that information, you would plan for the following percent of sales to occur each month:

February	11.5%
March	13.8%
April	26.4%
May	20.7%
June	13.8%
July	13.8%

Next, you would need to determine the total planned sales volume for the season. Using forecasting techniques described in Chapter 7, a 10 percent increase in sales is planned for the period. In some firms, top management may determine planned increases or decreases in planned sales and present them to you as a goal for your department or division.

Referring to last year's sales for the same period, you determine that total sales were $87,000. Therefore, planned sales for the current period would be $95,700 (10 percent of $87,000 = $8,700; the planned increase in sales that would be added to last year's sales; thus, $8,700 + $87,000 = $95,700).

Now, you must plan sales for each month of the current period. Using the planned percentage of total sales and the planned total sales figure ($95,700), you would make the following calculations:

	Planned % of Total Sales		Planned Total Sales		Planned Monthly Sales
February	11.5%	×	$95,700	=	$11,005
March	13.8%	×	$95,700	=	$13,207
April	26.4%	×	$95,700	=	$25,265
May	20.7%	×	$95,700	=	$19,810
June	13.8%	×	$95,700	=	$13,207
July	13.8%	×	$95,700	=	$13,206

These figures would then be entered on the six-month merchandise plan (on the Planned line) as follows:

Sales	February	March	April	May	June	July	Totals
Last Year	$10,000	$12,000	$23,000	$18,000	$12,000	$12,000	$87,000
Planned	**$11,005**	**$13,207**	**$25,265**	**$19,810**	**$13,207**	**$13,206**	**$95,700**
Revised							
Actual							

As you have learned, there is space to record any revisions in the plan as well as actual sales for the month. Keeping accurate records will improve your planning efforts in the future.

Planned BOM Inventory

Your next step in preparing a six-month merchandise plan is to determine the amount of stock required to meet the planned sales. You want to have sufficient stock on hand to meet customer demand. There must be an adequate opening merchandise assortment on hand which is in sufficient quantity to meet anticipated customer demand.

The stock-to-sales method of inventory planning requires that the buyer define a relationship between planned BOM inventory for a given month and the planned sales for that month. Using the stock-to-sales ratio method for planning stock levels, planned BOM inventory can be calculated using the following formula:

Planned BOM Inventory = Planned Sales × Stock-to-Sales Ratio

From trade sources and an examination of past years' sales and inventory data, you calculate the following stock-to-sales ratios:

February	3.1
March	2.8
April	2.0
May	1.8
June	1.8
July	1.8

Using these stock-to-sales ratios and planned sales for the current year, which were previously calculated, planned BOM inventory for each month can be calculated as follows:

	Stock-to-Sales Ratio		Planned Monthly Sales		Planned Monthly BOM Inventory
February	3.1	×	$11,005	=	$34,116
March	2.8	×	$13,207	=	$36,980
April	2.0	×	$25,265	=	$50,530
May	1.8	×	$19,810	=	$35,658
June	1.8	×	$13,207	=	$23,773
July	1.8	×	$13,206	=	$23,773

These figures would then be entered on the six-month merchandise plan (on the Planned line) as follows:

BOM	February	March	April	May	June	July	Totals
Last Year	$31,000	$33,600	$46,000	$32,400	$21,600	$21,600	$186,200
Planned	$34,116	$36,980	$50,530	$35,658	$23,773	$23,773	$204,830
Revised							
Actual							

Planned EOM Inventory

The EOM stock for any month is simply the planned BOM stock for the following month. On the sample six-month merchandise plan, planned EOM inventory levels would be as follows:

February EOM = $36,980 (March BOM)
March EOM   = $50,530 (April BOM)
April EOM   = $35,658 (May BOM)
May EOM   = $23,773 (June BOM)
June EOM   = $23,773 (July BOM)
July EOM   = –

Because the BOM stock for August is unknown, you do not know the planned EOM for July. Therefore, you must plan an estimated EOM stock for the period. For our sample six-month merchandise plan, the EOM for the period is estimated to be $21,000.

These figures would then be entered on the six-month merchandise plan (on the Planned line) as follows:

EOM	February	March	April	May	June	July	Totals
Last Year	$33,600	$46,000	$32,400	$21,600	$21,600	$20,000	$175,200
Planned	**$36,980**	**$50,530**	**$35,658**	**$23,773**	**$23,773**	**$21,000**	**$191,714**
Revised							
Actual							

Planned Reductions

The next component of the six-month merchandise plan to be planned is reductions. There are several types of reductions: markdowns, employee discounts, and shrinkage, usually inventory shortages from shoplifting or employee theft. Estimates for these reductions are based on past experience and are presented as a percent of planned sales on the six-month merchandise plan. For the sample plan that you are completing, the planned reductions are:

Planned Markdown Percentage   = 6.8%
Planned Shortage Percentage   = 2.1%
Planned Employee Discount Percentage = 1.1%

Therefore, total reductions are planned to be 10 percent of sales. Total reductions in dollars can be calculated by multiplying total planned sales by the reduction percent. Total reductions equal $9,570 ($95,700 × 10%).

Based on past records, you have determined that reductions each month have occurred according to the following breakdown:

February	11.5%
March	7.0%
April	15.0%
May	18.5%
June	22.1%
July	25.9%

Again, internal or external conditions affecting the current year may cause you to make adjustments in these figures. You can calculate planned reductions for each month as follows:

	% Reductions Planned for the Month		Total Planned Reductions		Planned Monthly Reductions
February	11.5%	×	$9,570	=	$1,100
March	7.0%	×	$9,570	=	$670
April	15.0%	×	$9,570	=	$1,436
May	18.5%	×	$9,570	=	$1,770
June	22.1%	×	$9,570	=	$2,115
July	25.9%	×	$9,570	=	$2,479

These figures would then be entered on the six-month merchandise plan (on the Planned line) as follows:

Reductions	February	March	April	May	June	July	Totals
Last Year	$1,001	$609	$1,305	$1,609	$1,923	$2,253	$8,700
Planned	**$1,100**	**$670**	**$1,436**	**$1,770**	**$2,115**	**$2,479**	**$9,570**
Revised							
Actual							

Planned Purchases at Retail

Planned purchases each month should be adequate to implement the six-month merchandise plan. On the merchandise plan, purchases must be planned at retail first because all the other figures are based on retail. The following formula is used to calculate planned purchases at retail:

Planned Purchases = Planned Sales + Planned EOM + Planned Reductions − Planned BOM

Using this formula and the data that you have already entered on the merchandise plan, planned purchases at retail can be calculated as follows:

	Planned Sales		Planned EOM		Planned Reductions		Planned BOM at Retail		Planned Purchases
Feb	$11,005	+	$36,980	+	$1,100	−	$34,116	=	$14,969
Mar	$13,207	+	$50,530	+	$670	−	$36,980	=	$27,427
April	$25,265	+	$35,658	+	$1,436	−	$50,530	=	$11,829
May	$19,810	+	$23,773	+	$1,770	−	$35,658	=	$9,695
June	$13,207	+	$23,773	+	$2,115	−	$23,773	=	$15,322
July	$13,206	+	$21,000	+	$2,479	−	$23,773	=	$12,912

These figures would then be entered on the six-month merchandise plan (on the Planned line) as follows:

Planned Purchases at Retail	February	March	April	May	June	July	Totals
Last Year	$13,209	$25,705	$11,009	$9,123	$14,253	$19,100	$92,399
Planned	**$14,969**	**$27,427**	**$11,829**	**$9,695**	**$15,322**	**$12,912**	**$92,154**
Revised							
Actual							

Planned Purchases at Cost

From the seasonal data, initial markup for the period is planned at 46.3 percent. Using the formula that follows, planned purchases at cost can be calculated.

Planned Purchases at Cost = (100% − Initial Markup %) × Planned Purchases at Retail

The cost of planned purchases for each month can be calculated as follows:

	(100% − Initial Markup %)		Planned Purchases at Retail		Planned Purchases at Cost
February	(100% − .463)	×	$14,969	=	$ 8,038
March	(100% − .463)	×	$27,427	=	$14,728
April	(100% − .463)	×	$11,829	=	$ 6,352
May	(100% − .463)	×	$ 9,695	=	$ 5,206
June	(100% − .463)	×	$15,322	=	$ 8,228
July	(100% − .463)	×	$12,912	=	$ 6,934

These figures would then be entered on the six-month merchandise plan (on the Planned line) as follows:

Planned Puchases at Cost	February	March	April	May	June	July	Totals
Last Year	$7,093	$13,803	$5,912	$4,899	$7,654	$10,257	$49,618
Planned	**$8,038**	**$14,728**	**$6,352**	**$5,206**	**$8,228**	**$6,934**	**$49,486**
Revised							
Actual							

The planned purchases at cost let buyers know how much money they will have to spend on merchandise for the season as well as individual months. Examine Figure 8.3 to view the entire six-month merchandise plan that you have just prepared.

Each month you must also enter actual figures to assist with future planning. Actual monthly figures can also aid you in making revisions to your plan if they are necessary. If sales are greater than planned, you will need to make larger purchases for the rest of the season to maintain the inventory level shown in the merchandise plan. However, if sales are less than planned, you must decrease the amount of purchases.

BASIC STOCK PLANNING

Some classifications of merchandise do not vary much from season to season in appearance, construction, or price. Such goods are known as basic merchandise. For basic merchandise, planned purchases can be calculated *without* using a six-month merchandise plan. A **basic**

Dept Name _____ Dept No. _____

		PLAN (This Year)	ACTUAL (Last Year)
SIX-MONTH MERCHANDISING PLAN	Workroom cost		
	Cash discount %		
	Season stock turnover		
	Shortage %		
	Average stock		
	Markdown %		

SPRING 20 ____		FEB	MAR	APR	MAY	JUNE	JULY	SEASON
FALL 20 ____		AUG	SEP	OCT	NOV	DEC	JAN	TOTAL
SALES $	Last Year	10,000	12,000	23,000	18,000	12,000	12,000	$87,000
	Plan	11,005	13,207	25,265	19,810	13,207	13,206	$95,700
	% of Increase							
	Revised							
	Actual							
RETAIL STOCK (BOM)	Last Year	31,000	33,600	46,000	32,400	21,600	21,600	$186,200
	Plan	34,116	36,980	50,530	35,658	23,773	23,773	$204,830
	Revised							
	Actual							
RETAIL STOCK (EOM)	Last Year	33,600	46,000	32,400	21,600	21,600	20,000	$175,200
	Plan	36,980	50,530	35,658	23,773	23,773	21,000	$191,714
	Revised							
	Actual							
REDUCTIONS $	Last Year	1,001	609	1,305	1,609	1,923	2,253	$8,700
	Plan	1,100	670	1,436	1,770	2,115	2,479	$9,570
	Revised							
	Actual							
PURCHASES AT RETAIL	Last Year	13,209	25,705	11,009	9,123	14,253	19,100	$92,399
	Plan	14,969	27,424	11,829	9,695	15,322	12,912	$92,154
	Revised							
	Actual							
PURCHASES AT COST	Last Year	7,093	13,803	5,912	4,899	7,654	10,257	$49,618
	Plan	8,038	14,728	6,352	5,206	8,228	6,934	$49,486
	Revised							
	Actual							

Comments

_____

Merchandise Manager _____ Buyer _____
Controller _____

Figure 8.3   A completed six-month merchandising plan.

stock plan is a tool many retailers use in planning purchases of basic merchandise. The purpose of the plan is to determine the amount of merchandise a retailer must have on hand or on order to have a sufficient amount of merchandise available during the period. To make these calculations, you must gather information about the average sales volume each week, reorder period, delivery period, and reserve stock levels.

The following formula is used to calculate the maximum number of any basic merchandise item that should be on hand and on order at any given point:

Maximum = Sales Volume per Week (Reorder Period + Delivery Period) + Reserve

Let's examine each of the elements of this formula.

Sales Volume per Week. You must first determine the weekly unit sales of each item by analyzing past sales records.

Reorder Period. The *reorder period* is the amount of time between orders for merchandise. Lengthy periods between reorder periods require ordering larger quantities of merchandise or keeping goods in storage.

Delivery Period. The *delivery period* is the time between when the order is placed and the time the merchandise is on the sales floor. Enough merchandise must be available in the store to cover the time it takes the vendor to deliver merchandise once it has been ordered.

Reserve. The *reserve* is the amount of merchandise necessary to meet unanticipated sales. Out-of-stock positions can cause your store to lose sales and profits; therefore, many buyers purchase additional merchandise to cover unanticipated sales to prevent customers from being lost to the competition.

Maximum. The *maximum* is the amount of merchandise that must be on hand or on order at any reordering point. The maximum must be sufficient to provide merchandise for sale while goods are being delivered. The stock on hand never reaches the maximum because sales will occur during the time it takes for the new order to be received.

Minimum. The *minimum* is the point at which reorders should be placed. The formula for determining minimum is as follows:

Minimum = Sales Volume per Week × Delivery Period + Reserve

In using the basic stock plan, buyers will develop a basic stock list. The *basic stock list* provides information such as description of the item, the retail price, the cost to the store, the maximum, the rate of sale, and the minimum reorder quantity.

Table 8.1: Missy Spring Merchandising Plans

Description	Act. Sales	Plan Sales	% of Dept/St.	% Over Last Yr.	Plan BOM 2008	Planned Month Purchases	% Fresh	Stock to Sales Ratio
Dresses								
February	$56.4	$64.0	11.4%	13%	$241.5	$121.4	42%	3.8
March	$101.9	$106.2	18.9%	4%	$287.5	$117.1	41%	2.7
April	$105.1	$120.7	21.4%	15%	$287.5	$93.8	38%	2.4
May	$82.9	$90.0	16.0%	9%	$245.0	$98.7	41%	2.7
June	$88.7	$101.2	18.0%	14%	$238.1	$97.1	46%	2.4
July	$68.2	$80.7	14.3%	18%	$209.3	$106.5	51%	2.6
August	$61.3	$69.9	12.4%	14%	$207.0			3.0
Dresses–Spring Season	$503.2	$562.8	26.6%	12%	$1,715.9	$634.6	43%	2.7

Plan Turn = 2.30

					Mark Downs				
Description	Season 2007 Act. EOM	Season 2008 Plan EOM	% of Store	% Over Last Yr.	Season 2007	Season 2008	% of Store	% Over Last Yr.	Plan % of Sales
Dresses									
February	$113.8	$287.5	24.4%	153%	$11.9	$11.4	19.6%	–5%	17.7%
March	$173.2	$287.5	28.3%	66%	$4.4	$10.9	23.1%	148%	10.3%
April	$241.9	$245.0	27.7%	1%	$7.1	$15.6	31.3%	120%	13.0%
May	$203.5	$238.1	27.8%	17%	$11.8	$15.6	26.5%	32%	17.3%
June	$151.7	$209.3	25.8%	38%	$31.6	$24.7	22.4%	–22%	24.4%
July	$112.0	$207.0	22.9%	85%	$38.1	$28.1	22.5%	–26%	34.8%
August									
Dresses–Spring Sesaon	$996.1	$1,474.4	26.1%	48%	$104.9	$106.3	23.7%	1%	18.9%

This form illustrates a store's merchandising plans for misses dresses during a six-month period.

OPEN-TO-BUY PLANNING

In the six-month merchandise plan (Table 8.1), you established the dollar amount of purchases that were to be made each month. However, not all the required monthly stock is purchased at the beginning of the month.

Definition of Open-to-Buy

Purchase decisions are distributed throughout the month in order to take advantage of new merchandise lines, to reorder fast-selling merchandise, or to acquire off-price merchandise to use in promotional sales. In addition, you may have outstanding orders, commitments from vendors that have not been delivered. The value of these outstanding orders will reduce the planned purchases for the month. As a result, you must be able to calculate, on a specific date during the month, the amount of merchandise to be purchased during the remainder of the month. The remaining purchases are defined as open-to-buy. *Open-to-buy* is the amount the buyer has left to spend for a period, and it is reduced each time a purchase is made.

Open-to-Buy Calculations

Although the open-to-buy figures are not listed on the six-month merchandise plan, they are calculated using the planned purchases at cost.

PROBLEM ILLUSTRATION

Your department has the following information:

Planned Sales	$22,000
Planned BOM	$33,000
Planned Reductions	$2,000
Planned EOM	$35,000
Stock on Order at Cost	$4,000
Initial Markup Percent	44.6%

Your first step is to calculate planned purchases at retail using the formula previously described:

Planned Purchases = Planned Sales + Planned EOM + Planned Reductions − Planned BOM

Thus:

$22,000 + $35,000 + $2,000 − $33,000 = $26,000

Then convert planned purchases at retail to planned purchases at cost as follows:

Planned Purchases at Cost = (100% − Initial Markup %) × Planned Purchases at Retail

Planned Purchases at Cost = (100% − 44.6%) × $26,000

Planned Purchases at Cost = $14,404

Next, determine open-to-buy:

Open-to-Buy = Planned Purchases − Merchandise on Order

Open-to-Buy = $14,404 − $4,000

Open-to-Buy = $10,404

Therefore, for the month given, the buyer would still have $10,404 to spend during the month.

Benefits and Uses of Open-to-Buy

The open-to-buy concept has two main goals. First, the buyer is assured that a specified relationship between stock on hand and planned sales is maintained. Second, buyers are able to determine how to adjust merchandise purchases to reflect changes in sales, reductions, and purchases. Open-to-buy allows you to determine if additional purchases during a period conform with the planned purchases for the period.

If effectively used, open-to-buy allows the buyer to:

• Limit overbuying and underbuying;
• prevent loss of sales due to inadequate amount of stock;
• maintain purchases within budgeted limits;
• reduce markdowns;
• increase sales;

- improve stock turnover; and
- hold back purchase dollars to reorder fast-selling merchandise, to take advantage of off-price merchandise, or to sample new merchandise.

Open-to-buy can also be used to determine problem areas. The most common problem is the buyer being in an overbought position. For example, if the open-to-buy in dollars is less than what you need to offer an adequate assortment, you are ***overbought*** for that period. Being overbought usually results because you made inaccurate sales forecasts, which caused your planned purchases to be incorrect, or you failed to recognize sales or fashion trends and had the wrong merchandise in stock.

Being overbought usually increases markdowns, decreases maintained markups, decreases stock turnover, and decreases profit. If you find yourself in an overbought position, you may want to implement any of the following strategies:

- Analyze ways to increase sales through better training of salespeople, additional sales promotions, or moving merchandise on the sales floor.
- Increase the amount of markdowns for the period, which should increase sales; however, changes in planned reductions will also cause other components of the merchandise plan to change.
- Cancel outstanding orders, if possible. However, you must realize that sometimes orders cannot be cancelled because of the sales contract the buyer has signed. Order cancellations also cause hard feelings to develop between the vendor and your store.
- A measure of last resort may be to increase purchases because the original plan has proven to be inaccurate. New merchandise may be needed to generate sales.

SUMMARY POINTS

- Buyers are responsible for providing the right merchandise, at the right place, at the right time, in the right quantities, and at the right price. To accomplish these goals, buyers must prepare merchandise plans (budgets) and assortment plans.
- Merchandise plans are developed using top-down planning, bottom-up planning, or a combination of both. Typically, merchandise plans are developed for a six-month period.

• Sales forecasting and stock planning are the key elements of merchandise plans. Sales forecasting involves examining past store records and current internal and external factors affecting sales. All other merchandising decisions are planned in relation to sales; therefore, if a sales forecast is in error, other decisions will be in error, too.

• Merchandise in stock must meet customer demand by offering customers variety. Yet stock levels must be small enough to ensure a reasonable return on the store's investment.

• The six-month merchandise plan is the tool used by buyers that translates profit objectives into a framework for merchandise planning and control.

• Successful merchandise planning should result in increased turnover, reduced amount of markdowns, improved ability to maintain markups, maximized profits, and a minimum investment in inventory.

• Components of the six-month merchandise plan include sales, BOM inventory, EOM inventory, reductions, purchases at retail, and purchases at cost. The plan shows the buyer how much should be spent on new inventory purchases to achieve planned sales.

• Basic merchandise planning can be accomplished by developing a basic stock plan, which is used to determine the maximum amount of merchandise that must be on hand or on order at any reordering point.

• Buyers use merchandise plans and the amount of merchandise on order to determine open-to-buy, which is the amount of money the buyer has left to spend for a period and is reduced each time a purchase is made.

REVIEW ACTIVITIES

Developing Your Retail Buying Vocabulary

Consult the Glossary if you did not add the following terms to your vocabulary.

Basic stock list	Minimum
Basic stock plan	Open-to-buy
BOM inventory	Overbought
Bottom-up planning	Reductions
Delivery period	Reorder period
EOM inventory	Reserve
Maximum	Six-month merchandise plan
Merchandise plan	Top-down planning

Understanding What You Read

1. What is the major benefit of top-down planning?
2. Why do many retailers use a combination of top-down and bottom-up planning?
3. List several internal and external factors that should be considered along with past sales records when forecasting sales.
4. On what will the accuracy of sales forecasts depend?
5. How will holidays affect merchandise planning from one year to the next?
6. For what two periods are six-month merchandise plans typically developed?
7. What is the purpose of "Revised (This Year)" on the six-month merchandise plan?
8. What is the first and most important calculation of the six-month merchandise plan?
9. How is planned EOM inventory on a six-month merchandise plan determined?
10. What are three types of reductions?
11. What is the drawback of lengthy periods between reorders of basic stock?
12. When would open-to-buy equal planned purchases at cost?
13. What would cause a buyer to be overbought?

Analyzing and Applying What You Read

1. Your store uses only top-down planning in developing merchandise plan goals. Outline arguments that you would use to convince top management to incorporate bottom-up planning in the process.
2. Your department is in an overbought position. What arguments could you use to make additional purchases?

Application Exercises

1. Prepare a six-month merchandise plan based on the information given for last year.
   a. First, plan BOM inventory using last year's stock-to-sales ratios.

	Last Year Monthly Sales	Last Year BOM Stock
February	$12,000	$25,000
March	$14,000	$30,000
April	$18,000	$38,000
May	$19,000	$40,000
June	$18,000	$39,000
July	$19,000	$41,000

b. Then, use last year's monthly stock-to-sales ratios to plan BOM inventory levels.

c. Now, plan monthly reductions for the period. Reductions are planned at 8 percent and will be distributed as follows:

February	10%
March	5%
April	5%
May	15%
June	30%
July	35%

d. Next, plan monthly EOM stock for each month. Ending inventory for the season is planned at $43,000.

e. Now, plan purchases at retail. Then, convert this figure to cost. The initial markup percentage is planned at 46.4 percent.

2. A small business places reorders every two weeks. Once orders are placed, four weeks are typically required for delivery. The weekly sales rate of an item is 30. Calculate the following:

a. Reserve.

b. Maximum.

c. Minimum.

3. Planned purchases at cost for the month of February are $21,000. Two purchase orders are outstanding. The first is for $550, and the second is for $2,150. What is the open-to-buy?

Spreadsheet Skills

1. Use a spreadsheet program to answer the questions presented in the Application Exercises above.

2. In *Making Buying Decisions: Using the Computer As a Tool*, complete problems related to the following concepts:

a. Merchandising Concept 8–2 (Calculate Planned Purchases).
b. Merchandising Concept 8–3 (Develop a Six-Month Buying Plan).
c. Merchandising Concept 11–1 (Calculate Open-to-Buy).

Internet Connection

1. Search the Internet for sales predictions related to the upcoming holiday season. How do these predictions compare with previous forecasts?
2. Search the Internet for recent retail sales by month. Calculate the percentage increase or decrease from month to month.

SNAPSHOT

RMSA: Retail Merchandising Service Automation

Retail Merchandising Service Automation (RMSA) provides sophisticated planning and management information services to independent retailers nationwide. The firm also develops and markets management information systems specifically designed for the retailing industry with the objective of solving problems, increasing the quality of merchandise inventory decisions, and improving the financial performance of its clients. RMSA has assembled a team of managers that has substantial expertise in merchandising, data processing, software development, and management training. These disciplines have been utilized to develop highly automated, integrated systems to assist retailers in planning, monitoring, and making decisions related to merchandise management. To assist in making these forecasts, RMSA has created a retail database that combines more than 50 years of historical merchandising data with the intelligence necessary to offer planning services customized to the individual store location, type, and size.

RMSA has developed a strong reputation in the retailing industry and is an acknowledged industry leader in fashion merchandise planning and management information services, providing services to thousands of clients throughout the United States. The types of retailers that comprise RMSA's client base include general merchandise stores, women's stores, menswear stores, shoe stores, and sporting goods stores, as well as other types of retailers, such as cycling, golf, gift, jewelry, and college bookstores.

In a nutshell, here's how RMSA helps its clients. The client retailer transmits pertinent information about previous business to RMSA. This includes information on sales, markdowns, receipts at cost and retail, transfers, retail inventory, and goods on order. The data are then processed with RMSA's proprietary software and combined with its industry database. The software captures and formulates the data, creating a forecast specifically for the client. The forecast is then reviewed by an RMSA account specialist who fine-tunes it and works with the client to make adjustments to ensure optimal results. The report identifies how much the client needs to buy and the proper flow of receiving merchandise. Armed with this information, the retail client can concentrate on selecting merchandise that truly meets customer needs. Each month, an RMSA merchandising analyst reviews the updated forecast with the client and helps the client create and implement a customized plan to purchase merchandise that will sell at optimal margins.

Typically, RMSA stores have maintained a higher margin compared with the industry. Using the system, retailers have been able to manage data more quickly and efficiently, allowing them to turn inventory at rates twice as fast as the industry average. One client states that "RMSA's services tell us how much to bring in, what's moving or not, and what our sell-through really is. As a result, we've lowered our average inventory and significantly lowered our cost of goods."

Buyers and merchandisers at independent retail stores may certainly want to consider RMSA or similar services before they begin merchandise planning. Small independents must constantly be alert to merchandising techniques that will allow them to successfully compete with larger retailers on the scene.

Based on information from www.rmsa.com

TRENDWATCH

Merchandise Planning: Taking the Holiday Pulse

Each year, one of the key components of merchandise planning for retailers is forecasting holiday sales during the fourth quarter; many retailers count on this quarter for as much as half the year's profit. Several factors may influence holiday shopping over the next few years, including energy prices, high debt, and slow income growth. Rising gasoline prices and heating fuel costs will also impact holiday shopping. Moreover, household debt is high and real disposable income growth has been slow, potentially leaving some consumers with less to spend. Consumer confidence, another factor that influences retail sales, has also declined in recent months. However, in past years, even with these problems, consumers have been fairly resilient. They have taken a number of economic challenges in stride and have continued purchasing during the holidays.

Each year buyers and forecasters grapple with predictions about what shoppers will do during this critical period. They usually are faced with how to interpret mixed signals from consumers and the economy. Many years, indicators are all over the board. Job growth could be good, but retail sales could only be so-so during September and October. Consumer confidence could be high, but has fallen slightly since the summer. The Dow Jones average could be diving and could shake consumer confidence. Often, buyers must build their merchandise plans based on murky conditions such as these.

Buyers can also examine consumer polls, and there are dozens during this time of the year. Often, even these poll results add to the uncertainty. For example, one year the International Mass Retail Association predicted spending would jump 7 percent from the previous year. At the same time, a *Money*/ABC poll reported that the majority of consumers would spend about the same as the previous year, but that a lack of confidence in the economy could cause them to scale back their purchasing. And, the National Retail Federation was predicting that consumer spending would follow the previous year's patterns.

Retail analyst firms, such as PriceWaterhouseCoopers, also issue predictions each year. Many retail buyers closely monitor forecasts from Visa because that company processes $17 out of every $100 spent in the United States by the firm's 500 million credit card holders.

With such mixed messages, buyers must make their own predictions about holiday sales. In fact, some stores may experience much higher or lower growth than predicted for the entire industry. Predictions for better merchandise planning can be based on local consumer surveys. A question such as "Approximately how much will your household spend in total on gifts this holiday season?" can be followed by "Is this more, less, or about the same amount of money your household spent in total gifts last holiday season?" Then by asking the amount of change, predictions can be made about local sales for the season. Similar questions can also be geared toward specific product categories.

Analyzing responses to questions such as these enables buyers to develop merchandise plans based on customer input. Along with national or regional predictions, buyers can then make better forecasts. Merchandise planning that results in overbuying results in heavy markdowns and promotions to move excess inventories. If planning results in underbuying, potential sales and profits will be lost. More than likely it will be too late to place reorders for that season.

Buyers must use as many tools as possible in taking the pulse of consumers before the holiday season begins. Their decisions will have a critical impact on the store's profitability for the year.

BASED ON:

Albright, Mark. (2007, January 17). Sagging sales likely to persist. *The St. Petersburg Times* (St. Petersburg, FL), 2D.

First holiday shopping forecasts arrive. (2006, October 19). *E-Marketer*, 1.

Holiday sales forecast is encouraging. (2006, October 2). *MMR*, 1–2.

Moin, David. (2005, July 27). Retail holiday forecast: modest sales increases amid consumer worries. *Women's Wear Daily*, 1.

Online to outpace overall holiday sales growth fourfold. (2006, December 26). *Information Week*, NA.

Chapter 9

Developing Assortment Plans

PERFORMANCE OBJECTIVES

Upon completion of this chapter, you should be able to:

- Identify the purposes of assortment planning.
- Describe how assortment planning differs by product categories.
- Describe how store policies affect assortment planning.
- Differentiate between stock breadth and stock depth.
- Explain how to determine when a product line should be expanded.
- Describe merchandise classification systems.
- Identify key merchandise selection factors used by consumers when purchasing merchandise.
- Explain how model stock plans are developed.
- Prepare an assortment plan.

The merchandising decisions related to product assortments that buyers make will have a strong impact on whether the store projects the desired image and attracts consumers in the identified target market. In fact, assortment planning decisions will have a strong impact on the store's overall performance.

Because no one retailer can provide all the product choices that are available in the marketplace to its customers, buyers must make decisions about which items to carry. In addition, most products will be available in a wide selection of options such as models, colors, and styles. Buyers will have to make those choices when deciding what to offer their customers. Merchandise selection should not be left to chance; it requires a careful analysis of (1) your store's goals and objectives, (2) types of products offered, (3) past sales records, (4) target market, and (5) other internal and external factors likely to affect sales.

In the previous chapter, you learned how a merchandise buying plan was developed. This dollar plan must be translated into a specific assortment plan of merchandise. In this chapter, you will learn how merchandise assortments are planned. Factors affecting merchandise assortments will be examined, and merchandise classification systems will be described.

PLANNING MERCHANDISE ASSORTMENTS

Buyers want to have enough products to meet customer demand without having to take markdowns due to having excess inventory. Maintaining such a balanced inventory requires skill and experience and takes considerable planning. As a buyer, you must prepare a detailed assortment plan for each item that you will be purchasing. You must also work within the framework established by your merchandise plan because quantity purchases for all items of merchandise must not exceed your dollar plan. Comprehensive and detailed assortment plans will also provide you with a merchandising control tool that can be used with the buying plan to help calculate your open-to-buy.

Assortment planning involves determining the specific quantities and characteristics of each product that you will be purchasing in relation to specific factors such as brands, colors, sizes, and materials. Figure 9.1 illustrates assortment planning for men's sports coats. You must develop an assortment plan that best matches the needs of your customers without having an excess amount of inventory in stock.

Figure 9.1   Assortment plans involve purchasing products of different brands, colors, sizes, and materials.

Assortment plans must be developed for all types of merchandise. For example, men's shirts can be purchased in many colors, sizes, sleeve lengths, materials, and styles.

The goal of assortment planning is to maintain a balanced assortment of merchandise that will meet the needs of as many customers as possible; therefore, an understanding of the various types of customers served by your store or department is essential to merchandise planning. Reliance on past sales records alone will be impractical for developing assortment plans for fashion merchandise because trends are volatile and change quickly. Changing consumer interests and buying habits must be analyzed using trade papers, trade association information, reporting services, and consultations with fashion coordinators and manufacturers.

Assortment planning also forces you to make plans based on the floor or shelf space available for the merchandise. In most instances, you will not have the space to carry the entire assortment of every product available. For example, supermarkets used to carry only Coke, Pepsi, and several other flavors of soft drinks. Today, however, each of these brands is available in sugar-free and caffeine-free varieties. In addition, they are available in an assortment of many different sizes and containers. Most grocery store managers are not able to offer the entire assortment of all soft drinks available on the market.

Continuously increasing the number of items in a product assortment presents a major problem to hardline retailers and supermarkets. Rarely will the product category be given more floor or shelf space when new varieties of the product are introduced; therefore, smaller quantities of each item must be purchased, which increases the likelihood of stockouts. In fashion stores, whatever sells best gets the space.

FACTORS AFFECTING MERCHANDISE ASSORTMENTS

When planning merchandise assortments, you will want to provide a variety of merchandise that is best suited to your customer's needs and is consistent with your store's image. As you develop the assortment plan, several key factors must be considered. They include (1) type of merchandise carried, (2) store policies, and (3) variety of merchandise available.

Type of Merchandise

The type of merchandise your store or department carries will affect your assortment planning. As you have learned, many methods are used to categorize merchandise, and each one requires the development of a different type of assortment plan.

Fashion or Basic Merchandise. Merchandise can be grouped into two broad classifications—fashion or basic. Fashion merchandise has high demand over a relatively short period of time, usually a season. Appeal for fashion merchandise is limited, which causes customer demand to end abruptly. To maximize sales, fashion buyers must quickly identify "best-sellers" in their merchandise assortments and place reorders immediately. As the selling season progresses, few or no reorders should be placed. Customer demand could end quickly, leaving the store in an overstocked position, and then even substantial markdowns may not move unwanted merchandise. Read the Snapshot titled, "Fashion Forecasting: Donegar Creative Services," to learn more about how buyers forecast new fashions.

Basic merchandise includes items that customers buy year in and year out and expect the store to have in stock at all times. For example, nails, hammers, stationery, men's white shirts, sheets, socks, and thousands of other items are considered basic merchandise items.

Buying basic merchandise is accomplished rather easily by checking past sales records and determining sales trends from previous years. Buyers know there is little danger of basic merchandise items not selling so there is less likelihood of overbuying merchandise that will not sell; but if these items remain in stock too long, they will become shopworn. With basic merchandise items, the size of your assortment will be limited by the selling space and storage space that you have available.

Some basic merchandise items may be classified as *seasonal basics*—products desired by customers only during certain times of the year. Customer demand, however, is fairly consistent from one year to the next. Examples of seasonal staples would include Easter egg dye, Christmas ornaments, kites, overcoats, and swimwear (Figure 9.2). Planning for seasonal basics requires that you keep precise records for the period in which these items sell and clearly identify the length of the selling period. Without planning, you will probably become overstocked and not sell out of inventory when the season is over.

Figure 9.2   The selling season for some products is so short that buyers may not be able to place a reorder.

Planning and control are essential for both fashion and basic merchandise. However, fashion goods must be monitored more frequently than basic goods. Fashion merchandise is usually surveyed on a weekly basis, whereas basic merchandise does not require such frequent attention.

Convenience or Specialty Products. Convenience goods are items that customers expect the store to have readily available. These items are usually inexpensive and may include products such as candy, hardware, health and beauty aids, and stationery. For convenience goods, a large assortment is usually not required because most customers will make a purchase regardless of which brand is available.

Specialty goods are products that customers will usually accept only in well-known brands. Examples of specialty goods could include silverware, china, appliances, designer apparel, and cosmetics. You will want to identify the brand loyalty of your customers and determine which brands are demanded by the majority of your customers as well as which brands are substitutable for others in the customer's mind.

Store Policies

Store management is responsible for establishing and specifying merchandising policies that best serve the interests and preferences of your store's target customers. These policies will serve as guidelines as you develop and maintain merchandise assortment plans and will affect the quality, exclusivity, and brands of your purchases.

Quality and Price Range. Purchasing decisions throughout the store should be implemented to create the desired store image and attract the target customers that have been identified by management. If quality is a strong appeal to your target customers, store policies should be developed to bring into the store only products constructed from the best materials available. If your customers are more price conscious, the highest-quality materials may not be as important as providing products in the desired price ranges.

Price range and quality usually are related to each other; however, many times there is no specific correlation between the two. Because your store cannot offer merchandise at all price ranges, you must determine which price ranges will be demanded by the majority of your customers.

Exclusivity. Many buyers will add products to their assortments that will not be available at other stores in their trading area because many customers prefer shopping at stores that have the reputation for carrying exclusives. You may negotiate with suppliers to be the only outlet for an item, or you can ensure exclusivity by carrying private brands. Obviously, exclusivity is desired by most stores because their image tends to be enhanced.

Brands. Store policies will also determine the mix of national and private brand names from which you can select. Many stores today, such as Dillard's, are offering national brand names almost exclusively; other stores, such as The Gap and The Limited, offer only private brand merchandise. In most product classifications, national brands dominate sales; and due to national advertising support, they are better known to customers. In fact, many customers are presold on nationally advertised merchandise before they enter the store. In addition, national brands represent quality to many customers.

On the other hand, private brands are usually more profitable to retailers because they have more control over merchandising decisions related to the products. Private brands are less expensive than national brands, and store loyalty is guaranteed because the competition will not have the product. Retailers, however, must create their own promotional plans for private brands.

Some supermarkets and drug stores are adding another brand classification to their assortments—generics. *Generics* are usually unbranded items in plain packages that receive secondary shelf locations and obtain little or no advertising support. The advantage for the customer is that generics are priced well below other brands; however, for many customers a question remains about the quality of these brands.

Variety of Merchandise Available

Within the constraints of a specified dollar investment in inventory, you must offer a variety of merchandise by carrying a number of different product lines. A *product line* is a broad category of products having similar characteristics and similar uses. Liz Claiborne and Ralph Lauren are both well-known apparel lines that offer many different items, all carrying the same label. Over the past years, there has been a rapid increase in the number of product lines as well as the number of products within existing product lines, making merchandise selection more complex. Rarely will any store be able to offer all the available choices within a product line, but in some instances, the manufacturer may require that your store carry a full product line if its merchandise is to be sold in your store.

In relation to the product lines carried, you must also make two decisions:

• What will be the stock breadth?
• What will be the stock depth?

Breadth. *Breadth* relates to the number of product lines carried or to the number of brands carried within a product classification. The breadth of your stock can usually be described as narrow, broad, or somewhere in between. For example, one store may offer four brands of men's dress shirts (broad breadth), whereas another store may offer only one brand (narrow breadth). Broad stock breadth allows the retailer to appeal to a larger market, but a narrow stock breadth usually allows the store to offer fewer brands in a larger number of styles, colors, sizes, and materials.

Depth. The number of choices offered customers within each brand or product classification is known as ***depth***. Many stores emphasize large stocks of a few product categories or brands. Stores find such assortment plans easier to stock, and customers are more likely to find what they want in the products offered for sale; however, customers are not offered a wide selection of brands, which may cause some of them to go to a competitor's store. Such an assortment would be described as a ***narrow and deep*** assortment plan.

On the other hand, stores may offer wide stock breadth and very little depth—a ***broad and shallow*** assortment plan. This would be the case for a men's clothing store that offers several brands of men's shirts, all of which are either blue or white.

A ***balanced assortment*** occurs when the breadth and depth meet the demands of your customers. Broad assortment plans are usually offered early in the season when new styles are being tested for customer acceptance. A broad and shallow assortment plan gives you the opportunity to experiment with several brands without making a heavy financial commitment. As customer demand becomes more clearly defined during the selling season, the assortment is likely to become narrow and deep.

Customers also vary in the amount of merchandise they want to examine before making a purchase. Some of them may know exactly what item they want, whereas other consumers may want to view many similar items before making a purchase. Some types of merchandise, such as apparel, require that the store carry a wide variety. Customers who are more fashion conscious require a wide choice.

Unbalanced assortment plans must be corrected as soon as possible to improve the overall performance of your store or department. You must ensure that an adequate product assortment is stocked and inventory shortages are minimized. While furthering the goals of your store, your assortment plan must satisfy customers. Most retailers have the tendency to stock too many similar brands and classifications. When one item is a substitute for another, there usually is no need to stock both.

To satisfy your customers and remain ahead of your competition, new products must be continuously added to your assortment while others are deleted. As you add items to the assortment, some goods will probably have to be eliminated from your stock because of limited floor space. Product lines will also need be eliminated before they become obsolete or outdated.

You can increase stock breadth by adding other product lines or additional items in an existing product line; however, new products may divert sales from your present assortment. *Cannibalization* occurs when potential sales of existing products are lost to new items. A careful evaluation of sales is required if product variety is increased to determine if total sales increased and if profits rose. For example, carrying five classifications of a product will not necessarily yield greater sales or profits than stocking three varieties. Carrying too many classifications would probably result in a shallow assortment offered for each product that could result in stockouts.

MERCHANDISE CLASSIFICATIONS

Every retail store is filled with a wide variety of merchandise in many different varieties. A merchandise classification system is needed to provide the means for better planning and control of this inventory.

Classifications and Subclassifications

Most retailers group the merchandise they carry into *classifications,* which refer to the particular kinds of goods in a store or department. For example, the shoe department could carry men's and women's shoes. Each of these broad product categories could be further divided into *subclassifications*. For example, men's shoes could be broken down into dress shoes, casual shoes, athletic shoes, work shoes, and boots; and subclassifications can also be developed for each of these categories. In the men's shoe category, athletic shoes could be classified as running shoes, court shoes, or cleated shoes. The type and size of your store or department, the image you want to project, your target market, and the financial resources available will all affect the number of classifications and subclassifications needed. For example, the variety and assortment of shoes would be much greater in a department that caters only to one specific group of customers (Table 9.1). Departments carrying

---

Table 9.1: Examples of Shoe Classifications

Men's Shoes	Women's Shoes
Dress Shoes	Evening Shoes
Oxfords	High Heels
Slip-ons	Medium Heels
	Low Heels
Casual Shoes	
Oxfords	Dress Shoes
Slip-ons	High Heels
	Medium Heels
Athletic Shoes	Low Heels
Running Shoes	
Court Shoes	Tailored Shoes
Cleated Shoes	High Heels
	Medium Heels
Work Shoes	Low Heels
Regular Toe	Wedge Heels
Steel Toe	
	Casual Shoes
Boots	Medium Heels
Dress Boots	Low Heels
Casual Boots	Wedge Heels
Western Boots	
Weather Boots	Dress Sandals
Work Boots	High Heels
	Medium Heels
	Casual Sandals
	Medium Heels
	Low Heels
	Fashion Flats
	Fashion Boots
	Weather Boots
	Duty Boots
	Athletic Shoes
	Slippers

---

shoes for men, women, and children would not be able to offer a complete assortment in each category. As each classification is planned, it must be large enough to develop a separate assortment plan; otherwise, it should be labeled a subclassification of a broader merchandise classification.

For merchandising and control purposes, each classification and subclassification is usually assigned an identification number. The

National Retail Federation has developed a ***Standard Classification of Merchandise*** coding system that classifies merchandise using four-digit codes.

Each classification code is divided into subclassifications. For example, 1000 is the code for adult female apparel, which is subdivided into other areas, such as:

1100	Cloth and All-Weather Coats
1200	Natural and Synthetic Leather and Fur Outerwear
1300	Women's, Misses, and Juniors' Dresses and Suits
1400	Formals
1500	Bridal, Maternity, and Uniforms
1600	Sportswear Tops

Each of these subclassifications can be further subdivided. For example, code 1600 (Sportswear Tops) can be broken down as:

1611	Skirts
1612	Blouses
1613	Cut and Sewn Knit Tops
1614	Sweaters

This coding system has not yet become universally accepted, but the concept has had great impact on the way retailers arrange inventory data and maintain inventory counts.

Closely associated with merchandise classifications is unit control, an inventory control system that tracks the movement of specific units of merchandise. Unit control information is essential to assortment planning. By using detailed inventory information, you can readily achieve a balance between sales and inventory in stock. Analysis of unit control records will also enable you to decide which items in the merchandise assortment to increase, eliminate, or reprice. Classifying merchandise and maintaining a unit control system also gives you the ability to make comparisons with other stores.

As a buyer, you should monitor the merchandise classification system used by your store to determine if it continues to meet your needs and the needs of your customers. Frequently ask yourself, "Does the classification system reflect the way in which my customers buy merchandise?"

Selection Factors

Each subclassification of merchandise can also be broken down by various *selection factors,* which are product characteristics most important to your customers as they make their purchasing decisions. Usually, a customer's purchase is based on a combination of characteristics such as brand, price, size, color, and material. Characteristics important to the purchase of a product will differ depending on the product type and the target market. For example, when buying a tennis racquet, a customer may be interested only in brand and price; however, when buying a suit, the same customer may be interested in brand, price, size, color, and material. In addition, there may be other important product characteristics to consider. For example, when purchasing a new suit, styling may be important to the customer: "Is it double breasted?" or "Is there a vented or nonvented back?"

You must identify the selection factors that are most important as customers purchase each item of merchandise that you stock. Your merchandise buying plan can also be used to determine the number of selection factors that can be represented in your assortment plan. For example, budgets may limit the number of brands you will be able to offer as well as the variety of each brand. Key selection factors that will be examined include (1) brand, (2) price, (3) size, (4) color, and (5) material.

Brand. You must determine if your customers exhibit brand loyalty when they purchase specific products. For example, do most of your customers ask to see lawn mowers or do they ask specifically to see John Deere mowers? If most of your customers are not brand loyal, you will not need to offer a broad selection of brands; you will be able to develop a wide assortment for one or two brands. In other words, you will be able to offer many more colors, sizes, models, or styles when only a few brands are offered. Stores carrying a large number of brands of each product type will probably have to limit the selection offered in each one.

Price. If one product classification has appeal to several income ranges, you will need to offer variations of that product at more than one price. Most retailers attempt to offer goods to customers in several different price ranges. The brands that you have selected to carry will also determine the price lines that would be available.

Some retailers offer several price lines at the beginning of a season and eliminate lines as the season progresses. Customers for higher-priced merchandise tend to buy in the early part of the season, and customers become less discriminating as the season advances. Customers at the end of the season are also more price conscious and are looking for lower-priced merchandise.

Size. For most products, size will also be an important selection factor. Size is not just important in apparel; size decisions must be made for home furnishings such as curtains and window treatments, appliances such as refrigerators, and even food packages. Product choices will confront you in almost all product categories. Table 9.2 illustrates size and price breakdowns for one brand of window blinds. Notice how the assortment is planned to include only the most popular sizes.

Size decisions for a product classification are based almost entirely on past records. Size requirements for customers remain fairly consistent from one period to another, and the size distribution of products sold during the past season is usually an indication of future demand. However, over a period of years, size requirements may change. For example, the average weight of women over age 30 has increased

Table 9.2: Assortment Plan by Selection Factors for Window Blinds				
Widths	**Lengths** **42"**	**50"**	**64"**	**72"**
17"	9.99			
23"	14.99		17.49	18.99
24"	14.99			17.99
25"			18.49	
26"	15.49		18.99	
27"			19.49	19.99
28"				19.99
29"	15.99		20.99	21.99
30"			21.49	22.99
31"	16.49		21.99	22.99
32"			21.99	23.99
33"			22.49	24.99
34"			22.99	25.49
35"	17.49	18.49	22.99	25.99
36"	18.99	19.99	25.49	27.99

five pounds over the past ten years, which has affected the sizes required for many customers. Read the Trendwatch titled, "All Shapes and Sizes: The Plus-Size Market Continues to Grow," to learn more about how the needs of this market are being met by retailers.

Color. You must also decide if color is an important consideration when your customers make purchases. You will need to decide which colors will be most important in the new season because you will be unable to offer all available colors. Nor can you simply buy colors that sold well in the past; fashion colors change from one season to the next. However, knowing past sales by color allows you to determine the degree to which your customers were fashion conscious when they accepted fashion colors in the past.

Before selecting colors, you will want to study current fashion trends, contact resident buying offices, and consult with your merchandise manager and the store's fashion coordinator. You must choose colors that complement the store's total "look" and that can be coordinated with other products offered for sale. You should never overstock fashion colors and neglect basic, more conventional colors. Even with fashion merchandise, basic colors usually account for a majority of sales.

Material. Knowledge of past sales will also help you in determining the material in which products should be stocked. For example, handbags may be offered in leather or vinyl. Shirts may be 100 percent cotton or a polyester/cotton blend. Luggage is also constructed of many different materials. In fact, almost every product is available in a number of different materials; however, if you are offering a wide selection of brands, sizes, and colors, you may not be able to offer customers a selection of material.

Let's examine how one retailer has implemented a merchandise assortment plan. One national men's clothing store chain offers three broad classifications of merchandise—suits, sport coats and slacks, and accessories (underwear, hosiery, shirts, and ties). Suits account for about 55 percent of its business and are available in three fashion categories in sizes ranging from 36S to 50XL. Fashion categories include (1) traditional American styling, (2) the International collection (nonvented coats with lower gorge and button stance), and (3) the British collection, featuring squared-off, pitched shoulders with either center or side vents.

Each of the three looks is available in two levels of quality/price—the top-of-the-line premier edition and the private store label. The top-of-the-line premier edition suits are 100 percent wool, fully lined, with piping, cigarette pocket, passport pocket, shirt-hugger bands with brace buttons, and pants lined to the knees. Prices start at $265. The premier label also includes another tier at $225—a suit with identical features except the fabric is a poly/wool blend.

The private store label starts at $195. These suits are primarily poly/wool blends, with piping, fully lined coats, and pants lined to the knee. Some basic suits in this category round out the line of suits available.

All retail stores must offer a balanced merchandise assortment that will meet the needs of the majority of their customers and must be based on a thorough understanding of customer needs. When customers come to the store and cannot find exactly the item they want in the right size, color, or material, they have made a frustrating and fruitless shopping trip. The store has also lost an almost-certain sale by not having a balanced merchandise assortment.

PREPARING AN ASSORTMENT PLAN

Because customers buy specific items of merchandise, dollar merchandise plans must be translated into some form of unit assortment plan. When you plan unit assortments, it is not a randomly selected collection of merchandise. Assortments of merchandise are balanced to customer needs while being bound by the financial constraints of the merchandise buying plan.

Assortment planning will result in establishing a ***model stock***, the desired assortment of stock broken down according to factors important to your target market, such as brand, price, material, color, and size. When developing model stocks you should be guided by current trends as well as by previous sales in order to purchase the goods that seem to best fit the needs of your store's customers. The objective of establishing a model stock is to maximize the sales and profits from your inventory investment.

Furthermore, a model stock does not have to be rigidly followed during the selling season. The plan should serve only as a guide because demand in regard to various selection factors will vary during the season. Adjustments are frequently made once the selling season is underway; reorders also change the nature of the model stock. Fashion buyers cannot be as specific as other buyers when developing model stocks. Dress buyers, for example, go to market knowing they can buy so many dozen dresses at the $39.99 range in assorted sizes. They do not determine other specifics, such as colors and styles, until they view the suppliers' offerings.

After you have determined the budget for merchandise purchases and examined store records, trends, and external factors affecting sales, you are ready to prepare an assortment plan that can be prepared using the following steps:

Step One. Decide what general classifications of products your store or department will carry. For example, you may decide to sell men's, women's, and children's apparel. You would then divide these classifications into subclassifications. For example, men's apparel could be broken down into suits, sport coats, blazers, neckwear, and so forth. By answering these questions, you will have determined the breadth of your product assortment. Examine Table 9.3 for a detailed list of other possible subclassifications for apparel.

Step Two. Determine the brands and price lines that you will carry for each of these subclassifications. Knowing characteristics of your target market is vital. You must know the brand preferences of your customers

---

Table 9.3: Examples of Apparel Merchandise Classifications

Menswear	Women's Wear	Children's Wear
Suits	Misses Dresses	Infant and Layette
Sport Coats	Junior Dresses	Toddler Boy
Blazers	Petite Dresses	Toddler Girl
Dress Slacks	After-Five Dresses	Girls Tops and Bottoms, 4–6x
Casual Slacks	Blouses	Girls Tops and Bottoms, 7–14
Top and Raincoats	Knit Tops	Girls Jeans
Dress Shirts	Novelty Tops	Boys Tops
Jackets	Sweaters	Boys Pants and Jeans
Sweaters	Skirts	Boys Suits and Sport Coats
Sport Shirts, Cut-n-Sewn	Pants	Activewear
Knit Shirts	Shorts	Outerwear
Neckwear	Blazers	Swimwear
Underwear, Hosiery	Swimwear	Sleepwear and Underwear
Belts	Activewear	Accessories
Swimwear	Suits	
Shorts	Coats	
	Jackets	
	Lingerie	
	Sleepwear	
	Handbags	

for each brand carried, and you will need to decide on the price lines that will be most appealing to your customers.

Step Three. Next, identify all the general characteristics of an item that customers may consider when purchasing it. For example, sweatshirts may be available in different colors, sizes, materials, and styles. Men's dress shirts have different colors, sizes, sleeve lengths, and collar styles and are made with different materials. The assortment plan that you develop should allow you to make purchases according to the most important of these characteristics in relation to the majority of your customers.

You cannot and do not need to plan for every possible customer; therefore, select major characteristics that present a balanced assortment. Your budget will also determine the breadth and depth of the assortment that you will be able to offer. For example, it would be possible to stock men's dress shirts from a size 14 neck to a size 27. However, the bulk of sales will be made at around size $15\frac{1}{2}$.

Step Four. Now you must decide on the proportion of one classification to another. In addition, you must determine the proportion in which each selection factor will be represented in your stock. For example, not all sizes or colors will have the same rate of sale. Nor will each color be equally popular in every size that is manufactured. For some selection factors, such as size, these proportions can be calculated by using past sales figures. For others, such as color, you will need to know how readily your customers accept new fashion colors as they are introduced.

Step Five. Calculate the specific number of units to purchase. Let's examine a problem that illustrates how an assortment plan is prepared.

PROBLEM ILLUSTRATION

Assume that your department is selling sweatshirts. From market research you realize that most of your customers for this product are not brand loyal. They will substitute one brand for another if you have the right size, color, and style for which they are looking. Past sales records indicate that Russell has been the most popular brand with your customers, and your merchandise buying plan indicates that you have $3,000 to spend on sweatshirts for the coming season. If you decide to stock only Russell sweatshirts costing $10 each, you will be able to purchase 300 sweatshirts. You must then calculate the specific unit breakdowns of these sweatshirts.

Russell has these sweatshirts in sizes from extra small to extra, extra large in 20 different colors. They also are available in 100 percent cotton or a polyester/cotton blend. Hooded and nonhooded sweatshirts are also available.

By examining past sales records, you determine that the size distribution of your customers has been:

Small	15%
Medium	20%
Large	45%
X-Large	20%

Basic colors of white and gray have been your best-sellers in the past, accounting for 20 percent and 35 percent of sales, respectively. Black has been a good seller too, with 15 percent of sales. You decide to supplement these three colors with two other colors (green and garnet) that are predicted to be very fashionable for the fall. Each of these will represent 15 percent of your assortment plan.

At this point, you decide to calculate the number of sweatshirts that you will purchase for each of the sizes and colors selected. These figures are presented below:

Size	Number	Color	Number
Small	45	White	9
		Gray	16
		Black	7
		Green	7
		Garnet	7
Medium	60	White	12
		Gray	21
		Black	9
		Green	9
		Garnet	9
Large	135	White	27
		Gray	47
		Black	20
		Green	20
		Garnet	20
X-Large	60	White	12
		Gray	21
		Black	9
		Green	9
		Garnet	9

Note, the number of sweatshirts purchased has been rounded. Forty-six small can be purchased, but only 134 large; however, the total order of 300 sweatshirts remains the same. After reviewing these figures, you decide to offer only hooded, 100 percent cotton sweatshirts. If you had broken the assortment down by offering both hooded and nonhooded, and all-cotton and cotton/polyester blends, you would not have been able to offer an adequate number of many of the sizes and colors. For example, if you had decided to offer each color in a breakdown of 80 percent nonhooded and 20 percent hooded, and 60 percent all cotton and 40 percent blends, you would be offering only one or two of some types, as the following chart illustrates:

Small
Garnet

	Material	Style
7	4 (all cotton)	3 (nonhooded)
		1 (hooded)
	3 (poly/cotton blend)	2 (nonhooded)
		1 (hooded)

As this example shows, you would be purchasing only one small, garnet, hooded sweatshirt made of 100 percent cotton and only one small, garnet, hooded sweatshirt made of a poly/cotton blend. Once these sweatshirts were sold, your assortment would be depleted in those areas. As you can see, offering too many selection factors makes buying much more complex. In addition, more frequent reordering would be necessary.

As you prepare your assortment plan, be sure to carry brands for which there is adequate customer demand and carry a complete assortment of these brands. Attempting to offer an assortment plan with too much depth in relation to your merchandise budget will result in stockouts and dissatisfied customers. Determining the assortment plan that best meets your customers' needs is not a simple matter; it will require exhaustive research and analysis of past records and current trends.

SUMMARY POINTS

- Assortment planning requires working within the framework established by the merchandise buying plan.
- Assortment planning must be based on attracting a specific target market and projecting the desired store image. Floor or shelf space available in the store will also affect assortment planning.

- Assortment plans will vary by types of merchandise. Assortment plans for fashion merchandise must be monitored on a frequent basis, whereas assortments of basic merchandise can be surveyed less frequently.
- The variety of merchandise available will also affect assortment plans. Many manufacturers offer product lines with a wide variety of options, whereas others offer only limited choices.
- For each product category, buyers must determine the assortment's breadth and depth.
- Assortments may be offered in either a broad and shallow or a narrow and deep plan.
- For fashion merchandise, buyers test the market early in the selling season by offering a broad and shallow assortment. As customer demand becomes more clearly defined during the selling season, the assortment is likely to become narrow and deep.
- Merchandise offered by retailers can be grouped into classifications and further subdivided into subclassifications. These breakdowns assist the retailer in maintaining inventory control records and in making comparisons with other stores.
- Each item of merchandise can be described in terms of selection factors. The most common selection factors include brand, price, size, color, and material.
- Assortment planning involves developing a model stock for the store that serves as a guide to the buyer who must monitor the market to detect changes in customer tastes and needs and make adjustments in the assortment plan as needed.

REVIEW ACTIVITIES

Developing Your Retail Buying Vocabulary

Consult the Glossary if you did not add the following terms to your vocabulary.

Assortment planning	Narrow and deep
Balanced assortment	Product line
Breadth	Seasonal basic
Broad and shallow	Selection factor
Cannibalization	Standard classification
Classification	of merchandise
Depth	Subclassification
Model stock	

Understanding What You Read

1. What is the goal of assortment planning?
2. Why is relying on past sales records not practical for fashion merchandise?
3. How does assortment planning differ between convenience and specialty goods?
4. What are the benefits of offering national brands as part of a store's merchandise assortment?
5. What is the benefit of offering a wider stock breadth?
6. What are the benefits and drawbacks of offering a narrow stock breadth?
7. Why would a fashion store probably offer a broad and shallow assortment at the beginning of a selling season?
8. When would increasing product lines not be practical for a store?
9. What are the benefits of implementing a merchandise classification system?
10. Describe the relationship of unit control and merchandise classification systems.
11. How does a buyer determine which selection factors to use when developing an assortment plan?
12. How does a store usually determine the size distribution of an assortment plan?
13. Describe how a fashion buyer would select the colors for a new assortment plan.
14. What are the objectives of establishing a model stock plan?
15. Why is more frequent reordering required as more selection factors are represented in an assortment plan?

Analyzing and Applying What You Read

1. For one of the apparel merchandise classifications presented in Table 9.3, develop a list of possible subclassifications. For each subclassification, identify the selection factors that would be important to a customer.
2. Select one item that can be found at a store that sells home furnishings or hardware. For that item, identify major brands and price ranges. Then, identify other selection factors that customers would consider before purchasing the item. Discuss whether most retailers would be able to offer a product assortment that would match all the selection factors for this product.

Application Exercises

1. You have the budget to purchase 100 sweatshirts for your store.
   All the sweatshirts will be purchased from Hanes for $12 each.
   The distribution of sizes will be as follows:

Small	12%
Medium	28%
Large	32%
X-Large	20%
XX-Large	8%

   a. Four colors will be represented in the assortment as follows:

Red	25%
Blue	25%
White	25%
Black	25%

   b. One-third of the assortment will be hooded, and the remainder
      will be nonhooded.
   c. Develop an assortment plan based on this information. Then,
      analyze the completed assortment plan. Is this an appropriate
      distribution for the assortment plan? If not, how could the
      distribution be improved?

2. You are the buyer for men's shirts at a local department store.
   You want to purchase short-sleeve, solid-color, 100 percent
   cotton shirts from two vendors, Gant and Arrow. You have a
   $20,000 budget that will be divided according to the following
   distribution—Gant, 75 percent, and Arrow, 25 percent. Each Gant
   shirt will cost $15, while each Arrow shirt will cost $21.

   a. Colors will be distributed in the following manner:

Gant	White	50%
	Blue	35%
	Yellow	10%
	Pink	5%
Arrow	White	70%
	Blue	30%

b. All colors will be purchased in the following size distribution:

14	5%
$14^1/_2$	5%
15	20%
$15^1/_2$	30%
16	15%
$16^1/_2$	15%
17	10%

c. First, calculate how many shirts of each brand will be purchased. Then, determine how many of each color will be purchased for each brand. Finally, calculate the number of each size that will be purchased by color and brand.

Spreadsheet Skills

1. Use a spreadsheet program to answer the questions in the Application Exercises above.
2. In *Making Buying Decisions: Using the Computer As a Tool*, complete problems related to Merchandising Concept 9–1 (Calculate Assortments to Be Purchased).

Internet Connection

1. On the Internet go to http://www.jcpenney.com and locate the company's offerings to the plus-size market. Describe the breadth and depth of the products offered for this market at this site. Select one other national retailer of women's apparel. Go to that site and locate that firm's offerings to the plus-size market. Compare the two retailers' plus-size product offerings.
2. For three products of your choice, identify two retailers on the Internet from whom each product can be purchased. Visit those sites and identify the breadth and depth of each product offered by the retailers that you have identified. Discuss the breadth and depth of the assortments offered: How do the Internet sites compare? How do the assortments offered on the Internet compare to assortments that can be found in bricks-and-mortar retailers.

SNAPSHOT

Fashion Forecasting: Doneger Creative Services

Retail buyers must constantly be involved with forecasting—what will customers want tomorrow? What will they want to buy next year? Forecasting such trends is a challenging job, and many buyers seek assistance from forecasting services. One such consultant is Doneger Creative Services, a division of the Doneger Group—a buying office located in New York and Los Angeles.

Doneger Creative Services primarily provides forecasting and analysis of trends and colors. They report on the apparel, accessories, and lifestyle markets in women's, men's, and youth product categories through printed publications, exclusive online content, and live presentations. These sources predict the direction for future colors and trends as well as report up-to-the-minute news on which clients can quickly act. Primary clients include retailers, manufacturers, and other style-related businesses.

What are some of the specific services that fashion forecasters like Doneger Creative Services offer? Some examples are provided below.

- Forecasting colors for each season is a critical element of the service. Doneger presents color direction for each season using dyed-to-specification color standards in key groupings, accompanied by inspirational collages, suggesting color combinations and applications for specific areas of a business.
- Organizing important elements of the design process that will serve as a foundation for the season is critical. Doneger typically addresses factors such as fabric, print and pattern, trim and detail, and shape and proportion. Material includes original sketches, runway images, and fabric swatches.
- Analyzing important themes that will emerge in coming seasons is another part of the forecast. Material provided by Doneger conveys influences and styling direction through trend collages, original color sketches, and fabric swatches. Emphasis is also placed on the season's important merchandising issues.
- Covering European markets and haute couture collections is another aspect of forecasting. Doneger identifies important concepts to come down the runways, tracks the hottest looks on U.S. and European streets and in store windows, and even provides a special St. Tropez street report.

Many fashion forecasters, like Doneger, provide seasonal live presentations on trends as well as supplemental presentations on lifestyle or industry topics. In addition, Doneger's clients can access information online at the company's Web site, which provides the most up-to-date information available.

Should you hire the services of a fashion forecaster? If you are making purchasing decisions in a dynamic, changing environment, the answer is probably yes. If the information provided helps you make better buying decisions, which translates into increased sales and customer satisfaction, it will be money well spent.

BASED ON:

Information from http://www.doneger.com

TRENDWATCH

All Shapes and Sizes: The Plus-Size Market Continues to Grow

In the United States, sales in the plus-size and big-and-tall markets are expected to balloon by nearly 41 percent by 2012. In 2006, plus-size sales accounted for approximately 40 percent of all U.S. women's and girls' clothing sales while the big-and-tall market accounted for nearly half of all men's and boys' clothing sales. Moreover, the fastest growth has been seen among the under-25 age group in recent years.

Despite the media's focus on razor-thin models, more than half of all Americans are overweight, with one in four people medically obese. Plus sizes are in more demand than ever before. While Lane Bryant, Catherine's, and Fashion Bug have continued to expand their plus-size merchandise, department stores are also increasing their product offerings in this area. Kohl's has even extended two of its private label lines, apt. 9 and Daisy Fuentes, to include plus sizes.

Celebrities have also lent their hands in championing the growth of the plus-size market. Rapper/actress Queen Latifah, supermodel Emme, and television personality Oprah Winfrey have all presented positive images of full-figured fashion in the media. Comedian Mo'Nique even launched a nationally televised plus-size beauty pageant.

Manufacturers are now realizing the value of catering to this previously overlooked market segment. In the past, the plus-size market has been an afterthought for many retail buyers. For example, many department stores placed their larger-size offerings in the basement or back of the store, and even limited the floor space targeted to this group. With nearly 50 percent of their customers nearing plus sizes, retailers are gradually bringing this merchandise out of the shadows, and this trend is expected to continue. Both manufacturers and retailers seem to be approaching this market with a new, more positive attitude.

To successfully target the plus-size market, buyers must purchase stylish and alluring merchandise. Selling plus-size clothing means offering fashion that fits not only the body shape, but also fits consumers' expectations of feeling good about the apparel they purchase. Customers in this market are no different than the regular-size shopper—they want the same brands and the same fashions.

To successfully market to this segment, retailers must determine how to best promote product offerings. Retailers have used labels like "woman" or "the forgotten woman" to say plus size without using those exact words. What are the best terms to use in promotional messages? In the male market, Casual Male XL changed its name from Casual Male Big & Tall because the company felt the new name would convey "confidence" instead of "freak."

Retail buyers must understand that even though the plus-size market retains the image of older shoppers, it is well represented across *all* age groups, with young people increasingly wearing plus sizes. Once these customers find a brand that works well for them, they keep purchasing that brand!

BASED ON:

Braverman, Beth. (2005, August 1). Plus-size market, giant opportunity. *National Jeweler*, 1–2.

Expanding plus-size market to grow 41 percent by 2012. (2007, July 2). *Just-style.com*.

Janov, Jill. (2005, October 1). As obesity rates soar, suppliers stretch into plus sizes. *Bicycle Retailer and Industry News*, 100–101.

Men's plus-size market fastest growing clothing sector. (2006, December 8). *Just-style.com*.

Plus-size market rockets by 50%. (2006, March 24). *Just-style.com*.

The plus-size market keeps growing. (2006, October). *Just-style.com*.

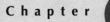

Chapter 10

Controlling Inventories

PERFORMANCE OBJECTIVES

Upon completion of this chapter, you should be able to:

- List the benefits of inventory control systems.
- Describe perpetual inventory control.
- Describe periodic inventory control.
- Differentiate between manual and computerized inventory control.
- Identify the basic information required for inventory control systems.
- Explain how buyers use inventory control systems.
- Differentiate between retail and cost methods of inventory valuation.
- Illustrate how FIFO and LIFO inventory valuations differ.
- Calculate GMROI.
- Describe Quick Response inventory management.
- Identify the technology required for Quick Response.
- Outline a plan for implementing Quick Response.
- Describe the benefits of implementing Quick Response.

Merchandise planning requires a good control system that provides a way to determine if a store or department is functioning according to a plan. Moreover, controls provide a basis to correct problems before they become disastrous for the store.

As a buyer you must constantly be aware of the amount of inventory in your store or department. Excessive inventory indicates there is a buying, selling, or pricing problem. For example, you may not have purchased the merchandise customers wanted to buy, or salespeople may not have provided an adequate selling effort, or the merchandise may not have been priced correctly in relationship to the product's quality. You will also need inventory information when calculating how much money is available for purchasing additional merchandise.

In this chapter you will learn about two types of inventory control systems—perpetual and periodic. Dollar control and unit control will be explained, and current trends in inventory management will be described.

INVENTORY CONTROL SYSTEMS

After deciding on the merchandise assortment that is to be carried, *inventory control systems* must be established. These controls involve the maintenance of stock levels in relation to changing consumer demand. The type of inventory control system used by a retailer will vary by type and size of the business and the kind and amount of information required. Inventory control for a department, such as hardware with thousands of different items, will probably be quite different from that for a product category such as apparel.

A good inventory control system offers the following benefits:

• The proper relationship between sales and inventory can better be well maintained. Without inventory control procedures in place, the store or department can become overstocked or understocked.

• Inventory control systems provide you with information needed to take markdowns by identifying slow-selling merchandise. Discovering such items early in the season will allow you to reduce prices or make a change in marketing strategy before consumer demand completely disappears.

• Merchandise control systems allow buyers to identify best-sellers early enough in the season so that reorders can be placed to increase total sales for the store or department.

• Merchandise shortages, **shrinkage**, can be identified using inventory control systems. Excessive shrinkage will indicate that more effective merchandise controls need to be implemented to reduce employee theft or shoplifting.

Buyers must establish a control process that allows them to analyze the current situation in relation to merchandise plans and correct any deviations. For example, you may compare actual inventory counts against planned inventory levels and determine that the store or department is overstocked. You must then decide what corrective actions are needed. Future merchandise orders may need to be reduced, prices may need to be decreased to increase sales, or salespeople may need additional training. Your job as a buyer is to decide on the most appropriate remedy.

The control system allows you to determine mistakes that have been made or identify areas that need your immediate attention. To be most effective, the inventory control system must also provide information in a timely manner to allow you to make decisions while problems can still be corrected. There are two basic types of inventory control systems—perpetual and periodic.

Perpetual Control

Retailers using a **_perpetual control system_** are recording business transactions such as sales, purchases, returns, and transfers on a continuous basis. At any point in time, stock levels can be calculated. Stores using perpetual control systems do not have to take actual counts of their stock except for regularly scheduled physical inventories. Two types of perpetual control systems include manual and computerized.

Manual. Although many retailers today have computerized their inventory control systems, some stores still maintain perpetual inventory control by manually recording transactions on inventory control forms. Inventory records are updated as transactions occur or on a daily or weekly basis by designated employees. Manual systems are slow, and many times employees responsible for updating inventory control forms are so late in completing them that the information is of little use to the buyer. Because data entries are made manually, they can be incorrect–providing inaccurate and misleading information to the buyer.

Computerized. Store computers can be programmed to maintain the same type of inventory information that manual systems provide. With such a system, merchandise information is automatically collected and processed for every transaction occurring at the POS (point-of-sale) register, providing the buyer or manager with up-to-date sales and inventory data. The computer has improved inventory control systems by improving speed, accuracy, and efficiency of recordkeeping.

Computerized systems require that each item of merchandise be coded to identify specific information about it, such as department, classification, vendor, style, color, size, or price. Identifying merchandise by such specific characteristics involves **_unit control_**. Most buyers need to know more about inventory than simply broad merchandise classifications. Maintaining a unit control system requires coding each item. SKU (stockkeeping unit) numbers identify a single item of merchandise within a merchandise classification. For example, an SKU number such as 95621 could identify the vendor (95), classification (6), size (2), and color (1). Today, many stores use the **_UPC_** (universal price code) already found on merchandise when it arrives from the supplier. Some retailers print their own bar codes once the merchandise arrives at the store. Read the Trendwatch titled "RFID: Can It Improve Retail Logistics?" to learn more about new trends being implemented by suppliers.

At the cash register, the code is "read" by a scanner (Figure 10.1), and the information updates the store's inventory records. There is less danger of salespeople making errors when merchandise is coded and scanners are used to record transactions. Problems can result

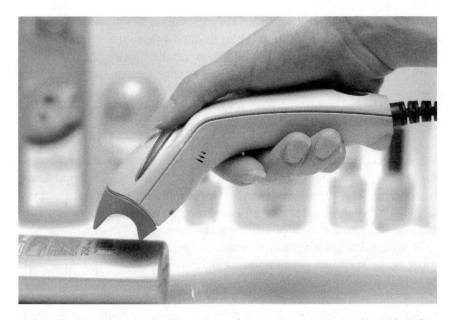

Figure 10.1   Bar codes can be scanned to track movement of merchandise in and out of a store.

from using computerized systems, however, if incorrect data are entered. For example, if price changes are inaccurately recorded, incorrect records and reports will result.

Today, some computerized systems include automatic reorder capabilities. The computer automatically signals when merchandise on hand and on order drops below a required level. Some systems can even send the purchase order electronically to the supplier.

Periodic Control

Periodic control systems are used by those retailers who take a physical inventory on a regular basis, which involves the actual counting and recording of information about the merchandise on hand at a specified time. Retailers take physical inventories for several reasons. The value of actual stock is needed in preparing a firm's financial statements such as profit and loss, and comparing physical inventory counts with store records allows the retailer to determine the amount of shrinkage that has occurred.

Methods of taking physical inventories vary among various types of retailers. Some retailers, such as large department stores, close while the inventory is being conducted. Most retailers take physical stock counts on an annual basis; however, others conduct stock counts every six months. Small stores may even conduct monthly counts. Most stores conducting annual physical inventories do so at the end of January–the end of a major selling season.

Careful preparation must be made to conduct physical inventories. Personnel conducting the inventory must completely understand inventory-taking procedures and the importance of their task. The importance of accuracy and thoroughness when counting and recording information must be emphasized to all employees. Some retailers even hire outside firms to conduct physical inventories.

Before taking a physical inventory, merchandise will need to be grouped by specific categories or classifications. Inventory takers must be supplied with inventory forms that allow them to record information such as product description, quantity, price, style, or vendor. Employees usually work in pairs with one person calling out information and one recording the data. Spot checks are normally taken by supervisors to ensure the accuracy of inventory counts.

ESTABLISHING AND USING INVENTORY CONTROL SYSTEMS

One of the primary responsibilities of a buyer will be to maintain inventory control systems that require the selection of categories by which data are gathered (Figure 10.2). Control categories must be narrow enough to determine opportunities and problems with specific lines of merchandise; yet they should also make comparisons with industry data easy. When establishing control categories, many retailers use Standard Merchandise Classifications that have been developed by the National Retail Federation. Merchandising and operating statistics of department and specialty stores for various classifications are also provided by this trade organization.

Information Required

Maintenance of inventory control requires information about purchases, sales, transfers, and returns. Single independent retail stores will not be maintaining information on transfers.

Figure 10.2   Inventory control systems must be in place on the selling floor and behind the scenes.

Purchases. Records must be kept of each unit of merchandise ordered and received by the store. Information from the store's receiving report can be used to update perpetual inventory control records either manually or by inputting the data into the store's computer.

Sales. If a manual inventory control system is being used, a sales check or a price-ticket stub identifying the item sold must be collected and the information recorded on the appropriate form. In stores with computerized POS registers, sales are automatically recorded and inventory records updated as each sales transaction is completed.

Transfers. At chain stores, merchandise is frequently transferred from one store to another. Stores using manual inventory control systems must record these merchandise *transfers*. Stores sending merchandise to another store will delete the items from their inventory records, whereas stores receiving the merchandise will add the items to their inventory records.

PART B - Return Goods Form

Within 60 days of original purchase: J.Crew gladly accepts returns of unworn, unwashed, or defective merchandise for full refund. Refunds must be accompanied by the original receipt and will be made in the form of the original payment. If the original receipt is unavailable, we'll make an exchange or issue a merchandise credit based on the current selling price. **After 60 days of original purchase:** J.Crew will gladly make an exchange or issue a merchandise credit for the price at the time of sale (with original receipt) or for the current selling price (without original receipt). For your convenience, catalog and internet purchases may be returned to any J.Crew retail store for immediate credit. For retail store returns, a government issued photo ID will be required for cash and check returns and returns without an original receipt. J.Crew Factory stores can only accept returns of items that were purchased at a J.Crew Factory location. J.Crew Retail stores can only accept returns of items that were purchased at a J.Crew Retail location or through the Catalog or Internet. Monogrammed or personalized items are not returnable or exchangeable. For our full return policy, please visit us at www.jcrew.com.

To return goods: Please detach Part B and follow instructions on the reverse side of Part A. If an item is damaged in shipment, save item(s) and packaging and phone us at **800 562 0258**.
For an exchange, use Part D on the reverse side of Part B, or phone **800 562 0258**.
Return reason code: Please fill in appropriate letter in the left-hand column below.

B. changed mind   **C.** just didn't like   **G.** too small   **M.** too large   **B.** wrong item shipped   **V.** arrived too late   **E.** defective, for our benefit please describe

Customer No. 532746259   Date 11/01/07   Order No. 107304051475

Reason Code	Item No.	Color	Size	Description
	86221	pro	9h-m	shoe,erin printed peep-toe hee
	85791	rpe	m	shirt,suzannah in liberty fabr
	86182	rpu	9h-m	shoe,lucia printed ballet flat

0110730405147
107304051475

Figure 10.3   Refund slips help retailers know why products were sent back.

Returns. Inventory control systems must also maintain records of *returns*, which include merchandise returned to vendors as well as merchandise that customers return to the store. Customers making returns to the store are usually issued a refund slip (Figure 10.3). A copy of this form is used to add merchandise back into stock when updating inventory records. When merchandise is returned to the vendor, a return form is also completed. Again, information from a copy of this form is used to delete merchandise from inventory records. Stores using computerized inventory control systems must enter data related to these returns in order to update inventory records.

Using Inventory Control Information

The accuracy of an inventory control system requires the careful recording of *every* item that enters or leaves the store or department. Mistakes result in inaccurate inventory records that decrease their usefulness to the buyer. The following are reasons for inaccuracies:

• Inaccurate beginning inventory counts,
• Improperly coded merchandise,
• Failure to record markdowns,
• Incorrect recording of sales, purchases, returns, or transfers, and
• Dishonesty of customers or employees.

Inventory control systems provide you with information on sales and merchandise in stock, providing information that will help you prepare for market trips. Facts, not guesses, are essential when determining sales trends to meet the wants and needs of your customers. Inventory control systems provide you with the means to regularly check actual sales against planned stock and sales projections.

You cannot rely on inventory records alone when determining purchases. Sales records do not show the requests made by customers for merchandise that was not in stock. For example, more sales might have been made if stock levels had not been depleted when customers came into the store to make a purchase.

If your store is using a computerized inventory control system, a number of reports can be generated on a daily or weekly basis to assist you in making merchandising decisions. Sales reports will show how rapidly or slowly inventory is being converted to sales, indicating whether adjustments need to be made in stock levels. Changes in

```
FORM SI203    1-14                              PREPARED 03/17 15:55           PAGE  2
CLASS 00002 DRESSES
```

STYLE DESCRIPTION COLOR	SIZE	ST	UNIT RETAIL	UNIT COST	ON ORDER	ON HAND	WTD	1-AGO	2-AGO	3-AGO	4-AGO	MTD	STD	LAST RECEIPT STAT
══════ VENDOR 000020														
80415 LIN BF SS JWLNK														
		01	120.00	59.00	0	1	0	2	2	0	0	4		
		TL	120.00	59.00	0	1	0	2	2	0	0	4		
81035 DRESS														
		01	47.00	59.25	0	0	0	0	0	0	0	0		
		TL	47.00	59.25	0	0	0	0	0	0	0	0		
81220 SS CHEX SHAPE DRS														
		01	132.00	65.00	0	1	0	2	1	1	0	3		
		TL	132.00	65.00	0	1	0	2	1	1	0	3		
81235 DRESS														
		01	50.00	63.00	0	0	0	0	0	0	0	0		
		02	50.00	63.00	0	0	0	0	0	0	0	0		
		TL	50.00	63.00	0	0	0	0	0	0	0	0		
81705 RAY/LIN BF COAT														
		01	150.00	74.00	0	4	0	1	0	0	0	1		
		02	150.00	74.00	0	3	0	0	0	0	0	0		
		TL	150.00	74.00	0	7	0	1	0	0	0	1		
82402 SS RAYON SKT BF DOTS														
		01	150.00	74.00	0	2	0	1-	2	0	1	1		
		02	150.00	74.00	0	2	0	1	0	0	0	1		
		TL	150.00	74.00	0	4	0	0	2	0	1	2		
84408 SS BASIC SKT COT/LIN														
		01	112.00	55.00	0	1	0	0	0	1	2	0		
		02	0.00	55.00	4	0	0	0	0	0	0	0		
		TL	112.00	55.00	4	1	0	0	0	1	2	0		
84412 DRESS														
		01	47.00	59.25	0	0	0	0	0	0	0	0		
		02	47.00	59.25	0	0	0	0	0	0	0	0		
		TL	47.00	59.25	0	0	0	0	0	0	0	0		
VENDOR TOTAL		01			0	9	0	4	5	2	3	9		
		02			4	5	0	1	0	0	0	1		
		TL			4	14	0	5	5	2	3	10		
══════ VENDOR 000038														
2015 REO COATDRESS L/S														
		01	136.00	99.00	0	0	0	0	0	0	0	0		
		02	136.00	99.00	0	2	0	0	0	0	0	0		
		TL	136.00	99.00	0	2	0	0	0	0	0	0		
2023 REO SB CREPE GLD BTN														
		01	111.00	81.00	0	0	0	0	0	0	1	0		
		02	111.00	81.00	0	0	0	0	0	0	0	0		
		TL	111.00	81.00	0	0	0	0	0	0	1	0		
D2015 CREPE DB COATDRESS														
		01	228.00	99.00	0	0	0	0	0	0	0	0		
		TL	228.00	99.00	0	0	0	0	0	0	0	0		
D2023 CREPE GOLD BTN FRT														
		01	111.00	81.00	0	0	0	0	0	0	1	0		
		02	111.00	81.00	0	0	0	0	0	0	0	0		
		TL	111.00	81.00	0	0	0	0	0	0	1	0		

Figure 10.4   Buyers use computer reports like this one to track inventory and sales.

consumer demand can also be detected. Reports can be generated to show unit sales for the current week, each of the past several weeks, month-to-date, or season-to-date. You may even receive reports that summarize sales for all styles of each vendor. Examples of computerized reports are shown in Figure 10.4.

Exception reports may also be obtained that show areas where sales or stock levels do not meet predetermined levels. You should carefully review these reports to determine why sales are higher or lower than planned. Immediate action must be planned to correct problem areas.

To be effective, inventory control systems require frequent reviews by the buyer; however, they should not be used as a substitute for experience. Merchandise control systems provide input into the decision-making process, but a buyer cannot rely solely on information from computer printouts. If used properly, inventory control systems will allow you to make more effective merchandising decisions.

INVENTORY CALCULATIONS

As you learned in previous chapters, most buyers develop a merchandise plan in advance of the selling season. The merchandise plan becomes the means by which actual results are evaluated. Once the selling season is under way, actual stock records can be used to control the amount of inventory on hand. Two types of inventory calculations that retailers often use are (1) stock on hand valuations and (2) GMROI, which measures the gross margin return on inventory.

Dollar Control Systems

Dollar control involves comparing the planned value of stock on hand with the value of stock on hand. These comparisons require that retailers place a value on inventory. Two methods are typically used for inventory valuation. They include the cost method and the retail method.

Cost Method. The *cost method* of inventory valuation requires that inventory records be maintained using cost figures–exactly what the retailer paid for the merchandise. Stores using this method usually include the cost of the merchandise using codes on the price ticket that customers and most employees cannot readily decipher. If costs remain constant, the cost method presents no problem; however, prices that retailers are charged for many products are continually changing. Because these prices change, stores using the cost method of inventory valuation have a choice in placing a value on the inventory. They can use either the LIFO or the FIFO method.

The **FIFO** (first in first out) method, assumes that the merchandise that was received first, sold first. This may not always occur. Many retailers use the **LIFO** (last in first out) method, which assumes that the merchandise that was received last was sold first. Such a situation does not likely occur, but in periods of rising wholesale prices, a lower inventory valuation results when this method is used because it is valued at lower prices.

PROBLEM ILLUSTRATION

Let's examine a situation to examine the differences in these two methods. Assume a department purchased 100 ties for $10 each on January 1 and purchased another 200 ties at $11 each on February 1. On March 1, inventory records revealed that 50 ties remained in stock. Dollar control requires that a value be placed on ending inventory.

Using FIFO, the ending inventory would be valued at the cost of the last ties purchased. In this instance, that would be $11. Therefore, the inventory would be valued at $550 ($11 × 50).

Using LIFO, the ending inventory would be valued at the cost of the first ties purchased. In this instance, that would be $10. Therefore, the inventory would be valued at $500 ($10 × 50).

For a buyer wanting to place the *lowest value on ending inventory*, the LIFO method would be best. Remember that when buyers develop six-month plans, they enter the value of beginning and ending inventories. Lower inventory values provide the buyer with opportunities to buy more merchandise. For this reason, the LIFO method is generally used by most retailers who use the cost method because of continually spiraling wholesale prices.

Retail Method. Today, most retail stores value inventory using the retail method. Stores using this method do not have to be concerned with changing wholesale prices, which may be difficult to determine and track. The **retail method** values the inventory using the current retail price. The retail value of all purchases, sales, transfers, and returns is recorded either manually or input into the computer system. Each change lowers or increases the value of current stock levels when the retail method is used.

Markdown, the reduction in the retail price of merchandise already in stock, is the key price change that must be recorded. Markdowns *decrease* the value of the inventory. *Markdown cancellations*, increases in retail price to offset all or any part of previously taken markdowns, usually occur when the retail price of merchandise has been reduced only temporarily for promotional purposes. Recording markdown cancellations *increases* the value of inventory. In some instances, the value of inventory may be increased by taking *additional markups*, increases in retail prices above those at which the goods were marked when they were first received into stock. Accuracy is vital when recording any of these changes in retail prices because mistakes could result in inventory overages or shortages.

GMROI—Measuring Profitability of Sales

Another inventory calculation that retail buyers examine is *GMROI* (gross margin return on inventory), which measures the profitability of a retailer's sales. It is a quick and easy way to measure how much cash a business is producing and how well it is using its investment in inventory. GMROI gives retailers a way to relate sales and the cash those sales are generating. In other words, GMROI integrates two performance measurements, gross margin and turnover, to create a single measure of performance.

On a daily basis, retailers plan and measure their business in terms of sales, but the ultimate measure of success for any business is profitable sales volume and the cash flow those sales produce. Profitable sales growth provides the cash a business needs to survive and grow. If it does not produce enough cash, it will fail and cease to exist. GMROI, stated in simple terms, attempts to answer a very basic business problem: "If I spend a dollar for merchandise to sell in my store, how much money do I need to get back if I wish to remain a viable business?" The objective is that a minimum dollar amount invested produces a maximum amount of gross margin.

Retailers calculate GMROI using the following formula:

GMROI = (Gross Margin Percentage × Turnover)/(1 − Markup Percentage)

Again, in simple terms retailers are measuring:

(How much they made on the sale × How long it takes to sell)/How much they had to pay for it

PROBLEM ILLUSTRATION

A business has a gross margin of 40 percent combined with a turnover rate of 2.5. It has a markup percentage of 50 percent. Calculate GMROI.

$$\text{GMROI} = (\text{Gross Margin Percentage} \times \text{Turnover})/(1 - \text{Markup Percentage})$$

$$\text{GMROI} = (.40 \times 2.5)/(1 - .50)$$

$$\text{GMROI} = 1/.50$$

$$\text{GMROI} = 2$$

GMROI should be viewed as more than a statistic; it is a driving force in the day-to-day management of inventories. In this formula, turnover measures the relationship between sales and stock levels. Both higher sales and managed inventories will boost turnover. The key is to increase sales without a corresponding increase in average inventory. It is important to realize that turnover represents the freshest, newest, and most wanted assortments to customers. In general, high turnover and high gross margin yield high GMROI, and low turnover and low gross margin yield low GMROI. Because high turnover and high gross margin are very desirable merchandising objectives, maximizing GMROI is an important goal for most buyers.

INVENTORY MANAGEMENT: QUICK RESPONSE

More than ever before retailers are seeking a competitive advantage by streamlining the flow of goods from suppliers. Many retailers are implementing an inventory management system that allows them to keep their shelves stocked with the fastest-selling items while reducing the cost of placing orders. The time between ordering and receiving merchandise is reduced, and the system allows the store to increase customer service by always having the right items in stock. This system is known as *Quick Response*.

By using POS computerized registers that are capable of automatically reordering specific items as they are sold, retailers can lower their inventory levels, and suppliers can increase their sales with a greater number of small shipments. Quick Response, however, is more than the use of technology to manage inventories—it is also a cooperative effort between retailers and their suppliers.

Ideally, Quick Response is a strategy whereby retailers can forecast today what they will sell tomorrow and have the merchandise in the store on time and in the right quantities, colors, sizes, and styles. The concept is quite simple—get the right merchandise in the store with a minimum amount of inventory. For retailers, Quick Response means monitoring sales down to the item level, spotting trends as they occur, and then quickly relaying this information to the supplier.

In today's intensely competitive marketplace, "quick" is important. Longer forecasting periods may result in merchandise being ordered that does not meet customer demand. Longer order periods and delivery periods also make it more difficult to keep merchandise in stock that customers want to purchase. Getting the quick results that Quick Response promises requires a partnership between supplier and retailer, as well as the implementation of new business practices.

To start, retailers must share sales information with suppliers to help them better plan production, and suppliers must be willing to meet new, stringent delivery demands. Using Quick Response strategies, a supplier would receive an electronic purchase order from a retailer. Almost immediately, the supplier would prepare a shipment attaching a bar-code label to each carton. As cartons are loaded onto trucks, bar codes are scanned to develop a shipping manifest that is sent to the retailer electronically. Retailers scan the bar codes of cartons as they arrive to ensure that the correct ones are received. The entire process is completed in the time required to move the goods to the retailer—usually a few days. Using traditional purchase orders and invoices would require weeks to complete the same process.

Requirements for Quick Response

Quick Response requires an alliance between the retailer and the supplier that is built on mutual trust and teamwork. The use and implementation of technology is also required, specifically the use of model stocks, bar coding/scanning, and electronic data interchange.

Model Stock Development. After the technology is in place to implement Quick Response, *model stocks* for each product classification are developed. Model stocks are based on the *ideal number* of any item that should be on hand. Lower inventory levels are required in the store because more frequent and smaller reorders will be placed using Quick

Response. Model stocks are adjusted periodically as indicated by the most current sales trends. Every item in the model stock is maintained in specific quantities by SKUs. Each product must also have a standard identification number, usually in the form of a bar code that is scanned at the POS register.

Bar Coding/Scanning. Implementing Quick Response also requires the use of *bar coding* and scanning. UPCs have become standardized in almost every part of the retail industry. A pattern of variable-width bars and spaces, representing a code of letters and numbers, is on most products when they arrive from the supplier. Some retailers, however, generate their own bar-codes using a bar code printer once the merchandise arrives from the supplier. The bar codes are scanned at the POS register, which enters the sale in the store's computer system. The retailer is then able to track merchandise on the item or SKU level.

Bar coding and scanning provide several benefits to the store and its customers, as well as the buyers. They include:

• Faster customer checkout because manual entry of the item information is eliminated.
• Ability to track merchandise down to the SKU level, which reduces stockouts.
• Elimination of the need to remark merchandise.
• Increased employee productivity because manual checking and marking procedures are eliminated.

Both bar coding and scanning are continuing to make major gains in the retail industry; however, the cost of investment in the equipment continues to be the primary barrier to implementing these technologies by small retailers. Read the Trendwatch titled "Scanners: How Accurate Are They?" to learn more about recent research measuring the accuracy of scanners in retail stores.

Electronic Data Interchange. The final requirement for Quick Response is *electronic data interchange* (EDI). EDI supports the communication of sales data and business documents, such as invoices and purchase orders, between retailers and suppliers. In fact, the computer systems can electronically send purchase orders that are triggered when specific items of merchandise are sold. Delays due to paper-handling are kept to a minimum. In addition to accelerating the ordering process, the major benefits of EDI are derived through reductions in clerical and administrative costs associated with data entry and tracking huge volumes of business documents.

Implementing Quick Response

Management cannot make all the changes required by Quick Response at once, and it should not even try. Usually, retailers develop a pilot program for only several product categories. Doing so allows them to identify everything that can go wrong. Most retailers have implemented Quick Response in basic merchandise areas first. Demand for basics is easier to forecast because of year-round demand; however, Quick Response promises significant benefits for fashion merchandise, too. In the fashion area, the approach most retailers take is to place smaller preseason orders and closely monitor initial sales. They quickly reorder fast sellers. Required changes in manufacturing processes are obvious, but Quick Response leads to increased sales for both the retailer and the supplier because retailers are more often in stock with merchandise desired by the customer. For the retailer, fewer markdowns result because only those styles for which significant demand has been demonstrated are reordered.

Implementation of Quick Response requires the following strategies:

- Inventory and sales must be tracked at the SKU level.
- Automatic replenishment systems must be used to constantly monitor inventory levels; therefore, smaller and more frequent deliveries are made.
- Suppliers must commit to a higher level of service through improved shipping accuracy and on-time deliveries.
- Retailers must cooperate more closely with suppliers by sharing sales data to improve production planning.

Implementing Quick Response requires defining new relationships with vendors, which is central to the concept. Without the right vendor relationships, Quick Response would not exist. This new relationship requires give-and-take by both the vendor and the retailer. Vendors cannot underproduce and short-ship to the retailer, nor can retailers make last-minute substitutions or requests for special ticketing or handling. The best Quick Response strategies are jointly developed by retailers and vendors.

Quick Response requires a change in how buyers and suppliers work and think, but all studies conducted in the area point to dramatic improvements in operating results. All retailers, however, have not readily adopted such merchandise management strategies. Two key barriers have kept some retailers from implementing Quick Response. They are:

- Lack of knowledge of how to implement Quick Response or a basic fear of technology, and
- Perceived beliefs that suppliers will not uphold their end of the agreement.

Measuring the Impact of Quick Response

Results of numerous studies indicate the potential for incredible industrywide savings with the implementation of Quick Response. The impact of Quick Response can be seen not only above the gross margin line (through increased sales and decreased markdowns), but also below the line, with significant reductions in operating expenses. The following are some of the areas where benefits have been achieved by retailers implementing Quick Response:

Sales. Sales are up in basic, seasonal, and fashion merchandise. By tracking merchandise on an item level, buyers can quickly react to actual customer demand. Industry leaders are increasing their in-stock positions from the 70 to 80 percent range to more than 95 percent.

Markdowns. By stocking more of what customers want and less of what they do not want, markdowns decrease—an average of 30 percent in basic merchandise and 40 percent in fashion merchandise.

Merchandising Expenses. EDI with automatic replenishment systems reduces the amount of time to create, communicate, and track purchase orders by as much as 80 percent. Bar coding also eliminates the need to reticket promotional merchandise.

Administrative Expenses. EDI significantly reduces the amount of data entry for both retailers and vendors. At the same time, clerical costs for the retailer can be cut by as much as two-thirds.

Interest on Inventory. Perhaps the easiest-to-measure bottom-line benefit of Quick Response is reduced inventory. Traditionally, retailers have kept large amounts of inventory throughout the pipeline—in transit, on hand, and in storage. By increasing inventory turns, there is a significant savings in inventory carrying costs.

These benefits come at a cost, however. Purchasing hardware and software can be expensive. In addition, implementing Quick Response requires that management provide education and training for store employees. Read the Snapshot titled, "VF Brands: Implementing Quick Response," to learn more about how one manufacturer has benefited from Quick Response.

Buyers and retailers must sit down and talk about how to do business differently, not just how to install the technology. The resistance to change is best overcome by a systematic, step-by-step implementation plan. First, points of resistance must be overcome. For many companies, this means converting the buyers. Buyers must realize that the system frees them to do what they do best—determining what is going to sell in the coming months. The primary mission of buyers does not change. They are still responsible for understanding customer demand, analyzing sales trends, merchandising products, and maintaining the correct image for the store in the marketplace. Buyers are also increasingly responsible for managing bottom-line profitability—that means responsibility for inventory turns and related costs.

SUMMARY POINTS

- Inventory control involves the maintenance of stock levels in relation to changing consumer demand.
- Buyers must establish controls that allow them to analyze current inventories in relation to merchandise plans and take corrective action if needed.
- Buyers use either perpetual or periodic methods when establishing inventory controls.

- Maintaining inventory control systems requires the selection of categories by which data are gathered. Maintenance of inventory control requires information about purchases, sales, transfers, and returns.
- Inventory control systems provide buyers with information about sales and merchandise in stock as they prepare for market trips.
- Two inventory calculations used by retailers include stock-on-hand valuations and GMROI. Stock on hand can be valued using FIFO, LIFO, or retail methods. GMROI measures the profitability of a retailer's sales.
- Quick Response is an inventory control system that many retailers and vendors are implementing to shorten the time between ordering and receiving merchandise.
- Implementation of Quick Response requires the use of bar coding and electronic data interchange.

REVIEW ACTIVITIES

Developing Your Retail Buying Vocabulary

Consult the Glossary if you did not add the following terms to your vocabulary.

Additional markup	Markdown cancellation
Bar coding	Model stock
Cost method	Periodic control system
Dollar control	Perpetual control system
Electronic data interchange	Quick Response
Exception report	Retail method
FIFO	Return
GMROI	Shrinkage
Inventory control systems	Transfer
LIFO	Unit control
Markdown	UPC

Understanding What You Read

1. How are perpetual inventory systems maintained manually?
2. When can information from perpetual inventory systems provide misleading information to buyers?
3. What are the key advantages that computerized inventory systems provide when compared with manual systems?

4. How can errors occur in computerized inventory systems?
5. When do most retailers conduct physical inventories?
6. Explain how returns affect inventory counts.
7. Why do most retailers use the retail method of inventory valuation?
8. Describe how shrinkage is determined using inventory control records.
9. Using a retail method of inventory, what type of price changes would increase the value of inventory?
10. Using a retail method of inventory, what type of price changes would decrease the value of inventory?
11. Why is a "quick" response by suppliers so important to buyers?
12. What are the benefits of scanning to both retailers and their customers?
13. What steps are required to implement EDI?
14. What are the benefits of using EDI?
15. Describe specific benefits enjoyed by businesses using Quick Response.

Analyzing and Applying What You Read

1. After analyzing inventory control records, a buyer determines he or she is overstocked in 80 percent of the merchandise categories carried. Explain possible causes of this problem. Present a plan that could improve future inventory levels.
2. The owner of a small sporting goods store is considering changing from periodic inventory control to perpetual control. Outline the benefits and drawbacks of each plan. Present your decision as if you were a consultant and the rationale for your recommendation.
3. Outline the arguments you would use to convince your store manager to implement Quick Response.

Application Exercises

1. a. The children's department made the following purchases:

   Jan. 1: 20 pants purchased at $20 each

   Feb. 1: 20 pants purchased at $20 each

   Mar. 1: 50 pants purchased at $20 each

   Apr. 1: 20 pants purchased at $23 each

   b. On April 30, 15 pants remained in stock. What is the inventory value of these pants based on both LIFO and FIFO?

2. a. At the end of the fall season, Department 58 had a gross margin of 41 percent combined with a turnover rate of 2.2. It has a markup percentage of 49 percent.
   b. At the end of the spring season, Department 58 had a gross margin of 41 percent combined with a turnover rate of 2.3. It has a markup percentage of 48 percent.
   c. Which season produced the highest GMROI?

Internet Connection

1. Use a search engine on the Internet to locate companies that are selling scanners to be used at retail businesses. Develop a report describing the different product features that are available.
2. Use the Internet to develop a list of three firms that are currently using Quick Response. Provide the URL address for each source.

SNAPSHOT

VF Brands: Implementing Quick Response

Since the early 1990s, implementing Quick Response has been common practice at VF Brands. In fact, the firm, one of the country's largest apparel manufacturers, was among the early proponents of implementing Quick Response. Currently, the majority of its retail clients use some flow replenishment technology. In fact, more than 90 percent of VF's Wrangler products are shipped using Quick Response. VF management is intent on fine-tuning every aspect of Quick Response in an effort to squeeze more and more time out of the order cycle. The ultimate goal is 24-hour replenishment.

One of the most recent steps taken toward that goal was a change in the way merchandise is prepacked for shipping. In the past, items were shipped in multiples of two or more. Therefore, merchandise could not be replaced on a one-for-one basis. Now VF Brands is packing all basic merchandise in single packs. Prepacks as a concept is dead.

Management points out that VF's Quick Response partners have experienced sales increases of nearly 40 percent and inventory turns that double. For example, prior to implementing Quick Response, retailers turned stock in the bra area roughly once a season and had an in-stock position of 65 to 70 percent. Now, they are reporting 1.25 to 1.5 turnovers per season while maintaining a 92 to 97 percent in-stock position. Most importantly, fewer customers are leaving a store without finding what they want. Having the right item, in the right size, in stock when a shopper is looking for it could mean the difference between building loyalty or losing a customer.

The goal at VF Brands is to replace the product on the retail shelf as quickly as possible. For retail accounts that provide daily sales information to VF—and that is most of them—goods can be replenished at the store level within four days from the time the customer buys the product. In fact, the firm has the ability to receive sales in the morning, create an order, and ship it within 24 hours. By comparison, in the 1980s, VF took about 30 days to turn an order into a product on the selling floor.

One of the biggest benefits of Quick Response partnerships is gaining access to almost 100 percent of retail sales data by SKU (stockkeeping unit). This has allowed VF to drive the size-planning process. In the past, VF would often find a retailer holding large inventories, yet still be 30 percent out of stock on the best-selling merchandise. Sales were lost because stores had been stocked with the wrong sizes and colors.

Retailers, manufacturers, and their customers will all reap the benefits of implementing Quick Response. Expenses are reduced, and customers are likely to find the merchandise they want in stock, when they want to make a purchase.

BASED ON:

Lloyd, Brenda. (2007, February 12). Outdoor brands drive profits at VF Corp. *Daily News Record*, 36.

Sorkin, Andrew Ross and Barbaro, Michael. (2007, July 27). Apparel maker VF acquires jeans and activewear brands. *The New York Times*, C2.

VF brand solutions. (2002, December). *Impressions*, SP11.

VF Corporation–Chairman, President, CEO Interview. (2005, July 21). *CEO Wire*.

TRENDWATCH

Scanners: How Accurate Are They?

Since the first scanner was installed at a grocery store in 1974, price scanning at checkouts has received both praise and criticism. The elimination of item pricing has netted retailers substantial savings. For example, retailers save 1 to 2 percent of costs in checkout, eliminate item pricing, and reduce the number of employees. Additional savings also accrue with improved efficiency in automatic ordering, improved shelf allocation, improved sales analysis, and better item tracking. For customers, the implementation of scanner technology provides faster store checkout, more detailed receipts, and price reductions resulting from retailers passing along cost savings. Customers have also been promised more accurate pricing as they go through the checkout; however, there have been many reports that retailers may have not delivered on this last promise.

Academic, government, and industry studies, as well as media stories and news reports, have found pricing errors at the checkout to varying degrees. The major problem of comparing these studies was that widely varying methods were used to collect information. For example, some of the studies have concentrated solely on advertised/sale items, whereas others have sampled prices across a store's entire inventory. Some studies have concentrated on one city or county, whereas others have used a national sample. In addition, many of the studies have dealt with pricing accuracy only in one specific retail category, such as grocery stores.

Standardized examination procedures were adopted by the National Conference on Weights and Measures (NCWM) in 1995. The NCWM price verification procedure is based on the assumption that some pricing errors are inevitable due to human or other errors; therefore, the procedure provides that a store "passes" an inspection if 98 percent or more of the items sampled are priced accurately.

The staff at the Federal Trade Commission invited seven states to participate in a joint national study of pricing accuracy. A pricing accuracy rate of 95.18 percent was found. Of the 17,298 items checked, 2.58 percent (446 items) scanned lower than the posted or advertised price, and 2.24 percent (388 items) scanned higher than the posted or advertised price, for a total error rate of 4.82 percent. One hundred percent pricing accuracy was achieved by 66 (22.45 percent) of the stores sampled. A 98 percent accuracy level was attained by 44.9 percent of the stores, and thus would have complied with requirements of the NCWM procedure.

As the FTC was conducting this initial price check study, similar research was being conducted by the author of this text. That pricing accuracy study found that the average price accuracy rate for all stores inspected was 96.13 percent. A total of 5,663 errors was found among the 146,518 items inspected, representing an error percentage of 3.87 percent. Thirty-seven percent of the stores inspected had no errors among the items checked; 58 percent of the stores reached a 98 percent accuracy level.

The findings of these research studies indicate that pricing accuracy is higher than many media reports would lead consumers to believe. Many retailers, however, must strive to improve pricing practices in their stores because many of them are not reaching a 98-percent accuracy rate. In the final analysis, retailers must continue to improve pricing accuracy at the checkout in order to take full advantage of the benefits that the use of scanners provides, both to their stores and to their customers.

BASED ON:

Clodfelter, Richard. (1998). Pricing accuracy at grocery stores and other retail stores using scanners. *International Journal of Retail and Distribution Management*, 26 (11), 412–420.

Federal Trade Commission. (1998). *Price Check II*. Washington, DC: FTC.

Federal Trade Commission. (1996). *A Report by the Staff of the Federal Trade Commission, Technology Services of the National Institute of Standards and Technology*. Washington, DC: FTC.

National Conference on Weights and Measures. (1995). *Examination Procedure for Price Verification*. Gaithersburg, MD: National Institute of Standards and Technology.

TRENDWATCH

RFID: Can It Improve Retail Logistics?

One of the newest retail technologies is RFID (radio frequency identification). RFID tags hold a code called the Electronic Product Code (EPC), which is a unique number that identifies the specific item tagged. RFID tags are more powerful than the conventional bar code.

The tags house a microchip and an antenna with which remote readers are able to communicate. A retailer can follow a tagged item from place to place and even place it geographically. The RFID tag reader can be placed anywhere within a store or warehouse and reliably read a tag up to a 30-foot distance away.

Over the past three years, the number of Wal-Mart stores using RFID has increased tenfold, from 100 stores in 2004 to 1,000 stores in 2007. For retailers overall, the pace of RFID usage has slowed. In fact, plans for RFID installation in Wal-Mart distribution centers is behind schedule and expansion plans for Target have been delayed. However, most retail experts believe that the technology is set to grow exponentially in the next few years.

One of the biggest pushes for adoption of RFID technologies has come from Wal-Mart. In 2006, Wal-Mart announced that RFID pilots resulted in a 16 percent reduction in the number of times products went out of stock, and the company's findings showed that RFID use improved the efficiency of moving products from the backroom to the store shelves by 60 percent. While the implementation of RFID technology into retailing has not come as quickly as many had hoped, there continues to be signs that the technology is getting closer to becoming more widespread.

Selexyz, Netherlands largest bookseller, is one of the first major retailers implementing RFID. The firm introduced the system in an effort to reduce labor costs, improve stock control, and make the store's customer experience more rewarding. For Selexyz, RFID technology follows a customized path—tracking each book from the central warehouse to each store. At that point, the software reconciles the shipping notice with the books that have actually been received, keeps tabs on each book as it moves through the store, and is able to identify books incorrectly shelved in wrong sections. One of the rewards to Selexyz has been a 50 percent increase in customer sales at in-store kiosks that can identify each book that is in the store as well as its exact location. The accuracy achieved by the RFID system approaches 100 percent. Any errors have been part of the remaining manual processes or tags becoming detached. The RFID tags used by Selexyz each cost about ten cents when purchased in quantities of 500,000. In smaller quantities, the tags cost from 20 to 40 cents each, but pressure from suppliers is forcing chip manufacturers to strive for a target of five cents per tag in this decade.

Retailers do benefit. During a pilot at New Balance stores, inventory accuracy increased and out-of-stocks were reduced. Restocking time by sales associates on the floor, receiving time for incoming merchandise, and store shrinkage were all reduced while the accuracy of receiving reports increased.

Some states are reacting to the threat of privacy loss that RFID presents. One state has proposed the Identity Information Protection Act to prohibit use of RFIDs that can be read remotely and without a person's knowledge. This could include all state identity documents, such as drivers' licenses, student IDs, and medical cards. Several organizations, including SmartCode Research, have taken on the mission of finding a solution for reducing privacy concerns by targeting RFID tags.

As the demand for shorter lead times in the flow of products increase, the use of RFID technology is bound to increase as well.

BASED ON:

Ayling, Joe. (2006, August 3). RFID revolution only just beginning. *Just-food.com*.

Cacere, Lora. (2007, May 2). Three years of retail RFID pilots. *Forbes.com*.

Davison, John. (2006, January 19). The future of IT in retailing–how retailers can keep the customer satisfied. *Computing*, 24.

Fontanella, John. (2007, April 4). RFID and the search for perfect logistics. *Forbes.com*.

Malone, Robert. (2006, May 24). RFID speeds order fulfillment. *Forbes.com*.

Malone, Robert. (2006, October 24). Smart store. *Forbes.com*

Malone, Robert. (2006, December 17). Can RFID invade your privacy? *Forbes.com*.

New Balance store: testing ground for RFID benefits. (2007, June). *Apparel*, SS3.

RFID's day still coming, just later than expected. (2006, November 6). *Chain Drug Review*, 37.

Purchasing Merchandise

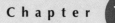

Selecting Vendors and Building Partnerships

PERFORMANCE OBJECTIVES

Upon completion of this chapter, you should be able to:

- Identify how buyers locate new vendors.
- List and describe different types of vendors.
- Explain criteria that buyers use to select vendors.
- Describe methods that buyers use to evaluate vendors.
- Outline procedures for developing buyer–vendor partnerships.
- Recognize that strong buyer–vendor partnerships are needed for retailers to be successful.

After you have developed your merchandise plan, you will need to locate sources of supply, or *vendors*, to provide the merchandise that will satisfy the wants and needs of your customers. Manufacturers, wholesalers, jobbers, and manufacturers' representatives are just some of the vendors from which you can choose. There are numerous types of vendors for each category of merchandise that you will be purchasing for your store, and it will be an important part of your job to select the right ones. As you will learn, profitable buying decisions are based on choosing both the right merchandise and the right vendor. In addition, much of your success as a buyer will hinge on your ability to deal with vendors and develop a strong partnership relationship with them.

In this chapter, you will learn about the different types of vendors with which buyers will conduct business, as well as the criteria used to select those vendors. Emphasis is also be placed on developing and maintaining strong buyer–vendor partnerships.

TYPES OF VENDORS

For some product categories, you must not only choose from many different vendors, but you must also decide whether to purchase directly from the producer or from a *middleman*, who acts as an intermediary between the buyer and seller. Again, careful analysis should allow you to choose the one that best meets your needs. Vendors are typically classified as (1) manufacturers, (2) wholesalers, (3) manufacturers' representatives/brokers, and (4) rack jobbers.

Manufacturers

Selecting a manufacturer as your source of supply may not be your decision to make. The minimum order required by many manufacturers is so large that your store may be unable to make a purchase directly. If so, you will be forced to make your purchases from some type of middleman.

Buyers of fashion goods typically make purchases directly from manufacturers or their representatives in the market. Because of the rapidity of the change in most fashion goods, styles could change if the merchandise had to go through other middlemen. Also, most fashion goods are produced just before the selling season, which requires that they reach the market with a minimum of handling and delay.

Those retailers who want to establish their own private brands also place their orders directly with manufacturers who are willing to make minor changes in their products if a large enough order is being placed. Thus, purchasing private brands directly from the manufacturer allows the retailer to secure merchandise that will not be available in other retail stores. In addition to purchase quotas, some manufacturers may also establish both promotion and pricing requirements for goods they sell directly to the retailer. You will need to analyze such policies before making the purchase agreement. The chief benefit of purchasing direct is that costs are lower because middlemen are eliminated from the distribution process.

Wholesalers

You may choose a wholesaler as the source of merchandise that you are unable to purchase directly from a manufacturer. A *wholesaler* is an organization that purchases merchandise from a manufacturer in large quantities and resells the goods in smaller amounts to retailers. Wholesalers are also known as *merchant middlemen* because they take possession of the goods they purchase from manufacturers.

A local wholesaler may be an ideal choice for your merchandise purchases if it maintains a broad assortment of merchandise that is ready for quick delivery. Also, most wholesalers will accept small orders, which allows you to experiment with new merchandise at a minimal risk because less of the store's capital is tied up in inventory. The store may also realize an improved stock turnover due to the smaller amounts of merchandise needed in stock because it can be quickly replenished from a nearby wholesaler.

Although most large retailers make purchases directly from the manufacturer, there are times when they need to purchase some merchandise from a wholesaler. For example, products with limited customer demand cannot be ordered directly from the manufacturer because the order would not be large enough. Quick shipments for emergency stock fill-ins also require that purchases be made at a nearby wholesaler.

In recent years, wholesalers are increasingly providing merchandising assistance to retailers in addition to just selling them merchandise. Such practices improve the working relationship between the retailer and the vendor, further developing a mutual partnership. The primary disadvantage of using a wholesaler, rather than buying direct from the manufacturer, is that merchandise will cost more because a middleman is involved in the buying process.

Manufacturers' Representatives/Brokers

You may also place an order through a *manufacturer's representative* or *broker* who acts as an agent for the manufacturer. These brokers are also known as *nonmerchant middlemen* because they do not take possession of the merchandise before selling it to the retailer. The manufacturer pays a fee to the representative or broker for bringing the producer and buyer together. The fee is usually a percentage of net sales that varies by product category, sales volume, and the number of services provided.

You can visit these vendors at showrooms in regional markets or trade shows, and most of them make personal calls on client stores. They typically represent several noncompeting lines from manufacturers across the country, thus saving you time and travel expenses by giving you the opportunity to view merchandise samples in a nearby showroom or your own store.

Rack Jobbers

Rack jobbers are a special type of vendor who services client stores themselves. They are chiefly found in the food industry, but some department stores use them in areas where special merchandising techniques are needed. As supermarkets extended their operations to nonfood lines such as cosmetics, toiletries, and housewares, they needed special assistance in purchasing and other merchandising decisions. They turned to rack jobbers.

Retail stores that use rack jobbers assign them rack or shelf space that they are responsible for keeping stocked with quick-turning merchandise. The store is visited by the rack jobber once or more a week to restock shelves and make any needed changes in the merchandise assortment being offered. Jobbers usually make better use of the space than would the store manager because they have had more experience in anticipating consumer demand, pricing the merchandise, and displaying it.

Although using a rack jobber may cost more than making purchases from a wholesaler, the retailer usually realizes a cost savings due to the benefits gained from the jobber's services. In most cases, these costs are only slightly higher because the rack jobber is a volume purchaser and is entitled to quantity discounts.

MAKING CONTACT WITH POTENTIAL VENDORS

One of the first questions new buyers will need to answer is, "Where can I locate vendors?" In some instances, you may have to initiate contact with potential vendors. In other situations, they may initiate contact with you.

Buyer-Initiated Contacts

A primary source of vendors will be found by visiting markets and trade shows (Figure 11.1); however, not all vendors have showrooms at regional markets or exhibit at trade shows. You may have to schedule appointments to personally visit some vendors.

If you are a client of a buying office, its representatives will be able to locate resources for you. In fact, buying offices are constantly scouting

Figure 11.1 Buyers can locate new vendors by visiting markets and trade shows.

the market for new vendors that could be of special interest to their client stores.

Reading current magazines and trade journals and subscribing to a retail reporting service are other ways to learn about potential new vendors in the market or learn more about established vendors. Many trade directories are also available that list and describe vendors.

Phone calls or e-mails to other buyers and conversations with them during market visits can also provide you with information that others have found to be beneficial. Shopping the competition's store can also help identify possible new suppliers.

Vendor-Initiated Contacts

Some vendors send sales representatives on frequent visits to retailers, whereas others rely on catalogs and bulletins for such contact. Many buyers for independent small stores tend to purchase from those vendors that assume the cost of the contact because of the expense and time involved in making market visits (Figure 11.2). They also prefer repre-

Figure 11.2 Many vendors have established specific merchandising and display criteria for their merchandise.

sentatives who call at regular intervals, follow up on their requests, and help maintain stock assortments in the store.

Most manufacturers' representatives contact their retail clients on a periodic basis to ensure there is an adequate supply of merchandise in the store. However, relying solely on representatives who visit your store does not allow you to compare merchandise offerings, prices, and services with those of other vendors.

Having the broadest possible market contacts with potential vendors will be most advantageous to you and your store. Changes are continuously occurring in the market, so it is essential that you maintain contact with other vendors even though you may not be making purchases from them. This practice allows you to determine if the quality and price of the merchandise you are purchasing is equal to or better than that of the competition.

Although a broad market coverage is important, most stores select a few vendors with whom to concentrate a large part of their purchases. These selected vendors are known as *key resources*. Concentrating your purchases ensures your importance to these vendors because of the size of your order. In addition, larger orders more easily qualify for quantity discounts. Because a mutual feeling of partnership develops when purchases are made repeatedly from the same vendor, your store will usually receive better service from the vendor. You always want to be open to new, exciting products from new vendors so do not overdo the concept of key resources.

After selecting key resources, most buyers distribute a certain amount of their purchases to other vendors in order to broaden their market contacts and to experiment with new merchandise or new vendors. This practice provides them with an alternative source of supply if the key resource is unable to meet an order. Having broader market coverage also allows the buyer to keep a close eye on what other vendors are offering.

CRITERIA FOR SELECTING VENDORS

Once you have identified the potential vendors from whom you can make your purchases, you will need to screen each of them. The following criteria should be considered as you select the vendors that are right for your customers and your store: (1) merchandise and prices offered, (2) vendor's distribution policies, (3) vendor's reputation and reliability, (4) terms offered, and (5) services offered.

Merchandise and Prices Offered

Your primary consideration should be whether the merchandise carried by the vendor is compatible with the needs and wants of your customers. If the merchandise is not right for your customers, the vendor should not be considered. You will also want to ensure that merchandise being offered meets the quality standards that both you and your customers expect. For example, when purchasing apparel, you will also be responsible for checking the quality of merchandise delivered to your store to make sure that it meets the quality of the samples you saw when the order was placed.

A wide assortment of merchandise offered by the vendor would be a key consideration for many retailers. Probably, you will also be looking for unique or distinctive merchandise. Having distinctive merchandise for your customers is a necessity if your store image is one of providing fashion leadership in the community. In this case, you must have new merchandise that has not yet gained acceptance from the masses. You may also look for vendors who distinguish their products in some way. Differences may occur in construction or styling or simply in the packaging provided by the vendor.

Another decision you need to make is whether to purchase national brands or develop private brands for your store. If you are looking for a particular brand of merchandise, selection of a vendor may be automatic. National brands have immediate recognition and usually ensure that a large number of customers already know about the product and want to purchase it. Private brands will offer your customers merchandise they cannot obtain at other stores, but there has been no national advertising campaign to presell your customers. For that reason, your costs are lower, allowing you higher markups.

Vendors' Distribution Policies

Choosing a vendor will also be affected by the distribution policies of the vendor. *Exclusive distribution* is a practice of some vendors whereby they sell the product to only one retailer in a trading area. Vendors benefit from an exclusive image that is created for the product. With exclusive distribution, the vendor usually retains some control over how the product is merchandised and promoted in the store.

Designer lines of cosmetics are frequently marketed through exclusive distribution. Also, owners of clothing stores in small communities frequently request exclusive distribution from vendors. They want to be able to offer their customers unique merchandise that cannot be found in competing stores in the town. Receiving exclusive distribution may be the factor that determines from which vendor you decide to make your purchases.

Some vendors use a similar practice known as *selective distribution* whereby they sell the product to one or more selected retailers in the same trading area. The number of stores selected is usually determined by the potential sales volume in the area. Again, because the number of stores is controlled, the vendor will usually place certain restrictions on retailers selling the product. For example, Ralph Lauren has established specific merchandising and display criteria for stores carrying the Polo line.

The price of the merchandise being offered by the vendor must also be a consideration as you decide from which vendor to make your purchases. The image and target customer of your store will dictate the price range of merchandise that you will be able to consider.

Vendors' Reputation and Reliability

Vendors vary in dependability with respect to the way they conduct business. Prompt delivery of the complete order will be an essential criterion by which to judge vendors. In addition, you will also want to determine a vendor's reputation for such areas as quality control and speed in handling complaints and adjustments. Talking with other buyers or consulting with your resident buying office will allow you to determine if a vendor with whom you are considering doing business is having major problems.

Terms Offered

Some retailers may want substantial cash discounts from vendors, whereas stores with limited financial resources may want more time in which to pay. Discounts offered by vendors you are considering should be at least equal to those prevailing in the industry. Some retailers choose vendors who are located near their store or near shipping routes to speed delivery. In addition to credit terms, most retailers are also interested in having shipping charges paid for by the vendor. Both credit and shipping terms are described in detail in Chapter 14.

Services Provided

Services provided by the vendor can be a deciding factor in determining from whom you will make your purchases. Services provided by vendors that may be valued by your store could include any or all of the following:

- *Cooperative Advertising Arrangements*. Many vendors will share the cost of local advertising with the retailer if their products are featured in ads (Figure 11.3).
- *Advertising Aids*. Vendors may provide copy suggestions, mats, and broadcast scripts for products your store purchases from them. Small stores may prefer vendors that provide signs, counter and window display units, fixturing, and other point-of-sale aids. Larger stores prefer the uniformity of their own fixturing.
- *Return and Exchange Privileges*. When choosing vendors, many buyers look for liberal return policies.

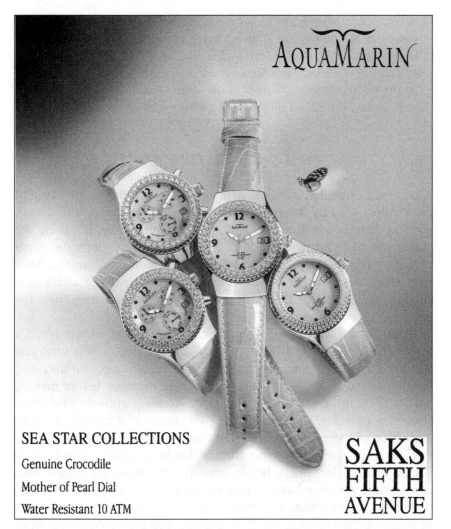

SEA STAR COLLECTIONS

Genuine Crocodile

Mother of Pearl Dial

Water Resistant 10 ATM

Figure 11.3 Example of cooperative advertising between Saks and Aqua-Marin.

- *Participation in Store Promotions.* Retailers want vendors who will participate in promotions planned by the store. For example, vendors may be asked to provide prizes for contests or clothing to be used in fashion shows.
- *Sales Training.* Some vendors will provide training for store salespeople when their products are purchased by the store. They may even establish awards programs for salespeople who sell above a specified quota of their products.

- *Assistance in Stock Control.* Bar coding of merchandise and improved computer technology are allowing many vendors to provide retailers help in conducting stock counts and developing model stocks.
- *Preticketing of Merchandise.* Some vendors will mark merchandise ordered by the retailer before it arrives at the store. Such a service saves the store money and allows shipments to move quickly to the sales floor.

ANALYZING VENDOR PERFORMANCE

A common error that some new buyers make is to eliminate many of the vendors used by the store in the past and start fresh. You do not want to dismiss a well-established vendor haphazardly, but there are reasons to seek out new vendors. For example, a vendor's standards may have slipped or its prices may have increased too rapidly. Also, your store may move toward a different target customer and a new vendor may be required, or a new and better resource may enter the field.

Relationships with vendors should not be disrupted arbitrarily. As a buyer, before deciding to drop a vendor and select a new one, you will need to carefully analyze the situation. In addition, you may also be required to check with your merchandise manager before making such a decision. Before disrupting your store's partnership relationship with a vendor, a systematic analysis needs to be conducted. Such a practice will strengthen your store's buyer–vendor relationships.

If several vendors offer you comparable merchandise, you have to decide which offer is best. If you have not previously purchased from the vendor, you may have to rely on what others have to say about the vendor's reputation. As a buyer, you will value your vendors, both in terms of the merchandise they provide and the profit potential of that merchandise.

If you are ordering from vendors with whom you have had prior experience, vendor profiles can be developed based on information you or the store have accumulated. You will want to develop a systematic method of evaluating the vendors that you use. One way to do this is by keeping a **vendor diary**–brief summaries of your dealings with each vendor with whom you do business. Even though the amount and type of information collected will vary from one buyer to another, certain basic data are essential. For each vendor you might want to record the following information:

- Total purchases for the year or season, at cost and original retail;
- returns to the vendor, if any;
- initial markup percentage;
- advertising allowances granted, if any;
- markdowns taken, by dollar value and as a percentage of sales;
- cash discounts as a percentage; and
- transportation expense as a percentage of purchases.

This information provides you with a good indication of how much a vendor has contributed to your store or department's sales volume and profit. In addition, you might want to consider other subjective factors such as:

- Customer opinions about the vendor's merchandise;
- reliability of the vendor's deliveries, including delivery of reorders;
- reliability of merchandise quality;
- promptness of the vendor in adjusting complaints; and
- services provided your store or department in such areas as conducting stock counts, preticketing of merchandise, and sales training.

You can use the information that you have collected in several ways to evaluate each vendor. Among them:

- Each vendor can be measured against its own performance when compared with prior years or seasons.
- Vendors can be measured against the performance of other vendors. For this reason, it is extremely important to record much of your data as a percentage.
- Vendors can be measured against their percentage of the store or department's total orders. For example, if a vendor accounts for 25 percent of the merchandise purchased by your store, did it also account for 25 percent of the profits earned?

Even though this process involves quantitative analysis (Table 11.1), you still make the final judgment. You must set standards about what is considered acceptable or unacceptable performance.

Remember that as you rate your vendors, they are also analyzing the profitability of doing business with your store. They rate your store or department on how you merchandise and sell their products as well as how fairly they have been treated.

Table 11.1: A sample analysis report of all products purchased from Vendor #125.

FORM SI-248

STYLE	VENDOR TRAK (R) CLASS	IMU PCT	FIRST RECVD STAT	BEG QTY	SLS QTY	MARKDOWNS PCT	MARKDOWNS QTY	RETURNS PCT	RETURNS QTY	REC QTY	END QTY	SALES RETAIL	GROSS PROFIT	GP PCT	PROJ GP PCT	SELL THRU	ON ORDER RANK
VENDOR 000125																	
3410 POLY/L A LAW L/S	00200	60.4%	10/16..C..	0	31	0.0%	1	13.9%	5	62	31	1602.	1013.	63.2%	61.9%	50.0%	01 H
5700 ASST PR/S-S JWL NCK	00200	56.5%	05/14ME....	0	48	14.9%	34	0.0%	0	48	0	1588.	796.	50.1%	50.1%	100.0%	02 H
7370 HARLEQUIN/FLANGE JWL	00200	55.3%	11/01....T	0	9	0.0%	0	0.0%	0	12	3	594.	328.	55.3%	55.3%	75.0%	03 H
9506 CHIFFON/ELAS WST SKT	00262	55.1%	11/13M.....	0	10	23.0%	8	16.7%	2	15	5	626.	321.	51.3%	44.6%	66.7%	04 H
7347 PLAID/FL JWL NK L/S	00200	55.3%	10/16M.C.T	0	7	17.1%	9	0.0%	0	8	1	434.	227.	52.4%	49.4%	87.5%	05 H
6508 ABSTR SPLSH/PLT COL	00200	52.2%	06/26M.....	0	10	36.7%	19	0.0%	0	10	0	518.	193.	37.3%	37.3%	100.0%	06 H
7369 PUZZLE/FLANGE JWLNK	00200	53.7%	11/01.....	0	5	0.0%	0	0.0%	0	11	6	330.	182.	55.3%	55.3%	45.5%	07 H
2502 ABSTR FL/V-CRSH DRAP	00200	55.3%	08/02M.....	0	5	5.1%	1	0.0%	0	5	0	314.	161.	51.4%	51.4%	100.0%	08 H
7367 ABSTR HNDTH/FL JWL	00200	55.3%	12/05..C.T	0	4	0.0%	0	0.0%	0	10	6	264.	146.	55.3%	55.3%	40.0%	09 H
6501U POLY/D B DRAPE FICHU	00200	62.5%	11/13	0	3	0.0%	0	0.0%	0	12	9	180.	112.	62.5%	62.5%	25.0%	10 H
7372U MULTI TRI/FLNG JWLNK	00200	55.3%	11/01M.....	0	3	0.0%	0	0.0%	0	10	7	198.	109.	55.3%	44.8%	30.0%	11 H
1302V POLY/S/S SHELL	00200	64.2%	12/10.....	0	1	0.0%	0	0.0%	0	3	2	38.	24.	64.2%	64.2%	33.3%	12 H
VENDOR TOTAL				0	136	9.9%	72	4.9%	7	206	70	6686.	3615.	54.1%	54.4%	66.0%	
FINAL TOTAL				0	136	9.9%	72	4.9%	7	206	70	6686.	3615.	54.1%	54.4%	66.0%	

DEVELOPING STRONG BUYER–VENDOR PARTNERSHIPS

Respect and cooperation between buyer and seller are necessary to ensure long-term profitability for both parties. Once you decide to place orders with a vendor, you both will need to work to build a strong partnership.

Vendors want to do business with buyers who pay bills promptly, accept goods they order, and do not return merchandise unless it has been authorized. Buyers seek to do business with vendors who ship the merchandise that was ordered in the right quantities and at the time specified. To achieve these goals, buyers and sellers need to act as partners, not adversaries.

Basis for Strong Partnerships with Vendors

You can build strong partnerships with your vendors by following simple courtesies such as:

- Being prompt in keeping appointments with vendors.
- Visiting with manufacturers' representatives who call on your store. There is probably always something new to learn about the market.
- Giving your full attention to their presentations.
- Promptly confirming or canceling any tentative orders you have placed. You should confirm in writing all agreements with vendors to avoid misunderstandings.
- Keeping the promises that you make. Orders should not be canceled before their cancellation date.
- Providing feedback to the vendor on how the merchandise has done in your store or department.
- Not making snap judgments when deciding to eliminate or change vendors. Changes should occur only after careful analysis on your part. Long-term performance by the vendor, not a temporary setback, should be the most important consideration.

Your success as a buyer will be based, in part, on your ability to establish good working relationships with your store's vendors.

Buyers' Expectations of Vendors

What do experienced buyers expect from their vendors? What makes an ideal relationship between a retailer and its vendors? Most buyers probably want the following:

Merchandising Help Through Technology. Most buyers need assistance in developing an assortment plan that would be specific to each store. Electronic data interchange (EDI) is really revolutionizing the business. It is vital that manufacturers have UPC (universal product codes) on their packages. Automatic reordering benefits the store because retailers using the system can carry less inventory and make quicker reorders than with manual counts. Automatic reorder systems also allow retailers to get a quicker handle on which sales trends are up or down.

Many buyers also want assistance in managing inventory and creating model stocks. The best way vendors can help most stores is by helping to eliminate the nonperformers and keeping retailers in stock on the items that perform well. Vendors can help buyers by analyzing sales reports and model stocks on a frequent basis. What is needed are vendors who continually service the stores, filling in stock based on sales.

Sales Training. Many buyers want vendors to provide in-store training and retraining of salespeople. Other buyers feel vendor-supplied sales training is not as helpful because of the high turnover of salespeople.

Fixturing and Visuals. Some buyers believe that vendors could do a much better job in participating in store fixturing at a reasonable and minimal cost. However, the higher the class of store, the less likely it is to use vendor-supplied fixturing. Many buyers want fixtures that do not have any vendor identification, whereas others have asked for funds from vendors to improve fixturing.

Packaging. Most buyers want packaging that is clear and self-explanatory. Packaging needs to be distinguished so that customers can say, "I know what I'm looking for—it's the one in the blue package." Some buyers feel that vendors need to reexamine the way they package products. For example, some products that are only shipped by the dozen, might if packaged by fewer units, provide a better assortment to their customers.

Timely Delivery. All buyers want "faster delivery" from vendors. Prompt shipment of orders and timely delivery are crucial. Timely delivery and merchandise quality and consistency should be "givens" that buyers can expect from any vendor.

Future Trends

The changes in retailing over the past few years have also contributed to changes in the relationships between retailers and vendors. Business troubles have forced the closing of hundreds of specialty stores, and mergers have consolidated many department stores. The move by Sears and other retailers to shift toward national brands has also had an impact on vendors.

Closer Buyer–Vendor Relationships. Most vendors and retailers are forming closer relationships. As retailers consolidate and merge, there is a tendency to develop stronger relationships with large vendors who can provide the quantities and service level that most small vendors would not be able to match. Yet, some vendors complain that consolidation in retailing may have given too much power to a handful of very large firms. Some of these large retailers have placed demands on vendors that they feel cannot be refused for fear of losing such a large account.

Closer relations between retailers and vendors are also a result of better communications. The vendor and the retailer must know each other's problems. Vendors must discuss with buyers the markups they need, the markdowns with which they can live, and the speed of inventory turns. Technological advances have also aided improved communication. Bar coding and computerized systems now allow vendors to give retailers accurate and up-to-date information on the status of their orders.

Consolidation of Vendors. Many small- and medium-sized vendors could also be in trouble. Just as in retailing, those vendors in the middle, with little to distinguish themselves, will face stiff competition from other vendors who appeal to specific retailing niches. Smaller vendors will need to increase their efforts to compete with the larger vendors. They will have to learn how to offset technological advantages of size by being more flexible and by customizing their approach to stores. The small vendor will have to find a way to do things for the retailer that the larger vendors, due to their size, are not going to be able to do.

Vendor-Owned Stores. Some vendors are using another approach—doing their own retailing with *vendor-owned stores*. Read the Snapshot, titled, "IKEA: Building a Global Empire," to learn more about one manufacturer's expansion plans. Manufacturers that open vendor-owned stores feel they can do a better job of selling their products than traditional retailers. For example, many fashion designers do not feel that department stores do justice to their lines. A designer may have 50 styles in a line, but a buyer may select only 11 of the 50. The designers feel that because department stores are not displaying their lines correctly, sales are not what they should be. Read the Trend-watch titled, "Manufacturers' Factory Outlet Stores," to learn more about another type of vendor-owned store.

Vendor-owned stores offer three key benefits. They include (1) the ability to display the entire line, (2) the ability to create an environment for the line according to the designer's concept, and (3) the ability to obtain feedback from customers on the entire line, not just pieces of the line. Rather than starting their own stores, other vendors are asking for an area specifically dedicated to their merchandise within a retail store. They also increase designer identification by not being thrown in with the rest of the store's assortments. For retailers, such a concept is acceptable only if they can justify a return in terms of sales per square foot. They will not give the space to any vendor who simply asks for it.

Vendor-owned stores must be viewed with more than mixed feelings by retailers. Retailers will need to keep a watchful eye on sales to determine the long-range effect of competition coming from these stores; they may erode sales. If vendor-owned stores are successful, many products may no longer be available to traditional retailers. These stores also mean more competition for retailers. Some companies, such as Liz Claiborne and Nike, say they are using vendor-owned stores as laboratories to test new products. This information is then shared with traditional retail clients.

Vendor-owned stores also face certain problems. Products being sold in vendor-owned stores are being dropped by some traditional retailers. Vendor-owned stores relying on a single manufacturer may experience a poor product mix, and buyers may become lazy in their search for new ideas and styles because their choices are limited. Many manufacturers have learned that retailing is a very different business from manufacturing–there have been failures as well as successes.

Today, there is a conscious effort by buyers to treat their vendors as valuable company assets. They are working to lessen past adversarial relationships and replace them with partnerships based on trust. Vendors continue to offer new products and use sales pitches to enhance their brands. Buyers continue to ask for more and better terms and deals; and, the relationships between the two continues to change.

SUMMARY POINTS

- Once they have made their merchandise buying plans, buyers must select vendors to supply needed merchandise.
- Vendors are typically classified as manufacturers, wholesalers, manufacturers' representatives, and rack jobbers. For many purchases, buyers must use middlemen to supply their needs.
- Buyers can initiate contacts with vendors through market visits, personal calls, or contacting their buying office. Vendors initiate contacts with buyers through bulletins, catalogs, and personal visits by manufacturers' representatives.
- Most buyers rely on key resources for the majority of their purchases in order to qualify for quantity discounts and receive better service; however, purchases are made with other vendors to broaden market contacts, keep key resources competitive, and experiment with new merchandise.
- Buyers select vendors based on the following criteria: merchandise and prices offered, vendor's distribution policies, vendor's reputation and reliability, terms offered, and services offered.
- Buyers should develop vendor diaries to evaluate each vendor in relation to predetermined goals in areas such as sales, returns, markups, and markdowns.
- After selecting vendors, buyers should work to develop strong buyer-vendor relationships. Buyers and vendors need to be partners, not adversaries.
- Many buyers want vendors to provide them with merchandising help through technology, sales training, fixturing and visuals, packaging, and timely delivery.
- Closer relationships between buyers and vendors will likely occur in the future.

REVIEW ACTIVITIES

Developing Your Retail Buying Vocabulary

Consult the Glossary if you did not add the following words to your vocabulary.

Broker	Rack jobber
Exclusive distribution	Selective distribution
Key resource	Vendor
Manufacturer's representative	Vendor diary
Merchant middleman	Vendor-owned store
Middleman	Wholesaler
Nonmerchant middleman	

Understanding What You Read

1. Describe why a retailer might require a buyer to get approval from top management before changing vendors.
2. What procedures should a buyer follow to locate new vendors?
3. Describe why retailers should not rely solely on vendors who have made the effort to contact them.
4. Describe why many buyers rely on key resources.
5. Can a buyer put too much reliance on key resources? Explain.
6. Identify types of retailers who would buy directly from a manufacturer.
7. Describe why fashion goods do not typically go through a wholesaler.
8. Identify types of retailers who would buy from a wholesaler.
9. Describe how manufacturers' representatives are paid.
10. What benefits do rack jobbers provide retailers?
11. What is the drawback to using a rack jobber?
12. Describe how identifying store image and target customers will allow buyers to narrow the choice of vendors from which they can choose.
13. Describe why clothing stores in small towns want exclusive distribution from vendors.
14. What are the drawbacks to exclusive and selective distribution?
15. Describe why many large retailers do not accept vendor-supplied fixtures.
16. What will small vendors have to do in the future to successfully compete with larger vendors?

17. What factors should be considered by the buyer when evaluating a vendor?
18. Describe why buyers should periodically evaluate all vendors.
19. Identify benefits that vendor-owned stores offer designers.
20. What can vendors do to strengthen their partnerships with buyers?

Analyzing and Applying What You Read

1. Describe why a newly hired buyer would want to change many of the vendors used by a store in the past. Describe the procedures you would follow before dismissing a vendor.
2. Describe why some buyers go to central markets often, whereas others go infrequently. What are the drawbacks of each practice?
3. You have recently signed a contract with a new vendor which you expect will develop into one of your store's key resources. Describe what you would do to ensure that the relationship develops into a strong partnership.
4. When would it be better to compare a vendor's performance with its own past performance rather than the performance of other vendors? Explain.
5. Describe why a strong buyer–vendor partnership is important to the vendor as well as the retailer.
6. Even though owners of vendor-owned stores say retailers have nothing to fear from them, why might retailers worry?

Internet Connection

1. Identify three manufacturers for products with which you are familiar. Access the manufacturers' Web sites (use a search engine, if necessary) and determine if these products can be purchased directly from the vendor online. Discuss the pros and cons of manufacturers selling directly to consumers.
2. Identify a wholesaler with which you are familiar. Use a search engine to locate a Web site for the firm. Compare and contrast how a wholesaler's Web site is similar as well as different from a traditional retail site.

SNAPSHOT

IKEA: Building a Global Empire

IKEA, the world's largest home furnishings chain, has successfully invaded the United States. The low-cost furniture store has now become the norm for consumers who are furnishing their first apartments. And, worldwide growth continues. In 2006, IKEA owned more than 254 stores in 35 countries, with 84,000 employees, and generated sales of $15.5 billion. The success of this global empire is based on a simple philosophy—offer a wide range of home furnishings that have good design and function at a price that the majority of consumers can afford.

Function, rather than fancy, has always guided IKEA design, which started out with light woods, birch and pine, combined with natural materials, such as cotton and linen. Although some of the newest designs may be more international, the firm still retains its identity with Scandinavia.

Virtually all IKEA furniture falls into the knocked-down category, requiring some work on the part of the customer. About 40 percent of the furniture and all the accessories and small items are self-serviced from stock on the selling floor. Other purchases are delivered to customers at the checkout area or to their homes in IKEA delivery trucks. A thick, full-color catalog remains IKEA's major marketing tool, and its production accounts for half the company's marketing budget.

Shopping at IKEA is meant to be a family outing—from the gigantic parking lots to the supervised playroom filled with multicolored balls, slides, and other fun things just inside the entrance. An inexpensive self-service restaurant specializing in Scandinavian fare, such as gravlax, is usually placed about midway through most stores.

IKEA opened its first store in the United States in a Philadelphia suburb in 1985 and met with immediate success. This store, however, was a little too quirky—its European bed sizes did not match American mattress and sheet sizes, for example. Although the first store was profitable, a quick expansion to seven U.S. stores put the chain in the red. Financial experts even suggest that if IKEA had been a public company, shareholders would have demanded it close operations in the United States. By 1997, however, with new product lines, IKEA was in the black.

With expansion, IKEA has defined a very specific wish list of its ideal customers. The ideal shoppers are between 20 and 49 years old, with a high school or college education. Their income is upward of $30,000. In terms of life stage, they run the gamut from college students to first-time homeowners to families with children. The retailer also looks for areas with more than 1.5 million people within a 30-mile radius.

In addition to the U.S. success, IKEA has been equally successful in other parts of the world. The company had an incredibly successful opening of a store in Moscow in April 2000, with over 40,000 visitors on its first day. A month after the opening, the store still packed in 100,000 visitors a week, and the firm has invested $79 million to build the largest IKEA store in Asia.

Presently, IKEA management intends to increase its presence in the United States. Headquarters has given the green light to opening two to three stores a year. The United States already accounts for 10 percent of company sales. Such expansion will make the North American division the fastest-growing division of the IKEA global empire.

Ambitious expansion plans, however face a new obstacle–Home Depot's Expo Design Centers, a home furnishings extension of the home improvement chain. There is also fresh competition from privately held Crate & Barrel, with a trendy CB2 spinoff. New product designs at Target are also providing direct competition.

IKEA continues to experiment to keep one step ahead. Fifteen to twenty in-house designers are employed, plus another 100 outside design resources. New products are continually reaching store shelves–such as Noguchi-inspired rice paper lamps and fabric furniture filled with air.

Experts agree that one factor primarily accounts for IKEA's success. The company has stayed consistent over time. The stores always occupy large spaces, offer modern furniture and home goods, provide outstanding service, and are kid-friendly, leading rivals to continually re-invent themselves to compete. IKEA has found a formula, perfected it, and leveraged it to the hilt. The firm's best marketing investment has been in satisfied customers who help sell IKEA to others. Management knows what has made IKEA successful, and it has delivered that concept successfully around the globe.

Based on:

Capell, Kerry. (2005, November 14). IKEA: how the Swedish retailer became a global cult brand. *Business Week*, 96.

Cassidy, William B. (2007, June 11). Savannah's Swede deal. *Traffic World*, 32.

Creativity key to growth. (2007, July 19). *Marketing Week*, 30.

Goldbogen, Jessica. (2000, April 10). Swedish invasion. *HFN: The Weekly Newspaper for the Home Furnishing Network*, 8.

Heller, Richard. (2000, September 4). The myth called Sweden. *Forbes*, 66.

IKEA: a household name. (2005, May 30). *The Journal of Commerce*, 28A.

TRENDWATCH

Manufacturers' Factory Outlet Stores

In the 1990s, manufacturers' outlet stores were rapidly expanding. Today, however, that growth has slowed. Most manufacturers have slowed their store openings, focusing more on managing existing stores and ensuring profitable growth.

Factory outlet stores are owned and operated by manufacturers who market and distribute their products at discounted prices. They are typically located in remote areas or near tourist areas. By opening their own stores in outlet centers, manufacturers can control their sales and the way their goods are presented.

In the early 1990s, as consumers became more demanding, the appearance of factory outlet stores changed. More sophisticated store designs, better ambiance, and more amenities contributed to the growth of outlet centers. Outlet center stores were no longer garishly lit spaces, filled with boxes heaped with clothing. In fact, *upscale* became the new buzzword for developers, as outlet centers took the form of upscale "villages" with a strong emphasis on brand names.

Most outlet stores have become well-arranged retail shops that provide attention to customer service and stock merchandise similar to that found in traditional retail stores. In fact, many outlet stores are barely distinguishable from stores in regional malls.

Today, manufacturers' outlet stores are facing strong competition from other retailers, particularly department stores in regional malls that have learned to compete by offering sales that feature frequent and deep discounts. No longer do consumers have to travel long distances to outlet stores in search of low prices—they may do as well at a sale in their local mall. This narrowing price gap has become one of the primary challenges facing factory outlet retailers.

Changing merchandise mixes at outlet stores have also had an impact on pricing and marketing strategies. In the past, much of the merchandise found at factory outlets was out-of-date or defective merchandise. That changed dramatically in the 1990s. Outlets today include designer and brand names such as Eddie Bauer, Geoffrey Beene, Liz Claiborne, J. Crew, Calvin Klein, Nike, Oshkosh B'Gosh, and Polo/Ralph Lauren.

Research reported in *Value Retail News* found that 37 percent of the merchandise shipments to outlet centers could be found in traditional retail stores at the same time, *but at the tail-end of their retail life span*. This merchandise often includes fashion duds or overproduced apparel, but some manufacturers even include parts of their current lines at full retail price. Converse, for example, uses outlets to showcase its current lines at full price. Thirty-two percent of the merchandise found in outlets were closeouts that included merchandise past the retail store season but still appropriate for many consumers. Seconds and irregulars accounted for only 18 percent of the merchandise carried. These merchandise defects may be minuscule or even nonexistent. In some situations, first-quality merchandise may have been labeled as defective out of desire to maintain good relations with full-price retailers carrying the line.

About half the apparel manufacturers now make goods specifically for outlet stores. For example, the Geoffrey Beene line of men's and women's sportswear, manufactured by Phillips-Van Heusen, exists only in factory outlet stores. Some manufacturers, however, still rely on outlet stores to only sell irregulars and closeouts. The focus of Croscill Factory Stores is selling cancelled orders, overruns, and irregulars. For this firm, sales at outlets continue to be a way to help mitigate losses from overproduction or irregulars without alienating their wholesale clients.

For a number of reasons, profits of manufacturers' outlet stores are being squeezed. Expenses for outlet centers have increased as "regular retail" amenities have been added in an attempt to meet the higher expectations of shoppers. In today's price-competitive marketplace, apparel retailers have not been able to raise prices, further cutting their margins. Explosive growth of outlets has also led to market saturation, and attractive, untapped markets have become scarce for new outlet stores.

BASED ON:

Clodfelter, Richard and Fowler, Deborah. (1999, Spring/Summer). A comparison of the pricing policies between manufacturers' retail apparel outlets and traditional retail stores. *Journal of Shopping Center Research*, 7–38.

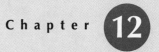
Locating Sources in Foreign Markets

PERFORMANCE OBJECTIVES:

Upon completion of this chapter, you should be able to:

- Identify reasons buyers purchase goods in foreign markets.
- Identify drawbacks buyers face when purchasing goods in foreign markets.
- Outline the factors to consider when determining the feasibility of purchasing goods in foreign markets.
- List and explain methods of locating foreign sources.
- Identify the components of calculating the landed cost of foreign merchandise.
- Identify special considerations buyers face when their stores expand into foreign markets.
- Recognize that a continual globalization of the marketplace is occurring.
- Cite examples of "Buy American" efforts.

You have spent days or even weeks researching the market and preparing your merchandise buying plan. Now, you have to make purchases that will put your plan into action, and that involves selecting the right merchandise for your customers. Merchandise selection is a continuous process that can take place at your desk, in a manufacturer's showroom, at a merchandise mart, or in foreign markets. Wherever you decide to make your purchases, you must ensure that the merchandise is what your customers will purchase once it is in your store. In addition, the amount of money that you have to spend will probably affect where you make your purchases.

In this chapter, the focus will be on selecting and making purchases from foreign sources. You will also examine the opportunities and drawbacks that these sources offer. Methods of locating foreign sources will be explained, and the impact of "Buy American" programs and the globalization of retailing will be described.

FOREIGN MARKETS

Buyers and retailers must constantly be alert to the evolving role that different countries play in the global marketplace. The growth or decline of a country can have a great impact on where buyers make purchases. In recent years, the big emerging markets of China and India have continued to experience robust economic growth. In

China, consumer spending continues to rise at a furious pace–making the world's third largest retail market very attractive to the world's retailers. The market in India has drawn attention also, but government restrictions in that country have limited the opportunities for buyers worldwide.

Total sales for the Top 250 Global Retailers reached $3.01 trillion in 2006; however, not every global company enjoyed strong growth. Forty-nine retailers of that group experienced declining sales. Ninety-three U.S.-based companies dominate the Top 250 list. The Top 10 Global Retailers are presented in Table 12.1.

Although international sales are becoming increasingly important to the growth strategies of many large retailers, foreign operations still account for only 14.4 percent of the Top 250 companies. Of this group, 104 have no international operations. The largest international retailer is France's Carrefour, with stores in just 29 countries, whereas multi-nationals in other industries might operate in 100 or more countries. Of the top five global economies, Japan remains the most insular. Among Japanese members of the Top 250 Global Retailers, two-thirds operate only in Japan.

For the United States, two agreements have dramatically affected trade with foreign markets. GATT (General Agreement on Tariffs and Trade) and NAFTA (North American Free Trade Agreement) have had far-reaching effects on what and how buyers purchase from foreign sources.

GATT (1994) reduced tariffs by about 40 percent on a large number of products and included new trading rules between the United States and 123 other countries; however, the elimination of trade barriers between the participating countries occurred gradually. The final result has been that buyers in the United States have access to markets all over the world. NAFTA (1994) will also gradually eliminate the trade barriers between the United States, Mexico, and Canada. Mexico is becoming an important country to U.S. buyers for sourcing products, especially apparel and textiles. With Mexico's close proximity to the United States, buyers should also be able to get their orders faster.

PURCHASING FROM FOREIGN SOURCES

Over 30 percent of the products purchased in the United States are imports from foreign markets. In this section, you will examine (1) the key reasons that have led buyers to turn to foreign sources and (2) the drawbacks of foreign sourcing.

Table 12.1: Top 10 Global Retailers

Rank	Name of Company	Country of Origin	Retail Sales (US $mil)	Formats
1	Wal-Mart Stores, Inc.	US	312,427	Cash&Carry/Warehouse Club, Discount Department Store, Hypermarkets/Supercenter/ Superstore, Supermarket
2	Carrefour S.A.	France	92,778	Cash&Carry/Warehouse Club, Convenience/Forecourt Store, Discount Store, Hypermarket/ Supercenter/Superstore, Supermarket
3	The Home Depot, Inc.	US	81,511	Home Improvement
4	Metro AG	Germany	69,134	Apparel/Footwear Specialty/ Cash&Carry/Warehouse Club, Department Store, Electronics Specialty, Hypermarket/ Supercenter/Superstore, Other Specialty, Supermarket
5	Tesco plc	UK	68,866	Convenience/Forecourt Store, Department Store, Hypermarket/Supercenter/ Superstore, Supermarket
6	Kroger	US	60,553	Convenience/Forecourt Store, Hypermarket/Supercenter/ Superstore, Other Specialty, Supermarket
7	Target Corp.	US	52,620	Discount Department Store, Hypermarket/Supercenter/ Superstore
8	Costco Wholesale Corp.	US	51,862	Cash&Carry/Warehouse Club
9	Sears Holdings Corp.	US	49,124	Department Store, Discount Department Store, Home Improvement, Hypermarket/ Supercenter/Superstore, Other Specialty
10	Schwarz Unternehmens Treuhand KG	Germany	45,891	Discount Store, Hypermarket/Supercenter/ Superstore

Source: *Stores*, January 2007.

Reasons to Buy from Foreign Sources

Almost every product imaginable is available in the United States; yet buyers seek out and purchase from foreign sources. Automobiles, cameras, TV sets, videotape players, and clothing are just some of the product categories that are coming from foreign markets in large quantities to compete with products manufactured in the United States. Why do buyers purchase from foreign sources? Key reasons include:

Unavailability of Merchandise. For some products, the only available sources may be in foreign markets. For example, almost no cameras are produced in the United States today. Many specialty food items must also be imported, as well as many wines and liquors. In addition, handmade products that cannot be replicated in this country are imported. When merchandise that customers want is unavailable from domestic sources, buyers must turn to foreign markets for those purchases.

Low Cost. Imports from foreign markets are often less expensive than similar merchandise purchased from domestic sources. Contributing to this low cost are typically much lower wages paid to factory workers in many third-world countries; however, the wages in many countries, such as Japan and Korea, are escalating.

Quality. Merchandise produced in the United States is of high quality; however, some countries are producing products of superior quality. The finest linen in the world is from Belgium and Ireland. Italy has some of the finest leather for clothing. Silks from China and cottons from India are world renowned. Many U.S. consumers also perceive foreign products to be of higher quality. Ask consumers to name top-performing automobiles, and they probably will mention BMW and Mercedes from Germany and Sweden's Volvo.

Uniqueness. Customers are always looking for something different. Foreign markets are one source of unique merchandise. Special handmade items with distinctive styling are not readily available from domestic sources. In the United States, customers seem to always be searching for new, different, unique products.

Fashion Trends. Globally, Europe is still a great influencer of fashion. Buyers from all over the world attend fashion shows in Paris and Milan to discover new trends. Making foreign purchases allows buyers the opportunity to offer their customers what is new and exciting and keep their store in a fashion leadership position. Read the Snapshot titled, "Zara: Providing Style and Rapid Response," to learn more about how one international retailer has dramatically changed the fashion cycle.

Drawbacks to Buying from Foreign Sources

If you choose to make purchases from foreign sources, you must realize that there are some drawbacks. These problems should not scare you away from foreign sources, but should simply make you cautious. Some typical drawbacks include:

Early Purchase Commitment Required. Because of the long lead time needed to guarantee delivery of imports, purchases of foreign products must be made much earlier than with domestic sources, and that makes sales forecasting more difficult. Trends are much more difficult to forecast over longer periods of time; however, trade journals, fashion forecasters, buying offices, and reporting services can all be helpful to buyers in predicting long-range trends.

Delivery Problems. Delivery of merchandise purchased from foreign sources is also subject to unforeseen shipping delays caused by events such as dock strikes and weather problems. Because of the delivery distances involved with foreign sourcing, there may be an inability to check on the location of shipments in transit. In addition, the delivery of reorders is nearly impossible for fashion merchandise. The season could be over before the reorder arrives. Completion dates for delivery of merchandise should be a part of any contract you sign. Penalties should be negotiated in case the merchandise arrives late.

Size Discrepancies. Measurements vary in the global marketplace. Goods purchased from many foreign markets may not be compatible with sizes found in the United States. As shown in Table 12.2, S-M-L means

Table 12.2: Clothes Size Guide

Clothing sizes in the United States are different than those found in the rest of the world. Therefore, it is important to know what your size is in U.S. measurements before you shop in the States. Here is a clothing guide to help you find your size. All sizes are approximate.

Women

Dresses and Suits

European	34	36	38	40	42	44	46	48
UK	6	8	10	12	14	16	18	20
USA	4	6	8	10	12	14	16	18

Shoes

European	38	38	39	39	40	41
UK	4½	5	5½	6	6½	7
USA	6	6½	7	7½	8	8½

Men

Suits and Overcoats

European	46	48	50	52	54	56	58
UK	36	38	40	42	44	46	48
USA	36	38	40	42	44	46	48

Shirts

European	36	37	38	39	41	42	43
UK	14	14½	15	15½	16	16½	17
USA	14	14½	15	15½	16	16½	17

Shoes

European	41	42	43	44	45	46
UK	7	7½	8½	9½	10½	11
USA	8	8½	9½	10½	11½	12

Socks

European	39	40	41	42	43	44
UK	9½	10	10½	11	11½	12
USA	9½	10	10½	11	11½	12

Children

European	125	135	150	155	160
UK (cm)	43	48	55	58	60
USA (ins)	4	6	8	10	12

Source: *Stores*, January 2007.

different sizes in different countries. Providing specific dimensions to the manufacturer is the most effective way to overcome this drawback.

Added Expense and Time Involved. Foreign markets are not as convenient as domestic markets when you need to make personal buying trips. Much more time is needed to visit many foreign markets because of the difficulty in moving from one vendor to another. You may have to go to different parts of a city or even to different cities to see lines and compare product offerings.

Funds Tied Up. When making foreign purchases, the retailer's capital funds have to be tied up for longer periods of time than when purchasing domestically. Factories in foreign countries usually require payment before the goods leave the country. Most domestic manufacturers, however, will extend credit terms, allowing the retailer to wait a period of time after goods have been delivered before having to remit payment.

Making the Decision to Buy from Foreign Sources

Buyers in the United States considering foreign sourcing can locate exciting alternatives in the global marketplace; however, before making the decision to use foreign sources, you should consider the following guidelines:

- Ensure that products from a foreign source are a logical extension of your current product assortment.
- Consider foreign sourcing only when the cost of a product has made it uncompetitive for you to purchase it in domestic markets.
- Recognize that lines of communication will be longer with foreign sourcing.
- Carefully study shipping arrangements from the foreign source.
- Be aware of all costs involved with foreign sourcing.
- Start small and slowly. Test some foreign products before making large merchandise commitments.
- Initially, keep alternative sources of supply.

Before purchasing merchandise from foreign sources, you must ensure that all costs associated with purchasing the goods are considered. Constant monitoring of U.S.-foreign trade regulations, tax regulations, quotas, and shipping costs will be required. Only by knowing such information can you make informed comparisons with products produced in the United States.

Most of the goods imported into the United States are subject to a tax, known as a *duty* or *tariff*. The key reason for these taxes is to lower the number of imports by making them cost more than goods produced domestically. Duties are charged as a percent of a product's value and vary according to the type of merchandise and the country of origin.

Many U.S. retailers pay unnecessary import fees because of bureaucratic rules governing imports. They may be able to realize considerable savings by carefully completing descriptions on purchase orders and invoices. One critical step in calculating duties is the precise description of the products being shipped. For example, a home center retailer importing tiles could save 33 percent on certain duties by precisely describing the merchandise purchased. The duty rate on tile varies from 20 percent on glazed mosaic floor tile to 13.5 percent for roofing tile, while the tariff on nonmosaic floor tile is 19 percent. Simply writing the word "tiles" on an invoice would result in a higher tariff. Purchasing apparel requires the same precise descriptions; tariff rates vary for a "blouse" and a "top."

Properly noting a product's country of origin can also reduce import duties. Rates vary depending on where the product is purchased. At one time, the same ceramic tile on which you would pay a 13.5 percent duty from Italy would have a duty of 4.3 percent if from Israel, would be duty-free if from Brazil, and would have a 55 percent duty if from Czech Republic. As retailers compete in an increasingly global market, monitoring import fees will become more important as a means of bolstering profit margins.

Countries that have been granted normal trade relations status qualify for lower tariffs. In 1998, this classification officially replaced *most favored-nation status*, a term that still remains in widespread use. Such status allows imports from these countries to be taxed at a lower level. To illustrate the impact of most-favored-nation status, consider the following example. Before receiving this special status, tariffs added $1.07 to the cost of a 750-milliliter bottle of Stolichnaya Russian vodka sold in the United States. That tariff was lowered to 8 cents a bottle under the new trade status.

Quotas also have an impact on the number of imports coming into this country and on the price consumers pay. A *quota* is a predetermined amount of merchandise that a country's government allows to be imported for a specific product category. Quotas are another means of protecting U.S. manufacturers from third-world countries that can produce products much less expensively than in the United States because wage rates are far less. When imports are restricted, price tends to rise for the goods if demand is high while supply is limited. Quotas have been used to protect many industries in this country, especially the automobile and apparel industries. Examine Figure 12.1 to see how quickly sheet production has moved offshore.

The buyer must calculate all these expenses when comparing the cost of foreign merchandise to merchandise produced in the United States. Buyers must know the landed cost of foreign merchandise. *Landed cost* is the final cost for foreign merchandise and includes the following expenses: (1) merchandise cost, (2) duties and tariffs, (3) commissions, (4) insurance, (5) storage expenses, and (6) transportation charges.

LOCATING FOREIGN SOURCES

You can use a number of methods to locate foreign sources. As a buyer, you can: (1) make personal buying trips to foreign markets, or (2) use intermediaries.

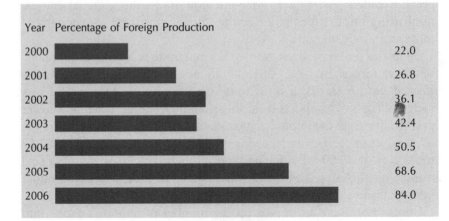

Year	Percentage of Foreign Production	
2000		22.0
2001		26.8
2002		36.1
2003		42.4
2004		50.5
2005		68.6
2006		84.0

Figure 12.1 Percent of sheets from foreign sources sold in the United States.

Making Personal Buying Trips

Many buyers are developing import programs that will provide their stores with unique merchandise brands from foreign markets. One way to develop these brands is to make personal contacts in foreign markets. Because direct negotiation is needed, fashion merchandise is typically purchased in this manner; however, only large retail organizations can afford the significant expense of sending buyers directly into foreign markets. If you are considering personal buying trips, you should realize there are problems to overcome, among them, language and social/cultural differences. Data presented in Table 12.3 provides etiquette tips visiting other countries.

Language. Buyers must have a knowledge of the language of the country where they are negotiating purchases. Being able to communicate without an interpreter has tremendous value when negotiating and will make misunderstandings less likely to occur. Although English is becoming the international language of trade, many small countries may not enjoy the luxury of having a large number of English-speaking representatives.

Social and Cultural Awareness. Buyers must be aware that cultures vary around the world. A sign or gesture may destroy a deal that a buyer has been negotiating. Removing your shoes in someone's home is considered proper etiquette in Japan, but it would likely be frowned on in the United States.

Foreign buying trips require planning similar to the plans you would make for a buying trip in the United States. One unique feature of planning for the foreign buying trip is that you must present a letter of credit to foreign suppliers. A **letter of credit** is a promise from the purchaser's bank to the seller that money is available to purchase the goods ordered.

In addition to visiting foreign factories, your market trip could include visits to expositions and trade shows in foreign markets. These shows are similar to ones held in the United States; they run for a few days or a week and attract buyers and retailers from around the world.

Buyers from the United States may also be able to contact some foreign sources without making a trip to a foreign country. Some foreign manufacturers are opening offices in U.S. central markets.

Table 12.3: Etiquette Tips for Visiting Other Countries

Cambodia	Never touch or pass something over the head of a Cambodian because the head is considered sacred.
China	As in most Asian cultures, avoid waving or pointing chopsticks, putting them vertically in a rice bowl, or tapping them on the bowl. These actions are considered extremely rude.
India	Avoid giving gifts made from leather because many Hindus are vegetarian and consider cows sacred. Keep this in mind when taking Indian clients to restaurants. Do not wink because it is seen as a sexual gesture.
Japan	Never write on a business card or shove the card into your back pocket when you are with the giver. This is considered disrespectful. Hold the card with both hands and read it carefully.
Malaysia	If you receive an invitation from a business associate from Malaysia, always respond in writing. Avoid using your left hand because it is considered unclean.
Philippines	Never refer to a female hosting an event as the "hostess," which translates to prostitute.
Singapore	If you plan to give a gift, always give it to the company. A gift to one person is considered a bribe.
Vietnam	Shake hands only with someone of the same sex who initiates it. Physical contact between men and women in public is frowned upon.
France	Always remain calm, polite, and courteous during business meetings. Never appear overly friendly because this could be construed as suspicious. Never ask personal questions.
Greece	If you need to signal a taxi, holding up five fingers is considered an offensive gesture if the palm faces outward. Face your palm inward with closed fingers.
Mexico	If visiting a business associate's home, do not bring up business unless the associate does.
Spain	Always request your check when dining out in Spain. It is considered rude for wait staff to bring your bill beforehand.

Source: *Business Etiquette for Dummies.*

Using Intermediaries

For most buyers, making personal buying trips to foreign markets may not be an option. Expenses and time involved would be too great for their store. In addition, some buyers who make trips to foreign markets may not be comfortable with the language and customs. In both cases, buyers could use ***intermediaries*** or middlemen. Several kinds of intermediaries are available.

Foreign Buying Offices. *Commissionaires* or foreign buying offices operate in foreign markets and function similarly to domestic buying offices. Staff members of the foreign buying office live in the local area, so they can provide the store buyer with an understanding of the language and customs of the foreign market. They are also much more familiar with markets than a store buyer who is spending only a week or two there. In addition, representatives from these buying offices can reorder merchandise for the store buyer and make arrangements for merchandise storage. They are constantly scouting foreign markets for the best available merchandise. A fee is typically charged based on a percentage of total purchases.

U.S. Buying Offices. Many U.S. buying offices are represented in major foreign markets and bring imported merchandise to client stores. Buying offices are providing such services as more retailers have become interested in developing import programs.

Importers. You may find that merchandise costs only a little more from ***importers*** located in the United States when compared with making a foreign market trip yourself. Importers may be able to qualify for quantity discounts and pass the savings along to the buyer. Many import wholesalers take the initial risk by making purchases in foreign markets and import merchandise to store in their warehouses in the United States. Buyers are then better able to compare the cost of foreign merchandise to merchandise available from domestic sources.

GLOBALIZATION OF RETAILING

The globalization of retailing is proceeding in many ways, including the transfer of retail techniques, ideas, and practices, and an increasing number of retailers are emerging as truly global firms. Most visible is the rising number of retailers trading outside their home markets, which is primarily caused by constrained growth in mature, domestic markets. Read the Snapshot titled, "Wal-Mart Exits Germany: What Are the Challenges of Global Expansion?" to learn more about the challenges retailers face when expanding to other countires.

Today, buyers can choose resources from around the world. Trade barriers between countries are falling, and virtually every retailer in the United States buys some foreign-produced products. Most retailers in the United States are also facing competition from businesses headquartered in other countries. For instance, The Gap and Benetton are already locked in a battle for the same consumers. To thrive in the twenty-first century, retailers must realize that a global marketplace exists. Not only will U.S. retailers continue to expand globally, but also local markets will be more open to foreign competition.

Domestically, the automobile and apparel industries have already been affected by the global expansion of markets. For both industries, foreign competition from the Far East has become a dominant force in the U.S. market, and many domestic factories have closed due to the influx of foreign competition. Foreign manufacturers, however, cannot take their market share for granted; they must continually monitor the marketplace and keep an eye on competition—from both the United States and other countries.

In the early 1990s, the United States signed NAFTA—the North American Free Trade Agreement—with Mexico and Canada. Gradually, this *free trade agreement* will eliminate all tariffs between the countries. Opinions about whether or not initial steps have been successful vary, depending on the source contacted. The trade agreement has produced both winners and losers, with most firms likely finding themselves somewhere in between. U.S. consumers have benefited from less expensive retail prices, but many domestic jobs have been lost.

A closer examination of the apparel industry illustrates some of the changes that are occurring. The Far East-Southeast Asia region has become the leading importer of apparel and textile products in both the United States and Europe. Apparel factories in Taiwan, the Republic of Korea, and Hong Kong have prospered; however, their continued prosperity may be threatened. Recent political strife in this area of the world has made the commercial future of some of these countries less bright. Wage rates in these countries have also increased substantially, causing prices of exports to increase dramatically. And new competition is entering the world marketplace for apparel from countries such as Bangladesh, the Philippines, Sri Lanka, and Turkey, where wage rates remain low. In addition, many apparel importers in the United States are looking to the Caribbean Basin as a sourcing alternative. The proximity of the region to the U.S. mainland would give them a much greater degree of control. Although this area offers a large labor supply, it is not yet able to produce the quality and quantity of the higher-end goods currently produced in the Far East.

As a buyer, you will need to constantly monitor the global marketplace for the right merchandise at the right price. Changes in the market may occur virtually overnight. Foreign sources will also have to monitor the American marketplace if they are to supply the products that consumers want and need. Read the Trendwatch titled, "Recalled Products: What Went Wrong?" to learn more about recent recalls of products made in China.

Globalization of retailing presents several concerns to buyers. When U.S. firms expand into foreign markets, decisions must be made about the merchandise mix. "Should it remain largely American?" or "Should products reflect local tastes?" are two key questions buyers must answer as they move into foreign markets. Expansion also presents problems involving the logistics of supplying stores.

Expansion into international retail markets is both appealing and challenging for many U.S. retailers. Interested retailers must decide if they want to expand by purchasing an existing foreign firm or exporting a store format that has an identity unfamiliar to customers there. Another dilemma facing U.S. buyers whose stores have added foreign units is whether or not to use the same merchandise sources as for their domestic stores. Talbot's, for example, has expanded to Japan and has decided not to change its merchandise sources. Buyers from Japanese stores come to the United States four times a year to review merchandise samples. One difference between merchandising policies in Talbot's Japanese and U.S. stores is that even more of Talbot's private brand labels are offered in Japan in an attempt to establish the name as an important retailer.

Retail buyers also face key differences in planning product assortments for stores in foreign markets. For example, Talbot's in Japan operates in 2,100-square-foot stores that are about half the size of a Talbot's store in the United States. One reason is that retail space is expensive, but less inventory is also required to stock the stores there. A wide assortment of sizes is not necessary. Whereas sizes in U.S. stores range from 4 to 18, Japanese stores usually need to stock only three or four sizes. Before expanding to foreign markets, U.S. retailers must evaluate all aspects of the market to determine if their retail concept will travel well to other markets. There are also some foreign companies exporting their retail concepts to the United States. Benetton, a specialty clothing store, and IKEA, a Swedish furniture retailer, are two foreign retailers who have expanded successfully to the United States.

What does the future hold in the global marketplace? Consider the following developments that may have an impact on buying:

• Four large trading blocs have emerged. They include (1) the Western Hemisphere, (2) the European Union, (3) Russia and its former satellite countries, and (4) Japan and the Western Pacific Rim. Trade within these blocs will probably flourish, while trade may grow more difficult between these blocs.
• NAFTA will become the model for new trade pacts with other countries. Free trade agreements are likely to result in lower prices for many products and a larger market for all goods.
• Political and economic turmoil in the Far East will probably limit trade growth between the United States and the Far East.
• American cultural dominance will continue to expand throughout the world. Sales of branded goods that are associated with American culture will continue to grow in the global market.

"BUY AMERICAN" CAMPAIGNS

As a reaction to the domestic job losses caused by the increasing use of imported products and materials, many businesses and organizations have undertaken "Buy American" strategies (Figure 12.2). Nationalistic marketing to promote American-made products is a trend that started during the 1984 Olympics and heightened for the Statue of Liberty celebration in 1986. The most ambitious advertising "Buy American" campaigns come from the apparel and automobile industries, market segments most hurt by imports. Read the Trendwatch titled, "'Buy American' Campaigns," to learn more about efforts to get customers to buy American-made products.

U.S. textile, apparel, and home furnishings industries are making the most of their campaign called "Crafted with Pride in the USA." Retailers are also picking up the theme by stocking and promoting American-made products, whenever possible. For example, in 1985 Wal-Mart became the first major retailer to launch an ongoing "Buy American" campaign based on both patriotism and the desire to create jobs. This campaign was also one way to communicate the chain's support for U.S. manufacturing. Management said it wanted to sell more goods that were manufactured domestically and made a concerted effort to create more U.S. jobs using a number of strategies. For example, Wal-Mart offered U.S. manufacturers the chance to replicate items that the chain acquired from foreign sources. If they could do so on a cost-effective basis, Wal-Mart purchased from the firm.

Wal-Mart worked closely with domestic suppliers, encouraging them to produce goods for the chain. Efforts were also made to promote locally made products in the stores. The company sought out domestic suppliers and welcomed any business propositions they had to offer.

What were the results of the campaign? Eighteen months after "Buy American" began, Wal-Mart reported that due to the campaign it had bought an additional $400 million worth of merchandise by either switching to domestic suppliers or retaining suppliers who were supposed to be phased out, and about 43,000 jobs had been created or retained that otherwise would have been sent to foreign shores.

Figure 12.2 Many retailers feature "Buy American" displays in their stores.

For example, Mr. Coffee was able to convert four of its products from overseas production to U.S. production. Fieldcrest Cannon started making a 12-pack of washcloths that Wal-Mart used to buy from Taiwan. And, 85 percent of the dress shirts being sold in Wal-Mart were being produced domestically.

After three years of implementation, Wal-Mart estimated that $1.2 billion "Buy American" purchases had been made. However, Wal-Mart realizes that the U.S.-made option is not always viable, and the company does not exempt foreign suppliers when the price and quality of goods are better than what is available domestically.

The "Buy American" campaign also has more appeal to certain segments of the population. The campaign has strong appeal to blue-collar workers, who have been most seriously affected by unemployment caused by imports. They blame foreign competitors for plant shutdowns. Women and older Americans have also been targets of the campaign.

Some buying offices have also developed sourcing strategies to increase the use of domestic sources. Product quality, however, remains their prime consideration. Typically, buying staffs are instructed to find the best product, at the best price, no matter where it can be sourced.

One controversy caused by "Buy American" campaigns is trying to define what qualifies as an American-made product. For example, is it a TV made by U.S.-based Zenith at a plant in Mexico, or a General Motors car assembled at a California factory co-owned by Toyota? Increasingly, there is no such thing as an "American" product. U.S. brands are often foreign owned, and foreign brands can be manufactured in the United States.

Retailers that have emphasized "Buy American" campaigns have come under heavy media scrutiny. In fact, Wal-Mart was a target of investigations by both *NBC Dateline* and *60 Minutes*. These broadcasts showed racks of clothing under "Made in the USA" signs that bore foreign labels. Videos showed flustered executives vehemently denying allegations that their commitment to sell U.S. products was phony and hypocritical. Wal-Mart apologized for signs being in the wrong areas, and removed from its stores a jacket with a label that contained a U.S. flag but read "Made in Bangladesh."

Experience has shown that domestic manufacturers need to become more responsive to what their customers are asking them to produce. They must quicken their response time in anticipating the wants and needs of American consumers and give consumers the choices they want at competitive prices.

SUMMARY POINTS

- Merchandise selection occurs at a buyer's desk, in central markets, in a manufacturer's showroom, at a merchandise mart, or at a trade show.
- Buyers also have a choice of domestic or foreign sources.
- Buyers purchase foreign merchandise because of (1) unavailability of some merchandise in the United States, (2) low cost, (3) quality, (4) uniqueness, and (5) fashion trends.
- Drawbacks to purchasing foreign merchandise include (1) early purchase commitment required, (2) delivery problems, (3) size discrepancies, (4) added expenses and time involved, and (5) funds tied up for longer periods of time.
- Foreign sources can be located by making personal buying trips; however, personal buying trips require that buyers have familiarity with both the language and customs of the country they are visiting.
- Buyers can also obtain merchandise from foreign markets by using intermediaries such as foreign buying offices, domestic buying offices, or importers.
- The landed cost of merchandise must be calculated by buyers in order to compare foreign merchandise costs with domestic merchandise costs.
- Today, buyers can select goods from a global marketplace rather than just domestic sources. U.S. retailers are also facing competition from foreign sources.

REVIEW ACTIVITIES

Developing Your Retail Buying Vocabulary

Consult the Glossary if you did not add the following terms to your vocabulary.

Commissionaire	Landed cost
Duty	Letter of credit
Free trade agreement	Most-favored-nation status
Importer	Quota
Intermediary	Tariff

Understanding What You Read

1. Which countries are the source of most apparel and textile imports in the United States?
2. Which countries are providing competition to Far East apparel manufacturers?
3. Identify foreign products that are unavailable for buyers to purchase in the U.S. market.
4. List reasons buyers have for purchasing foreign products.
5. Why could delivery problems be more severe for foreign merchandise than for domestic merchandise?
6. After deciding to make purchases from foreign sources, why should retailers keep contact with alternative sources of supply?
7. Why would most buyers who consider purchasing foreign products go through intermediaries?
8. List the components of landed cost of foreign merchandise.
9. What is the primary purpose of most tariffs and quotas?
10. How could buyers save money on tariffs when merchandise is described on purchase orders and invoices?
11. Give examples of U.S. retailers who have expanded into foreign markets.
12. Give examples of foreign retailers who have expanded into the U.S market.

Analyzing and Applying What You Read

1. You are the buyer for several lines of footballs that have been purchased from domestic sources. Market research has revealed that your customers make an effort to purchase American-made products. Describe plans that your store could initiate to make your customers aware of where your footballs were purchased.
2. Research reveals that only 17 percent of Americans strictly avoid purchasing imports. Does this indicate that "Buy American" campaigns have not been successful? Explain.
3. Should the United States tighten quotas against apparel manufacturers from the Far East? After listing the pros and cons, present arguments to support your final decision.
4. You are a retailer interested in expanding into foreign markets. Would you expand with your existing store or purchase an existing retailer there? Support your decision.

Internet Connection

1. On the Internet, access the U.S. Department of Labor site at www.dol.gov.esa. Report on the apparel industry partnership agreement in relation to manufacturers and sweatshops.
2. On the Internet, access Social Accountability International at cepaa.org. Report on the goals and activities of this organization in relation to sweatshops.
3. On the Internet, access the Office of Textiles and Apparel (OTEXA) at otexa.ita.doc.gov. Report on how OTEXA promotes U.S. exports of textiles and apparel products.
4. On the Internet, access the U.S. International Trade Commission at dataweb.usitc.gov. Report on how tariff rates with Mexico will change as NAFTA is fully implemented.

SNAPSHOT

Zara: Providing Style and Rapid Response

Zara, the trendy Spanish clothing chain that produces "fashions for the masses" of young, hip, urban consumers, is joining a group of aggressive international retailers that has targeted the United States. Zara currently has 820 stores in 60 countries.

Some clothing retailers bemoan the fickleness of fashion, but Zara thrives on it. The firm has pioneered the concept of "live collections," which are designed, manufactured, distributed, and sold almost as quickly as their customers' fleeting enthusiasm. Traditionally, fashion collections are designed only four times a year, and major retailers outsource most of their production to low-cost subcontractors in far-off developing countries. Zara, however, ignores this old logic. For quick turnaround, some two-thirds of its clothes are made at a company-owned facility in Spain, and stores around the globe are restocked twice a week with an astounding 12,000 different designs a year.

Recognizing that what is "in" today may be "out" next month, Zara has organized a design and fulfillment network capable of meeting two key objectives. The firm creates fashion ideas that resonate with customers, and moves those ideas from the drawing board to store shelves in 10 to 15 days—a lightening pace by industry standards. Zara meets the first objective by getting its designers and store personnel out of their offices and into the plazas, discos, and universities where consumers congregate. That information then gets fed back to Zara's headquarters—often using hand-held computers that transmit images as well as data. The designs that emerge from these customer contacts then enter a fast-paced production and logistical system.

Customers love the results—they queue up in long lines outside stores on designated delivery days. They understand that if they like something in Zara, they must buy it then because it will probably not be there the following week. Zara's women's wear is broken down into three collections: (1) Woman, the most expensive line; (2) Basic, which offers casual apparel for smaller budgets; and (3) Trafaluc, the trendiest and hippest Zara has to offer.

The company is hugely profitable, achieving the same profit margins—and higher sales per square foot—than larger rivals such as The Gap. Although The Gap is in no immediate danger of being knocked from its pedestal, there are signs that consumers may finally be tiring of khakis and one-pocket T-shirts.

Several other factors have contributed to the success of Zara. The firm does not have to carry the cost of high inventory levels, and it gets a big revenue boost by putting fresh fashion on shelves so rapidly. Most retailers depend on advertising. Zara shuns the medium altogether, preferring to invest in prime locations.

Zara derives its competitive advantage from an astute use of information and technology. The company is building its growth on speed, customization, supply-chain management, and information sharing, which has transformed the relatively low-profile retailer into a global powerhouse. Unless other apparel retailers can duplicate this approach, they may not be in business ten years from now.

BASED ON:

Capell, Kerry. (2006, September 4). Fashion Conquistador. *Business Week.com*.

Crawford, Leslie. (2000, September 26). Putting on the style with rapid response. *The Financial Times*, 17.

Ferdows, Kasra, Lewis, Michael, and Machuca, José. (2004, November). *Harvard Business Review*, 104–110.

Folpe, Jane M. (2000, September 4). Zara has a made-to-order plan for success. *Fortune*, 80.

Ryan, Thomas J. (2006, January). Uncovering Zara. *Apparel Magazine*, 27.

Shining examples. (2006, June 17). *Economist*, 4–6.

SNAPSHOT

Wal-Mart Exits Germany: What Are the Challenges of Global Expansion?

In July 2006, Wal-Mart announced that after nine years of operating stores in Germany, the company would sell its 85 stores there to Metro, a German rival. By selling the stores, Wal-Mart expected to take a $1 billion loss. That year, Wal-Mart already operated 2,700 stores in 14 countries outside the United States. Why did the world-dominant retailer fail when expanding into the German market?

Germany represents the third-largest global retail market after the United States and Japan. Wal-Mart had high hopes for expansion into the German market, but never made a profit during its stay in the country. In fact, the company only captured 2 to 3 percent of the German market.

Wal-Mart entered Germany through two acquisitions, which saddled the company with some undesirable locations. Moreover, some of the stores were poorly designed. Other challenges facing Wal-Mart in Germany included restrictive building codes and the scarcity of available land for new stores. However, the major reason may be that company officials misjudged the culture of German consumers. For instance, Wal-Marts in Germany adopted the U.S. custom of bagging groceries, but many German consumers found this practice distasteful because they did not want strangers handling their food. The Wal-Mart policy of having employees smile and greet customers seemed unnatural to many Germans. Also, many German consumers believed that signage and product organization in many Wal-Mart stores needed to be reworked.

Wal-Mart built its reputation in the United States on low prices, but the company found that its prices were often undercut in Germany by local rivals such as Aldi and Lidl. Wal-Mart may not have been successful in competing with low prices because having too few stores made it difficult to leverage operating costs against sales revenues. For example, Aldi has more than 4,000 stores, which gave that firm a huge advantage in handling logistics and advertising more cost-effectively.

In the final analysis, the biggest problem was that Wal-Mart underestimated the competition. The company went into a market with a low-price offering in an arena that already was dominated by low-price retailers. Even when Wal-Mart's prices beat the competition, the differences were many times too small to motivate consumers to travel to a supercenter, a format that has never been fully accepted by German consumers who prefer shopping at smaller stores.

Global expansion has become very important to Wal-Mart and other domestic retailers as they near saturation in the United States. Therefore, Wal-Mart is not likely to retreat from global expansion plans, but the company has to be more careful about how it addresses cultural differences and consumer behavior in different global markets. Firms like Wal-Mart must realize that one formula does not fit all markets. Global retailers cannot win in every market; they have to carefully select the spots on the international stage where expansion prospects are the best.

Retail analysts predict that expansion prospects for Wal-Mart are much better in Latin America and China. In fact, the company continues to grow and expand in Brazil (295 stores), Canada (278 stores), and Mexico (774 stores).

BASED ON:

Bowers, Katherine. (2006, October 23). Analysts see the upside in Wal-Mart's China plans. *HFN The Weekly Newspaper for the Home Furnishing Network*, 9.

Edelson, Sharon and Drier, Melissa. (2006, July 31). Wal-Mart exiting Germany. *Women's Wear Daily*, 16.

Norton, Kate. (2006, July 31). Wal-Mart's German retreat. *Business Week Online*.

Summer woes for Wal-Mart. (2006, September). *Retail Merchandiser*, 6.

Wal-Mart plans to exit Germany. (2006, August 7). *Supermarket News*, 1.

TRENDWATCH

Recalled Products: What Went Wrong?

- March 2007: Menu Foods, Inc. of Streetsville, Ontario, recalled 60 million cans and packages of pet food contaminated in China with melamine, a substance used in plastics and flame-resistant materials.
- March 2007: Hong Chang Corp. of Santa Fe Springs, California, recalled 282 22-pound boxes of monkfish, which originated in China and were distributed in California, Hawaii, and Illinois because they contained a deadly toxin.
- June 2007: The FDA (Food and Drug Administration) warns U.S. consumers not to use any toothpaste manufactured in China because it contains a poisonous chemical used in antifreeze as a solvent.
- June 2007: The National Highway Traffic Safety Administration orders a tiny importer, Foreign Tire Sales Inc. of Union, New Jersey, to recall up to 450,000 light truck tires made in China since 2002 because a defect could cause dangerous tire separation.

• August 2007: Mattel Inc. recalls 83 Fisher-Price products, 1.5 million units, made in China because they were finished with lead paint.

What went wrong? These events awakened both China and the United States to a latent crisis and raised the looming question as to who is legally responsible when lead paint ends up on a toy sold in the United States. Companies have started to find out and are learning that the liability is here. U.S. regulators generally hold U.S. importers responsible for ensuring that foreign-made products meet American safety standards. Some companies will not be able to withstand the repercussions. For example, Foreign Tire Sales, the 16-employee family-owned business mentioned above, is hurtling toward bankruptcy as it faces a $90 million projected recall. The company sued the Chinese supplier, which denied any defect. However, even if U.S. plaintiffs win default judgments against foreign firms, it is unclear whether they will be able to enforce them anywhere. Moreover, in Chinese courts, tiny awards and frequently hostile local judges often make litigation pointless.

Menu Foods, another firm mentioned above, faces class-action suits and big-name retailers they supply are also named as defendants—should Menu Foods run out of insurance coverage. As these events occurred in the United States, China suspended imports of some animal products from seven U.S. firms. A Chinese agency said the food was contaminated with salmonella.

Recalls are not always the result of shoddy production monitoring. Mattel goes to great lengths to try to ensure that the companies it does business with operate properly and ethically, even subjecting them to outside audits from the International Center for Corporate Accountability. Mattel's crisis illustrates just how difficult it is for U.S. companies purchasing foreign products to keep tabs on all their suppliers around the world.

To what extent will these recalls have on sales? It is still unclear, but other toymakers and retailers have already begun advertising the fact that their toys are made in the United States. Retailers and particularly buyers must be alert and more carefully select suppliers for the products they sell. Repeated product recalls will undermine consumer confidence and reduce sales—something no retail buyer wants to occur.

On the other hand, if Chinese exporters want to stay in business, they will have to become accountable for injuries to U.S. consumers and businesses. To stay in the world market, China will have to stand behind the products its companies' manufacture and that means stronger regulation and more accountability.

BASED ON:

Carey, John. (2007, July 30). NOT made in China. *Business Week.com*.

China finds tainted food products from U.S. (2007, July 15). *Las Vegas Review-Journal*, 20A.

D'Innocenzio, Anne. (2007, August 15). Recalls stagger Mattel. *The State*, B1.

Horovitz, Bruce, Farrell, Greg, and Carty, Sharon. (2007, August 15). Mattel's stellar reputation tainted. *USA Today*, 1B.

Palmeri, Christopher. (2007, August 15). What went wrong at Mattel. *Business Week Online*.

Parloff, Roger. (2007, July 23). China's newest export: lawsuits. *Fortune*, 48.

Recalled products. (2007, August 13). Recalled products. *Business Insurance*, 25.

Wal-Mart supplier recalls dog food on salmonella concerns. (2007, June 7). *Progressive Grocer, NA*.

TRENDWATCH

"Buy American" Campaigns

When surveyed, most U.S. consumers today say they prefer to buy American brands and products. But, with imports totaling more than a trillion dollars each year, buying American may no longer be practical in some instances and impossible in others. Moreover, other considerations, such as quality, style, and price—particularly price—often take precedence with consumers.

Especially in the automotive market, it is nearly impossible for the average consumer to guess where many vehicles have been assembled, let alone determine from what country the parts came. What appears to be a domestic car may have been built outside of the United States, and what appears to be a foreign car may have been built in a consumer's local neighborhood. To help buyers, the U.S. Congress passed the American Automobile Labeling Act in October, 1992, requiring manufacturers to identify a vehicle's final assembly point. By making consumers aware of where their vehicles were made, proponents of the Act hoped to spur a "Buy American" sentiment; however, that did not occur.

Another factor probably contributed to this neutral "Buy American" sentiment. In the late 1970s and 1980s, Honda, Nissan, and Toyota offered automobiles with superior quality, reliability, and excellent fuel mileage at competitive prices that translated to superior resale values.

Later, in its advertising campaign, General Motors admitted to and apologized for producing poor-quality cars during those years. The damage, however, may have already been done.

Today, younger shoppers may be the least likely consumers to care whether the products they purchase are made in the United States. These shoppers grew up in a global economy. With factory closures and layoffs, it is also increasingly unlikely that they or their parents work for a manufacturing company. "Buy American" campaigns have the least impact on these consumers.

Even when American consumers like to support products made in the United States, most are not willing to pay a higher price if it is made here. We live in a very price-conscious society. During the beginnings of the Iraq War, there was lots of press about people boycotting products made in France because that country did not support the war, but those actions were short-lived and ineffective. For the most part today, consumers do not ask where a product is made.

However, consumers can take some action. Shoppers that want to guarantee that they are purchasing American-made products can go online. Established in 1999, *BuyAmerican.com* began with 50 vendors offering their American-made products for sale online. The site currently represents more than 600 U.S. manufacturers selling over 27,000 American-made products. There are several online sites with similar missions.

In the final analysis, American consumers may never embrace "Buy American" hype. Consumers care about price today. Suppliers care about producing a quality product with the greatest efficiency and cost savings. And, retailers care about getting the best product at the lowest possible price.

BASED ON:

Americans dislike flag-waving promos. (2003, October 12). *Convenience Store News*, 10.

Dolliver, Mark. (2007, January 15). Buy American or shun American? *AdWeek*, 34.

Drickhamer, David. (2003, September). Bye-bye to "Buy American?" *Industry Week*, 25–29.

Is made in America important to your customers? Or do they really care where a product is manufactured? (2004, January). *Gifts & Decorative Accessories*, 244.

Lisanti, Tony. (1998, May 25). Bye-bye "Buy American." *Discount Store News*, 11.

Pinto, David. ((2004, August 23). It's time to revive "Buy American." *MMR*, 33.

Turkel, Stanley. (2002, August). How American-owned can you get?" *Lodging Hospitality*, 13.

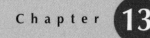

Making Market Visits and Negotiating with Vendors

PERFORMANCE OBJECTIVES

Upon completion of this chapter, you should be able to:

- Identify the purposes of buying trips.
- Describe the planning steps required before making a buying trip.
- Identify a buyer's typical activities during a buying trip.
- Recognize that buyers can prepare for negotiations before face-to-face meetings occur with vendors.
- Develop objectives for negotiations.
- List and describe frequently used negotiation tactics.
- Identify terms on which most negotiations with vendors will focus.
- Recognize that the outcome of negotiations should be to develop a long-term partnership with the vendor.

Once buyers have identified potential suppliers, their next step is to prepare to visit the market. As you have learned, that market can be located locally or in some other country, and today, markets can even be found online. Before you arrive at the market, you must begin developing your negotiation skills. Successful negotiations with vendors begin with adequate preparations while you are in the office.

In this chapter you will learn about the planning steps required for making a market visit and how to prepare for negotiations. Development of negotiating strategies and tactics are described, and the desired outcomes of negotiation are presented.

PREPARING FOR A MARKET VISIT

Due to their closeness and accessibility, most buyers begin searching for merchandise in domestic markets. However, as you learned in Chapter 12, lower costs are the primary reason that buyers seek out appropriate foreign markets today. As they prepare for trips to either foreign or domestic markets, buyers will typically find central markets, merchandise/apparel marts, and expositions/trade shows. After deciding which type of market they will be visiting, buyers must clearly define their purpose and thoroughly plan any trip that will take place outside their offices.

Types of Markets

A *central market* is a city where a large number of key suppliers are located. New York and Hong Kong are key supply cities for many types of merchandise, particularly apparel. As pictured in Figure 13.1, the garment district in New York City contains thousands of showrooms that display apparel, textiles, fabrics, and many other apparel accessories. That city is still considered the major apparel market in the United States. Central markets also exist for other products. For example, key U.S. furniture markets are located in High Point, North Carolina, and Las Vegas, Nevada, as well as locations in Germany and China. Read the Trendwatch titled, "Which Furniture Market Will Dominate?" to learn more about the rivalry developing between High Point and Las Vegas.

In some cities, buyers will find a single complex (a *merchandise/apparel mart*) like the one shown in Figure 13.2. At these marts, it is easy for buyers to view all merchandise lines available and make compar-

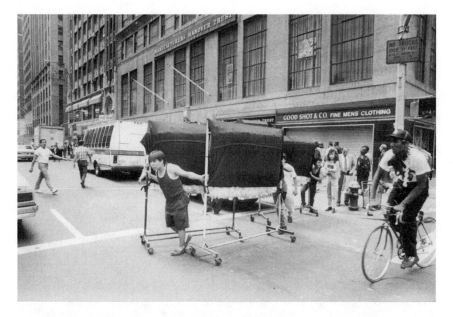

Figure 13.1   The garment center in New York contains showrooms with many types of merchandise, particularly apparel.

isons. Since manufacturers or their representatives lease showroom space, the marts function as a one-stop shop so that buyers do not have to go to different sections of a city to locate suppliers. Marts located near buyers also allow them the opportunity to make quicker and more frequent buying trips. Marts present several market weeks during the year, and registered buyers are sent guides detailing vendors available, lines carried, and their location in the mart. Large marts can be found in Atlanta, Chicago, Dallas, Los Angeles, and Miami.

For other product categories, buyers can locate ***trade shows/expositions***. These shows are typically held at convention centers or exhibition halls in large cities to showcase the latest merchandise in a particular product category. For example, yearly shows are held in areas such as toys, electronics, groceries, automobiles, and computers. Buyers are able to easily compare vendor offerings while attending these shows and have the opportunity to identify new trends and resources in the market. Trade shows and expositions are usually held for only a few days each year, so your calendar must be left open for this time. Read the Snapshot titled, "The American International Toy Fair," to learn more about the toy industry's annual show.

Figure 13.2 All vendors are located under one roof at various merchandise marts around the country.

Purposes of Buying Trips

Buyers make market visits for a number of reasons. Some of the key reasons include:

- To obtain merchandise for the upcoming season,
- To gain knowledge about trends and new merchandise,
- To evaluate new resources and merchandise offerings from vendors,
- To seek out special values for an upcoming promotion—special deals that could be featured in new promotional events or sales,
- To replenish stock in order to fill in sections of stock that have been selling well, and
- To attend previews of new vendor lines. Fashion designers and manufacturers of such products as automobiles, electronics, and computers typically have special shows for buyers to preview changes in styles and models.

Frequency of Market Trips

The purposes of your buying trip will determine the frequency of your market visits. Most buyers usually visit foreign or central markets only once or twice a year and make other trips to regional markets to supplement their assortments. If they are not located a great distance from a market, buyers may make more frequent buying trips. When and how often you make market visits will also depend on a number of other factors, as follows:

Season of the Year. Most buyers will make market visits depending on the season of the year. Market weeks, shown in Figure 13.3, are planned around a particular season such as fall/winter or spring/summer. Each product category has a specific number of major selling seasons, depending on changes in styles and models. If new styles develop for each season, frequent trips may be required.

Type of Merchandise. Buyers of all types of products make market visits. Fashion buyers will need to make more frequent visits because of the rapidity with which fashion changes, but even with fashion merchandise there are more shows for some product lines and fewer for others. For example, there might be five shows annually for women's wear and only two for menswear.

Size of Store or Department. Large firms will require more market visits than would smaller stores in order to keep the merchandise

Figure 13.3   Cover of market guide for AmericasMart.

assortments fully stocked. Larger stores tend to have a higher merchandise turnover, which requires more frequent market visits.

Store's Merchandise Policies. Stores that want to maintain a fashion leadership position will certainly need to make frequent market visits.

Proximity to a Market. Being located a distance from the market city may necessitate fewer market trips because of the time and expenses involved. Some buyers substitute trips to regional merchandise/apparel marts rather than going to foreign or central markets for all their needs.

Business Conditions. Business slowdowns may negatively affect sales to such an extent that some market trips may not be needed. On the other hand, slowdowns may be an opportune time to make market trips to locate new and exciting merchandise that might spur sales.

Planning the Market Trip

Like any business activity, your buying trip should be thoroughly planned. As many details of the trip as possible should be arranged before you leave so that your time in the market can be spent on merchandise-related decisions. Planning should involve the following steps:

1. You should have prepared a merchandise buying plan. If you go to market with facts about your inventory, sales, and customer preferences, your decisions will be based on facts and not feelings. Also, your vendors can provide you with more concrete assistance when they are provided with such information. Have a vendor analysis form completed for any firm you plan to visit if you have carried their products previously. Even with a buying plan, you will still have decisions to make on specific selections, particularly if you are making fashion purchases. Large stores may have a fashion coordinator to advise you on any trends in styles, colors, or silhouettes; otherwise, you need to have researched these trends yourself.

2. Make certain that you have obtained all approvals that you need for your buying plan. At many stores, both the merchandise manager and the finance officer will be required to approve of plans before buyers go on market visits.

3. If you have one, notify your buying office of your upcoming visit, and inform people there about your specific merchandising needs and vendors you would like to visit. Without a buying office, you will need to schedule visits with vendors yourself. Make sure that key resources are notified early so you will be assured of an appointment time that best fits your schedule. You may also want to examine market reports, trade journals, and other publications to identify new manufacturers or designers that you may want to visit. When you call for appointments, ask about the length of time the sales representative feels is adequate to review the merchandise line.

4. Determine how many days will be needed for your buying trip, and then arrange your hotel and travel reservations. These arrangements may be made for you if your store is a client of a buying office.

5. Establish a work schedule for your staff members while you are away. Prepare an itinerary of your market visits so you can be reached by your staff or management. While in the market, keep them informed of any changes in your plans. A good practice is to establish a regular call-in time so that any messages can be easily relayed to you.

Planning will make your buying trip more enjoyable and more profitable. In the market, you will find that you have the time needed to visit vendors and evaluate merchandise.

VISITING THE MARKET

Now that your trip has been thoroughly planned, you need to consider the activities in which you will participate while in the market. Most market trips are generally planned for a week or less, but on occasion you may need more time. While in the market, you will want to talk with representatives of your buying office, visit vendors and showrooms, tour factories, attend seminars or fashion shows, talk with other buyers, and tour outstanding retail stores in the market. Use your time wisely during market week; it is likely to be a hectic period. A sample week at the Denver market is shown in Figure 13.4. An exciting and stimulating atmosphere prevails; vendors are there to sell, and they will use a maximum of showmanship.

Working with a Buying Office

As you learned in previous chapters, buying offices perform many advisory and consultant services for client stores. Before your trip, people at the buying office can assist you with travel and hotel arrangements, and if you have informed them of your merchandising needs, they will have scouted the market and previewed merchandise lines for you. They can save you valuable time by eliminating visits to vendors whose lines are inappropriate for your needs.

Before visiting vendors or participating in other market activities, you will want to talk with the representatives of your buying office. You should make an effort to build a strong relationship with these individuals. The better you get to know them, the more assistance

THURSDAY
Show Hours: 9:00 a.m.–5:00 p.m. Mart Building Only

FRIDAY
Show Hours: 9:00 a.m.–6:30 p.m. Mart Building Only

Buyer Information Session
8:30 a.m.–9:00 a.m. Forum Meeting Room #2

"Moving Your Business onto the Web"
3:30 p.m.–4:30 p.m.

Buyer Appreciation Reception
6:30 p.m.–8:00 p.m.

This special evening is to say "thank you" to buyers for attending the Denver Show.

Complimentary hors d'oeuvres and cocktails with live background music set the scene for a comfortable, relaxing evening.

SATURDAY
Show Hours: 9:00 a.m.–6:00 p.m. All Buildings Open

"50 Great Visual Marketing Ideas in 50 Minutes"
8:30 a.m.–9:30 a.m

Buyer Information Session
10:30 a.m.–11:00 a.m.

"Merchandising the Misfits"
2:30 p.m.–3:30 p.m.

SUNDAY
Show Hours: 9:00 a.m.–6:00 p.m. All Buildings Open

"It's More than Just Price"
8:30 a.m.–9:30 a.m.

"Ways to WOW Your Customers and Keep Them Coming Back"
3:30 p.m.–4:30 p.m.

Figure 13.4   A sample week at the Denver Mart. *(continued on next page)*

(Figure 13.4 continued)

> Sunday Night Extravaganza
> 6:00 p.m.–8:00 p.m. Plaza at the Mart
>
> An evening of music and dancing, with a complimentary bar and buffet dinner for buyers and exhibitors!

MONDAY
Show Hours: 9:00 a.m.–6:00 p.m. All Buildings Open

> "Your Employees: Hiring, Firing, Retaining, Training"
> 9:00 a.m.–10:30 a.m.
>
> "Vendor Partnerships"
> 3:30 p.m.–4:30 p.m.
>
> Monday Night Party
> 6:00 p.m.–8:00 p.m. Plaza at the Mart
>
> Enjoy a night of music, a complimentary buffet dinner, beer and cash bar.

TUESDAY
Show Hours: 9:00 a.m.–4:00 p.m. All Buildings Open

WEDNESDAY

> Many of the Mart's permanent showrooms will be open for late buying opportunities. A list of participating showrooms will be available at the show.

they can be to you. By having a better understanding of your needs, buying offices can provide much more valuable assistance. You will want to review your merchandise buying plan with them and discuss the general market outlook. In addition, they will likely inform you of any new resources in the market. Some buying offices provide a room in which store buyers can view samples of merchandise from vendors. Again, valuable time can be saved by eliminating visits to vendors whose merchandise lines are inappropriate for your needs.

Representatives of buying offices may also present some ideas concerning resources, styles, colors, or fabrics, as shown in Table 13.1. Many buying offices also hold fashion shows or seminars for buyers from stores similar to yours. Take the time to participate in these activities.

Table 13.1: Examples of Home Fashions Information Buyers Would Learn in the Market

Concepts	Colors	Fabrics & Textures	Key Items
High Tech	Peacock	Stainless Steel	Frosted Glass
Balanced	Daffodil	Platinum/Chrome	Embossed Woods and
Contemporary	Cantaloupe	Polypropylene	Leathers
Pure and Simple	Squash	Leather	Etched Metals
Sleek	Coral	Shearing	Alternative Metals
Linear	Aqua	Scoring	Leather Furniture
Interlocking	Black	Overlays	Plastic Dinnerware,
Modular	Grey	Embossing	Drinkware, and
Tubular	Off Whites	Stamping	Furniture
Curves		Transparent Wax	

They offer you the opportunity to exchange ideas and opinions with other buyers who may be experiencing similar buying situations. They do not represent the competition, so you will not be giving away trade secrets.

Visiting Vendors

Whether the vendors to be visited are in a central market, regional merchandise mart, or trade show (Figure 13.5), there are certain procedures you should follow to make the visits successful. They include:

1. Establish a tentative itinerary each day. Do not be too rigid, because delays may occur.

2. Visit resources in a planned sequence. Determine which classifications of merchandise you will be viewing on the market trip. Then, make a list of vendors that you will visit for each classification. Many buyers examine merchandise for each classification separately, which helps them sort through their thoughts better at the end of the day. If you use such an approach, you would complete viewing one merchandise classification before moving to the next one; however, in central markets the location of resources may prevent using this approach. For example, several vendors that you wish to visit may be located in the same building; however, they may deal with different classifications of merchandise. During a visit in one office building, it would be an unwise use of your time not to visit all the vendors there. Viewing one classification at a time works well in merchandise/apparel marts,

Figure 13.5   Buyers must carefully record information that they learn when visiting each resource.

because similar vendors are located near each other—many times on the same floor. Many buyers also like to view the most expensive lines before lower-priced lines in order to better understand the components of a quality product.

3. Be on time for appointments. If you must cancel an appointment, call as early as possible. Do not rush through your market visits. Rushing through showrooms usually causes buyers to miss important items or overlook significant product features. Carefully viewing merchandise from a few carefully selected vendors is better than rushing through 20 to 30 vendors.

4. View all merchandise before placing orders. During your first viewing of the merchandise, take careful notes and make tentative choices. A second viewing of some lines may be required, but you will be able to reject many lines during the initial viewing.

5. Price the merchandise while viewing. Do not ask the price of merchandise you are viewing until you have thoroughly examined it. While viewing the merchandise, mentally attach a price to it. If the price quoted by the vendor is lower than you judged, it possibly is a good buy or you may have overlooked weaknesses in the item. If the price quoted is higher than you judged, you may have overlooked some features or the item may be overpriced.

6. Make careful notes. Your notes should include specific details about the merchandise, such as prices and size ranges; allowances and discounts permitted; and the name, address, and phone number of the vendor. Weigh all your intended purchases against your buying plan before placing any orders. Purchase orders need to be analyzed against your plan to ensure proper coverage of classifications, price lines, colors, sizes, and required areas. Make your selections in the quiet of your hotel room or back in your office at the store. Use your own order sheets when placing orders, because you will know that the required information is contained on the form.

Visiting Factories

While in the market you may want to visit the manufacturers of products carried in your store. Many times these factories are located near the central market, and such visits give you more detailed knowledge of the products your store is selling. Also, you are able to obtain a better idea of how the manufacturer operates. Such visits are especially useful if you plan to obtain any minor alterations in the merchandise.

You may also want to visit factories from which you are considering making purchases. These visits will allow you to determine if the manufacturer can handle the amount of work that would be required to produce the products you need. You would also be able to determine evidence of quality control steps taken by the manufacturer. Visit small manufacturers, too. From them you may be able to locate unusual and unique items.

Other Market Activities

While in the market, talk with other buyers to learn about their views of the current market and even the selections they have made for their stores. Much valuable information can be learned from informal conversations with fellow buyers.

Also allow time for nonmarket activities. Watch people in the streets or at group functions to detect any new fashion trends. Visit retail stores and window shop throughout your visit. You may even want to tour outstanding stores in the market city.

Visiting Online Showrooms

Today, buyers are able to visit some markets without ever leaving their offices. Retail business-to-business online showrooms are sprouting up at a dizzying pace these days on the Internet. These marketplaces bring multiple buyers and sellers together at a central hub, where they can collaborate and negotiate at a fraction of the cost and time previously needed for complex transactions. In addition, online showrooms provide easy reach for international and geographical areas without easy access to traditional markets.

Major competitors in the field currently include i2i Retail.com, Market 4Retail.com, and Tradeweave.com. Each of these marketplaces has developed a somewhat different interface with the buyer. At Market4 Retail.com, retail buyers can search, select, plan, collaborate, and negotiate directly with suppliers in a virtual marketplace. At i2i Retail, buyers are offered three methods of transaction—classifieds, auctions, and exchanges—allowing them to choose the one that best meets their needs. The auction is the heart of the Tradeweave marketplace.

In general, virtual showrooms make money by charging a percentage of the value of the transactions carried across their hubs. Often, the transaction fee is the responsibility of the seller, who can be charged from less than 1 percent to as much as 15 percent of the purchase price, depending on the products being sold.

For retailers, online marketplaces open the door to more variety and more partners without having to compromise efficiency. Most experts predict, however, that online showrooms will probably hold greater appeal for small and mid-sized retail firms and suppliers. The Internet will allow them to bypass the massive mainframes, the software applications, and the integration of various computer systems. All they need to do is use their computer to start interacting in the Internet's dynamic, real-time environment. Today, most retail analysts believe there is little doubt that the business-to-business segment of the Internet will dwarf business to consumer.

PREPARING TO NEGOTIATE

Before you arrive at the market, you should develop a negotiation plan in addition to your merchandise buying plan. The actual starting point of negotiation always precedes the face-to-face meeting by weeks or even months. ***Negotiation*** is more than an event, it is a process that involves gathering and using information to your advantage.

What images come to mind when the word "negotiation" is mentioned? For many people, the images they have are "dirty tricks" and endless haggling sessions in which only one side can emerge as the winner. As you will learn, negotiation involves much more. Most Americans do not seem to enjoy negotiating, but in many other countries, negotiation is a part of daily life. If you have ever traveled abroad and visited any of the many public markets, you know that everyone haggles over price; however, in the United States, many people tend to view haggling as an approach used by those who are cheap, petty, and noncooperative. Yet, there are many occasions when you have to negotiate.

Did you ever have to convince your parents to buy you a car? What arguments did you use? Did you stress to them what they would gain by purchasing the car for you? If they decided to purchase the car, who negotiated with the car dealer? Did you pay the sticker price? Probably not, if you negotiated.

In fact, almost every activity involving other people probably involves some form of negotiation. Rarely do two people agree on everything. If you are married, you probably have to negotiate such activities as who is going to shower first in the morning, what kind of new car will be purchased, where to go for dinner on weekends, when to purchase a new appliance, or where to spend your summer vacation. We all use negotiation every day.

Like most people, you learned to negotiate as a child when you first had to share your toys with your brothers and sisters or other children in the neighborhood. You had to negotiate who would get to play with them and for how long. Negotiation in business involves that same kind of give-and-take between two people. In other words, negotiation is the process of reaching a mutually satisfying agreement. Negotiation is also based on the premise that people are willing to give up something in order to get something else.

As a buyer you will be involved with negotiation every time you deal with a vendor. Your goals are to lower costs and improve terms and allowances, whereas the vendor's goals are to obtain your business with you paying the highest possible price. Each of you must be willing to give up something if agreements are to be reached during negotiations.

Before entering into any negotiations, you need to thoroughly understand the market, and the larger your impending purchase, the greater the need for research. You need to understand your customers' needs, competitive and economic conditions, and technical aspects of the products you are planning to purchase. You will want to frequently visit various types of vendors to make comparisons. You will also want to keep abreast of current trends by reading newspapers, magazines, and trade journals. In addition, an understanding of the manufacturing costs involved will enhance your ability to negotiate price concessions. Time spent on research is seldom wasted.

Analyze Your Position

Prepare yourself for negotiations with relevant facts. Have information such as your inventory position, desired profit margins, and current market trends for products that you are purchasing. Before negotiating, conduct a vendor analysis of every vendor with whom you plan to do business. Be sure you are able to justify your offers to vendors, and be ready to offer reasons that explain any concessions for which you are asking.

Determine the Vendor's Position

You will also need to research the vendor's position. Your buying office may be helpful in providing you with information about vendors with whom you will be dealing. Talking with buyers from noncompeting stores is another way to learn about vendors. Obtain as much information as possible from those buyers who have negotiated with the vendor in the past.

Knowing information about the vendor's firm will also be helpful as you plan your negotiations. For example, if manufacturers are doing well, vendors may be more generous in their negotiations with buyers. Or, if the firm is experiencing difficulties, the vendor may need to get rid of goods by offering special prices. Read the Snapshot titled, "Springs Industries: The Loss of Another U.S. Textile Manufacturer," to learn more about the problems faced by one vendor.

Develop Negotiation Skills

Negotiations require that you develop a variety of skills. Successful negotiation techniques come down to essentially one thing–understanding people. Good negotiators consider both their own firm's needs and those of the other party. Some characteristics of good negotiators include creativity, good listening skills, good organizational skills, and self-confidence. Good negotiators force themselves to exert diplomacy and tact. The best negotiators are good listeners who ask questions to get information or to stimulate and direct the other person's thinking.

A knowledge of human behavior is essential to anyone involved with negotiation. You must study people, because they—not terms or conditions—are the key to negotiations. Successful negotiators are sensitive to the needs of others. You need to study psychology, but more importantly, you need to listen and observe. Determine how people have previously reacted in similar situations. Elements of human behavior are predictable, but understanding those elements requires research and analysis.

You must be flexible, too. You will need to keep an open mind and always be ready to make changes in your appraisal of a situation. Above all, you will want to keep on friendly terms with the vendor. Alienation of the vendor, as a result of a negotiation, will only create additional problems for you in future business dealings.

Determine Objectives of Negotiations

Before entering negotiations, you will want to carefully develop your objectives. Know exactly what you want to achieve for each point on which you will be negotiating. In your preparation, you should answer the following questions:

- "What is the minimum that I can accept?"
- "What is the maximum I can ask for?"
- "What is the maximum I can give up?"
- "What is the least I can offer?"

Set your minimums and maximums in advance. Do not reveal them during your initial negotiations with the vendor, and stick to them. Once you have determined the minimum you can accept and the maximum you can give away, you will need to assess the maximums and minimums of the vendor. Never assume that vendors with whom you will be negotiating will be reasonable; their objectives might make sense only to them. Also, points that are important to you may be unimportant to the vendor.

SETTING THE STAGE FOR NEGOTIATING

Skillful negotiators know that the other person is not the enemy. Instead, the enemy is whatever will keep both sides from arriving at a positive outcome. Realize that people and circumstances change, so you must be prepared for change. As a buyer, you will be involved in thousands of negotiations, and it is doubtful if any two are ever alike.

Build Rapport

Communicating with friends is much easier than with strangers, so try to build a rapport with the vendor before you start negotiating. Even if you have met the vendor before, you will need to reestablish rapport. Establishing an open, warm atmosphere will help immeasurably when you get to tough issues.

Open your negotiations by focusing on small issues—the points that seem easiest to resolve. Exuding confidence plays a big part in negotiations, too. Be confident and enthusiastic. One way of gaining confidence and maintaining it throughout the negotiation is to ensure that your position is based on sound research. Do not come into negotiations unprepared.

Ask Questions

During negotiations you will also want to determine the vendor's needs. Ask questions, listen carefully, and give the vendor the opportunity to talk.

During your questioning, you will want to seek answers to two questions about the vendor:

- "What is the least the vendor can accept?"
- "What is the most the vendor can offer?"

Ask probing, open-ended questions, and keep asking questions until you learn everything you want to know. Be persistent. Listen carefully to the answers, because you may identify hidden messages. Your questions should be relevant and not offend the vendor, and you will want to lay a foundation as to why you want the information for which you are asking.

Ask questions to clarify what the vendor has said. Sometimes there is more to a situation than what is being said. You might say something like, "Let me make sure I understand you." Then, paraphrase what the vendor has said.

Listen and Watch for Nonverbal Clues

Effective negotiations depend on effective listening. Vendors may reveal clues about their minimums and maximums as they talk with you. By listening more and talking less in negotiations, you will increase your chances of gaining more information about the vendor's position. With enough information, you are more likely to get the results you want without giving up too much. Listening can be as persuasive as speaking.

Experienced negotiators also look for certain body signals and gestures. For example, vendors leaning back in their chairs and folding their arms may mean they object to something you have said. Be aware of the nonverbal clues you give to the vendor, too. Remain still during negotiations, sit with your shoulders squared, and look the vendor in the eye. You may need to practice these techniques, but they work.

DEVELOPING A NEGOTIATING STRATEGY

Achieving a common understanding is the nature and purpose of negotiations. In a successful negotiation, everybody wins. Unless both parties to an agreement come away feeling that they have made the best deal they could under the circumstances, there has been no real negotiation. There can be no losers when negotiations are successfully completed.

Negotiation is a competitive activity that should be carried on assertively, yet professionally. As you develop a negotiation strategy, you will want to analyze your personality traits and the traits of vendors with whom you will be negotiating. Then, you will want to develop tactics or techniques to use in order to reach your objectives. Keep in mind, however, that the vendor will also be developing strategy and tactics.

Personality Styles in Negotiations

Ask people like Donald Trump or Bill Gates about their negotiation style, and they may brag about their toughness. If you use "tough guy" tactics and bully vendors, they probably will not want to do business with you again, and neither will anyone else who hears about your tactics. Before negotiating, analyze your personality traits, and during negotiations, analyze the traits of the vendor. For successful negotiations to occur, both you and the vendor must be interested in collaboration.

Do you approach negotiations as if you are entering combat? If your only concern is winning, you may not be a successful negotiator for the long term. Some negotiators are not concerned with the relationship or its longevity; their goal is victory through power, threats, or even deception.

Do you concede easily when negotiating? Some people concede too easily on every issue; they try to maintain a low profile and avoid confrontation. Buyers or vendors who display this personality trait will not last long in their jobs.

Either of these traits are extreme examples of negotiation styles. You will want to develop traits that will allow you to become a ***collaborator***. That is, you want to view concerns as mutual problems and seek to arrive at solutions that allow both you and the vendor win.

Negotiation Tactics

Individuals should be aware of their objectives before selecting *tactics* for negotiations. Tactics should be based on becoming acquainted with negotiators and their organizations. The strategy and tactics that you select will be based to some extent on the power that you or the vendor possess. You both possess a certain level of power; however, neither side possesses complete power. Your store needs to purchase products from a vendor, but there are many other vendors. Vendors need to sell products to you, but there are other retailers who will make purchases from them. At times, economic and market conditions may give either you or the vendor more power. For example, during recessions, vendors may not be selling large quantities of merchandise, which gives you more power in the negotiation process. Conversely, when economic times are good and a large demand exists for the product that the vendor is selling, power lies with the vendor, who will be unlikely to make concessions. You need to understand the limits of your own power, and recognize the limits of the vendor's power. Never intimidate vendors with your store's clout. You may face lean times and will need them later.

Learn to recognize and react to negotiation tactics. Some of the more frequently used negotiation tactics follow:

- *Take It or Leave It*. This tactic is used when there is a deadlock or no time for further negotiation. Obviously, there is a risk that no agreement will be reached, and the other side may leave it. This tactic produces resentment if not handled carefully.
- *Limited Authority*. This tactic requires that the buyer say that he or she is authorized to pay up to $20 for a particular item, and higher prices would require the approval of the merchandising manager or controller.
- *But You Can Do a Little Better*. This tactic challenges the vendor to do a little better to finalize the deal.
- *But I Can't Make Up My Mind*. This tactic places the burden of convincing the buyer on the vendor. Often, the vendor will assume the buyer's role, summarize the issues, and point out the relative strengths and weaknesses. Ultimately, the vendor may be put into the position of assisting the buyer to make up his or her mind by improving the offer.
- *Facts and Data*. This tactic may determine the outcome of a negotiation. The individual with the most data can build the best case for his or her position.
- *What If?* This tactic uses questions such as the following: "What if I increase the purchase quantity?" "What if we combine similar items?" "What if I pay the invoice in 10 days instead of 30?" "What if we offer to extend the warranty period an additional six months?" "What if we offer an option to buy an additional unit at 20 percent discount?"
- *Let's Split the Difference*. This tactic requires that both the buyer and vendor relinquish an equal amount of a disputed difference. Usually this tactic is used when the difference is small and the end of the negotiation is near.
- *Time Pressure*. This tactic is also frequently used by both vendors and buyers. It is designed to make the other person give up something. The vendor may attempt to force you into an immediate decision with any of the following statements: "The price will increase next month." "The offer is good for only ten days." "Delivery is four weeks after the receipt of the order." "There is only limited inventory available." As a buyer, you may use time-pressure tactics, too. For example, you may say, "I'm returning home tomorrow, and I will need your final offer by the end of the day." Time-pressure tactics work for the person who has time; but an actual lack of time may work against you in negotiating.

Negotiation involves bargaining and compromise. A person entering negotiations should concentrate on tactics and only use compromise at the end. Being prepared to negotiate and taking the initiative are important for leverage during negotiating. Moreover, negotiating can be learned, and practice is the most effective way to sharpen negotiating skills.

Bargaining

The negotiation process involves bargaining and agreement between you and the vendor in relation to the business transaction. Try to see vendors' proposals from their point of view so that you can learn what is important to them.

One of the more formidable tools in negotiating is silence. People dislike silence and usually try to fill it with information. For example, suppose a vendor says to you, "I cannot guarantee this price will be available at the end of the month." If you remain silent, and let the vendor talk, he or she may reveal that this is not the real position.

Compromise is usually arrived at during the normal course of negotiating; however, the sole intent of negotiation should not be compromise. The real skill in negotiating is to work out a settlement that gives the other side just enough to make them willing to agree–but no more.

It is not wise to accept the first offer in a negotiation, because doing so does not test the other person's position. Avoid quick concessions. You risk giving up something unnecessarily if you hurry to expedite negotiations. Negotiations require a full discussion, not shortcuts.

The last 20 percent of negotiating time is believed to be when most concessions are made. If you have to make tradeoffs during negotiations, which you inevitably will, make sure you do not give up something that will derail your long-range strategy.

Negotiators often answer affirmatively too quickly when they could have bargained for a better deal. Learn to "flinch" as a standard reaction to any proposal made, then play the role of the reluctant buyer.

If you think negotiations are near an end but have not arrived at a decision, ask the vendor for a solution. Build on the partnership concept. In fact, the vendor may offer an alternative of which you had not been aware. At that stage of the negotiations, avoid **ultimatums**, one of the most common but least effective negotiating tactics. Even if the vendor gives in, he or she will resent you. If you ever plan to do business with the vendor again, and the chances are that you will, you cannot win if the other side loses. Your winning and the vendor losing cannot be good for future business. When you both win, you are likely to walk away from negotiations with more than a deal; you have acquired a relationship based on mutual respect. Negotiations should not be "winner take all." When you realize that, you are on your way to becoming a successful negotiator.

Negotiation Checklist

Before entering negotiations, make a list of areas to guide your negotiations. Be assertive, and ask for what you want in a straightforward manner. Some of the most important topics that you may negotiate include:

- Price
- Discounts
- Transportation terms
- Allowances
- Return privileges
- Exclusives
- Off-price
- Specification buying
- Private brands
- Vendor-supported promotions
- Delivery

These areas are more fully explored in Chapter 14. As a buyer, your responsibility is to negotiate for every allowance or service for which your store is eligible. That requires that you know what vendors have available.

Outcomes of Negotiation

Negotiating is a business relationship in action. It involves more than merely setting out to win some concessions from the other person. Although such an attitude may work in a single transaction, in an ongoing business relationship, the outcome must hold benefits for all parties. Furthermore, mutually beneficial solutions also should convey the perception of benefits. Great negotiators are outstanding problem solvers.

Negotiation is an essential business skill that involves the attitude you convey, the tactics you use, and the concern you show for the other person's feelings and needs. The objective is for both sides to win—to develop a long-term partnership. Understanding, acceptance, respect, trust, and a lasting business relationship will be the outcome of successful negotiations.

SUMMARY POINTS

- Central markets offer buyers access to a large number of key resources in close proximity to one another. Regional markets have developed to serve specific areas of the country by offering one-stop shopping to buyers at merchandise/apparel marts. Buyers can also locate sources at trade shows or expositions held yearly in many areas.
- Before planning a buying trip, buyers need to determine the purpose of the trip and develop a merchandise buying plan as well as a negotiation plan.
- The season, type of merchandise, size of store, its merchandise policies, proximity to markets, and business conditions will determine the frequency of a buyer's visits to market.
- In the market, buyers will want to talk with buying offices, visit vendors and showrooms, tour factories, attend seminars and fashion shows, talk with other buyers, and tour outstanding retail stores.
- When viewing lines, buyers must be systematic and take careful notes. Some buyers prefer to view all of one classification before moving to the next classification.
- Buyers must negotiate every time they deal with vendors.
- Negotiation is a process that begins *before* the face-to-face meeting between the vendor and buyer occurs. Before negotiating, buyers must gather and use information about their customers, competitive and economic conditions, and facts about products they will be purchasing.
- Before negotiating, buyers should learn about their vendors from buying offices and other buyers who have dealt with them in the past.
- Negotiation requires that buyers understand people and have good listening skills. Successful negotiators are self-confident and exhibit tact and diplomacy.

- Before negotiating, buyers should establish the minimum they can accept and the maximum they can give away. During negotiations, buyers must also assess the minimums and maximums of the vendor.
- Questions help the buyer determine the vendor's position during negotiations. Asking questions requires that buyers listen carefully in order to obtain more information about the vendor's position.
- The intent of negotiation should not be compromise. The real skill in negotiating is to work out a settlement that gives the other person's side just enough to make it willing to agree—but no more.
- Successful negotiators are collaborators. Their goal is for both sides in negotiations to "win."
- Various negotiation tactics are available for both the vendor and the buyer to use. The same tactics are frequently used by both sides to make the other side give up something.
- The end result of negotiation should be a mutually beneficial solution for both the buyer and the vendor.

REVIEW ACTIVITIES

Developing Your Retail Buying Vocabulary

Consult the Glossary if you did not add the following terms to your vocabulary.

Central Market	Negotiation
Collaborator	Tactics
Compromise	Trade Show
Exposition	Ultimatum
Merchandise/Apparel Mart	

Understanding What You Read

1. Describe what a buyer would typically find in a central market.
2. List and describe three purposes for making a buying trip.
3. For what reasons would a buyer make shorter and more frequent buying trips?
4. What should be developed first as a buying trip is planned?
5. Who may be required to approve a buyer's merchandise buying plan?

6. What services can a buying office provide buyers before they reach the market?

7. Why would buyers want to attend seminars sponsored by their buying office?

8. Describe the benefits of viewing an entire classification of merchandise before viewing other classifications.

9. Why do most Americans not enjoy negotiating?

10. Where does the starting point of any negotiation begin?

11. Why is knowing the vendor's position important to the negotiation process?

12. What four questions should buyers answer as they prepare for negotiations?

13. Describe ways to build rapport with vendors during negotiations.

14. While negotiating, what two questions about the vendor's position should the buyer attempt to answer?

15. Why is listening so important to the negotiation process?

16. Why should buyers not approach negotiations as if they are entering combat?

17. When should the "let's split the difference" tactic be used in negotiations?

18. Describe how both the buyer and the vendor can use time-pressure tactics.

19. Why should buyers never intimidate vendors by using their store's clout?

20. Why should buyers avoid quick concessions during negotiations?

21. Why should buyers ask the vendor for an alternative when the negotiation process seems to be stalled?

22. What should be the outcome of any negotiation?

Analyzing and Applying What You Read

1. What problems might result from buyers rushing through the viewing of a vendor's lines?

2. Why should buyers "price" a vendor's line of merchandise before inquiring about the cost?

3. Explain why the sole intention of negotiations should not be compromise.

4. Your research has revealed that the vendor with whom you will be negotiating has the reputation for heavy use of facts and statistical support. As a buyer, what should you do before meeting with the vendor?

How should you respond when the vendor begins pouring out all these data?

5. The vendor with whom you are negotiating has just hit you with a take-it-or-leave-it stand. He will sell dress shirts to you at $15.50 each and not a penny less. What should be your response? Explain.

6. Outline a plan that any new buyer could follow to practice the skills needed for successful negotiation.

Internet Connection

1. Access an auction site on the Internet, such as www.ebay.com. Record information about the negotiation process that is used (e.g, minimum bids, length of offers, etc.). In addition, report on how the site handles information on the reliability of the sellers.

2. On the Internet, access sites for two regional merchandise/apparel marts, such as www.denvermart.com. Record information about market dates and itineraries.

SNAPSHOT

The American International Toy Fair

Which toy will be the Tickle Me Elmo hit of this year? Every toy maker hopes the answer to that question will be found in its new product lines revealed in February each year at the American International Toy Fair held in New York City. At this annual trade show, the buzz is always about "which toy it will be?" But, it is impossible to know. Tickle Me Elmo was the surprise hit of 1996–selling out of stores nationwide well before the holidays. Moreover, thanks to the Elmo craze that year, sales of all plush dolls climbed 12 percent. An Elmo phenomenon, however, is not planned, and even the largest toy companies usually cannot predict what the "hits" are going to be.

A lot is riding on this event. Each year as the Toy Fair opens, manufacturers will show their new lines, and retailers will be scouting around for what will be the year's next big hit. The annual Toy Fair mixes business with outright silliness. Firms construct elaborate sets and hire teams of actors to push the products they hope will be big sellers for the year, especially during the holiday season. Men in suits lick lollipops and examine Furby's new friends. Executives discuss the merits of various dolls. Actresses sit in bedroom sets built just for the show and tickle the feet of toy infants. Public relations people blow bubbles. But, by the end of the show, millions of dollars in orders have been placed, and toy executives have a strong idea what the big hits of the year will be.

Most years, manufacturers depend heavily on licensed toys, linking their products to new movies from Hollywood. Today, it seems that every movie has products tied to it. Toy makers like movie-related products because they are identified with a heavily advertised entertainment package. But, each year manufacturers and retailers have to wait to see if kids respond to the new movies. They know these toys can be highly profitable. With the rerelease of the "Star Wars" trilogy in the late 1990s, Hasbro and Galoob Toys reissued their full line of action figures associated with the movies. They sold $425 million worth of toys based on 20-year-old characters.

Technology also has played a part in many of the new toys hitting the market in recent years. Perhaps the most surprising new category in recent years to reflect the influence of technology has been in the infant and preschool segments. A substantial part of the growth came from the creative use of computer chips in musical instrument toys such as Barney's Magical Banjo and preschool learning toys such as Vtech's AlphaBert.

Each year, retail buyers also place orders for classic toys; they know many parents purchase toys for their kids similar to the ones with which they played as children. Many manufacturers even update these classics with new interactive technology. For example, construction toy maker Lego went high-tech with the release of a CD-ROM game, "Adventures on Lego Island," which mixed technology with traditional Lego building.

For retail toy buyers, the Toy Fair represents the most important show they will attend each year. Yet, they must cut through the hype and make selections based on what they think will be hits with *their customers*. There is lots of pressure associated with those decisions— no retailer wants to be stuck with the toy no one wants at during the holidays.

BASED ON:

American International Toy Fair 2007. (2007, February 16). *eWeek*.

Graves, Pamela. (2007, January). American International Toy Fair. *Giftware News*, 16.

High-tech toys thrill at International Toy Fair. (2007, February 13). *eWeek.com*.

Keeping toy fair on track; media a big part of the merchandising mix as industry braces for next holiday season. (2007, February 12). *Television Week*, 18.

Palmeria, Chirstopher. (2007, February 13). Happier times in toyland. *Business Week Online*.

Personal kid tech in spotlight at New York Toy Fair. (2007, February 9). *Information Week*, NA.

Simon, Ellen. (2000, February 15). New York toy fair anticipates toys for the future. *Knight-Ridder/Tribune Business News*, NA.

TRENDWATCH

Which Furniture Market Will Dominate?

When the Las Vegas, Nevada, furniture market debuted in July 2005, questions immediately began to be asked about the future of the nearly 100-year-old International Furniture Market in High Point, North Carolina. In April and October of each year, High Point boasts over 2,500 exhibitors spread over 11.5 million square feet of display space in 186 buildings. The Market World Center in Las Vegas, which opened with 2.6 million square feet, has already announced plans to expand showroom space to nearly 12 million square feet by 2013—equalling the amount of space currently available in High Point. The inaugural Las Vegas market drew 62,000 people, which was not far from the 100,000 that the High Point market draws.

Attendance at both shows gives vendors the opportunity to develop new customers as well as develop face-to-face contact with clients whom they may have communicated with only through telemarketing or the Internet. For vendors, the High Point market offers lower rental fees per square foot. The average cost in Las Vegas is about $30 a foot, which is more than double the cost in High Point.

Buyers want to be able to access the entire spectrum of goods in a single market. For many of them, there is currently more product available at the High Point market than anywhere else in the world.

However, one advantage of the Las Vegas market is that "shows within a show" are presented simultaneously. For example, the Vegas Gift and Accessory Show provides a one-stop destination for gift buyers and suppliers with exhibits including tabletop, stationary, candles, frames, vases, and garden, while the Interior Lifestyle Show focuses on innovative and trend-oriented products.

Some analysts stress that High Point is a very "hardworking" trade show; buyers who attend are focused on business, not entertainment distractions. Some in the industry, however, refute this claim. A chief officer of one of the biggest furniture manufacturers in the world believes that Las Vegas is certainly on its way to becoming the dominant industry show. He believes that when buyers attend a furniture market they are working, but they want to be entertained too.

Other furniture executives have opposing views. They would rather send buyers to the market where they can get the most work done, a contest that is easily won by High Point. There is another noticeable difference between the two markets. Market days in Las Vegas start slow, then grow throughout the day–a trend that is in direct contrast to the way that a market day unfolds in High Point. Perhaps such actions could be attributed to the entertainment aspects of Las Vegas versus High Point.

Failing to recognize the importance of Las Vegas could be similar to the failure of some companies to accept China as a furniture source several years ago. Currently, the question of which market is winning or losing is up in the air. In the final analysis, success will be measured by which market buyers decide to attend.

BASED ON:

Evans, Matt. (2007, March 23). Future of furniture market dominance still undecided. *The Business Journal of the Greater Triad Area*, 1.

Miller, Hannah. (2005, September). High Point digs in its heels; the new Las Vegas furniture market made a big splash in July. *Wood and Wood Products*, 33.

Sloan, Carole. (2007, February 5). Buyers flock to Las Vegas market. *Home Textiles Today*, 1.

Thomas, Larry. (2007, February 5). Vegas business booms. *Furniture Today*, 1.

Vegas furniture market grows to 2.6 million square feet. (2006, June). *RTO.com*.

Vegas shows average 50,000. (2006, August 21). *Furniture Today*, 62.

SNAPSHOT

Springs Industries: The Loss of Another U.S. Textile Manufacturer

In June 2007, Springs Industries announced that it was closing the last of its South Carolina factories. The family-owned textile company was started 120 years ago in Fort Mill, South Carolina. Company co-CEO, Crandall Close Bowles, said, "The pace of change…has surprised me," in an interview reported in *The Charlotte Observer*. She said, "I would not have thought that we could have gotten to this point as quickly as we have." Bowles indicated that now sheets and towels for Springs would be made mostly in Brazil and other lower-wage countries. On January 1, 2005, the end of import limits, which had been in place for decades, unleashed foreign competition that Springs was never able to fend off.

The company announced that the goal of closing U.S. plants and moving operations to Argentina, Brazil, and Mexico was to reduce manufacturing costs. Factory wages average $1.40 per hour in Brazilian plants. That is about twice the rate that textile workers in China and India earn, but Brazil is much closer to U.S. markets so shipments reach store shelves faster. On the other hand, Springs' South Carolina factory workers were averaging about $15 per hour.

The move was designed to help Springs survive. The two other "Big Three" home furnishing companies have fared worse. In 2003, Pillowtex, formerly Fieldcrest-Cannon, blamed imports as a cause when it closed, eliminating thousands of jobs in the United States. That same year, West-Point Stevens filed for bankruptcy but has since been purchased.

In 2004, sales for Springs Industries were over $3.37 billion, well above their sales in 2000 of $2.28 billion. Sales picked up for Springs following the Pillowtex closures, but the company still lost nearly $17 million in 2004 on its sheet and towel business. It had difficulty booking orders at profitable prices.

In 2005, Springs' losses were nearly $96 million as the end of import limits on China and other countries allowed those countries to ship unlimited quantities of many textiles to the United States. For example, imports of sheets that year leaped 49 percent, while towel imports rose 36 percent. The big benefit of domestic production—quick delivery—could not offset large differences in product costs.

By the end of 2007, Springs had only one towel plant left in the United States, but still had other domestic factories producing products such as pillows, mattress pads, and bath rugs. In making the closure announcements, company officials said that the shift to foreign markets would allow Springs Industries "...to combine large-scale, high-efficiency, state-of-the-art facilities with competitive labor and energy costs, and give the company access to low-cost raw materials."

Springs employed more than 15,000 workers in North and South Carolina as recently as the mid-1990s. After the shutdowns, Springs will have only about 700 workers in the Carolinas, mostly at distribution facilities and at two sales and administrative offices.

How quickly will other domestic factories follow Springs offshore? How soon will it be impossible for retail buyers to find domestic sources for textiles?

BASED ON:

End of era for Springs. (2007, August 2). *Rock Hill Herald*, B1.

Hopkins, Stella M. (2007, June 27). Springs ends 120 years of SC manufacturing. *The Charlotte Observer*, A1.

Hopkins, Stella M. (2007, August 1). Springs lives on in a changing world. *The Charlotte Observer*, D1, D6.

Shoulberg, Warren. (2006, June 19). *HFN The Weekly Newspaper for the Home Furnishing Network*, 1.

Making the Purchase

PERFORMANCE OBJECTIVES

Upon completion of this chapter, you should be able to:

- Describe techniques for price negotiations in the market.
- List and describe types of discounts for which buyers can negotiate.
- List and describe types of FOB (free-on-board) terms.
- Identify and describe allowances and return privileges that vendors may grant buyers.
- Recognize the impact of private brands on retailing.
- Describe special buying situations (e.g., job lots, off-price, seconds, and irregulars).
- List and describe types of orders placed by buyers.
- Identify key parts of a purchase order.

After you have decided what to order and have developed a clear understanding of the negotiation process, you and the vendor must agree on the price of the merchandise and terms of the order. In this chapter, you will learn about the terms for which buyers negotiate. Special buying situations are described, and how orders are placed with vendors is explained.

NEGOTIATING TERMS OF THE SALE

The most important terms that you will negotiate include (1) price, (2) discounts, (3) transportation, (4) allowances, and (5) return privileges.

Price

Price negotiation really starts before you go to market. You should learn as much as you can about market conditions and individual vendors with whom you will be negotiating. For example, economic slowdowns or internal troubles that a manufacturer may be facing are indications that the vendor may be willing to offer price concessions. If you know that the merchandise is already manufactured and subject to becoming outdated, you may have a better opportunity to negotiate price reductions. Also, by having an understanding of the manufacturing costs involved, you will have a better idea of how much the vendor may be willing to reduce prices.

While viewing merchandise in the market, you will want to estimate its retail value before inquiring about the cost. If the price quoted by the vendor is lower than you judged, it possibly is a good buy or you may have overlooked weaknesses in the item. If the price quoted is higher than you judged, you may have overlooked some features or the item may be overpriced. You could practice this technique by predicting retail prices in stores where you shop.

In the market, compare price quotes offered by different vendors. Shop the market thoroughly; some vendors may be willing to reduce their price to meet the competition. Most buyers, however, do not simply select the vendor with the lowest price. You will also want to check other criteria such as the vendor's dependability, delivery times, discounts, or allowances offered.

Many price reductions that vendors offer are based on increasing the quantity of merchandise purchased. You may not be able to increase total purchases, but you may be able to consolidate orders with one resource to qualify for larger quantity discounts. Also, some price reductions may be offered in the form of free deals. For example, you may be offered two free cases of a product when 100 cases are purchased.

In all price negotiations, vendors must be concerned with not violating the Robinson–Patman Act of 1936, which outlawed price discrimination in interstate commerce. All price reductions must be offered on a "proportionally equal" basis to all buyers. The manufacturer must be able to justify any price reductions given a buyer that result from differences in the seller's manufacturing costs, selling costs, or delivery costs. For example, if the seller's cost to deliver a large shipment to Retailer A is actually less than making a small delivery to Retailer B, the vendor could pass on this difference in the form of a price reduction to Retailer A.

In relation to price, you may also negotiate a **_price decline guarantee_** that protects the store if market prices drop over a stated period of time. For example, a buyer may purchase computers for $1,000 each on March 1; the manufacturer may then drop the price to $950 on March 15. With a price decline guarantee, the buyer would be protected against such price reductions for a period of time after the order was signed. In this case, the vendor would credit or refund the buyer's store $50 for each computer purchased.

Discounts

Probably the most important terms that you will negotiate are discounts, a reduction in the price of the merchandise. You must determine the types of discounts offered by each vendor, and where possible, attempt to qualify for them. There are several types of discounts for which you may qualify.

Quantity Discounts. Often vendors will offer *quantity discounts* to buyers to entice them to order more merchandise. Some buyers place an order for the estimated quantity of merchandise they will need for the entire season, with a cancellation date approved by the vendor. The buyer is able to place an order for a larger quantity for discount purposes.

Vendors offer buyers quantity discounts because they save money in handling and processing orders in large quantities. By offering quantity discounts, manufacturers can benefit from lower production costs–they can order raw materials in larger quantities and plan their operating schedules more efficiently. Also, completing the order forms for a large order takes about the same amount of time as for a small order. An example of a quantity discount would be a vendor offering a 2 percent discount for orders of more than 125 dozen. The quota could be expressed in units or dollar amounts.

Seasonal Discounts. Some buyers may be offered *seasonal discounts* for making purchases in advance of a selling season. Seasonal discounts may be offered on such products as skis, air conditioners, or lawn mowers. Manufacturers benefit because they are able to plan their production schedules more efficiently and keep skilled employees working throughout the year. An example of a seasonal discount would be a vendor offering a 2 percent discount to buyers who place orders for next year's lawn mowers in October. Seasonal discounts are attractive, but you must be certain that styles or models will not change noticeably by the time the merchandise arrives at the store.

Trade Discounts. Many times buyers are offered *trade discounts* based on the manufacturer's list price. Manufacturers may quote trade discounts as a series of discounts. For example, an item with a list price of $1,000 may be offered with discounts of 40 percent and 10 percent—which is *not* a 50 percent discount. Instead, each discount is computed on the amount that remains after the preceding discount has been taken. With the example given, the 40 percent discount is calculated first, and is $400. That amount is subtracted from the list price, for a total of $600. Then, a 10 percent discount is taken on the $600, which equals $60. The cost to the buyer would be $540 ($600−$60).

Cash Discounts. Manufacturers also grant ***cash discounts*** to retailers for early payment of invoices. Manufacturers want payments as quickly as possible, and most retail managers want buyers to negotiate for cash discounts because of the price advantages they offer the store in the marketplace. Discounts can turn a breakeven year into a profitable one, so a store cannot afford to ignore them. Typically, cash discount terms are expressed in a form such as "2/10 net 30," which means that a 2 percent discount will be granted if the buyer pays the invoice within 10 days of the invoice date. If the invoice is not paid within that period, the total amount is due in 30 days.

Several dating terms are used to determine the amount of time given to the retailer to take advantage of the cash discount. The most commonly used are as follows:

- *Ordinary dating terms* are the most common type of cash discount. The amount of time to take advantage of a discount is calculated from the invoice date. The preceding example illustrated ordinary dating terms.
- *ROG (receipt of goods) dating terms* allow the buyer to calculate the discount period from the day the merchandise was received in the store rather than from the invoice date. These terms are written "2/10 net 30 ROG." In this situation the buyer would have 10 days from the delivery date to take advantage of the 2 percent discount offered.
- *EOM (end-of-month) dating terms* allow the buyer to calculate the discount period from the end of the month. These terms are written "2/10 net 30 EOM." In this situation the buyer would have 10 days from the end of the month in which the invoice was written to take advantage of the 2 percent discount offered. There is one exception. If the invoice date falls on the 25th day of the month or later, the last day to take advantage of the discount is calculated from the end of the following month rather than from the month in which the invoice was written.
- *Extra dating terms* give the buyer a specified number of additional days in which to pay the invoice and earn the cash discount. The terms are

usually written "2/10 net 30 60X." In this situation, the buyer would have 10 days from the invoice plus an additional 60 days to take advantage of the 2 percent discount offered.

- *Advance dating terms* indicate that the invoice is dated for some specified time in the future. For example, an invoice for lawn mowers shipped on January 14 may have terms of "2/10 net 30 as of May 1." In this situation, the buyer would have 10 days from the date given (May 1) to take advantage of the cash discount.

Anticipation is an extra discount that some manufacturers give buyers for paying an invoice *in advance of the cash discount date*. Anticipation is usually taken only if your store has ready cash available.

Buyers may not always be given discount terms. If a vendor is uncertain of a buyer's credit, merchandise is sent *COD* (collect on delivery), which means that the transportation company will collect the amount of the invoice when the goods are delivered.

Transportation

Transportation terms may also need to be negotiated. If your store is to pay the cost of shipment, you will want to specify how the merchandise is to be shipped. Time and cost are important considerations as you select methods of shipment. If the merchandise is needed quickly, you will want to select the fastest method of shipment possible; however, speed is usually associated with more expense.

Just as with discounts, there are a number of transportation terms available. Each transportation term indicates who is to pay the shipping charges and when the buyer takes title to the goods. Title of the goods is important because it indicates who is responsible for goods while they are in shipment. *FOB*–free on board–is the term associated with transportation charges. Commonly used transportation terms include the following:

- *FOB origin (factory)* are the most commonly used terms under which merchandise is shipped. Title passes to the buyer when the seller delivers goods to the transportation carrier. Transportation charges as well as other expenses and risks are the responsibility of the buyer.
- *FOB destination (store)* are terms that indicate that the manufacturer pays the shipping charges, and title passes to the buyer when the merchandise is delivered to the retail store. For a buyer, FOB destination terms are ideal.

• *FOB **destination, charges reversed*** indicates that the buyer pays the shipping charges, but the seller assumes responsibility for the goods while they are in transit.

• *FOB **destination, freight prepaid*** indicates that the seller will pay the freight charges, but the buyer takes title to the goods as soon as they are shipped.

• *FOB **shipping point*** indicates that the manufacturer has title to the goods and will pay shipping costs until the merchandise reaches a distribution point. From that point, the buyer takes title to the goods and pays transportation charges until they reach the store.

Allowances

Many vendors may also grant special allowances to buyers. ***Cooperative (coop) advertising*** is one of the most common. If the buyer runs an advertisement featuring the manufacturer's products, the manufacturer will agree to pay a percentage of the ad's cost. Usually the vendor will require proof that the ad ran before credit is issued. With coop advertising, vendors may exercise some control on the kind of advertising that the store can use. Coop advertising provides one way for the store to reduce its promotion budget; however, there are problems. The advertising may disrupt the store's current advertising program, and the retailer may be tempted to promote only those products for which coop advertising is given.

In grocery stores, some vendors are willing to pay for preferred selling space. Research has determined the value of specific spaces in the store, so vendors are willing to pay for preferred space that could increase sales volume. Vendor-supported promotions are frequently used for groceries, automobiles, and cosmetics. Vendors may be willing to provide advertising, in-store entertainment, free products, or public relations surrounding an in-store promotion.

Today, many buyers also negotiate for floor-ready merchandise shipped from the manufacturer that already includes price tags and source tags designed to curb shoplifting. Read the Trendwatch titled, "Source Tagging: Bargaining for Floor-Ready Merchandise," to learn more about this trend.

Return Privileges

Some vendors may agree to accept returns of merchandise that did not sell. Return privileges are frequently used by vendors when they are selling new merchandise of which the retailer may be unsure. Vendors may agree to accept the return of merchandise if it has not sold within a specified period of time. Vendors offering returns must realize that this practice may result in excessive returns of unsold merchandise at the end of the season. Two frequently used terms for returns are:

- **On memorandum,** which indicates that the merchandise coming into the store has a return privilege with it. The store pays for the merchandise but has the opportunity to return any unsold items at the end of a specified period.
- **On consignment,** which indicates the buyer will take merchandise into the store but will pay for it only when it sells. The buyer can then return any unsold merchandise. On consignment allows the store to increase inventory without increasing capital investment; but, slow-selling merchandise may occupy valuable selling space.

NEGOTIATING SPECIAL BUYING SITUATIONS

Your negotiations with vendors may also involve special situations, some of which are described in this section. They include private brands, specification buying, promotional buying, job lots, off-price buying, and seconds and irregulars. Read the Snapshot titled, "Liz Claiborne," to learn about how one vendor is changing the rules.

Private Brands

For many years, retailers offered only national brands as part of their product assortments. For the stores, the benefits were that national brands had already gained widespread customer acceptance, and being associated with national brands tended to increase the store's prestige. In addition, most manufacturers backed up national brands with extensive promotional campaigns. One problem, however, developed for retailers–the products lacked exclusivity. Sameness was created in the marketplace because competitors were all selling the same brands.

As retailers began experimenting with ways to distinguish themselves, some turned to *private brands,* which allowed them to avoid direct competition. Private brands are developed by retailers in order to offer unique merchandise to their customers. Read the Trendwatch titled, "Private Labels Spell Profits," to learn more about trends in this area.

Before you decide to offer private brands, however, you must conduct research to determine their feasibility in your market. You need to identify buying motives that cause your customers to choose one brand over another. With an understanding of your customers' needs, you can provide the product mix that will best meet those needs.

Brands must mean something to your customer. In other words, they must add value. If your store decides to replace national brands with similar products under your store's private brand, quality must be controlled. Private brands must be of sufficiently high quality that they can be compared with national brands. Today, consumers are more sophisticated and look beyond low prices when purchasing products; they look at workmanship and quality.

If your store decides to offer private brands, several questions must be answered. You must determine the percent of your total merchandise assortment that will be private brands, and you must decide what name should appear on the label—the store's name or some other "signature." Today, most stores are moving away from using the store's name as the private brand.

Instituting a private brand program also requires capital. Manufacturers may require larger quantity purchases because changes may be required before your label is placed on the product. In addition, your store must conduct promotional campaigns to make consumers aware of your new brand.

Advertising and visual merchandising play a crucial role in making private brands recognizable and meaningful to consumers. Most retailers advertise national brands alongside their private brands. Promotion also is needed to build customer preference, which requires that private brands be given treatment similar to national brands. JCPenney displays its private brands prominently alongside national brands, stressing their quality and features. Macy's has created such an effective private brand in Morgan Taylor that many people believe she is a real woman.

The quality of private brands is also critical. Before adding a private brand, buyers must take steps to guarantee customer satisfaction. Product testing ensures that colors stay true, that the fit is right, and the fabric is long-wearing. Most retailers also advertise national brands alongside their private brands. Figure 14.1 illustrates some of the tests that could be performed on a shirt.

Many private brands outperform national brands, but they must be distinctive to be successful. Private brands cannot be simply knockoffs

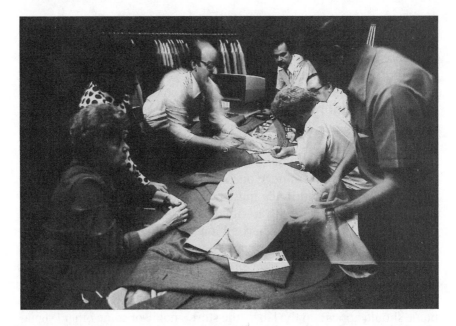

Figure 14.1   Buyers must test the quality of products that are shown in the market.

of a national brand. When your store decides to develop private brands, you may take your designs to a manufacturer or rely on the manufacturer for product development. Some buying offices will also help with private brand development programs.

Your store might develop private brands because of the possibility of higher markups, but that will be a short-sighted reaction unless private brands meet the needs of your customers. Private brands also allow stores more control of merchandising decisions, such as price and promotion.

To be successful, your private brands must offer exclusivity, at a special price, and be well made in order to compete effectively with national brands. In the past, too many retailers have regarded private brands as brands that should be cheap, low-priced products. Quality and consistency is the key today. There is even a trend toward upscaling private brands and packaging them to appeal to a specific market niche. Increasingly fragmented consumer markets present an opportunity for new brands, including private brands targeted to specific consumer segments.

What are the trends of private brands in today's marketplace? The debate continues over private label versus national brands in many stores.

Some retailers strongly support private labels, while others oppose them vehemently. Some retailers, such as The Limited, Eddie Bauer, Benetton, and The Gap, carry 100 percent private labels, whereas other retailers have few or no private brands.

Most retail executives feel that national brands benefit them in the long run. If a Claiborne blouse does not sell, it may have to be marked down only 15 percent, whereas a private brand blouse may have to be discounted 30 to 40 percent in order to move it out of the store.

There have been highly publicized increases in the use of private brands at stores such as Kmart, which continues to build private brands associated with personalities. Its Jaclyn Smith apparel collection has been successful, as has the At Home with Martha Stewart collection of bed linens and accessories. In this way, Kmart is using private brands to develop a fashion image.

There have been equally publicized decreases in the use of private brands. Sears is the most notable, as it switched to Sears Brand Central. In previous decades, Sears had built its reputation on many of its private brands such as Kenmore (appliances), Craftsman (tools and lawn and garden), Diehard (auto batteries), Road Handler (tires), Toughskins (boy's jeans), Trader Bay (men's sportswear), and Cheryl Tiegs (women's sportswear). Today, Sears carries over 1,000 national brands along with a mix of private brands.

After a period of decline, private brands have been growing in supermarkets. Today, most supermarket operators are reporting increases in the number of private brands being offered. For years, private brands for food were plagued by consumer concerns about product quality. Primarily this occurred because past emphasis had traditionally been placed on low prices. Store owners have now realized that it is not price alone that sells products; consistency and value must be there, too.

Improvements in packaging have also boosted private brand business in supermarkets. For most stores, updated packages have translated into increased sales, and more emphasis on advertising and promotion has also improved the image of private brands. Many grocery store ads now feature 20 percent private brands.

Grocery store owners have also realized that price differences between private brands and national brands cannot be either too high or too low. They know that pricing too low can do more harm than good, because consumers will then question the quality of the product. Although consumers expect national brands to cost more, the private brand should be priced no less than 20 percent under the national brand–less than that, and the consumer will gravitate to the national brand. On the other hand, if there is a 30 to 35 percent difference, the consumer will think there is something wrong with the private brand.

Most retailers are not likely to give up national brands entirely. They feel that national brands create the energy and drive trends in the marketplace. Private brands, however, will continue to be presented as an alternative in the merchandise mix.

Specification Buying

Rather than developing private brands, some buyers may become involved in *specification buying*. In some situations, buyers may suggest specifications or changes that upgrade the quality of the merchandise, its workmanship, or styling. Some specification buying involves no upgrades but simply making the merchandise different from similar goods carried by the competition.

If your store does specification buying, you may need product development personnel. In addition, specification buying requires a sales volume large enough to warrant the manufacturer making the suggested changes. You must also be concerned with quality control when conducting this type of buying.

Promotional Buying

Promotional buying involves purchasing merchandise to be featured in the store's promotions, and it is usually a part of the buyer's overall merchandise plan. Because most retailers have frequent promotions during the year, buyers must scout the market for special promotional buys to feature in those promotions. Typically, you will be interested in locating merchandise that can be offered to your customers at a price lower than its regular selling price. You must carefully calculate your needs so that excess merchandise is not left after the promotion is completed. Also, before bringing new merchandise into the store, you should analyze your current stock to determine if the price of any items could be reduced as part of the promotion. Customers will more easily recognize value when the merchandise on sale had previously been sold in the store.

Job Lots

While in the market, you may also be offered a job lot by a vendor. A *job lot* is an assortment of merchandise that the vendor has been unable to sell at regular prices and therefore offers it at a reduced price. The job lot will frequently contain merchandise of different value, so you should determine the retail price that could be realized for selling the goods quickly. If the estimated margin on the job lot does not reach the department's plan, you should consider other purchases.

There are other dangers in purchasing job lots. A poor assortment of sizes, colors, and styles may be offered. The quality may be excellent but your customers may not want to purchase the items in the job lot. If your store already carries the items in the job lot, there is less danger involved because the merchandise can be added to your existing merchandise lines. Another danger occurs when job lots are offered to the buyer near the end of the selling season. Even though a bargain price is offered, the merchandise will arrive at your store so late in the season that you may not be able to sell it without taking more markdowns.

You must also determine the effect of any job lot purchases on your existing lines. Cannibalization of the line may occur. In other words, the sale merchandise from the job lot may take away sales from existing merchandise in the store. As a result, planned margins are not maintained because you may be forced to take heavy markdowns on merchandise already in the store.

Off-Price

Buyers for some stores may specialize in buying *off-price*, which occurs when retailers purchase manufacturers' overruns at deep discounts for the purpose of offering consumers low prices on name brand merchandise. Stores such as Burlington Coat Factory, Marshall's, Syms, S&K, and T.J. Maxx are retailers that offer off-price merchandise. Some vendors have even established their own factory outlet stores to sell their own overruns. Prices at off-price stores are about 20 to 30 percent less than those at department stores selling the same merchandise.

Buying off-price requires that you wait longer into the selling season before making purchases. Customers of off-price stores are more concerned with price, rather than being the first to have a new fashion. By waiting into the selling season to make their purchases, buyers can usually find overruns in the market or vendors willing to sell products at a lower price.

Seconds and Irregulars

In the market, you may also be offered merchandise with slight imperfections or minor damage. For example, small pulls or snags may appear in apparel. The nature of the manufacturing process results in a certain amount of goods in this category. Manufacturers may inform buyers of the availability of these products through trade paper advertisements or through market representatives.

Imperfect or damaged merchandise is typically classified as *irregulars* or *seconds*. Irregulars have slight imperfections not visible to the naked eye. Seconds contain more obvious imperfections or damage. Because they are available at low prices, buyers purchase them to offer products to their customers at enormous savings. Some outlet stores stock seconds and irregulars exclusively.

There are dangers with purchasing seconds and irregulars. There must be a demand for these products by your customers that should coordinate with other products and fit into the merchandising policies of your store. Some buyers will not purchase irregulars or seconds because they may damage the quality image that the store has worked to develop.

Stores that offer seconds and irregulars usually sell them in an area set off from other first-quality merchandise. A special tag is usually attached to the item informing customers that the item is an irregular or a second. Large department stores usually put the merchandise in their budget departments.

PLACING THE ORDER

After you have made the decision to purchase merchandise and agreed to terms and conditions, you are ready to complete the purchase order. The purchase order is a contract between a buyer and a vendor and must be completed carefully to avoid any costly mistakes. The manufacturer's representative will provide order forms, but most buyers prefer to use their own. Because each form is different, there is a danger of some essential information being omitted.

Types of Orders

Buyers may place several types of orders, as follows:

- *Regular orders* are placed by the buyer directly with the vendor.
- *Reorders* are additional orders for merchandise previously purchased. Some fashion retailers are limiting reorders and placing orders for new merchandise to have continuously fresh and exciting stock moving into the store.
- *Special orders* are placed to satisfy the needs of individual customers.
- *Advance orders* are regular orders whose delivery is negotiated for some time in the future. Special discounts may be given to buyers who are willing to place orders early.
- *Open orders* are usually placed with the buying office. The buyer will select the vendor that is best suited to fill the requirements specified by the store.
- *Back orders* are placed by the buyer for shipments or parts of orders that the vendor had been unable to fill in the past.

Parts of the Purchase Order

Each purchase order is usually marked with a serial number. Other information that is found on most orders includes (Figure 14.2):

- Name and address of the store
- Date of the purchase order
- Vendor's name and address
- Where the goods are to be delivered, if not the store
- Terms of sale (dating and FOB terms)
- Cancellation date for the order
- Department number
- Classification number
- Description of the merchandise, including quantity, stock number, unit price, and total price
- Signature of the buyer or other authorized signatures
- Special instructions

Typically buyers will have a number of copies of the purchase order. The original is given to the vendor, and a copy remains with

PURCHASE ORDER

THE ABOVE ORDER NUMBER MUST BE SHOWN ON ALL INVOICES AND PACKAGES.

RESOURCE CODE

DATE

TERMS:

RESOURCE: _____

ADDRESS _____

CITY _____ STATE _____ ZIP _____

SPECIAL INSTRUCTIONS

LABEL INSTRUCTIONS
☐ MFG. LABEL
☐ STORE LABEL
☐ BOTH
OBTAIN LABELS FROM:

WHEN SHIP: ☐
AS READY
STARTING
COMPLETE
AUTOMATICALLY CANCEL
AFTER
Without Written Notice

INDICATE BY LETTER IN THE FIRST COLUMN OF EACH SECTION, THE SIZE RANGE BEING USED.

MERCHANDISE INDICATED BELOW SHIPS TO STORE SHOWN ABOVE UNLESS OTHERWISE SPECIFIED IN SPECIAL INSTRUCTIONS.

ALL SIZES OF A COLOR MUST BE SHIPPED COMPLETE IN ONE SHIPMENT.

STORE CODE

SHIPPING INSTRUCTIONS
☐ UPS
☐ UPS BLUE
☐ P.P.
☐ EXPRESS
☐ FREIGHT
☐ AIR FREIGHT
☐ OTHER

INSURE ☐ YES ☐ NO

REORDER LEAD TIME IN WEEKS (CIRCLE ONE) 1 2 3 4 5

CHECK SEASON ✓
SPring
SUmmer
TRansition
FAll
HOliday
BAsic
PRomotional

1 2 3 4 5 6 7 8

LENGTH - INSEAM
WIDTH - SLEEVE

CLASS | STYLE | DESCRIPTION | COLOR CODE | QTY. | RETAIL PRICE | UNIT COST | TOTAL COST

TOTAL →

AUTHORIZED SIGNATURE

1. We are not responsible for purchases unless made out on this order form and duly authorized by a responsible signature.
2. If the terms specified on this order do not appear on, or agree with, the seller's invoice as rendered, seller agrees that purchaser may change the invoice to conform with this order and make payment accordingly.
3. Merchandise arriving after date specified, or not as ordered, is subject to refusal or return of part or all without prior notice, at vendor's expense for both incoming and outgoing shipping charges.
4. In the event the seller is unable to deliver any part or all of the merchandise called for by this order, seller agrees to notify purchaser immediately.
5. Goods received on or after the 20th of the month will be paid as if billed the 1st of the following month.

Figure 14.2 A sample purchase order used by retail buyers.

the buyer. In larger stores, additional copies may be sent to (1) receiving, which checks incoming merchandise on arrival at the store, and (2) the finance department, which pays for merchandise that has been ordered.

Sometimes it may be better to wait until you have returned from a market visit before completing purchase orders. You then have the opportunity for reconsideration, the ability to review your order without pressure from the vendor or other market activities.

Follow Up of Orders

After the order is written, you still have certain responsibilities to ensure that the merchandise arrives at the store. For example, you may need to check with the manufacturers or transportation companies when merchandise does not arrive on time. Before special promotions, you may want to contact the manufacturer to ensure that the amount of merchandise needed will be arriving on time. You may also have to trace delayed or lost shipments.

Buyers also may be involved with *quality checks* to ensure that the merchandise shipped is identical to the quality of the merchandise seen in the market. Other store employees can be responsible for *quantity checks* that involve counting the number of items received as well as checking for correct sizes, colors, and models. These numbers are compared with both the purchase order and the invoice to determine that (1) merchandise received was actually ordered, and (2) the store was billed correctly. If goods are to be returned to the vendor, proper forms must be completed. Different action may be required if other types of discrepancies are found.

Vendors should notify buyers if they are sending substitutions. On occasion, the vendor may be unable to complete the order exactly as requested, but may be able to send merchandise that is nearly identical. Buyers should have the opportunity to decline substitutions before they are ever shipped. By accepting merchandise that was not ordered, you would be establishing a dangerous policy for your store.

Throughout the negotiation and ordering process, you will want to build a partnership with your vendors based on mutual respect, fair treatment, and honesty. Part of your success will depend on the cooperation and understanding that you develop with your vendors.

SUMMARY POINTS

- Buyers must shop the market thoroughly to compare prices from vendors. Buyers may actually realize price reductions on merchandise through discounts, free deals, or other allowances granted the vendor.
- Buyers should be aggressive when seeking discounts from vendors. Discounts may turn a breakeven year into a profitable one. Types of discounts offered by vendors include quantity, seasonal, trade, and cash.
- When negotiating dating terms, buyers can negotiate discount percentages as well as the number of days in which the bill is to be paid. Types of dating terms include ordinary, EOM, ROG, extra, and advance.
- Buyers will also negotiate transportation terms. In addition, buyers may determine the method of shipment to be used. FOB destination terms are the most favorable for the buyer.
- Buyers may also negotiate for cooperative advertising and return privileges.
- Private brands allow buyers to establish exclusives for their store; however, advertising and visual merchandising are crucial to developing sales for private brands.
- When considering job lots, off-price buying, and seconds and irregulars, buyers must determine if the products will deliver the desired markup and how they will affect sales of other products.
- Buyers complete purchase orders, which become a legal contract between the store and the vendor.
- When merchandise arrives in the store, both quality checks and quantity checks should be conducted.

REVIEW ACTIVITIES

Developing Your Retail Buying Vocabulary

Consult the Glossary if you did not add the following terms to your vocabulary.

Advance dating terms	Off-price
Anticipation	On consignment
Cash discount	On memorandum
COD	Ordinary dating terms
Cooperative advertising	Price decline guarantee

EOM dating terms   Private brand
Extra dating terms   Promotional buying
FOB   Quality check
FOB destination, charges reversed   Quantity check
FOB destination, freight prepaid   Quantity discount
FOB destination (store)   ROG dating terms
FOB origin (factory)   Seasonal discount
FOB shipping point   Seconds
Irregulars   Specification buying
Job lot   Trade discount

Understanding What You Read

1. Under the Robinson–Patman Act how are manufacturers able to charge lower prices to large retailers?
2. Give examples of products for which price decline guarantees would be desired.
3. Why are manufacturers willing to offer seasonal discounts to buyers?
4. On merchandise with a list price totaling $2,520, a wholesale buyer is offered trade discounts of 40 percent and 15 percent. For what dollar amount will the buyer be billed?
5. Why are manufacturers willing to offer cash discounts to buyers?
6. In most cases, why would ROG terms be better for a buyer than ordinary dating terms?
7. The invoice date is January 5 and the delivery date is January 6. Terms of the order are 2/10 net 30 EOM. When is the last day the buyer can pay the bill and still receive a discount?
8. When could a buyer be in a position to take advantage of anticipation?
9. Goods are sent from the manufacturer with the following terms: 2/10 net 30 FOB factory. Who pays the shipping charges?
10. What are the dangers to the retailer of accepting cooperative advertising allowances?
11. When would a seller most often grant a buyer on-memorandum terms?
12. Why do retailers offer private brands?
13. How should a retailer promote private brands?
14. Why have Sears and other retailers reduced the number of private brands they carry?

15. Why did sales of private brand products slow down in supermarkets for several years?
16. Describe how private brands should be priced in relation to national brands.
17. What are the dangers involved with purchasing job lots?
18. What are the dangers involved with purchasing seconds and irregulars?
19. When would a buyer issue an open order?
20. Why do some buyers return to their hotel rooms or their offices before completing purchase orders?

Analyzing and Applying What You Read

1. A vendor has offered you a choice of the following terms on a purchase that is under negotiation:

   2/10 net 30
   2/10 net 30 ROG
   2/10 net 30 EOM

   Which terms will be best for you? Explain.
2. A retail store in Charlotte, North Carolina, places an order with a factory in New York. The order is delivered to the store on August 10 with an invoice date of August 5. Terms were 3/15 net 30 FOB Charlotte. Including shipping charges if they owe any, how much would the retailer owe if it paid the bill on August 19?
3. Your store manager is considering offering some private brands in menswear. As the buyer for that department, you have been asked to prepare a proposal recommending the action to be taken. After listing the pros and cons of establishing private brands, present arguments to support your final decision.
4. Describe techniques that department stores and specialty stores could use to effectively compete with off-price retailers.

Spreadsheet Skills

1. Use a spreadsheet program to develop a spreadsheet that will calculate extensions (e.g., purchasing 12 dozen priced at $56.44 a dozen) and total the purchase for five items.

2. In *Making Buying Decisions: Using the Computer As a Tool*, complete problems related to Merchandising Concept 10.1 (Calculate Cost and Retail Extensions with Markup Percentages).

Internet Connection

1. On the Internet, access a site for a department store, such as www.jcpenney.com. Record information about private brands offered for sale. Report on such factors as the brands offered, their prices, and types of promotion these private brands received.

SNAPSHOT

Liz Claiborne

In 2007, New York-based apparel maker Liz Claiborne announced plans to cut 800 jobs, which accounted for about 9 percent of the company's workforce. In addition, the firm was considering selling, licensing, or shutting down 16 of its brands. Those under review included well-known labels, such as Dana Buchman, Ellen Tracy, Emma James, and Tapemeasure.

What caused such a dramatic overhaul? What caused this once go-to fashion line among career women to falter? Earnings in early 2007 plunged 65 percent. One key reason for those losses could be traced to Liz Claiborne's decision to develop a product line for JCPenney. Macy's, Liz Claiborne's biggest client, was not pleased with that move because it would make the Liz Claiborne brand less exclusive. Macy's response was to slash orders for the Liz Claiborne brand by millions of dollars.

A shrinking department store market, compounded by the power struggle with Macy's, forced Liz Claiborne into these current decisions. Moreover, more and more department stores are moving to their own private labels. In addition, Liz Claiborne was burdened by a number of tired, bland lines that were not growing in the overcrowded American apparel market. Some industry analysts even felt that huge chunks of the firm's brand offerings had little or no future potential.

With the company overhaul, Liz Claiborne's structure was divided into two sections—a "direct brand" division to oversee their retail chains, such as Lucky Brand Jeans, and a "partner brand" division to manage department store labels, such as Ellen Tracy. The move is designed to reduce the firm's dependence on department stores. Plans are to grow Liz Claiborne's "direct brands" by opening hundreds of new stores for those brands. The firm opened 125 new locations in 2007.

The aim is to cut costs and free Liz Claiborne to focus on more profitable fashion lines. Company representatives have said that future growth will be fueled by Kate Spade, Juicy Couture, Lucky Brand Jeans, and Mexx. Overall, the goal is to revamp and relaunch Liz Claiborne to make it a brand that women want to buy. Sales of the firm's brands are expected to grow from about $2.2 billion in 2007 to $3 billion by 2010.

Liz Claiborne has several options dealing with its "partner brands." They could retire a label or sell it to a competitor, such as Kellwood Co., or they could seek exclusive licensing deals with individual chains, similar to the arrangement with JCPenney for its Liz & Co. brand. The brands being reviewed include C&C California, Dana Buchman, Ellen Tracy, Emma James, Enyce, First Issue, Intuitions, JH Collectibles, Kensie, Laundry by Design, Mac & Jac, prAna, Sigrid Olsen, Stamp 10, Tapemeasure, and Tint.

The overall plan is to wean Liz Claiborne off its reliance on department stores by emphasizing its own retail stores. The firm will focus on promising brands like Juicy Couture and Lucky Brand, market them heavily, and control their images. In other words, Liz Claiborne will act more like a retailer.

Will this strategy work? Will more Lucky Brand stores succeed? Can Kate Spade become the next Coach? Only time will tell. Retailers, and ultimately consumers, will be the final judge about whether these strategic moves are on target.

BASED ON:

Beckett, Whitney. (2007, July 31). Liz faces challenges selling off 16 brands. *Women's Wear Daily*, 1.

Beckett, Whitney. (2007, August 1). Liz Claiborne posts 65 percent earnings drop. *Women's Wear Daily*, 2.

Cordova, Elizabeth Butler. (2007, July 9). Claiborne plans belt-tightening. *Crain's New York Business*, 1.

D'Innocenzio, Anne. (2007, July 12). Major overhaul at Liz Claiborne cuts up to 9 percent of jobs. *USA Today*, 4B.

Greenberg, Julee. (2007, July 12). Claiborne's laundry day. *Women's Wear Daily*, 9.

Liz Claiborne raises the bar on brands. (2007, July 13). *Just-style.com*.

TRENDWATCH

Source Tagging: Bargaining for Floor-Ready Merchandise

One new area on which buyers will be negotiating is source tagging of merchandise. Source tagging allows retailers to protect their merchandise without having to go through the time-consuming process of attaching traditional shoplifting prevention tags. Source tagging has already transformed the antishoplifting strategy of drug stores, home centers, and music stores. The concept is now beginning to make its way into the apparel industry. For apparel, the basic principle is that tags are embedded into and literally enveloped by the fabric that comprises the labels. Tags are deactivated at the point of sale.

Proponents of apparel source tagging claim it should yield retailers several benefits. Retailers adopting the concept will enjoy enhanced access to floor-ready merchandise, because the tags will have been affixed to clothing before it arrives at distribution centers or stores. Through source tagging, EAS (electronic article surveillance) tags are inserted during manufacturing or packaging, thus saving retailers thousands of dollars and labor hours annually. Unlike hard tags, source tags need not be removed from garments at the point of sale, thereby speeding checkout and increasing customer satisfaction, while conserving the time of sales associates.

There are also other benefits. Source tagging is not as easy to defeat as traditional theft-prevention tags. Also, hard tags can detract from a garment's overall appearance, make goods difficult for customers to try on, and interfere with effective displays. Retailers that use source tagging will probably see more shoplifting attempts, because more traditional tags are much more highly visible; but, apprehensions should also increase when source tags are used.

With source tagging, retailers are able to take merchandise out from locked showcases and highlight items in self-service fixtures. Sales increases for one retailer were phenomenal once eight categories of merchandise were brought out from under lock and key.

For many retailers, source tagging has become a prime strategy in their war on shrinkage. But, a major problem still persists. There are three different technologies from which to choose. Some vendors are all but giving away the equipment in order to establish a toehold with retailers for their tags. One reason is that the equipment market is small compared

with potential sales of tags. For the vendors of these competing technologies, the key lies in selling their systems to major retail accounts,
with the goal of establishing critical mass toward overall acceptance
of their technology. For example, Sensormatic's acousto-magnetic
technology has been adopted by retailers, such as Musicland and
Home Depot, which has marshaled more than 100 suppliers to join in
a source-tagging program.

And, one other question remains—"Who will bear the cost of tagging
programs?" The answer will probably vary. Suppliers who have little
leverage with specific retailers will probably be asked to assume the entire
cost if they want those merchants to carry their lines. In other situations, retailers will either shoulder the expense themselves or work
out agreements with suppliers to split the bill. Whichever agreement
is reached will probably depend on the nature and longevity of the
retailer–vendor relationship.

The competitive advantage that source tagging provides is that floor-
ready merchandise has been priced, ticketed, and tagged before it arrives
at the store. Stores not using source tagging cannot turn inventory as
quickly. For most buyers, source tagging will probably be near the top
of their negotiation lists with vendors in the future.

BASED ON:
$5m apparel source tagging programme launched. (2007, June 28). *Just-style.com*.
Carrefour plans aggressive source tagging. (2006, April). *Security Technology & Design*, 14.
Rudnick, Michael. (2005, June 20). Federated looks to source tagging for supply-chain
     acceleration. *HFN The Weekly Newspaper for the Home Furnishing Network*, 59.
Source tagging and implementing item-level labels. (2007, June). *Apparel*, SS5.
Source tagging step. (2006, March 20). *MMR*, 38.

TRENDWATCH

Private Labels Spell Profits

Private labels keep growing and creating more competition for national
brands. And, private labels are not always the least expensive brands
today. As private labels grow, they may one day be their suppliers' biggest
competitors. This trend also means that some buyers are increasingly
becoming brand managers by taking responsibility for such things as
trend tracking, product innovation, creating and maintaining the brand's

image and identity, and developing expertise in brand marketing, brand repositioning, and brand renewal.

Private labels have penetrated almost every type of retail store, but the market share in supermarkets has been the strongest, controlling almost 16 percent of the U.S. food industry. One private label manufacturer, Ralcorp Holdings Inc. of St. Louis, Missouri, has had total sales surge by nearly 60 percent in recent years due to increasing sales of its private label cereals, cookies, and jellies. The firm's products are sold under the labels of various retailers and grocers. Private labels for other manufacturers have also grabbed large market shares in categories such as milk, cheese, and eggs. Moreover, private labels are also getting a boost from missteps by some national brands. For example, private label peanut butter got a boost from ConAgra's recent recall of its Peter Pan and Great Value peanut butter products amid concerns about salmonella contamination.

Private labels usually carry a bigger profit margin for retailers than national brands. They also give customers more options and help retailers attract and retain customers by building brand loyalty. Other retailers cannot carry a competitor's private label. Private labels give stores another way to differentiate themselves from the competition. But for private labels to be successful, they must be promoted so that customers get to know them.

Today's private labels are alive with innovation from a greater emphasis on the quality of products and ingredients to increased sophistication of packaging and marketing. Most retailers are seeing private labels as an integral part of their business operations and have even begun transforming the marketing of these brands. Publix, a grocery store chain in the Southeast, recently offered a free private label item to customers who purchased the same item from a national brand.

In recent years, retailers are moving away from producing basic commodity products toward more premium products. For example, private label products in supermarkets have shed their dowdy image and now feature high-quality packaging that does not look out of place next to national brands. However, the move toward the higher end of the market has its perils—retailers risk closing the price differential between national brands and private labels. If there is little price difference between the two, most consumers will probably opt for the national brand.

Retailers must realize that when competing for customers with private labels, customers will not make future purchases of the products based on price alone. Private label brands must be used again and again by customers to create an emotional bond with the products. In the final analysis, private labels are simply brands to most customers. For customers to repurchase them, they must satisfy their needs in terms of both quality and price.

BASED ON:

Chadwick, Chad. (2007, June 25). Managing private label as a brand in its own right. *Drug Store News*, 18–21.

Daniel, Fran. (2007, August 19). Done right, private label spells profit. *Winston-Salem Journal*, B1.

Gabrielsen, Tommy and Sorgard, Lars. (2007, February). Private labels, price rivalry, and public policy. *European Economic Review*, 403–425.

Orgel, David. (2007, June 18). Potential private-label surge seen. *Supermarket News.com*.

Private labels changing food industry. (2007, July 19). *Gourmet Retailer*, 1.

Reinhold, Emma. (2007, July). Trading places: private label has come a long way in a short time. *European Cosmetic Markets*, 279–282.

Retailers to be suppliers' competitors? (2003, July). *Private Label Buyer*, 12.

Motivating Customers to Buy

Pricing the Merchandise

PERFORMANCE OBJECTIVES

Upon completion of this chapter, you should be able to:

- Identify the elements of retail price.
- Calculate initial markup percentage.
- Calculate retail price using markup based on retail.
- Identify factors affecting retail price.
- Describe the benefits and limitations of price lining.
- Describe the impact of store image on pricing decisions.
- Describe the methods used to evaluate pricing decisions.
- Identify types of adjustments to retail price.
- Distinguish between markdown percentage and off-retail percentage.
- Calculate markdown percents and off-retail percents.

Once merchandise has been purchased for the store, its retail price must be determined. This price must cover the cost of the merchandise and the expenses of doing business while providing a profit for the store. Yet, retail price must be attractive to consumers and priced competitively for market conditions. There is no formula for determining the best retail price, but through an analysis of customer buying behavior, past sales records, anticipated expenses, and economic and market conditions, you will be able to arrive at an appropriate price for the merchandise.

Price is the value placed on what is exchanged. In other words, price quantifies the value of products or services and is a major determinant of the amount of merchandise that will be sold by your store or department. Moreover, price is usually the element of retail strategy that can be changed quickly in response to changes in economic and market conditions.

In this chapter, you will learn about the mathematical calculations necessary for establishing retail prices. Factors affecting retail price are described, and adjustments to retail prices are explained.

ESTABLISHING RETAIL PRICES

Retail price includes (1) the cost of merchandise, plus (2) an additional amount known as markup. Markup must be large enough to cover the operating expenses of the retail organization while providing a profit.

Elements of Retail Price

Cost of goods includes the actual cost of the merchandise plus transportation charges involved in getting the merchandise from the vendor to the store. *Markup* is added to the cost of goods to determine retail price.

To plan the most appropriate markup, you will need to estimate both expenses and profit. These estimates also require that you have already made a sales forecast. When planning expenses, you must realize that some of them will not change, while others will increase or decrease in relation to sales. Typically, expenses are classified as fixed or variable. *Fixed expenses* do not vary regardless of how much merchandise the store sells. Examples of fixed expenses include mortgage and insurance payments. *Variable expenses* change in a direct relationship to sales. Such expenses normally increase or decrease as sales increase or decrease. Examples of variable expenses would be commissions, delivery expenses, supplies, and advertising. Past records and industry averages can be used to estimate expenses required for estimated sales levels.

The profit goal must also be planned before merchandise is priced. Profit earned by retailers varies by type of business. Grocery stores that turn over merchandise quite rapidly may earn a profit of less than 2 percent of sales, whereas specialty stores with much slower turnover may have more than 5 percent profit. The National Retail Federation reports average profit percentages for many categories of retail businesses, and these figures can be used as one measure of retail control.

If the amount of markup is not carefully planned, the resulting retail prices may be too high and the merchandise may not sell. Or, if markups are too low, not enough revenue will be generated to cover expenses and provide a profit for the store.

Determining Markup Percentage

Based on these elements, the following formula expresses the elements of retail price:

Retail Price = Cost + Markup

This formula can also be rearranged to calculate cost or markup as follows:

$$Cost = Retail\ Price - Markup$$

$$Markup = Retail\ Price - Cost$$

All components in the formula can be expressed as a dollar figure or as a percentage. In most situations, you will probably be more interested in the markup percentage rather than the markup in dollars. Percentages provide a better control method when comparing results with past store records or industry averages.

Typically, markup is expressed as a percentage of retail. The formula is expressed as follows:

$$Markup\ Percentage = Markup\ in\ Dollars/Retail\ Price$$

Let's examine one situation to make this calculation. Assume that the cost of an item of merchandise is $40 and the markup is $35. Markup percentage based on retail would be 46.7 percent ($35/$75 the retail price).

Planning Initial Markup Percentage

As a buyer, how can you plan the most appropriate markup? You must make estimates about the elements of retail price as well as any planned reductions in price. They include sales, expenses, profit, reductions, and cash discounts. You can determine an initial markup percentage using the following formula:

$$Initial\ Markup\ Percentage = \frac{Expenses + Profit + Reductions - Cash\ Discounts}{Sales + Reductions}$$

Let's examine this formula more closely. First, you must realize that all these figures are "planned," or predictions based on an expected level of sales. Inaccurate predictions will lead to inaccurate pricing decisions.

Sales. The sales level should be planned first. As you have already learned, sales forecasts are based on past sales records as well as changes

Figure 15.1 Excess consumer demand can increase sales and lower retail prices.

in internal and external conditions. The other components of this calculation are based on an expected level of sales (Figure 15.1).

Expenses. You must plan both fixed and variable expenses associated with expected sales levels. Estimates of the impact of sales on variable expenses must be made.

Profit. The amount of profit the store wishes to obtain from the sales volume must also be estimated. Again, past store records or industry averages could be used to make this prediction.

Reductions. When determining initial markup, you must also consider planned reductions that your store or department will experience. *Reductions* include markdowns, employee discounts, consumer discounts, and shrinkage.

• *Markdowns* are reductions in the original retail price. Almost every business must plan for markdowns because customers may not buy the merchandise at its original price; it may become shopworn; or the price may need to be reduced to clear the merchandise from inventory at the end of the season. Markdowns will be explained more fully in the section of this chapter dealing with adjustments to retail price. Original retail prices must be high enough to allow for markdowns to be taken and still result in the planned sales volume and profit.

• Discounts also reduce the original retail price of some items that are sold. Discounts may be given to employees or special groups of consumers such as senior citizens. You must have some estimate of how many discounts will occur during the period for which you are planning.

• *Shrinkage* includes reductions in inventory not accounted for by sales. Employee theft and shoplifting are the major causes of shrinkage. When making your estimates, you must realize that shrinkage will occur and probably cannot be controlled entirely. Estimated shrinkage is included in the initial markup calculation and will raise the planned retail price.

• Cash discounts may be given by some vendors to retailers who pay for merchandise at an early date. When cash discounts are provided, retail price can be lowered, because these discounts reduce the expenses of doing business. In the initial markup formula, cash discounts are subtracted.

The components of the initial markup formula can be estimated either as a dollar amount or as a percentage of sales. Let's examine examples using both approaches.

PROBLEM ILLUSTRATION

Assume that a store plans sales of $50,000 with a profit of $2,500. Markdowns are planned at $5,000 and shrinkage is planned at $500. No employee or consumer discounts have occurred. Expenses are planned at $15,000. Using the initial markup formula, markup percentage can be calculated as follows:

Initial Markup Percent = $15,000 + $2,500 + $5,500/$50,000 + $5,500

Initial Markup Percent = $23,000/$55,500

Initial Markup Percent = .414

Initial Markup Percent = 41.4%

When planning markup, many stores make predictions based on estimated percentages of retail sales. The assumption is that even though the dollar figure will change based on different sales predictions, the percentage of sales will remain fairly constant.

PROBLEM ILLUSTRATION

Expenses may be planned at 30 percent of sales, and the store desires a 5 percent profit. Markdowns are estimated to be 10 percent of sales, and shrinkage is estimated to be 1 percent. Using the same formula, initial markup can be calculated from these percentages as follows:

Initial Markup Percent = .30 + .05 + .11/1.00 + .11

Initial Markup Percent = .46/1.11

Initial Markup Percent = .414

Initial Markup Percent = 41.4%

(*Note*: When using percentages, the sales percent will always equal 100.)

Seldom will you apply the same markup to all products carried in the store. Markups below the planned initial markup may be necessary for some items, while substantially higher markups can be achieved on other items. Also, products having the same cost may differ greatly in customer appeal and consequently will require different markups. Some fashion apparel and perishable items may require large markups to offset drastic markdowns or high spoilage rates. Even though different markups are used, the overall goal is to achieve the planned markup goal for the store or department.

Once the initial markup percentage has been established, retail prices for individual items can be calculated. As you learned, retail price is the cost of merchandise plus the desired markup. Many times, the markup percent for your store will already have been established by management. Your task will be to determine the retail price of an item when its cost and markup are known.

Because we are dealing with markup percents based on retail, the retail percentage will always equal 100 percent. Let's use this information to establish a retail price. In the example that has been presented, a 41.4 percent markup is planned. Assuming the cost of an item is $50, what would be the retail price? First, supply the information you already know, as follows:

	$	%
Cost	$50	
+ Markup		41.4%
= Retail Price		100%

We also know that the cost percent is 58.6 percent (100% − 41.4%). Remember that the formula can be rearranged to calculate cost as follows: Cost = Retail − Markup. The formula works for percentages as well as dollar amounts. Now, using simple algebra, you can determine the retail price. You know that 58.6% of retail price equals $50 (the cost). This information can be expressed as:

$$.586 \times \text{Retail Price} = \$50.00$$

$$\text{Retail Price} = \$50.00/.586$$

$$\text{Retail Price} = \$85.32$$

Some businesses use ***keystoning*** to establish retail price. They simply double cost to determine the retail price. The resulting markup will always be 50 percent based on retail. In competitive market situations, keystoning may result in pricing the merchandise much higher than the competition, which would result in fewer sales. In some instances, keystoning may not cover operating expenses or provide a profit for the business.

FACTORS AFFECTING RETAIL PRICE

Obviously, costs and operating expenses must be considered when establishing retail prices. A store cannot survive if prices do not cover these costs and expenses and yield a profit. In most situations, these considerations are considered a minimum or ***price floor*** below which the product cannot be priced.

The preceding explanation of establishing retail prices is based on a cost orientation, whereby a calculated markup is added to the cost of the merchandise. However, such mathematical calculations do not consider other important factors that retailers would consider before establishing a retail price. They include (1) target market, (2) store policies, (3) competition, and (4) economic conditions.

Target Market

The overall objectives established by management determine the store's target market. As a buyer you must understand how your store is positioned in the marketplace, and you must determine how your customers

Figure 15.2 How is this store positioned in the marketplace? What types of customers will it attract?

view price (Figure 15.2). Some customers relate higher prices to higher quality for some products such as apparel and electronics. Knowing your target market also establishes the price range in the store or department. Fashion-conscious customers are eager to purchase the most current styles and are willing to pay a higher price for them, whereas price-conscious customers will scour the market for the lowest prices available. In the final analysis, you must determine whether your customers will recognize the value they will receive based on the price you place on the merchandise.

Store Policies

Management will also determine both the store image and policies that will be implemented to create the desired image. Store policies must be used to guide pricing decisions. You would develop a strategy to implement store policies and create the desired image.

Stores wanting to create a prestige image may use price skimming as the cornerstone of their pricing policy. Stores using *skimming* charge the highest possible price that customers who most desire the product will pay. The policy is used by many stores when new products are introduced, and it can also be used as a tool to limit demand when there is a short supply of the product available.

Discounters use *penetration* policies. They are concerned with penetrating a market quickly with low prices to produce large unit sales volumes. A small amount of profit is made on each item, but many more units are sold, which can result in higher overall profits for the store. Stores use this policy when they want to gain market share quickly. Also, lower prices tend to discourage many competitors from entering the market.

Some retailers even use *loss leaders*, pricing specific products at a point that will not generate any profits. The purpose of loss leaders is to build store traffic. Once in the store, retailers hope customers will make other purchases. Some retailers also believe that loss leaders give customers the impression that all the store's prices are low. However, using loss leaders requires considerable skill. Management must determine if customers are indeed making other purchases. Many customers buy the special items and then leave without making other purchases. Also, too large a reduction may suggest damaged or inferior goods to some customers.

Retailers also establish pricing strategy based on anticipated emotional responses of customers. They most commonly use odd or even pricing. *Odd-cent pricing* attempts to influence customer's perceptions of the retail price by ending it with certain numbers. Users of the technique assume more customers will purchase a product at $9.99 rather than $10.00. It is thought that they view the price as $9.00 plus a few pennies because they pay more attention to the dollar figure rather than the cents. Research studies, however, suggest that odd-cent pricing has little effect on sales. Discounters typically use odd-cent pricing while prestige stores use even pricing.

Stores attempting to create a prestige or upscale image often price products using *even pricing*. For example, they would use a retail price of $32.00 rather than $31.95. Even prices tend to enhance the upscale image of many products such as jewelry and fragrances.

Stores may also implement a policy known as *price lining,* which will dictate pricing decisions. Price lining consists of selecting certain prices and carrying assortments of merchandise only at those prices. For example, men's white shirts may be carried at $19.95, $29.95, and $39.95.

Price lining developed because customers desire a choice when purchasing most merchandise; however, buyers must ensure that customers can distinguish the difference among the items offered for sale. Fewer price lines reduce the consumer's confusion and allow salespeople to become more familiar with the merchandise and more aware of the differences that exist. Buyers can more easily select merchandise because their selections must be priced at preset price levels.

Price lines are usually established through a careful analysis of past sales, selecting those prices representing the bulk of sales. Many retailers establish three *price points* for many items of merchandise, which could be broadly classified as good, better, or best; however, such relative terms have specific meaning for only a particular category of merchandise.

Let's examine an illustration of how one price point may be developed. Assume that a buyer has purchased scarves from four vendors at the following unit costs:

Scarves from Vendor 1 at $5.80 each.
Scarves from Vendor 2 at $5.33 each.
Scarves from Vendor 3 at $5.00 each.
Scarves from Vendor 4 at $5.13 each.

If a predetermined markup percentage were applied to each of these scarves, four different, but similar retail prices, would be calculated. Confusion would result for both the customer and the sales staff. Most buyers would establish one price point, such as $10.99, thus reducing confusion resulting from customers attempting to determine slight differences that might exist among the scarves.

The major limitation of price lining is that the price point requirements sometimes hampers the buyer's efforts to obtain adequate assortments. There is also difficulty in maintaining uniform quality.

A storewide single price policy is an extreme example of price lining. Under this policy, everything in the store is sold for the same price. This approach is usually found in stores that carry only inexpensive merchandise. Read the Snapshot titled, "Dollar Tree: Successfully Pricing Items for a Dollar," to learn more about how one retailer has adopted this pricing policy.

Competition

Retailers must also examine the competition's prices when establishing retail prices. You must decide to price at, below, or above the competition. A pricing strategy based on the competition's prices requires that you closely monitor price changes as they occur in the market-place.

Pricing to Meet the Competition. Stores using this strategy deemphasize price as a merchandising tool. Factors such as service and location are stressed to customers.

Pricing Below the Competition. Some retailers attempt to establish retail prices below those of competitors. To do so, however, requires that the merchandise be purchased at a lower cost or that operating expenses be less than those of the competitors. Some retailers may stock private brand merchandise, which cannot be as easily compared with similar products carried by competitors. Because private brand merchandise usually costs the store less, higher profit margins are obtained.

Attempting to underprice the competition may bring disastrous results if the store becomes involved in a price war. A *price war* develops when several competing retailers try to undersell each other. The stores in such a war keep reducing their prices to attract each other's customers. Lowering prices to beat the competition strains profitability, and if price is the store's only competitive tool, it may not be able to attract customers who desire more service or larger product assortments. Read the Trendwatch titled "Outlet Centers: Do They Deliver Lower Prices?" to learn more about pricing strategies used at outlet centers.

Pricing Above the Competition. Some retailers attempt to create a prestige image by pricing above competitor's prices for similar merchandise; however, customers must perceive extra value for the higher prices. Usually stores with higher prices are offering free services (such as delivery and alterations), exclusive merchandise, higher-quality merchandise, or more personalized sales attention.

Economic Conditions

Pricing decisions must also be made in relation to economic conditions. For example, during economic slowdowns, prices are lowered to generate more sales. Supply and demand also have an impact on retail prices. When demand for a product is greater than supply, retailers can charge higher prices. The reverse is also true; prices must be lowered when supply exceeds demand. For example, during the winter when the supply of tomatoes is low, prices skyrocket, but during the summer when tomatoes are abundant, prices plummet.

ADJUSTMENTS TO RETAIL PRICE

Retail prices must be adjusted frequently to meet changing conditions. Three typical price adjustments are (1) markdowns, (2) markdown cancellations, and (3) additional markups.

Markdowns

Every item of merchandise probably will not sell at its original retail price; thus, markdowns are a critical element of merchandising decisions. Because markdowns have such a significant impact on the revenues of a store or department, they must be carefully planned and controlled.

Reasons for Markdowns. Buying, pricing, and selling errors can all result in markdowns. In addition, some markdowns occur as a sales promotion tool to attract customers.

- Overbuying occurs when the buyer has overestimated customer demand. In order to move the excess inventory, price reductions are used. Carefully maintaining sales records and analyzing current trends will help you avoid this problem.
- Sometimes merchandise is priced higher than customers are willing to pay. Overpricing most frequently occurs when new merchandise that the store has never carried is purchased.
- Faulty selling practices are another reason for markdowns. Sometimes salespeople do not give proper sales efforts to a product. They may not point out new merchandise to customers when it arrives; consequently, the merchandise remains in stock until it is too late to sell at original prices.
- Markdowns also occur at the end of the season when only odds and ends of a particular line are left in stock. For example, only a few small

and extra-large sweatshirts may be left. These items are marked down to clear them from stock so fresh stock can be added to inventory.

• Also, some merchandise may have been in stock so long that it has become soiled or damaged. Price reductions are needed to move these goods.

Timing of Markdowns. There is disagreement among retailers on the best time to take markdowns. Some retailers delay markdowns as long as possible, hoping to sell the merchandise at the original retail price. Other retailers wait until late in the season before taking markdowns to establish in the customer's mind that "special sales" will occur at the same time each year. Some of these retailers, such as Filene's Basement in Boston, are well known for their ***automatic markdowns*** at the end of the selling season. For example, goods that remain unsold after 12 days are repriced at 75 percent of their original price; after 6 more days, at 50 percent; after another 6 days, at 25 percent; and after a final 6 days, they are given to charity. Even though customers know a larger markdown will occur later, many of them make purchases early to ensure they can get the merchandise before it is sold.

Most retailers believe markdowns should be taken early to keep a fresh supply of goods flowing into the store. Also, early markdowns tend to be smaller than markdowns taken later in the season. For fashion goods, markdowns should be taken as soon as sales begin to fall off. Basic or staple merchandise items should be marked down before the goods have been in stock too long and have become shopworn.

To be effective, a markdown must be large enough to induce customers to buy merchandise. For example, marking an item down from $15 to $14 is probably not adequate to generate new customer interest in the product.

Recording Markdowns. As a buyer, you will need to maintain information about the number and amount of markdowns taken. Knowledge of past markdowns is essential for planning initial markup. Also, markdown information is needed as a check on shrinkage. Moreover, knowing about specific markdowns gives you information about which products are having to be marked down to generate sales. Future purchases of these products should be curtailed.

Buyers are also interested in the ***markdown percentage*** during a selling season. To calculate this figure, you must know the total amount of markdowns and total amount of sales. The markdown percentage can be calculated using the following formula:

Markdown Percent = Dollar Markdown/Total Sales

PROBLEM ILLUSTRATION

Assume 100 ties were originally purchased at $10 each, and marked to sell at $20 each. At the end of the season, all the ties sold at that price except ten, which were marked down to $12 and finally sold. Total markdowns are $80 (10 ties × $8 markdown). Total sales were $1,920 ($1,800 for 90 ties at $20 each plus $120 for 10 ties at $12 each). Substituting in the formula, markdown percent is calculated as follows:

Markdown percent = Dollar Markdown/Total sales

Markdown percent = $80/$1,920

Markdown percent = .04166

Markdown percent = 4.2%

For retail accounting procedures, you will calculate markdown percent as described, but for advertising purposes, an *off-retail percentage* is calculated. Off-retail is calculated using the following formula:

Off-Retail Percentage = Markdown/Original Retail Price

For the previous example, each of the last ten ties was marked down $8.00 from an original retail price of $20. The off-retail percent that would be advertised would be 40 percent ($8/$20).

Markdown Cancellations

For many promotions involving markdowns early in the selling season, all items in stock that were marked down probably will not sell at the reduced price. A promotion such as a Presidents' Day Sale, for example, may last for only a few days. At the end of the sale, merchandise is repriced, usually at the original retail price. A *markdown cancellation* has occurred.

You would need to record such cancellations. Assume that 100 items that had an original retail price of $12 each were marked down $2 each for a special sale. Ninety of the items sold at the sale price, and the others were repriced at $12 when the sale was over. A $20 markdown cancellation would be recorded for this item ($2 price increase × 10 remaining in stock).

Additional Markups

During periods of rising prices, many retailers may find it necessary to increase original retail prices. *Additional markups*, or increases in retail prices, are most likely to occur for basic merchandise items as wholesale prices increase. Merchandise already on the sales floor may be remarked to reflect price increases of new purchases (Figure 15.3). Fashion merchandise would less likely have additional markups during the season because the selling period is so short.

Figure 15.3 Fashion merchandise is usually remarked during the selling season based on sales.

EVALUATING PRICING DECISIONS

Retailers must evaluate the effectiveness of pricing decisions once they have been made. Pricing decisions are usually evaluated against the pricing objectives the organization planned to achieve. Three key measures of the success of pricing decisions are (1) market share, (2) profit, and (3) markup achieved.

Market Share

Market share describes a store's sales in relation to total sales in the industry or one specific trading area. A store's objective may be to maintain or increase market share. However, the organization with the largest market share is not always the most profitable. Stores may have had to lower prices to build market share, and lower prices could have resulted in lower profits.

Profit

All stores want to maximize profits with the retail prices they establish. Management usually states profit objectives as a percentage of sales. Actual profits can be compared with industry averages or past records. You may also express your objective as a percent increase in profits from one period to the next.

Markup Achieved

Buyers will be evaluated on how well they achieved their markup goals at a specified sales level. The markup formula included a profit estimate; therefore, if markup is achieved at the desired sales level, profits will result.

SUMMARY POINTS

- Retail price must cover the cost of the merchandise as well as the expenses of doing business, while providing a profit for the store.

- Markup is calculated by estimating store expenses and planned profit. Both can be planned using past store records and industry averages obtained from trade associations.
- Markup percent is usually more significant to a buyer than markup in dollars.
- The initial markup percent can be planned by first making a sales forecast, then estimating expenses, profit, reductions, and cash discounts planned for that sales volume.
- Seldom will a store apply the same markup to all the products carried. Even though different markups are used, the overall objective will be to achieve the planned markup goal.
- In addition to mathematical calculations, other factors must be considered before establishing retail prices. They include the target market, store policies, the competition, and economic conditions.
- Price skimming and penetration pricing are the policies used most often when introducing a new product. Skimming yields fewer sales but at a higher markup, whereas the goal of penetration pricing is volume sales at a low markup.
- Price lining essentially dictates pricing decisions. Price points are established, and only merchandise to be priced at those levels is bought for the store.
- Adjustments are made to retail prices through markdowns, markdown cancellations, and additional markups.
- The success of pricing decisions will be measured against market share, profit, and markups achieved.

REVIEW ACTIVITIES

Developing Your Retail Buying Vocabulary

Consult the Glossary if you did not add the following terms to your vocabulary.

Additional markup	Odd-cent pricing
Automatic markdown	Off-retail percentage
Cost of goods	Penetration
Even pricing	Price floor
Fixed expenses	Price lining
Keystoning	Price point
Loss leaders	Price war

Markdown   Reductions
Markdown cancellation   Shrinkage
Markdown percentage   Skimming
Markup   Variable expenses

Understanding What You Read

1. What are the two elements of retail price?
2. Describe the difference between fixed and variable expenses.
3. List four types of reductions.
4. Why do most stores not apply a uniform markup percent to all products they carry?
5. Why does fashion apparel typically require larger markups than basic merchandise?
6. Describe situations when price skimming would be most appropriate.
7. Describe situations when penetration pricing would be most appropriate.
8. Why are loss leaders used by some retailers?
9. What are the benefits of price lining?
10. What are the drawbacks of pricing lining?
11. What is the rationale for using odd-cent pricing?
12. What is the rationale for using even pricing?
13. When is pricing above the competition a feasible pricing strategy?
14. How can a retail store price the same product for less than the competition is charging?
15. Describe how supply and demand affect retail price.
16. How will a store determine if correct pricing decisions have been made?
17. List and explain three causes of markdowns.
18. What are the benefits of taking markdowns early?
19. Explain why some retail stores take markdowns only at the end of the season.
20. Why do stores use additional markups?

Application Exercises

1. Calculate the initial markup percent for the following situations:
   a. Sales = $60,000
      Expenses = $25,000
      Profit goal = $8,000
   b. Expenses = 38%

Reductions = 10%

Cash discounts = 1%

Profit goal = 5%

c. Sales = $185,000

Reductions = $12,000

Expenses = $53,000

Cash discounts = $18,000

Profit goal = $15,000

d. Profit goal = 7%

Reductions = 18%

Cash discounts = 4%

Expenses = 33%

2. Calculate the retail price for the following situations:

a. Markup percent = 45%

Cost = $14

b. Markup percent = 60%

Cost = $2

3. Calculate the (1) amount of markdown in dollars, (2) markdown cancellations, and (3) markdown percent for the following situation:

Original Retail	Sale Price	On Hand Start of Sale	Units Sold	Retail Price After Sale
$50	$40	36	20	$50
$35	$27	36	20	$35
$30	$20	48	25	$30
$20	$15	52	15	$20

4. Calculate the off-retail percent that can be advertised for the following situations:

a. Original retail = $50

Sales price = $35

b. Cost = $25

Initial markup = $25

Markdown = $5

c. Cost = $125

Initial markup = $120

Sales price = $230

Spreadsheet Skills

1. Use a spreadsheet program to answer the questions in the *Application Exercises* above.
2. In *Making Buying Decisions: Using the Computer As a Tool*, complete problems related to Merchandising Concepts 2–1 (Calculate Retail Price); 2–2 (Calculate Desired Cost *n*), and 2–3 (Calculate the Markup Percentage).
3. In *Making Buying Decisions: Using the Computer As a Tool*, complete problems related to Merchandising Concept 3–1 (Calculate Initial Markup Percentages).
4. In *Making Buying Decisions: Using the Computer As a Tool*, complete problems related to Merchandising Concepts 5–1 (Calculate Total Dollar Markdowns); 5–2 (Calculate Markdown Percentages), 5–3 (Calculate Off-Retail Percentages), and 5–4 (Calculate Markdown Cancellations).

Internet Connection

1. On the Internet, access a site for an outlet store near you. Record the prices for five products offered at the outlet store. Compare those prices to retail prices at nearby stores in traditional malls or shopping centers. Report your findings. Who delivered the lowest prices?
2. On the Internet, use a search engine to locate the Web sites for one-price stores. Report on the types of sites that you located (e.g., types of products, prices, ability to purchase online).

SNAPSHOT

Dollar Tree: Successfully Pricing Items for a Dollar

The corner five-and-dime store was supposed to have been killed off by the superstores long ago, but that has not occurred. In fact, several strong players, known as "dollar stores," are proving that there is money to be made simply "living off the crumbs of Wal-Mart." Moreover, growth at these stores has been phenomenal. One of these stores, Dollar Tree, has been named a "Star Performer" by *Retail Merchandiser*, a monthly trade magazine, and has even landed at number 79 on the National Retail Federation list of the nation's top 100 retailers.

Traditional discount stores, such as Wal-Mart and Kmart, have been upscaling their merchandise and their presentation, as well as bringing in more special labels like Martha Stewart. As they have made these moves, there was an unfilled need and companies like Dollar Tree have taken advantage of the opening.

Currently Dollar Tree operates 3,219 stores in 48 states and the majority were profitable within a year. Most of these stores are about the size of one department in a superstore and have average net sales of $1 million yearly.

As Dollar Tree has grown, the stores' merchandise mix has also changed. Only about 12 percent is now closeout merchandise. Dollar Tree imports many of its products itself, made to specifications or specially packaged for the company. In addition, the stores are always full of seasonal merchandise. Dollar Tree buyers understand overseas manufacturing and have been skilled at negotiating with vendors. As the company has grown, its leverage with vendors has also increased. Buyers are able to negotiate deals that translate into better value for the firm's customers. Dollar Tree buyers also look for trends in gift stores, such as Hallmark, and in souvenir shops and then have items based on those trends made for Dollar Tree. In addition, buyers develop relationships with first-run vendors, producers of parallel brands, so instead of Fantastik, Dollar Tree sells Fabulous.

Dollar Tree continues to have success in generating merchandise excitement through an ever-changing mix of variety and seasonal merchandise. The addition of more basic consumable products that are frequently purchased has contributed to increases in both traffic and sales.

Dollar Tree sets itself apart from rivals like Family Dollar and Dollar General with one clear strategy—everything costs exactly $1. The competition offers items at many different price points. One other difference is that stores like Dollar General and Family Dollar tend to be destinations in themselves—often in neighborhood strip malls. Dollar Trees are often in larger malls, including some enclosed malls, and often near stores such as Wal-Mart and Target. This means that sales at Dollar Tree depend more on how many people are shopping at those malls. A general downturn in retail sales would have negative results on Dollar Tree, too.

Dollar Tree, like most low-priced, limited-assortment retailers, is already well entrenched among low-income households, but recently has experienced strong increases in penetration across all income groups. Sixty-seven percent of Americans shop one-price stores regularly, and that trend seems likely to increase.

BASED ON:
Dollar Tree benefits from "exceptional execution." (2007, May 7). *MMR*, 8.
Dollar Tree lives up to expectations. (2007, January 8). *MMR*, 46.
Dollar Tree stores: Dollars and sense. (2001, January 8). *Forbes*, 152.
Tarnowski, Joseph. (2006, September 15). Dueling for dollars: the dollar store channel is expanding to new markets. *Progressive Grocer*, 95–98.

TRENDWATCH

Outlet Centers: Do They Deliver Lower Prices?

Growth for outlet centers has slowed dramatically in recent years. Profits of outlet center retailers have also been squeezed. Expenses have increased as "regular retail" amenities have been added in an attempt to meet the higher expectations of shoppers. Moreover, explosive growth of outlets in the 1980s has led to market saturation; and attractive untapped markets have become scarce for new outlet centers.

Outlet centers have built their promotions around savings claims of 20 to 75 percent. Do they, in fact, deliver lower prices than traditional retail stores? Outlet-to-retail price comparisons have been difficult. Outlet stores typically market a product's "suggested retail price" on the tag, but quite possibly, no retailer ever ordered that item or used that suggested retail price. For example, Toys Unlimited advertised an Ice Capades Barbie for $8.99 with a suggested retail price of $14.99, but a spokesperson at Mattel said the approximate retail price was $10.75, and Toys "R" Us had it for $9.99. Another doll, Li'l Miss Magic Hair, was being promoted for $14.99–reduced from a suggested retail price of $34.99. Mattel quoted the approximate retail price at $27, and customers could buy it for $20.99 at Toys "R" Us.

Limited research on price savings at outlet centers has found similar results, but most of these investigations have compared only a small number of items. A study of price differences by *Value Retail News* staffers found that prices at outlet centers (where goods could be matched) were only 20 percent below the department store prices. Although most outlet centers promise savings of up to 75 percent off retail prices, the average discounts are about 20 to 25 percent.

In a survey conducted by *Value Retail News*, manufacturers reported discounts at their outlet stores averaged 40 percent. When shoppers were questioned, though, they *estimated* the average discount at closer to 25 percent. Respondents to a *Consumer Reports* survey found prices were higher than they expected on nearly one-third of their visits to outlet malls.

Consumers have become conditioned not to buy unless a discount is dangled. As a result, the price gap between various types of retail stores has been shrinking. Pricing strategies are also changing, with many outlets reducing their emphasis on deep discounts to focus on moderate discounts of 20 to 25 percent. The outlet industry's price leadership has eroded. More conveniently located, traditional retailers, offering everyday value-pricing or engaging in frequent sales promotions, are providing competition for outlet centers.

Overall, merchandise found in the luxury/designer categories may be the best outlet buys these days. For example, Coach handbags that run between $100 and $400 do not go on sale in retail stores. But in the company's outlets, quality irregulars and discontinued styles are marked down 25 percent. At Esprit outlets, goods arrive just six to eight weeks behind the department stores and are sold at a 30 to 70 percent discount. An additional markdown may be taken a month later. St. John Knits is about nine months behind the retail stores at its three East Coast locations; but because the line's devotees wear the items for years, at 50 percent off the lag might not matter.

Low prices and a wide selection of merchandise are what attract customers to outlets today. In fact, 90 percent of customers surveyed by *Value Retail News* said they were satisfied with their savings, and almost 60 percent of respondents to a recent *Consumer Reports* survey were highly satisfied with their experience. Only 11 percent were at all dissatisfied. Outlet shoppers are convinced they are getting bargains, and they enjoy the challenge of finding markdowns and special deals even within this discount venue.

BASED ON:

Clodfelter, Richard, and Fowler, Deborah. (1999, Spring/Summer). A comparison of the pricing policies between manufacturers' retail apparel outlets and traditional retail Stores. *Journal of Shopping Center Research*, 7–38.

Chapter 16

Promoting the Merchandise

PERFORMANCE OBJECTIVES

Upon completion of this chapter, you should be able to:

- Describe the purposes of promotional activities.
- Identify the elements of the promotional mix.
- Describe the buyer's role in planning and implementing promotional activities
- Explain how objectives are established for promotional activities.
- Describe how promotional budgets are prepared.
- Identify how merchandise is selected for promotional activities.
- Describe how schedules are established for promotional activities.
- Identify how promotional activities are evaluated.
- Explain how a store's promotional activities are coordinated.

Buyers may have purchased the "right" merchandise for their customers and offered it at the "right" price, but without promotional activities, sales and profits will not be maximized. Because merchandise does not sell itself, you must be knowledgeable about the sales promotion activities used by your store. In many retail stores, products are exactly the same or quite similar to those of the competition. Promotion provides you with the tools to distinguish your store from the competition.

The buyer's role in promotional activities will vary considerably from store to store. In small, independent stores, the owner will perform almost all business functions, including the buying and promotion of merchandise. At large retail stores, there will probably be other individuals or even promotion departments to assist with planning and implementing promotional efforts. Promotion managers, advertising managers, artists, copywriters, and display assistants are just some of the individuals involved with promotional planning. At large retail organizations, buyers only assist in planning promotional activities; other individuals will implement the plans. Buyers must select merchandise for promotion, purchase merchandise needed to support promotional activities, and negotiate with suppliers who could support or expand the store's promotional activities.

In this chapter, you will learn about the elements that must be considered when planning promotional activities. The steps involved in developing and coordinating a promotional campaign are also described.

RETAIL PROMOTIONAL ACTIVITIES

Sales promotions are an integral part of all retail store operations, and buyers need to be involved in promotion decisions. Promotion must be developed based on the buyer's knowledge of customer motivations and preferences as well as product information he or she has available. In these areas, the buyer will be invaluable in the development of sales promotion activities.

Sales promotion involves the communicating of information about products, services, images, and ideas to influence a consumer's purchase behavior. In other words, sales promotion includes all those activities executed by retailers to provide information to customers that leads to sales. The store's promotional activities are designed to create customer confidence that will lead to continued customer patronage.

All promotional activities should have the following general objectives:

• To produce sales and maximize profits,
• To generate customer loyalty and continued patronage, and
• To project or enhance the store's image.

Regardless of their size or location, most retail stores use a combination of promotional activities to inform consumers about products and persuade them to make purchases. These different promotional methods are known as the *promotional mix*. Key promotional mix elements include:

• Advertising,
• Visual merchandising,
• Personal selling,
• Publicity,
• Special events, and
• Other sales promotion activities.

By coordinating these elements, a single, unified message will be presented to your customers.

Advertising

One of the most often used elements of the promotional mix is *advertising*, a paid, nonpersonal promotional message for a product, service, or idea by an identified sponsor. Advertising usually has the following purposes:

- Increase sales volume,
- Increase store traffic,
- Attract new customers,
- Introduce new products or services,
- Develop a demand for private brands,
- Reinforce customer satisfaction,
- Increase sales volume during slow periods, and
- Presell the merchandise.

At large retail stores, buyers initiate the preparation of advertising by completing a request for advertising that includes specific details about the merchandise as well as benefits the merchandise offers customers. At small stores, the owner will probably be responsible for developing advertising or securing such services through various media or advertising agencies. *Media*, the methods selected to transmit an advertising message, could include both print and broadcast channels. Selection of the most appropriate media should be based on the following factors:

- Product to be advertised,
- Trading area of the store,
- Media used by the competition,
- The selling season,
- Type of customer to be reached, and
- Budget available.

Visual Merchandising

Store layout and displays are also key elements of your promotional plan. *Visual merchandising* includes the layout of store facilities and the placement of merchandise in the store to stimulate customer desire (Figure 16.1).

Many times, buyers have the responsibility for requesting displays to feature merchandise they have purchased and to project current trends and styles that best represent the store's target customers. The buyer's job in planning visual merchandising is to ensure that the desired message comes through about the merchandise. As you make suggestions for displays consider the following:

Figure 16.1
Effective displays
must be planned
to stimulate
sales of products
the buyer has
purchased.

- Display new merchandise prominently. Do not let clearance displays dilute the impact of featured displays.
- State prices clearly in the displays if they are important to your customers.
- Use feature displays to help customers visualize using the product(s) themselves. For fashion goods, tell a story with the merchandise–show the entire look, not just pieces of merchandise. Use appropriate accessories from other departments.
- Give maximum visibility to displays of advertised merchandise.

Visual merchandising is one of the least expensive and most powerful forms of promotion that is available to your store; use the tool effectively. When requesting visual merchandising, you should offer ideas for possible displays. Keep an idea file of display examples from resident buying offices, suppliers, photographs of showroom displays, or sketches of interior and window displays of central market stores similar to yours.

Personal Selling

One of the key ways in which retailers distinguish themselves from competitors is by providing a high level of customer service. Today, many retailers are emphasizing service rather than relying on heavy promotions with one sale after another. Small retailers, in particular, cannot always compete with large stores on price, but they can compete by satisfying customers through better personal selling. **Personal selling** is the one-on-one communication between a customer and a salesperson for the purpose of satisfying customer wants and needs through products presented for sale.

Buyers do not usually make sales themselves; their responsibility is to help sales associates make sales. The responsibilities of buyers in this area would be to:

- Provide product information to sales associates that will help sell a product.
- Emphasize product selling points to sales associates at store meetings or in written communications.
- Visit the sales floor to observe customers and work with sales associates. In contacts with sales associates, you should learn about customer reactions to merchandise offered. Experienced sales associates are also valuable sources of information about customer wants.

Distributing product information is an important part of the buyer's job. Keeping sales associates informed about product features and benefits builds their interest and enthusiasm as well as sales, so you need to provide them with as much product information as possible. Knowledgeable and enthusiastic sales associates pass on that energy to their customers. Most of the product information that you will need can be obtained from suppliers. In addition, some suppliers provide training sessions for sales associates where they learn important product information as well as techniques for selling the products.

Today, most retailers are working to improve personal selling and customer service in their stores. The management of Parisian so strongly believes that the action in retailing is on the selling floor that their sales associates have business cards—not just to give to their customers but to enhance their own feeling of importance. Nordstrom's has a reputation in the retailing industry for providing outstanding customer service.

Customer service is also being enhanced at self-service stores. Anyone entering a Wal-Mart knows that personal selling starts at the front door. Customers encounter greeters who welcome shoppers, give advice on where to find merchandise, and mark merchandise being returned. On their way out, customers are thanked for their patronage. The people-greeting practice is one of many ingredients that has made Wal-Mart extremely successful in retailing.

At newly remodeled Kmarts across the country, different types of customer call boxes are being installed. After a customer pushes a button on the box, a prerecorded message is heard alerting the staff that a customer needs assistance in the area of the call box. If there is no response after 45 seconds, another message is automatically broadcast.

Publicity

You may also obtain promotion for your merchandise through *publicity*, the free and voluntary mention of a company, product, or service by the media. The basic elements that differentiate advertising from publicity are payment and sponsorship. Advertising is a paid promotional message, whereas publicity is free; and advertising identifies a sponsor, but publicity does not.

To obtain publicity, you must have something newsworthy and of interest to the general public. Most publicity is obtained when a company contacts the media by sending a press release. Typical *press releases* are announcements of new products, such as new automobiles, new models of computers, or new designer fashions. Announcements about the opening of a new business or a new branch store would probably receive publicity in many communities, and *special events* that involve customers are also good possibilities for publicity.

Your publicity release should include the following information:

Who: The company or persons involved.
What: The important event.
When: The date and time
Where: The location.
Why: The reason for the event.

Publicity is rarely used as the only promotional mix element; it is used to supplement other promotional activities that are planned.

Special Events

Stores also plan special events that are not part of their everyday merchandising activities to tie together the theme of a promotional campaign. Examples of special events could include fashion shows, book signings, and seminars on upcoming trends (Figure 16.2).

Figure 16.2 Retailers can use special events, such as celebrities visiting the store, to stimulate sales.

One of the most famous special events is Macy's annual Thanksgiving Parade in New York City. Although hard to measure, most retailers generally agree that without such events, sales would probably be lower. Special events create excitement and enthusiasm for the store and its products. Read the Trendwatch titled, "Victoria's Secret: Using the Web as a Promotional Tool," to learn more about how retailers are using the Internet for special promotional events through Webcasting.

Other Sales Promotion Activities

Stores can also use other sales promotional activities such as special sales, coupons, and premiums (Figure 16.3). Sales promotion activities give customers additional reasons to buy. As an example, Kmart has tested a new sales promotion technique–TV monitors above checkout lanes that entertain customers while making a sales pitch. The program/advertising

Figure 16.3 Coupons are issued by some stores at the cash register to stimulate future sales.

ratio usually runs at 70 percent to 30 percent. Individual stores have the ability to customize the programming based on time of day and store demographics. Many grocery stores also use instant coupon machines that can be attached to the shelf edge in front of the item being promoted. The device is now crossing into the discount and general merchandise environment.

When deciding on the right mix, you will need to consider:

- The success or failure of the previous year's mix of promotional activities,
- the image that the store desires,
- the store's target customer,
- store objectives, and
- the competitive environment.

DEVELOPING A PROMOTIONAL PLAN

Once you have identified the elements of the promotional mix that will be used to promote your merchandise, you will want to determine how the various elements can be most effectively combined to reach your goals. These combined promotional activities will comprise your ***promotional campaign***, a planned and coordinated series of promotional activities built around a specific theme for the purpose of reaching the desired goals of the business. Campaigns require that promotions be targeted, comprehensive, and well planned (Figure 16.4).

A successful promotional campaign requires thorough planning and a careful execution of the following steps:

- Establish objectives,
- Prepare the budget,
- Select merchandise for promotion,
- Establish a schedule for promotional activities,
- Prepare the promotional message, and
- Evaluate promotional activities.

Establish Objectives

Your first step in developing a promotional plan is deciding what you are trying to accomplish. Specific objectives should be established for

Figure 16.4 Promotional campaigns, such as the Macy's Flower Show, reflect the selected theme in the entire store.

each element of the promotional mix. There may be many other possible goals and objectives, but the ultimate goal of all promotional activities is to increase the store's sales and maximize profits. Advertising, special events, and publicity encourage customers to come to the store, while visual merchandising, personal selling, and other sales promotions persuade customers to buy the merchandise.

A well-planned promotional campaign will not necessarily result in improved sales and profits unless the other elements of the marketing mix (price, place, and product) are coordinated with promotion. For example, prices may be too high, the product may not be located in the most appropriate location on the sales floor, or there may be an inadequate assortment of sizes and colors desired by customers.

As you develop objectives for the promotional campaign, they should be stated in specific terms of what is to be accomplished. Above all, objectives should provide a standard against which the performance of your store or department can be measured. The following are examples of objectives that could be established for a promotional campaign:

- To increase store traffic by 20 percent during the slowest day of the week.
- To increase sales by 5 percent for the week.
- To educate customers on how to use a new product.
- To make 75 percent of your target customers aware of upcoming special events.

The promotional objective of many retailers is to establish a specific image in the marketplace. Read the Snapshot titled, "Lillian Vernon: Promoting an Image Through Catalogs," to learn about how this retailer uses catalogs to establish its desired image.

Prepare the Budget

The next step in planning the promotional campaign will be to develop a budget to implement the objectives that have been planned. The **_promotional budget_** is a plan of how much money will be spent on promotional activities during a specific period. Planned sales are usually the basis of this budget. For most retailers, promotional expenditures average 1 to 4 percent of sales, but this amount will vary by the type and size of the retailer. Once the promotional budget is determined, the amount allocated to each promotional activity must be established. The exact percentage allocated will depend on other factors such as promotional objectives and the promotional activities of the competition.

Store management will usually prepare a promotional budget for a six-month period. During the season the budget may need to be adjusted, depending on actual sales, by increasing, reducing, or reallocating funds when sales do not meet predictions.

One method that many stores use to increase their promotional budgets is through ***cooperative advertising,*** whereby manufacturers share the advertising costs with retailers that promote their products; however, not all suppliers offer cooperative advertising. Management expects buyers to negotiate with suppliers for cooperative advertising to expand the store's promotional dollars. Before paying for the advertising, the manufacturer will require proof that certain specifications are met. A copy of the advertisement is sent along with a statement indicating the manufacturer's share of the advertising expenditure.

There are problems with accepting cooperative advertising for the store. You must be careful not to be lured by cooperative advertising into buying the wrong merchandise. Overbuying leads to markdowns, and excessive price reductions can severely cut the store's profits. Some buyers become so preoccupied with obtaining advertising allowances that they accept second-rate merchandise. When making purchases, you must be sure that you are buying the best merchandise, not the merchandise with the best cooperative advertising. In addition, cooperative advertising may not fit the store's overall plan, and it may not be coordinated with the store's other planned promotions. Furthermore, taking advantage of cooperative advertising requires additional recordkeeping.

There are advantages to obtaining cooperative advertising. It gives both the manufacturer and the retailer additional exposure by sharing the advertising expense. You may be also able to increase the impact of your advertising message by placing larger and more frequent ads. Increased advertising purchases may qualify your store for a lower rate on all its advertising. For the manufacturer, the prestige of the store's name reinforces the acceptance of the product on a local level. Buyers may also be able to negotiate with suppliers for other promotional materials such as premiums, point-of-sale displays, and even display fixtures. A problem with some of these items is that the manufacturer's name will be prominently displayed, which may not fit the image your store is attempting to develop.

Select Merchandise for Promotion

Your next decision is to determine what merchandise will be featured in the promotional activities. Generally, items selected tie in with themes that have been selected by the promotion department. Promotional objectives will influence the merchandise featured in promotions, but the following should also be considered:

- Select fast-selling, popular items or styles that are on their way to becoming best-sellers.
- Promote products that will attract immediate interest or tie in with seasonal promotions.
- Select items to promote that vendors will also be heavily promoting.
- Select merchandise that will be easier to write about and easier for customers to visually picture. The promotion department must be able to communicate the value and desirability of the product to customers.
- Select new items. A business with an image of fashion leadership will promote the newest styles.
- Select merchandise that has distinct price appeal. Sales will probably be needed at the end of the season to make room for fresh goods. Markdowns must be advertised to attract customers.
- Promote private brands in order for them to gain customer acceptance.

There are some products that should not be selected for promotion. They include:

- Do not rely on promotional efforts to correct buying errors. Promotions will not convince customers to purchase products they do not want.
- Old and obsolete merchandise should not be promoted.
- Merchandise that cannot be quickly reordered should not be promoted. Customer demand may be higher than anticipated, and many customers may be upset if they cannot obtain the advertised merchandise in a reasonable length of time.
- Goods previously advertised and still in stock should not be selected for promotion.
- Do not choose merchandise to promote that has been initially rejected by consumers or that has passed its peak.

Not every item of merchandise is worthy of promotion; promotional activities cannot sell merchandise that customers do not want. For promotional campaigns, select representative items that will bring the largest number of customers to your department or store. The buyer is the best-qualified store employee to select the most appropriate merchandise.

Establish the Schedule

A schedule or timetable of promotional activities must also be prepared. You will need to decide how often promotion will be needed and then develop a ***promotional calendar***, a written timetable for a long-range promotional campaign. The calendar will include:

- When promotional activities will occur,
- What merchandise will be promoted,
- Which promotion mix elements will be used,
- Who will be responsible for the activity, and
- How much is to be budgeted.

Many promotions are held in November and December during the busy holiday season; however, retailers also use other holidays such as Presidents' Day and the Fourth of July to hold many promotions. Grocery store sales occur usually on Thursday, Friday, and Saturday, so promotion is massed on Wednesday and Thursday; but many supermarkets use promotion to build sales during other parts of the week.

Promotions for specific classifications of merchandise are scheduled at the same time for most seasons. Promotions for swimwear, for example, usually begin in February, and "Back-to-School" promotions begin in July. Some retailers even create their own promotion periods such as a "Founder's Day" sale or "Midnight Madness" sale. In addition, promotions may be scheduled to supplement manufacturers' promotions.

When scheduling your promotional activities, you will want to ensure that the maximum number of customers will be exposed to your message. If radio has been selected as a medium to deliver your promotional message, you must ensure that times are selected for advertisements that will deliver the maximum number of potential listeners who comprise your target market. In other words, you must be concerned with both reach and frequency. ***Reach*** refers to the number of people who will be exposed to one or more promotional messages. ***Frequency*** is a measure of how often a customer is exposed to a promotional message. Most of the time it will take more than one advertisement to get your message across to the desired audience.

Prepare the Promotional Message

Now you must determine what message you want delivered through your promotion. Your message must appeal to your target customers by stressing the reasons they have for buying the product. Keep the message concise; do not try to overload the customer with information. Stress a few facts about the merchandise that will be of the most interest to customers. Mention product *features*–selling points that make the product unique–but emphasize the benefits of each product. Customers buy benefits, not product features. Above all, make the message believable to the customer.

As a buyer, you will have the responsibility of providing the promotion department with information about all products being promoted. It will need to know how the product is used, product features as well as benefits, and the materials, colors, sizes, and brands in which the product is available. You will want to stress to the copywriter, artist, and display staff the reasons why you bought the merchandise and why you think customers will buy it. Your enthusiasm for the products must reach the individuals responsible for implementing the promotional activities.

Evaluate each promotional message using the following criteria:

- Does the message attract attention? Will it be seen or heard by your target customers?
- Will the message stimulate interest? Attention is brief, but interest must be developed by providing enough information to the customer.
- Does the message build the customer's desire for the product? Are product benefits stressed?
- Will the message gain customer conviction? In other words, does the message convince customers to buy the product?
- Finally, does the message induce action? Does it get customers to make the purchase *now*? The use of dated coupons or limited-time offers are methods many retailers use to get customers to make the purchase rather than wait.

Evaluate Promotional Activities

Even though there are numerous methods available with which to evaluate the effectiveness of promotional activities, determining how a specific activity influenced sales is difficult. Customers may not immediately respond to many promotions. They may visit a store months after a promotional activity has occurred and make a purchase.

Store records are vital to evaluating the effectiveness of promotional activities. Records of what and how many of each item sold must be maintained as well as any special circumstances that might have affected sales, such as weather conditions, competitor's advertising, and other promotions that were used at the same time. You will also want to examine unit sales as well as dollar volume that occur after a specific promotional activity. Some retailers also count the number of customers entering the store while a promotional activity is being conducted. If coupons are used, they can be counted, and if more than one medium was used to deliver the coupons, they could be coded differently for each medium, thus allowing you to determine the most effective medium at reaching your target customer. Some small store owners even ask customers which promotional activities caused them to buy the product.

The ultimate goal of promotional activities is to sell merchandise, but the desired store image should also be reinforced through products selected for promotion, store interiors, displays, and customer service provided by sales associates. In large retail stores, the promotion department will make the final decision about where, when, and how merchandise will be promoted. The key role of the buyer will be to select suitable merchandise for promotion, suggest promotional ideas, and provide the promotion department with product information.

COORDINATION OF PROMOTIONAL ACTIVITIES

A coordinated promotional campaign is essential to obtaining your desired objectives. Plans should ensure the maximum exposure to the largest number of potential customers. Advertising, special events, and other sales promotions should create sufficient interest and desire to bring customers into the store. Visual merchandising should remind customers why they came to the store, and informed sales associates should be able to persuade customers to buy. Often, sales are lost because sales associates are not informed about the merchandise being promoted.

Regardless of the size of the store, one individual should control the promotional decisions. Someone must be delegated the responsibility to follow through on each planned promotional activity. For example, when advertising is being run, someone must check the advertising proofs, see that copies of the ad are posted, ensure that sufficient merchandise is in stock, and check with visual merchandising to ensure that displays will be constructed. Responsibilities must be explicitly assigned. An assignment sheet should be developed that includes the names and responsibilities of all persons participating in the promotional campaign, and the list should be circulated to all departments involved with the promotional activity. Advertising should be reinforced with displays featuring advertised items, and sales associates must also be thoroughly briefed on the objectives of the promotion and selling points of the merchandise.

Sales associates must be informed about forthcoming promotional campaigns, and special training may be necessary if the promotion involves new products. Receiving personnel must be informed of promotions to ensure that items are stocked in sufficient quantities and with correct prices. Visual merchandising workers need advance notice in order to create displays to coordinate with the theme of the promotion.

Particularly important to the coordination of promotional activities is working with sales associates. Promotional activities are designed to help sell merchandise, but it is the sales associate who completes the sale. Personal selling is needed to adapt the promotional message to individual customer needs. Sales associates should know:

- What promotional activities are being conducted,
- Why the merchandise was selected for promotion,
- Where and when the promotional activities will occur,
- How the promotional activities will be coordinated,
- What features and benefits of the merchandise being promoted should be emphasized to customers, and
- What questions they should anticipate from the customer regarding the advertised merchandise.

Promotional activities for all products must be coordinated. Some products, such as men's fragrances, can be easily promoted using a series of activities. These products typically sell much better in special areas exclusively designed for fragrances. Some TV advertising is done in which the store tags the national fragrance ads with the store's name. A card with a sample of the fragrance may be included in monthly bills. This promotional technique makes men more willing to come in and sample the fragrance. Buyers also work with vendors to create promotions and other in-store events.

Advertising, special events, and other sales promotions should create sufficient interest and desire to bring customers into the store. Visual merchandising should remind customers why they came to the store, and informed sales associates should be able to persuade customers to buy.

SUMMARY POINTS

- The buyer's role in sales promotion will vary considerably from store to store.
- Key roles for the buyer will be to select merchandise for promotion, purchase merchandise needed to support promotional activities, and negotiate with suppliers to support the store's promotional activities.
- Key functions of sales promotion activities will be to produce sales and maximize profits, to generate customer loyalty, and to project the store's image. To accomplish these objectives, many different elements of the promotional mix can be used.
- Key promotional mix elements include advertising, visual merchandising, personal selling, publicity, special events, and other sales promotion activities. These elements must be combined in a coordinated manner that will provide a single, unified promotion message to customers.
- Buyers must request advertising and visual merchandising for new merchandise they have purchased. In addition, they must provide the promotion department with product information as well as information about customer preferences. Product information must also be provided to salespersons.
- A successful promotional campaign requires thorough planning and a careful execution of the following steps: establishing objectives, preparing a budget, selecting merchandise for promotion, establishing a schedule for promotional activities, preparing the promotional message, and evaluating the promotional campaign.
- Promotional activities for a campaign should ensure the maximum exposure of the firm's advertising message to the largest number of potential customers.
- One individual in the store should control all promotional decisions because a coordinated campaign is essential to obtaining the store's desired objectives.

REVIEW ACTIVITIES

Developing Your Retail Buying Vocabulary

Consult the Glossary if you did not add the following terms to your vocabulary.

Advertising	Promotional calendar
Cooperative advertising	Promotional campaign
Features	Promotional mix
Frequency	Publicity
Media	Reach
Personal selling	Sales promotion
Press release	Special events
Promotional budget	Visual merchandising

Understanding What You Read

1. How does the buyer's role in promotional planning differ at small and large retail stores?
2. Why should the buyer be involved in promotional planning?
3. What should be the objectives of all promotional activities?
4. List the key elements of the promotional mix.
5. What are the general goals of advertising?
6. What are the basic elements that differentiate advertising and publicity?
7. What is the purpose of a publicity release?
8. What information should be included in a publicity release?
9. How are the elements of the promotional mix selected for a promotional campaign?
10. Why must objectives for a promotional campaign be stated in specific terms?
11. What method is normally used to calculate the amount to budget for promotional campaigns?
12. For what period of time is the promotional budget usually planned?
13. Why is management interested in buyers securing cooperative advertising?
14. List advantages and disadvantages of retailers using cooperative advertising.

15. What type of merchandise is generally selected for promotion?
16. What type of merchandise should not be selected for promotion?
17. What are some factors that will affect the schedule of promotional activities?
18. Describe methods used to evaluate the impact of promotional activities.
19. Explain how promotional activities should be coordinated with sales associates.
20. Why must promotional activities be coordinated with suppliers?

Analyzing and Applying What You Read

1. As streaming video improves and is used more often to present fashion shows, such as the Webcasts held by Victoria's Secret, the potential exists for buyers to view fashion shows on their computers rather than visiting market cities. Discuss the pros and cons of buyers using the Web to view new lines of fashion merchandise.
2. Using the following outline, complete a promotional plan for a retail business with which you are familiar.
   a. Describe the retail store and target market for which the promotional plan will be executed.
   b. Establish objectives for the promotional plan.
   c. List merchandise that will be promoted.
   d. Develop a budget for the promotional plan.
   e. Describe the promotional activities that will be used in the campaign.
   f. Develop a schedule (timetable) for the events.
   g. Develop a responsibility sheet showing who is assigned responsibility to accomplish each activity.
   h. Describe how the results of each promotional activity will be evaluated as well as the benefits to the store.

Internet Connection

1. If VictoriasSecret.com is presenting a Webcast of a fashion show during the semester, view it online. Make a list of any problems that occur during the Webcast. Discuss whether these problems can be outweighed by the benefits that Webcasting provides retailers.

2. Visit the Web sites of five different retailers. Make a list of promotional tools that are used to attract and retain customers (e.g., sweepstakes, free gifts). Evaluate the effectiveness of each promotional activity.

SNAPSHOT

Lillian Vernon: Promoting an Image Through Catalogs

In 1951, Lillian Vernon founded a mail-order business on her kitchen table with $2,000 in wedding gift money. She placed an ad for personalized belts and handbags in a magazine and filled orders from home. The promotion succeeded, and a retail giant was born. Today, the Lillian Vernon company offers low-price lines that include household, gardening, and children's products sold via catalog and at lillian-vernon.com. These products are primarily aimed at middle-aged mothers who are employed outside the home. It is a concept that has succeeded. The company was recently sold and is now part of a private company that does not release specific sales figures, but indications are that sales are still above plan.

But, it is still hard to separate Lillian Vernon, the person, from Lillian Vernon, the company. In fact, that is what makes the catalog so distinctive and is why it has survived. Throughout its first 55 years of existence, Lillian Vernon had a vision that she was able to implement flawlessly. She really seemed to know what the average customer wants and needs. Product selection and promotion for the company were based on that vision.

Yet the company does not rest on past laurels. As the next 55 years of growth begins, the firm is already actively competing online—leveraging the famous company name. The Web site even allows customers to create their own catalog. Customers plug in keywords and price ranges and receive a list of items that fits those criteria. The Web will be just another way the company attempts to give customers exactly what they want. In addition, new product lines for the catalog are being considered with the use of extensive database analysis and market research, which have been critical to the success of the company. Throughout her career in catalogs, Lillian Vernon has listened to her customers, who have been quick to tell the company when it has made a mistake.

Based on the experience of Lillian Vernon, a catalog should offer at least 100 products, run approximately 24 pages, and have a mailing list of at least 200,000 customers. Vernon suggests doing at least two, preferably four, mailings a year, and carrying an inventory of 33 percent of the items being sold, depending on where the buyers have sourced the products. Company management believes that inventories should be kept low until sales can be projected accurately. In fact, inventory levels are invaluable guides to the health of a cataloguer, as they are for any retailer. If foreign sources are used, more coverage would be needed.

Catalogs, such as Lillian Vernon, succeed or fail on the quality of the products offered; therefore, the role of the buyer is paramount to its success. Buyers, however, must recognize that customers will reject a product the buyers may have considered a "winner." Just as in traditional retail stores, such a failure should not discourage buyers or make them reluctant to make the next purchase.

Lillian Vernon believes that how well merchandise is presented—the design and production of the catalog—also has a lot to do with how well customers receive it. The company's most successful catalogs have been those with distinctive personalities. Sharp images come when a catalog bears the stamp of a single person's spirit and taste. In the case of the Lillian Vernon catalog, it has been her own.

Since the first catalog in 1960, the company has spent much time and thought in establishing the identify of the catalog. After all, it was through those pages that the company communicated with its customers, and they judged the company by the catalog. Lillian Vernon insisted that the catalog have a distinctive personality and that the merchandise offered give the catalog uniqueness. In general, the goal of the catalog has been to offer merchandise that is original, affordable, attractive, useful, and fun.

Promotions must also fit the image of the catalog. Some catalogs use sweepstakes to bring in customers. Such promotions have never been used at Lillian Vernon because management does not feel they fit the image of the catalog. However, Lillian Vernon found that gifts did work for the company as a promotional tool. On the 16th anniversary of the catalog, customers were given a free gift with their purchases. The gifts ranged from the decorative to accessories to useful household items. For years, the company gave the gifts, but one year decided to stop. Customers complained, and sales went down. Lillian Vernon quickly discovered that gifts did, indeed, enhance sales.

Lillian Vernon is a prime example that all retailers should concentrate on the products they know how to sell and on the market with which they are familiar. A sound vision must be developed and successfully implemented through product selection and coordinated promotion efforts.

BASED ON:

Leveraging famous name. (2000, June 19). *Advertising Age*, 46.

Lillian Vernon celebrates with parties, catalogs. (2004, October 4). *Brandweek*, 8.

Lillian Vernon's heart is still in business she sold. (2005, February 19). *The Virginian Pilot* (Norfolk, VA), D2.

Lillian Vernon joins forces with Catalog Vision. (2007, April 16). *DM News*, 17.

Mail-order maven Lillian Vernon turns over company to new owners. (2005, February 19). *The Virginian Pilot*, D2.

Vernon, Lillian. (1996). *An Eye for Winners*. New York: Harper Business Publishers.

Zisko, Allison. (2004, October 11). Lillian Vernon catalog enters a new chapter. *HFN The Weekly Newspaper for the Home Furnishing Network*, 14.

TRENDWATCH

Victoria's Secret: Using the Web as a Promotion Tool

Today, many retailers are developing a 360-degree approach to their stores and products. In other words, customers can reach them anywhere and anytime. Web sites are used to support a store's catalog, the catalog supports the stores, and vice versa. The goal is to be build an online and catalog business that operates seamlessly with traditional stores. Such strategic moves make it easier for customers to access a retailer and make purchases when it is most convenient for them. Implementing online sites also provides retailers with a prime promotional tool.

Victoria's Secret is one retailer that has been successfully implementing this type of strategy for several years. Management had several key goals when its Web site was initiated. The primary goal was to maximize all channels of distribution, including retail stores, catalogs, direct mail/e-mail campaigns, and a Web site. The second goal was to develop new business opportunities that included using the Internet for breakthrough marketing campaigns, such as Webcasts. Overall, the Web site was designed to add strength to the existing Victoria's Secret brand and generate more sales through additional channels.

Victoria's Secret had a strong reputation to uphold when management decided to enter the world of e-tailing. In implementing Web strategies, management wanted to combine all elements of the business to present a consistent and single message to customers. When the Web site recently featured "Body by Victoria" bras, for example, so did the catalog and store windows. Management has strived to employ a singular promotional image and brand message across the three platforms and has been able to reach all types of customers.

For Victoria's Secret, the Web site has been a very successful promotional tool. The company received more than 1 million new requests for catalogs via the site, and the more than 1.7 million registered users of the Web site receive regular updates on specials and promotional exclusives. According to company management, the most productive promotional program for the Web site has been via e-mail. The company sends exclusive offers to Web shoppers and has acquired a significant response rate with minimal acquisition costs.

Management has also used the Web to move from the catwalk to the laptop. Victoria's Secret's first-ever fashion show Webcast was a record-breaking event, with over 1 million visits the day of the event and 2 million visits during the next 30 days after the live show. It took just a single TV ad during the Super Bowl inviting consumers to a live lingerie show Webcast; the viewers came in droves. But despite its success, technological difficulties marred the experience for some customers. Many customers were unable to log on. Customers who logged on saw the usual twitchy, postage-stamp display. But the Webcast put the company on the Web map and showed other retailers the power of combining traditional and online promotions.

Planning began for the next Webcast just days after the first one was completed. Improvements were made in the technology, resulting in more than 2 million viewers of Victoria's Secret Cannes 2000 Fashion Show Webcast—without any problems. According to company executives, a significant increase was made in streaming capacity, resulting in more rapid content delivery. Another groundbreaking technological innovation that debuted during the 2000 fashion show Webcast was a "shop while you watch" feature. As viewers watched the Webcast on the left of their browser window, screens featuring items like those being modeled appeared on the right. Shoppers had the option of selecting items to purchase from these pages by simply clicking to add them to their shopping baskets. When the show was over customers proceeded to checkout, at which point they were required to specify colors, sizes, and quantities.

Victoria's Secret plans to continue Webcasting its annual fashion show as part of its tradition of using cutting-edge technology to extend the store's brand to consumers around the world. The fashion show Webcasts will become a key part of the company's promotional strategy. They will serve to increase global awareness of and enthusiasm for the retailer, creating business opportunities in local and global markets through the VictoriasSecret.com Web site.

BASED ON:

Dinakar, S. (2007, July 23). Victoria's Secret. *Forbes Global*, 24.

Mack, Ann M. (2000, May 15). Victoria's Secret improves technology for cybercast. *ADWeek Eastern Edition*, 96.

Reda, Susan. (2000, July). Technology team brings Victoria's Secret webcast to huge audience. *Stores*, 54–57.

Victoria's IT secret? (2000, June 7). *Planet IT*, 1.

Victoria's Secret improves technology for cybercast. (2000, May 15). *Brandweek*, 92.

Victoria's Secret reveals 283 percent rise in Web traffic. (2000, May 26). *Business Wire*, 55.

Appendix A
Basic Retail Math Formulas

Basic Pricing Calculations

$ Markup = $ Retail − $ cost

$ Retail = $ Cost + $ Markup

$ Cost = $ Retail − $ Markup

Markup % Based on Retail = $ Markup / $ Retail

Initial Markup % = Expenses + Profit + Reductions − Cash Discounts / Sales + Reductions

$ Retail = Cost $ / (100% − Markup % Based on Retail)

Markdown $ = Original Retail Price − Final Retail Price

Markdown % = Markdown $ / Sales $

Off-Retail % = Markdown $ / Original Retail Price

Calculating Planned Stock Levels

Stock-to-Sales Ratio Method
   Stock-to-Sales Ratio = Value of Inventory / Actual Sales
   BOM Inventory = Stock-to-Sales Ratio × Planned Sales

Maximum = Sales Volume Per Week (Reorder Period + Delivery Period) + Reserve

Minimum = Reserve + (Rate of Sale × Delivery Period)

Stock Turnover Rate = Sales / Average Stock

Merchandise Planning Calculations

Planned Purchases at Retail = Planned Sales + Planned Reductions + Planned EOM + Planned BOM

Planned Purchases (Cost) = Planned Purchases at Retail × (100% − Markup %)

$ Open-to-Buy = Planned Purchases − Merchandise on Order

Unit Open-to-Buy = Unit Planned Purchases − Units on Order

Profit Calculations

Net Sales = Gross Sales − Customer Returns and Allowances

Profit (Loss) = Net Sales − Cost of Goods Sold − Expenses

Profit % = Profit $ / Net Sales

Appendix B
Decision Making

Buyers must constantly make decisions in their job; therefore, they must develop their ability to solve business problems using a logical framework. Decisions are a part of our day-to-day living. Some decisions will be easy to make, while other decisions will require much more thought. While you will make some decisions alone, some will require you to get help from other people or to work with others to reach a decision.

Closely related to the number of decisions that you make each day is the number of alternatives from which you have to choose. More alternatives make it more difficult to make a decision. As the number of alternatives increases, information becomes vital to effective decision making.

Without being consciously aware of it, you use a decision-making process automatically. In fact, the steps you use to make decisions in your daily life are similar to ones used in business. One way to approach the decision-making process is by following these four steps:

1. Identify the problem
2. List and evaluate alternatives
3. Select the best alternative
4. Implement your decision and follow up

Identify the Problem. Too many individuals rarely show a great deal of interest in planning how to solve a problem; they want to immediately start working on a solution. They incorrectly believe that planning is not very important to the decision-making process; however, evidence indicates that people who spend time clearly identifying the problem make better decisions.

If you are working with a group (other buyers, sales associates, managers, etc.), you need to make sure that everyone has the same perceptions of the problem or the decision that has to be made. If you have three people in your group, you may have three different perceptions. You also need to share with others in the group how the issue or problem will affect them. We all tend to become more personally involved in the solution if we can see a connection between ourselves and the problem.

Moreover, your group will also want to state an objective for the problem in measurable terms. For example, you may want to "Increase sales 10 percent by November 15." No matter what decisions you make to increase sales, you will know if you succeeded or failed. Once you have agreed on what the problem is and how you will evaluate results, you are ready to develop a strategy to solve the problem.

List and Evaluate Alternatives. There will be many alternative ways to achieve your objective, and you need to identify and evaluate each one. The more input you receive usually leads to more effective decision making.

Brainstorming is a process that many groups use to identify alternatives. All ideas presented have potential value to your organization and must be considered. Brainstorming is like sowing seeds. Some of these seeds, just like some ideas, will be good and bear fruit; others will not. The result may be that inappropriate ideas may be presented; however, many good ideas may be triggered by some suggestions that seem "offbeat."

No idea is too ridiculous to be written down. If you do not write ideas down, good ideas may get lost. During the brainstorming process, ideas should be listed but not evaluated.

Next, you will want to screen good ideas and eliminate bad ones. You will want to remove the frivolous from the serious and reduce the list to a workable number. You will want to evaluate each alternative against criteria such as:

- Is the suggestion feasible? Can it be done?
- Can the suggestion be implemented during your allotted time frame?
- Do you have the resources available to implement the suggestion?
- Has the suggestion been tried before? With what results?
- Is the suggestion practical?

Once you have reduced alternatives to a manageable number, you should carefully review both the positive and negative consequences of each of the remaining alternatives. Consider all information that is available.

Select the Best Alternative. Now you are ready to choose a solution–you have got to make a decision. In most situations, this will be much easier for individuals than groups. Group decision making is a much slower process because more people must be consulted. Votes by members may be required to make a decision. If so, your group must decide on whether a decision will be based on a simple majority or require unanimous agreement, or something in between.

Implement the Decision and Follow up. After deciding which alternative will be used, an action plan needs to be developed to list what is going to be done by whom and when it is to be accomplished.

Decision making is worthless without follow-up and feedback. There is a need to monitor how the action went. Decision making does not end when the decision is implemented. You need to examine and evaluate the results. You need to know what went right as well as what went wrong. In this way, you can identify opportunities for improvement that will make future decision making easier in this area.

Using Group Decision Making. Many of the decisions your organization faces will have to be made by groups rather than individuals. However, group decision making can be frustrating as you try to achieve unanimity or consensus with group members. You must realize that not all decisions should be made by groups. There is a place for individual as well as group decision making in all organizations. Groups should be used for decision making when they can contribute to the solution of the problem. For example, some problems are so complex that they cannot be handled easily by a single individual. Also, if implementation of the decision requires group members, it is best to involve them in decision making. People tend to carry out decisions that they helped make.

Group decision making has both advantages and disadvantages over individual problem solving. Key advantages of group decision making include the following:

- There is more information in a group than any one of its members possesses. Therefore, if a problem situation requires using knowledge, groups have an advantage over individuals.
- Individuals get into ruts in their thinking. Because group members will not have identical approaches, each member can contribute by moving others out of their ruts.
- Many problems require solutions that depend on the support of others to be effective. When groups solve such problems, a greater number of members feel responsible for making the solution work.

However, there are drawbacks when using group decision making. They include the following:

- People tend to conform. The desire to be a good group member causes some members to be silent and not voice their disagreement. This causes consensus to be reached without a complete examination of all alternatives.
- Some groups become controlled by a dominant individual. That individual may have a great persuasive ability or just stubborn persistence when dominating discussion. This individual may not be the best problem-solver in the group. Also, the leader may exert a major influence on the outcome of any discussion because of the position he or she holds.
- In general, more time is required for a group to reach a decision than for a single individual to reach a decision. If the problem requires a quick decision, individual decisions are needed.

Use the previous criteria to determine if the problem that you or your organization is facing should be handled by one person or a group. Then proceed with the decision-making process.

Glossary

additional markup an increase in the retail price of an item, above the price at which it was marked to sell on arrival at the store

advance dating terms dating an invoice for a specified time in the future, thus discount calculations are made from that date, rather than from the invoice or delivery dates

advertising a paid, nonpersonal promotional message for a product, service, or idea by an identified sponsor

anticipation an extra discount that some manufacturers allow buyers to take for paying an invoice in advance of the cash discount date

assistant buyer an individual who aids buyers in performing their duties; may be buyers in training

associated (cooperative) buying office a buying office that is owned, operated, and controlled by a group of stores that it represents

assortment planning involves determining the specific quantities and characteristics of each product being purchased, in relation to specific factors such as brands, colors, and sizes

automatic markdown placing a predetermined markdown on merchandise that remains unsold after a given period of time

automatic reordering system involves the use of computers and bar coding to generate weekly merchandise orders that are based on sales, in relation to model stock plans

availability refers to the amount of effort customers are willing to exert to obtain a particular product

average stock calculated by dividing the sum of the value of inventory at predetermined periods of time by the total number of those time periods

balanced assortment an assortment of merchandise which meets the needs of as many customers as possible, with a minimum investment in inventory

bar coding using a pattern of variable width bars and spaces on merchandise to identify a product being scanned

basic merchandise items that customers buy year in and year out and which they expect the retail store to have in stock at all times

basic stock list a list that provides the buyer with information such as merchandise descriptions, retail price, cost, rate of sale, and the maximum and minimum reorder quantity

basic stock plan a plan used to determine the amount of merchandise that a retailer must have on hand or on order to ensure a sufficient amount of merchandise being available during a given period of time

behavioristic data includes information about consumers' buying activities, such as the time they typically make purchases or the average amount of their purchases

BOM inventory amount of stock on hand at the beginning of the month

BOM stock level amount of inventory at the beginning of the month

bottom-up planning involves estimating total sales for a store by adding together the planned sales figures that have been developed by each department manager

breadth relates to the number of product lines or to the number of brands that is carried by a store or department within a product classification

bricks-and-mortar refers to traditional retail presence as a physical storefront

broad and shallow refers to offering a wide selection of brands with little depth

broker an individual who acts as an agent for the manufacturer when dealing with retailers

buyer individual in a retail firm whose primary job is to purchase merchandise

buying the business activity that involves selecting and purchasing products to satisfy the wants and needs of consumers

buying office an organization that is located in a major market center with the purpose of providing buying advice and other market-related services to client stores

COD collect-on-delivery, which means that the transportation company will collect the amount of the invoice when goods are delivered to the retailer

cannibalization occurs when potential sales of existing products are lost when new items are added to a store's inventory

career path/ladder diagrams that show job progressions for a specific career

cash discount discount granted to retailers for paying an invoice early

centralized buying occurs when all buying activities are performed from a retailer's central headquarters

central market a city in which a large number of key suppliers for a product line are located

central merchandising plan occurs when a central office representing a group of stores has complete responsibility for the selection and purchase of merchandise for all the stores

chain store two or more retail stores under single ownership

classic a style that is in demand continuously even though minor changes may be made in the product

classification refers to the particular kinds of goods in a store or department

clicks-and-mortar refers to retailers developing an on-line presence in addition to their traditional storefronts

collaborator a negotiator who views concerns as mutual problems; seeks to arrive at solutions where both parties win

commission (merchandise broker) buying office a type of independent buying office that is paid by the manufacturers it represents, rather than by retail clients

commissionaire a buyer who operates in foreign markets and function similarly to domestic buying offices

comparison shopper firms that shop competing stores to provide information on the merchandise assortments, prices, and promotion of other retailers on the area

compromise an agreement based on both sides in a negotiation giving in on some of their demands

concentrated target marketing involves a retailer focusing on one market segment

consumer advisory panels consists of typical customers who make suggestions about policies, services, and merchandise assortments.

convenience product an item that customers expect the store to have readily available at all times

cooperative advertising allowances offered by some vendors to retailers whereby they will share the cost of any advertising that features the vendor's products

cost of goods includes the actual cost of the merchandise, plus transportation charges involved in getting the merchandise from the vendor to the store and any workroom costs

cost method a method of inventory valuation that requires stock records to be maintained using cost, not retail, prices

customer database an organized collection of comprehensive data about individual customers

data information

data mining searching through warehoused data to find trends and patterns that might otherwise have gone unnoticed

data warehousing involves electronically storing customer and operations data

database marketing activities that provide retailers with ongoing intelligence based on tracking and analyzing customer behavior

decline stage the last stage of the product life cycle that occurs when the target market shrinks, and price-cutting minimizes profit margins

delivery period the time between when an order is placed and when the merchandise is available on the sales floor

demographic data include characteristics of customers such as age, sex, family size, income, education, occupation, and race

demographic trend trend related to characteristics of consumers, such as marital status and birthrates

department store a business that sells all kinds of merchandise for the individual and the home

departmentalization organizing different store activities into departments or divisions

depth the number of choices offered to customers within each brand or product classification

destination store a store that consumers make a planned effort to shop

direct marketing direct connection with carefully targeted individual customers to both obtain immediate response and cultivate lasting customer relationships

discount department store retailers that emphasize one-stop shopping to meet the needs of all family members, but appeal to consumers who value savings over service

dollar control inventory planning based on a planned dollar value of stock, rather than specific units of stock

durability refers to how long a product will last

durables products (such as cars, furniture, and appliances) that are capable of surviving many uses and typically last for years

duty a tax on merchandise imported into a country

EOM dating terms dating terms that allow the buyer to calculate cash discounts from the end of the month

EOM inventory stock available at the end of the month

early adopters a consumer who purchases fashion merchandise in the early stages of the product life cycle

electronic data interchange the use of technology to support the communication of sales data and business documents, such as invoices and purchase orders, between retailers and suppliers

emotional buying motive buying motive that involves customers' feelings, rather than logic

even pricing a strategy to create an upscale image for a product by pricing it with even numbers such as $32.00

exception report computer-generated report that is produced when sales or stock levels do not meet planned levels

exclusive distribution a practice of some vendors to sell a product to only one retailer in a trading area

exports goods shipped to other countries

exposition show held at a convention center or exhibition hall on a periodic basis to showcase the latest merchandise in a particular product category

external forces forces occurring outside a business, such as economic and competitive conditions

extra dating terms dating terms that give the buyer a specified number of additional days in which to pay an invoice and earn a cash discount

fad a short-lived fashion

FIFO first in, first out method of inventory control that assumes that the merchandise that was received first, sold first

FOB destination (store) transportation term that indicates the manufacturer pays the shipping charges, and title passes to the buyer when the merchandise is delivered

FOB destination, charges reversed transportation term that indicates the buyer pays the shipping charges, and the seller assumes responsibility for the goods while they are in shipment

FOB destination, freight prepaid transportation term that indicates the seller will pay the freight charges, but the buyer takes title to them as soon as they are shipped

FOB origin (factory) transportation term where title passes to the buyer when the seller delivers goods to the transportation carrier; freight charges are the responsibility of the buyer

FOB shipping point transportation term that indicates the manufacturer has title to the goods and is responsible for shipping costs until the merchandise reaches a distribution point where the buyer takes title to the goods and pays transportation charges until they reach the store

fashion the prevailing style that is accepted and used by a particular group of people at a particular time in a particular place

fashion forecaster a business consultant who predicts long-range fashion trends

fashion merchandise merchandise that has a high demand over a relatively short period of time, usually a season

features selling points that make a product unique

fixed expenses expenses that do not vary regardless of how much merchandise is sold

forecasting involves predicting what con-sumers will probably do under a given set of conditions

free trade agreement an agreement between countries to eliminate tariffs on merchandise being traded

frequency a measure of how often a customer is exposed to a promotional message

functional departmentalization refers to activities of a similar nature being grouped together into a major area of responsibility and headed by an individual who reports to the owner or chief executive of the store

GMROI a measurement of the profitability of a retailer's sales

generic brand unbranded merchandise

generics products without a brand name

geographic data include information on where consumers live such as zip codes, neighborhoods, cities, counties, states, or regions

geographic departmentalization refers to an organizational structure based on geographic areas (e.g., a retailer having a north, south, east, and west division, each headed by an executive)

growth stage the stage in the product life cycle where innovators have recommended the purchase of a new product to their friends, causing increased sales and product variations

hard lines all merchandise carried by a store with the exception of apparel and accessories and fashions for the home (e.g., hardware, sporting goods, appliances, furniture, lawn and garden)

haute couture high fashion, or those styles first accepted by the fashion leaders

hot item merchandise that is difficult to keep in stock because of tremendous customer demand for it

hypermarkets megasupermarkets and general merchandise stores that stock everything from food to appliances

image the perceptions consumers have about a retail store

import merchandise purchased from foreign sources and brought into a country

importer business that purchases merchandise from foreign sources and then sells it to domestic retailers

impulse product a product that is purchased by a consumer often because of an irresistible urge

independent buying office a buying office that is privately owned and operated

innovator a consumers who is more likely to purchase a new style

intermediary a middleman

internal forces those activities within a business that will probably affect sales, such as increasing or decreasing advertising expenditures

introduction stage the stage in the product life cycle that occurs when products are usually accepted by only a few people

inventory control system involves the maintenance of stock levels in relation to changing consumer demand

irregulars merchandise that contains slight imperfections usually not visible to the naked eye

job lot an assortment of merchandise that the vendor has been unable to sell at regular prices; therefore, the entire lot is offered to the buyer at a reduced price

key resource vendor with whom retailers concentrate a large percentage of their purchases

keystoning a technique used by some small retailers to calculate retail price by doubling the cost of merchandise

kiosk a touch-activated computer terminal used for electronic retailing

LIFO last in, first out method of inventory control that assumes the merchandise that was received last was sold first

laggard a consumer who accepts a style when it is in the decline stage of the product life cycle

landed cost the importer's final cost for foreign merchandise, which includes the merchandise cost, duties and tariffs, commissions, insurance, storage expenses, and transportation charges

late adopter a consumer who accepts a fashion when its past its peak

letter of credit a promise from the purchaser's bank to the seller guaranteeing payment for shipments

licensed product a product that is designed and sold through identification with a celebrity or corporate name, logo, slogan, or fictional character

long-term forecast forecasting for more than a year

loss leader pricing technique that involves pricing a product below cost in order to generate store traffic

management training program program offered by retail stores to college graduates pursuing a management career in retailing

manufacturer's representative an agent for a manufacturer who deals with retailers

markdown reduction in the retail price of merchandise already in stock

markdown cancellation increases in the retail price to offset all or part of previously taken markdowns

markdown percentage a control tool used by buyers that is calculated by dividing total dollar markdowns by total sales

market a group of people with the ability, desire, and willingness to buy—a store's potential customers

market basket analysis describes data-mining solutions that identify the correlation among items in a customer's shopping basket

market segment a group of potential customers that has similar needs or other important characteristics

market segmentation dividing the total market into segments

marketing concept the belief that all business activities should be geared toward satisfying the wants and needs of consumers

marketing research the systematic process of gathering, recording, and analyzing information about problems related to marketing

markup the amount of money added to the cost of goods to calculate retail price

mass customization providing individual customers with products that have been mass produced, yet still giving them "exactly what they want"

maturity stage the stage of the product life cycle that occurs when sales reach maximum levels and all types of retailers carry the product

maximum the amount of merchandise that must be on hand or on order at any reordering point

media the methods selected to transmit an advertising message

merchandise/apparel mart a single building or complex of buildings located in many cities that offers retail buyers one-stop shopping

merchandise manager the individual in a retail store who is responsible for managing the buying function

merchandise mix the types or mix of products that are available for customers to purchase

merchandise plan a projection in dollars of the sales goals for the store or department, over a specified period of time

merchant middleman the middleman who takes possession of goods that it purchases from manufacturers, before selling them to retailers

middleman an intermediary between the buyer and seller

minimum the point at which merchandise reorders should be placed

model stock the desired merchandise assortment, broken down according to the selection factors that are important to a store's customers

most-favored-nation status status granted to certain countries that allows them to qualify for lower tariffs on their exports

multisegment target marketing involves a retailer focusing on several different market segments

narrow and deep refers to stocking large amounts of a few product categories or brands

national brand a product sold almost everywhere in the country, such as Arrow shirts or Levi jeans

negotiation the process of reaching a mutually satisfying agreement

networking involves identifying and communicating with individuals who can be helpful in a job search

niche a segment of a larger consumer market

nondurables products that are used up in a few uses or simply become out-of-date when styles change

nonmerchant middleman a middleman who does not take possession of merchandise from the manufacturer before selling it to the retailer

obsolescence the outmoding of a product due to a change in fashion before its usefulness has been exhausted

odd-cent pricing a pricing technique used by some retailers to create the perception of a lower price in the customer's mind by using odd cents such as $5.99

off-price occurs when retailers purchase manufacturers' overruns at deep discounts for the purpose of offering consumers low prices on name-brand merchandise

off-retail percentage percentage used for advertising purposes that is calculated by dividing the amount of markdown by the original retail price

on consignment term that indicates that the buyer will take merchandise into a store but will pay for it only when it sells

online retailing electronic retailing occurring over the Internet

on memorandum term that indicates the merchandise coming into the store has a return privilege with it

open-to-buy the dollar amount that the buyer has left to spend for a period

ordinary dating terms terms that indicate that cash discounts are calculated from the invoice date; the most common type of cash discount

organizational chart a diagram of a firm's internal structure, indicating all employees and their relationship to each other

outlet store a retail store that has typically sold slow-moving and out-of-date merchandise at discount prices

overbought a condition that exists when a buyer has purchased more than planned during a specific period of time

patronage buying motive a buying motive that involves customers choosing one store over another

penetration using low profit margins to generate greater sales; usually used to quickly gain market share

periodic control system inventory control on a seasonal basis, such as monthly or yearly

perpetual control system inventory control on a continuous basis

personal selling one-on-one communication between a customer and a sales associate for the purpose of satisfying customer wants and needs through products presented for sale

positioning identifying a group of consumers and developing retail activities to meet their needs

press release announcement sent by a retail store to the media for the purpose of obtaining publicity about new products, special events, new store openings, etc.

price agreement plan a plan whereby central buyers select the vendors from whom in-store buyers may make purchases

price decline guarantee terms that protects the store if market prices drop over a stated period of time; the vendor would credit or refund the buyer the amount of the price reduction that occurs

price floor the minimum price below which a product should not be priced

price lining selecting certain prices that appeal to target customers and only carrying merchandise assortments at those price points

price point certain price range that has been established by the store, such as good, better, and best

price war develops when a number of retailers attempt to under price each other; increased sales may result, but usually at the expense of profits

primary data data that originate with the specific research being undertaken

private brand brand of merchandise that is developed by retailers that allows them to offer unique merchandise to their customers

private buying office a buying office that is owned and operated by the one retail store that it represents

product life cycle a diagram that illustrates the expected behavior of a product over its life span

product line a broad category of products that have similar characteristics and uses

product-line departmentalization departmentalizing a retail store based on broad categories of merchandise such as furniture, appliances, children's wear, or jewelry

promotional budget a plan of how much money will be spent on promotional activities during a specific period

promotional buying purchasing merchandise that will be featured in a store's promotion plans

promotional calendar a written timetable for a long-range promotional campaign

promotional campaign a planned and coordinated series of promotional activities built around a specific theme

promotional mix different promotional methods that include advertising, visual merchandising, personal selling, publicity, special events, and other sales promotional activities

psychographic data include information on the lifestyles, interests, and opinions of consumers

psychographic trend a trend related to consumers' lifestyles, interests, and opinions, such as how they use their time

publicity the free and voluntary mention of a company, product, or service by the media

quality check checking merchandise that has been received in the store to ensure that it is identical to the quality of the merchandise ordered

quantitative performance standard evaluative criteria that have been established in numerical terms to measure a buyer's job performance

quantity check checking merchandise that has been received in the store to ensure that it is identical to the number ordered, as well as in correct sizes, colors, models, etc.

quantity discount a discount offered to buyers as an enticement for them to order a larger quantity

Quick Response an inventory management system based on a partnership between the retailer and the vendor that uses unit control and electronic data interchange to ensure a store will have the right items in stock

quota a predetermined amount of merchandise that a country's government will allow to be imported for a specific product category

ROG dating terms dating terms that allow the buyer to calculate discounts from the delivery date (receipt of goods) rather than the invoice date

rack jobber special type of vendor that services client stores where the vendor is assigned shelf space and the responsibility for keeping it stocked with quick-turning merchandise

rational buying motive a buying motive concerned with basic human needs such as food, clothing, and shelter

reach refers to the number of people who will be exposed to one or more promotional messages

reductions includes markdowns, employee and consumer discounts, and inventory shortages

reorder period the amount of time between merchandise orders

reporting service organization that reports on changing market trends that will probably affect buying decisions for a retail store

reserve the amount of merchandise kept in stock to meet unanticipated sales

retail method method of inventory valuation based on the retail price of merchandise in stock

retail strategy the overall framework or plan of action that guides a retailer

retailing all the business activities involved in the selling of goods and services to ultimate consumers

return merchandise that has been returned to the store by the customer, or merchandise that has been returned to the vendor by the retailer

SKU stock keeping unit; number that identifies a single item of merchandise within a merchandise classification

salaried (fixed-fee) buying office an independent buying office that is paid directly by the retail stores it represents

sales forecast a prediction of future sales for a specified period under a proposed marketing plan

sales promotion involves the communicating of information about products, services, images, and ideas to influence a consumer's purchase behavior

seasonal basic a product that is desired by customers consistently during certain times of the year (e.g., Easter egg dye or kites)

seasonal discount a discount offered to buyers for making purchases in advance of a selling season

secondary data data that have been gathered for some other purpose, but are applicable to solving the problem at hand

seconds merchandise that contains obvious imperfections or damages

selection factors product characteristic that is most important to a store's customers when they make their purchasing decisions

selective distribution occurs when vendors sell their products to only selected retailers within a trading area

shopping product a product for which consumers will make price, quality, suitability, and style comparisons

short-term forecast forecasting for a period of one year or less

shrinkage merchandise shortage, usually a result of shoplifting or employee theft

six-month merchandise plan a tool used by retailers to translate profit objectives into a six-month framework for merchandise planning and control

skimming a pricing policy that occurs when stores charge the highest price possible; lower sales will result, but the profit margin on each item is high

soft lines apparel and accessory product categories, as well as fashions for the home—items such as linens, curtains, or bathroom items

special events events that are not part of a store's everyday merchandising activities

specialized superstore superstore that offers one to three categories of merchandise in large assortments and at discount prices that are unmatched by any other retailer in the area

specialty product a product for which customers' buying behavior is geared to obtaining a particular product without regard to time, effort, or expense

specialty store retailer that primarily sells one specific product line

specification buying buying merchandise that is offered by the vendor, if certain specifications or changes are made

standard classification of merchandise coding system that classfies merchandise using four-digit codes.

stock-to-sales ratio a figure that indicates the relationship between planned sales and the amount of inventory required to produce those sales

Stock-to-Sales Ratio Method a method of stock planning that involves maintaining inventory in a specific ratio to sales

stock turnover rate the number of times that the average stock is sold during a given period of time

store brand a brand sold only at a specific store; also known as private brand

style a form of a product that is significantly different from other forms of that product

subclassification dividing merchandise classifications into other classifications (e.g., men's shoes could be broken down into dress shoes, casual shoes, athletic shoes, work shoes, and boots)

supermarket a departmentalized store, which sells groceries, dairy products, meats, and produce along with some nonfood items

superstore any store that is bigger than what is normally found in an area selling a specific category of merchandise

tactics techniques used to reach an objective

target market the specific group or groups of consumers on which a retailer focuses its marketing activities

tariff tax on goods coming into a country

top-down planning involves the top level of management estimating total sales for the upcoming period

trade association an organization of businesses that have similar characteristics for the purpose of providing various services to its members, such as updates on current trends and market conditions

trade discount a discount offered to buyers based on the manufacturer's list price

trade show show held at convention centers or exhibition halls on a periodic basis to showcase the latest merchandise in a particular product category

transfer merchandise that is either sent to or received from another store in a chain

trend a change or movement in a general direction

UPC universal product codes for merchandise that are found in bar codes on the merchandise

ultimatum a final proposal or offer which, if not accepted, will end negotiations

undifferentiated target marketing involves an attempt by retailers to please all consumers

unit control an inventory control system that tracks the movement of specific units of merchandise

variable expenses store expenses that change in a direct relationship to sales

velocity the speed with which products move through the product life cycle

vendor an organization or individual who supplies merchandise to retail stores

vendor diary brief summaries of a store's dealings with each vendor with whom it does business

vendor-owned store retail store owned and operated by the manufacturer

visual merchandising includes the layout of store facilities and the placement of merchandise in the store to stimulate customer desire

want slip system involves keeping a record of customer requests for merchandise not in stock, in order to make future purchases for the store

warehouse club huge warehouses that offer a limited number of product lines to customers in large quantities, usually with no frills, little sales assistance, no decor, and no deliveries

warehouse requisition plan a type of centralized buying that occurs when in-store buyers must make merchandise purchases from the chain's warehouse, which houses merchandise selections that have already been purchased by central buyers

wholesaler an organization that purchases merchandise from a manufacturer in large quantities and resells the goods in smaller amounts to retailers

Index

A

accuracy
  of forecasts, 194, 205, 206
  in inventory control, 282, 285,
    300–301
actual sales, 228
additional markups, 289, 436
advance dating terms, 398
advance orders, 407
advertising, 78, 105, 447–48, 461–62
  cooperative, 316, 317f, 399, 457
  Internet and, 135–36
  online, 16, 17f
  price and, 107
  private brands and, 401
  profitability and, 220
  reducing costs of, 216
  turnover and, 210
affinity analysis, 143
African Americans, 134
age groups, spending patterns and,
    132–34
  See also baby boomers
age range, population projections,
    130t
Albertson's grocery chain, 75, 123,
    125
Alcala's Western Wear, 84
Aldi (German retailer), 355
allowances, 399
AllRetailJobs.com, 63–64
Amazon.com, 11, 15–16

American Customer Satisfaction
    Index, 33
America's Research Group, 187
analysis
  market-based, 219–20
  price and performance, 143
  quantitative, 46–47, 319
  sales, 229
  vendor performance, 318–21
analytical ability, 50
Andersen Consulting's Retail Place,
    154
anticipation, 398
apparel industry, 413–14
  globalization of, 346
apparelsearch.com, 108
AquaMarin, 317f
assistant buyer, 42–43, 51, 55
assistant department manager, 55t
assistant store manager, 55t
associations, in data mining, 141–42
assortment, 72, 138, 222, 314
  job lot, 405
  private brands and, 401
assortment planning, 222, 249–75
  balance in, 257–58, 264
  breadth and depth in, 256–58, 266
  factors affecting, 252–58
  forecasting services and, 273–74
  merchandise classifications,
    258–64, 265
  plus-sizes and, 262–63, 274–75
  preparation, 264–68
  problem illustration, 266–68

assortment planning *(continued)*
  review activities, 269–72
  selection factors and, 261–64
  types of merchandise, 253–54
automatic markdowns, 434
automatic reordering systems,
  43–44, 281
automobile market, 167, 346
  Buy American campaign and,
    358–59
  smart cars, 164, 165, 183–84
availability, of products, 159
average stock, 208, 210

B

baby boomers, 132, 135*f*, 136
  aging of, 26, 153–54
back orders, 407
balanced assortment, 257–58
bar coding, 281, 291, 294, 301, 323
  Quick Response system and, 292
  UPC, 280, 292
bargaining, with vendors, 382
  See also negotiation, with vendors
basic merchandise, 39, 69, 253–54
  Quick Response systems and, 293
  wholesale prices of, 436
basic stock list, 237
basic stock planning, 235, 237
Bed Bath & Beyond, 89
behavioristic data, 8
Benetton, 107, 346, 348, 403
birthrates, 131
B.J.'s Wholesale Club, 19
Bloom stores, 124–25
BOM (beginning of the month)
    inventory, 225, 226
  planned, 230–31, 234
BOM (beginning of the month)
    stock levels, 207
Bottom Dollar, 124, 125

bottom-up planning, 223*f*, 224
Bowles, Crandall Close, 391
brand, 261
brand loyalty, 152, 254, 417
brand names, 174–75, 331
  See also national brands; private
    brands
Brazil, 356, 391
breadth, product line, 256–57, 265,
  266
bricks-and-morter retailers, 15
Bristol Farms, 125
broad and shallow assortment plan,
  257
broker, 310
budget
  approval of, 82, 101
  limits of, 261
  preparation of, 45, 222
  for promotion, 456–57
Burlington Coat Factory, 405
business casual, 162, 186–88
business conditions, 367
business owners, 19
*Business Publication Rates and
  Data,* 199
Buy American campaigns, 348–50,
  358–59
buyer, 37–66
  assistant buyer and, 42–43
  career paths, 51–54
  changing role of, 43–45, 65–66
  contacts with vendors, 311–12
  decision making by, 4
  duties and responsibilities, 41–42
  employment forecasts, 56–57
  fads and, 186
  job of, 37–45
  merchandise manager and, 45–47
  merchandising and, 28
  planning for career in, 47–58
  qualifications needed, 47–51
  quality testing by, 402*f*
  Quick Response systems and, 295

retail organizational structure and, 40–41
review activities, 60–61
specialization and, 41
trends and, 65–66
vendor relationships, 65–66, 318, 322–23
buying function, 67–92
centralized, 76–79
for chain stores, 75–79
departmentalization and, 79–81
at department stores, 71–72, 87–90
at different retail formats, 70–75
managing, 45–47
organizational structure and, 79–83
review activities, 86–87
at small independent retailers, 83–85, 90–92
types of products in, 67–70
buying motivation, 136–39
buying offices, 109–17
foreign, 345
market visits and, 367, 368, 370
purpose and importance of, 109
selecting, 114–16
services provided by, 111–13
trends influencing, 116–17
types of, 113–14
buying plans. *See* open-to-buy planning; six-month merchandise plan
buying trips, 343
See also market trips

C

Calvin Klein, 107, 331
Cambodia, 344*t*
Canada, 23, 122, 335, 356
NAFTA and, 346
cannibalization, 258
career ladders/paths, 53–54

career planning, 37
Caribbean Basin, sourcing in, 347
Carol Hoffman, 110*t*
Carrefour, 335, 336*t*
cash discounts, 316, 397–98, 426
cash flow, 289
casual Fridays, 162, 186–88
catalog database, 120–21
catalog manager, 55*t*
catalogue marketing, 12–13
Lillian Vernon, 466–68
online, 16
Web-based, 12, 13
catalogue retailers, 10, 11*f*
category killers, 20
category managers, 65
Catherine's, 274
celebrities, 274, 452*f*
Census Bureau, U.S., 98, 131, 132, 199, 200
on Hispanics, 151, 152
centralized buying, 76–79
drawbacks in, 78–79
central market, 363
central merchandise plan, 76–77
chain stores, 91
buying for, 75–79
merchandise transfers at, 283
See also grocery chains; *specific chains*
change, 163
revolutionary *vs.* evolutionary, 164
character licensing, 176*f*, 177
children, character licensing and, 176*f*, 177
children's wear, sizing of, 339*t*
China, 356, 391
economic growth in, 334–35
recalled products made in, 347, 356–58
Circuit City, 22
classic styles, 166
classifications, merchandise, 258–64, 265

clicks-and-morter retailers, 15. *See also* Internet retailing

closeouts, 331, 442

clustering, in data mining, 142

COD (collect on delivery), 398

coding, for merchandise, 260

collaborator, 380

college education, 50

color, assortment plan and, 263, 266, 267

commissionaires, 345

commission office, 113–14

communication
  buyer and, 49
  buyer-vendor, 323
  with buying office, 115, 116
  online, 16
  with sales associates, 75
  written, 79

comparison shoppers, 106–7

competition, 40, 197, 291
  fads and, 167
  fashion leadership and, 166
  marketing research and, 97
  meeting prices of, 107
  pricing and, 431–32
  product line and, 157
  small retailers and, 84
  source tagging and, 416

competitive price analysis, 142

compromise, in negotiation, 382–83

computer-aided design, 198

computer literacy, 50–51

computers, 323
  automatic reordering systems, 43–44
  database marketing and, 145
  data warehousing and, 139
  inventory control, 280–81, 285–86
  teen market, 133*f*, 135
  See also Internet

concentrated target marketing, 9–10

consolidation, 21–22, 65
  in buying departments, 45, 57
  of buying offices, 116

supermarkets and, 74
  of vendors, 323–24
  warehouse clubs and, 19

consumer advisory panels, 103, 105

Consumer Buying Indicators, 199

consumer demand, 101, 286

consumer focus groups, 121

consumer polls, 247

Consumer Reports, 444

consumers, 124–54
  brands and, 175
  changing demographics, 128–29
  confidence of, 247
  identifying changes, 130–36
  interviews of, 99*f*
  lifestyle trends, 134–36
  loyalty cards and, 123
  marketing concept and, 5–6
  motivation of, 136–39
  targeting, 6–9
  See also customers

control department, 80, 82, 101, 194

convenience, 138

convenience products, 159, 254

cooperative advertising, 316, 317*f*, 399, 457

coordination, 46, 194

cosmetics, 315

Costco, 19, 336*t*

cost method, inventory valuation, 287–88

cost of goods, 423

costs, foreign sourcing and, 337, 340, 342

cost savings, 311

coupons, 453*f*, 454, 461

Crafted with Pride in the USA, 348–50

Crate & Barrel, 329

Creative Marketplace, 198

creativity, 48

credit card information, 16, 34, 145
  sales forecasts and, 247

credit cards, 25

credit standing, 113, 340, 343

Croscill Factory Stores, 331

culture, American, 348

customer contacts, 354

customer database, 26–27, 35, 120
  data mining, 141–43
  data warehousing, 139–41

customer demand
  promotions and, 458
  seasonal basics and, 253

customer loyalty, 34, 145, 146, 254
  stockouts and, 299

customer loyalty cards, 122–23

customer needs, 144, 163
  assortment plan and, 264
  private brand and, 401, 417–18

customer profile, 97

customer relationships, 12

customers
  assortment plan and, 252
  brand preferences of, 265–66
  changing base, 25–26
  classification of, 34–35
  comparison shoppers, 106–7
  day-to-day contact with, 83
  purchase profiles of, 219
  style assessment, 104*f*
  targeting current, 34–35

customer satisfaction, 102, 145

customer service, 28, 88, 139, 450–51
  Lowe's and, 33
  small retailers and, 84–85, 90, 92
  value and, 23, 25

customer surveys, 35, 98, 103, 121, 136, 197

customization, 147, 178, 181–82

CVS Drug Stores, 123

D

data, 65, 96
  out-of-date, 199
  See also decision making, data for

database, merchandise management, 245–46

database marketing, 26–27, 143–47
  goals of, 146–47

data mining, 141–43

data warehousing, 139–41

dating terms, 397–98

decentralization, 79

decision making, 4–5, 473–75
  assortment planning and, 250
  customer analysis and, 140
  foreign sources and, 340–42
  group, 475
  pricing, 437
  product placement, 220
  product selection, 155–58
  promotion, 461
  risks in, 69
  in sales forecasts, 202–11

decision making, data for, 95–125, 141
  analyzing and interpreting, 99–100
  buying offices and, 109–17
  external sources of, 103–9
  internal sources of, 100–102
  loyalty cards, 122–23
  marketing research and, 96–100, 120–22
  review activities, 118–20

decline stage, in product life cycle, 171

décor merchandise, 163

delivery, 111, 237, 310
  costs, 65
  foreign sources and, 338
  timely, 323, 409

Dell Computers, 11

demographic data, 8, 26, 120, 195
  households, 131–32
  marital status and birthrates, 131

demographic trends, 128–29

departmentalization, 79–81

department manager, 55*t*

department stores, 58, 71–72
 budget departments, 406
 buyer role in, 40
 catalog sales by, 13
 centralized buying for, 76
 declining sales at, 22, 73*f*
 future of, 89–90
 inventory management in, 43, 44
 Liz Claiborne and, 414
 mergers of, 89
 plus sizes and, 275
 specialized, 72
 teen boards for, 103
 vendor-owned, 324
 warehousing for, 77
depth, product line, 257–58, 266
designer names, 331
designers, 324
destination stores, 23
 furniture stores as, 24*f*
digital catalogs, 16
Dillard's, 43, 89, 198, 255
direct marketing, 11–12
discount department stores, 72
discounters, 71, 74
 Bottom Dollar, 124, 125
 off-price retailers, 405–6
 pricing policies of, 430
 supercenters of, 18
discounts, 396–98
 cash, 82, 316, 397–98, 426
 estimating, 426
 quantity, 311, 314, 395, 396
 seasonal, 396
 trade, 396–97
disgruntled shoppers, 34
Disney corporation, 177
displays. *See* visual merchandising
distribution policies, 315
district manager, 55*t*
diversity
 retail formats and, 124–25
dollar control systems, 287
Dollar General, 89, 215, 216
Dollar Tree, 441–43
Donegar Consulting, 110*t*

Donegar Creative Services, 273–74
Donegar Group, 109, 110*t*, 273
Donnelly (research house), 145
Dow Jones average, 196*f*, 247
downward flow theory, 172–73
drive, 48
Dun & Bradstreet, 207
durability, 160
durables, 160
duty, 341

E

early adopters, 171, 185
EAS (electronic article surveillance),
 415–16
economic conditions
 forecasting and, 97*t*, 194, 195,
 196*f*, 200
 holiday sales and, 247
 pricing and, 432–33
Eddie Bauer, 13, 22, 73
 private labels of, 175, 403
EDI. *See* electronic data interchange
education, 50. *See also* training programs
Egghead Software, 12
electronic data interchange (EDI),
 292–93, 294–95, 322
electronic product code (EPC),
 301–2
electronic retailing, 13–17
e-mail, 66, 469
emotional buying motives, 138
employee training, 295
 See also sales associates
The Encyclopedia of Associations,
 199
enthusiasm, 48
environmental issues, 197
EOM (end of month) dating terms,
 397

EOM (end of month) inventory, 226
Ernst & Young (auditor), 217
e-tailing, 469
   See also Internet retailing
ethnic origin, 134
etiquette tips, 344*t*
Europe, fashion influence and, 338
even pricing, 430
evolutionary changes, 164
exception reports, 287
exchange privilege, 316
exclusive distribution, 315
exclusivity, private brands and, 158,
   255, 400, 402
expenses, price and, 423, 425
experience, 51
expositions, 364
   See also trade shows
external forces, 195
extra dating terms, 397–98

F

factory outlet stores, 330–31
factory visits, 373
fads, 166–68, 172*f*, 184–86
Family Dollar, 89, 215–16
Far East, competition from, 346, 348
fashion, 65, 161
   Latin-influenced, 152
   ripple effects of, 163
   trends and theories, 166
fashion adoption theories, 171–74
fashion appeal, 161–63
Fashion Bug, 274
fashion colors, 266
fashion coordinator, 55*t*
fashion cycle, 338
fashion designers, 324
fashion director, 55*t*
fashion forecasters, 107
fashion image, 403

   See also image
fashion leadership, 314, 338
fashion merchandise, 39, 69, 253–54
   markdowns on, 434
   markups on, 436
   Quick Response systems and, 293
   short sales life of, 77
fashion.net, 108
fashion news, 105
fashion show, Webcast, 469, 470
fashion trends, 338. *See also* trends
Federal Trade Commission, 300–301
FIFO (first in first out) method, 288
Filene's Basement, 434
finance officer, 101
Fingerhut, 142
fit, 182
fixed expenses, 423
fixed-fee office, 113
fixturing and visuals, 322
flexibility, 49, 377
FOB destination, charges reversed,
   399
FOB destination, freight prepaid,
   399
FOB destination (store), 398
FOB origin (factory), 398
FOB shipping point, 399
focus groups, 198
Food Lion supermarkets, 74–75,
   124
food retailing trends. *See* grocery
   store chains
footwear, customized, 182
forecasting, 174, 191–220, 246
   accuracy of, 194, 205, 206
   adjustments in, 202, 205
   for basic merchandise, 69
   buyer and, 65
   changes in sales potential, 200
   data mining and, 142, 197–99
   decisions in, 202–11
   demographic trends, 129
   developing, 195–202

forecasting *(continued)*
  economic data for, 97*t,* 194, 195,
    196*f,* 200
  fashion and, 39
  future direction of, 211
  holiday sales, 247–48
  inventory and, 202–3, 206–8
  market-based analysis, 219–20
  merchandise manager and, 201–2
  process for, 199–202
  review activities, 212–14
  sales records and, 193, 200, 203
  scope of, 192–94
  weather forecasts and, 217–18

forecasting services, 273–74

foreign sources, 333–59, 391–92
  Buy American campaigns and,
    348–50, 358–59
  buying decision and, 340–42
  Chinese recalls, 347, 356–58
  drawbacks to buying from, 338,
    340
  etiquette tips when visiting, 344*t*
  foreign markets and, 334–35
  globalization and, 345–48
  locating, 342–45
  lower wages and, 342, 346–47, 391
  purchasing from, 335, 337–42
  reasons to buy from, 337–38
  review activities, 351–53
  Zara and rapid response, 353–54

France, 344*t,* 359

FreddyandMa.com, 182

free on board. *See* FOB

free trade agreements, 335, 346, 348

frequency, promotions and, 459

functional departmentalization,
    79–80, 81*f*

funds, 340
  See also credit

furniture market, 363, 389–90

furniture stores, 24*f*
  See also IKEA

G

The Gap, 23, 40, 76, 255, 346, 354
  private labels of, 403

GATT (General Agreement on Tar-
    iffs and Trade), 335

General Nutrition Centers, 178

generic brands, 175, 256

geographic data, 8

geographic departmentalization, 81

Germany, Wal-Mart in, 346, 355

globalization, 23
  foreign sources and, 345–48
  Wal-Mart and, 356

global market, 334, 341
  Internet retailing and, 16

GMROI (gross margin return on
    inventory), 289–90

goal setting, 48

government agencies, 98

Great Britain, 122

Greece, 344*t*

green products, 185

grocery chains, 74–75, 122, 124
  assortment plan and, 252
  brand names at, 175
  instant coupons at, 454
  preferred selling space in, 399
  pricing, 403
  profit and turnover at, 413
  promotions by, 459
  trends in, 150–51
  See also supermarkets

gross margin, 220
  return on inventory (GMROI),
    289–90

growth stage, in product life cycle,
    170–71

H

Halston, 173

handbags, customized, 182

hard lines, 69
Harris poll, 198
haute couture, 172–73
HDA International, 110*t*
Henry Donegar Associates, 110*t*
Here & There (forecaster), 107, 110*t*
High Point (NC) furniture market in,
    389, 390
Hispanic market, 134, 151–52
holiday sales, forecasting, 247–48
Home Depot, 336*t*
    customer service at, 25
    Expo Design Centers, 329
    Lowes compared, 32–33
    small retailers and, 91
    source tagging at, 416
home fashions, 175, 371*t*
    décor merchandise, 163
Hong Kong, 346, 363
horizontal flow theory, 173
hot item, 112
human behavior, 377
human relations skills, 49
hypermarkets, 18

I

identification number, 259
Identity Information Protection Act,
    303
i2i Retail.com, 374
IKEA, 25, 328–29, 348
    as destination store, 23
image, 6, 177, 403
    assortment and, 250
    store, 90, 165–66, 185, 314, 457
importers, 345
import tax, 341
impulse products, 159
independent buying offices, 113
India, 334, 335, 344*t*, 391
information technology (IT), 82

initial markup percentage, 424–25,
    427
innovation, 48, 91, 164–65
innovators, 170
Inside Retailing (report), 108
interactive technology, 27, 31–32
intermediaries, 345
    See also middlemen
internal forces, 195, 203
International Mass Retail Associa-
    tion, 247
international sales, 335
    See also global market
Internet, 163
    advertising on, 135–36
    buying office and, 116
    e-mail and, 66
    job posts on, 58, 63–64
    online showrooms, 374
    product customization on, 178,
        181–82
    as research tool, 108
Internet (online) retailing, 15–17,
    359, 467, 469
    catalog retailing and, 12, 13
    direct marketing and, 12
    Lands' End, 31–32
internship programs, 51, 62–63
introduction stage, in product life
    cycle, 170
inventory, 467
    assortment planning and, 251
    BOM, 225, 226, 230–31, 234
    coding system for, 260
    sales forecasts and, 202–3, 206–8
    turnover of, 246
inventory control systems, 225,
    277–303
    accuracy in, 282, 285, 300–301
    automatic reordering systems,
        43–44, 281
    calculations in, 287–90
    carrying costs and, 295*f*
    computerized, 280–81, 285–86
    establishing and using, 282–87
    GMROI and, 289–90

inventory control systems
    (continued)
  markdowns and, 279, 289, 293, 294
  periodic systems, 281–82
  perpetual control, 279–81
  Quick Response, 290–95, 298–99
  return records, 284*f*, 285
  review activities, 296–98
  RFID technology and, 301–3
  scanners in, 280, 281*f*, 292,
      300–301
inventory records, 100–101
invoices, 82
irregulars, 406
IT. *See* information technology l

J

Jaclyn Smith brand, 158, 175, 403
Japan, 23, 122, 335, 344*t*
  Talbot's in, 347–48
JCPenney, 40, 72, 77
  buying decisions at, 79
  catalog marketing by, 12, 13
  centralized buying at, 76
  Hispanic market and, 134
  Liz Claiborne and, 413, 414
  national brands at, 158
  outlet stores of, 73
  private brand of, 175, 401
job lot, 405
job promotions, 52
jobs, 55–56*t*
  Internet search, 58, 63–64
  résumé for, 57–58, 64

K

key resources, 313–14
keystoning, 428
kiosks, 14–15, 178
Kmart, 18, 22, 72, 442
  customer call boxes at, 451
  private brands at, 158, 175, 403
  Sears and, 71, 89
  TV promotion monitors, 453
Kohl's, 72, 87–88, 89, 274
Korea, Republic of, 346
Kroger grocery chain, 18, 75, 336*t*

L

labor costs/wages
  foreign sources and, 342, 346–47,
    391
laggards, 171
landed cost, 342
Lands' End, 13, 140
  customization at, 181–82
  online sales of, 16, 31–32
  private brands at, 175
Lane Bryant, 76, 274
language, foreign sourcing and, 343
Las Vegas, furniture market in, 389,
  390
late adopters, 171
Latinos. *See* Hispanics
leadership, buyer, 49
letter of credit, 343
Levine, Leon, 215
liability, 357
licensed products, 175–77
lifestyle trends, 134–36, 197
LIFO (last in first out) method, 288
The Limited, 22, 76, 255
  private labels of, 403
"living large" lifestyle, 136
Liz Claiborne, 256, 324, 331, 403,
  413–14
L.L. Bean, 10, 13, 22
long-term forecasts, 193
loss leaders, 430
Lowe's, 20, 32–33, 91

loyalty, customer. *See* customer loyalty
loyalty cards, 122–23

M

Macy's, 71, 72, 89, 401, 413
  Flower Show, 455*f*
  Hispanic market and, 134
  internship program at, 51, 62–63
  private brand at, 175
  Thanksgiving Parade and, 453
magazines, 105
Magnolia Hi-Fi, 84–85
makeup, 152
Malaysia, 344*t*
management, 101, 198
  Buy American campaign and, 349
  career path in, 54*f*
  centralized buying and, 77
  fashion decisions and, 163
  jobs in, 53, 55–56*t*
  market segments and, 72
  merchandise selection and, 79
  positions in, 53
  price agreement plan and, 78
  product category and, 219
  promotional budget and, 457
  Quick Response systems and, 293
  strategy for, 6, 10
management trainee, 55*t*
management training program, 51
manual inventory control, 280
manufacturers, 309
  coop advertising and, 457
  outlet stores of, 330–31
  price reductions and, 395
  seconds and irregulars, 406
  visits to, 373
  See also vendor
manufacturer's representatives, 310
Margit Publications, 110*t*
marital status, 131

markdown cancellations, 289, 435–36
markdown percentage, 434–35
markdowns, 21, 425–26, 444
  controlling, 46
  data mining and, 143
  estimating, 417
  increase in, 241
  inventory control and, 279, 289, 293, 294
  of licensed products, 177
  opportunity identification, 143
  overbuying and, 241, 253, 433, 457
  reasons for, 433–34
  recording, 434–35
  reducing amount of, 225
  stock turnover and, 210
  timing of, 434
market, 6
  volatility of, 194
market-based analysis, 219–20
marketing concept, 5
marketing orientation, 5–10
marketing research, 96–100, 120–22
marketing research director, 55*t*
marketing strategies, 201, 202
  catalog, 10, 12–13
  database, 26–27, 143–47
  direct, 11–12
  inventory control and, 279
  kiosk, 14–15
Market4Retail.com, 374
market segment, 6–9, 72, 83
market segmentation, 8
market share, 437
market trends. *See* trends
market trips, 112
  frequency of, 365–67
  purposes of, 365
market visits, 312–13, 361–92
  buying office and, 367, 368, 370
  factory visits, 373
  furniture market, 363, 389–90
  negotiation strategies, 362, 374–84

market visits *(continued)*
  online showrooms, 374
  preparing for, 362–71
  sample week, 369–70
  types of markets and, 363–64
  visiting vendors, 371–73
market weeks, 364
markup percentage, 423–25, 431
markups, 315, 422–24, 426, 437
  additional, 289, 436
  data mining and, 143
  initial, 225, 235
  opportunity identification, 143
  private brand and, 402
Marshall's, 405
Maslow's hierarchy of needs, 137–38
mass customization, 147, 178, 181–82
material, selection of, 263–64
math formulas, 471–72
Mattel Inc., 357
maturity stage, in product life cycle, 171
maximum, 237
Mazur, Paul M., 80
media, 448
Mediamark Research, 132
members-only stores, 18–19
men's wear
  necktie sales, 187–88
  sizing of, 339t
Menu Foods, Inc., 356, 357
merchandise
  basic, 39, 69, 253–54, 293, 436
  market visits and, 365
  outlet store mix, 330–31
  preticketing of, 318
  pricing of, 372 *(See also* price and pricing)
  unavailability of, 337
  vendors and, 314–15
  See also fashion merchandise
merchandise analyst, 56t
merchandise/apparel mart, 363–64
merchandise assortment. *See* assortment

merchandise-broker office, 113–14
merchandise classifications, 258–64
  subclassifications and, 258–60, 261, 265
merchandise control systems, 287
  See also inventory control systems
merchandise manager, 45–47, 56t, 101
  sales forecasts and, 201–2
merchandise mix, 88, 155
merchandise plan, 223, 367
  assortment planning and, 251
  calculations for, 472
  central, 76–77
  inventory calculations and, 287
  See also planning
merchandise policies, 366
merchandise selection, 48, 158
merchandise transfers, 283
merchandising
  career path in, 53f, 56t
  knowledge and skills in, 49–51
  management of, 222–24
merchandising department, 80, 82–83
merchandising expenses, 294
merchandising systems, 88
merchant middlemen, 309–10
mergers and acquisitions, 57, 89, 109
Mervyn's, 44
meteorology, 217–18
Metro AG, 336t, 355
Metromail (research house), 145
Mexico, 23, 344t, 356, 391
  NAFTA and, 335, 346
microwave ovens, 167
middlemen, 308
  foreign sources and, 345
  merchant, 309–10
  nonmerchant, 310
minimum, 237
model stock, 264–65
  Quick Response and, 291–92
Money magazine, 12–13

most-favored-nation status, 341
movies, licensed products and, 177, 388
multicultural society, 26
multisegment target marketing, 10
multitasking, 134

N

NAFTA (North American Free Trade Agreement), 335, 346, 348
narrow and deep assortment plan, 257
national brands, 72, 88, 90, 158, 174–75
  private brands compared, 255–56, 315, 400, 401–3
National Conference on Weights and Measures (NCWM), 300–301
nationalistic marketing. *See* Buy American campaigns
National Retail Federation, 80, 106, 207, 247, 423
  merchandise classification and, 260
  top 100 retailers of, 442
needs, hierarchy of, 137–38
negotiation, with vendors, 362, 374–84
  bargaining and compromise in, 382–83
  building rapport in, 378
  checklist for, 383
  determining objectives in, 377
  developing strategy, 379–84
  nonverbal clues in, 379
  outcomes of, 383–84
  personality styles in, 380
  probing questions in, 378–79
  setting the stage for, 378–79
  skills to develop in, 376–77
  special buying situations, 400–406
  tactics in, 380–82
  terms of sale, 394–400
  vendor's position in, 376
  your position in, 376
Neiman Marcus, 6, 23, 89, 145
  buying office of, 114
networking, 57
New Balance, 302
newspapers, 98, 105
New York City, 109, 363, 387, 453
niche internet job sites, 64
niche marketing, 9, 135, 402
  further specialization in, 22–23
Nike, 167, 181, 324
nondurables, 160
nonmerchant middlemen, 310
Nordstrom Rack, 73
Nordstrom's, 25, 89, 451

O

obesity, 136, 274
obsolescence, 163
Occupational Outlook Handbook, 56
odd-cent pricing, 430
Office Depot, 20
off-price retailers, 405–6
off-retail percentage, 435
Old Navy, 76
on consignment, 400
one-stop shopping, 71, 74, 89, 138
  marts and, 364, 390
one-to-one marketing. *See* database marketing
online retailing, 15, 359, 467
  See also Internet retailing
Online Services, 110*t*
online showrooms, 374
on memorandum, 400
open orders, 407

open-to-buy planning, 239–41, 251
  benefits and uses of, 240–41
  calculations for, 239–40
  definition of, 239
operations department, 80
order cancellation, 241
ordinary dating terms, 397
organizational chart
outlet stores, 73–74, 330–31, 443–44
overbuying, 241, 253, 433, 457
over-55 market, 129, 132, 134
  See also baby boomers
overpricing, 433
overruns, 405
overstocking, 279

P

packaging, vendors and, 322–23,
  403
Parisian, 72, 450–51
partner brands, 414
partnerships with vendors, 310, 314,
  321, 442
  buyers and, 65–66
  negotiation and, 382, 384
  Quick Response systems and, 291,
    293, 299
  substitutions and, 409
Patagonia, 13
patronage buying motives, 138–39
penetration policies, 430
performance standards, 46–47
periodic control systems, 281–82
perpetual control system, 279–81
"perpetual sale" strategy, 21
personal computers, teens and, 133*f*
personality traits, 48
personal selling, 450–51, 462
personnel, 158
  See also sales associates

Philippines, 344*t*, 347
planned EOM inventory, 232, 234
planned net sales, 225
planned purchases at cost, 226,
  234–35, 240
planned purchases at retail, 226,
  233–34, 235, 240
planned reductions, 226, 232–33,
  234
planned sales, 228–30
planned stock levels, 471
planner/distributor, 44
planning, 221–48
  calculations for, 472
  forecasting and, 194
  merchandise manager and, 45
  open-to-buy, 239–41, 251
  review activities, 242–45
  six-month merchandise plan,
    224–35
  top-down *vs.* bottom-up, 223–24
  See also assortment planning
plus-size market, 262–63, 274–75
Polo, 73, 315
positioning, 6
POS (point-of-sale) cash register, 44,
  290, 292
press releases, 451
price agreement plan, 77–78
price analysis, competitive, 142
price and pricing, 88, 92, 421–44
  basic calculations, 471
  brand and, 417
  competition and, 431–32
  Dollar Tree, 441–43
  economic conditions, 432–33
  establishing retail prices, 422–26
  evaluating decisions, 437
  outlet stores and, 330
  retail price, 422–35
  review activities, 438–41
  scanner errors, 300–301
  vendors and, 314, 372
  Wal-Mart and, 355
  See also markup

price cutting, 216, 217

price decline guarantee, 395

price discrimination, 395

price floor, 428

price lines, 266

price lining, 430–31

price negotiation, 394–95

Price Point Buying, 110*t*

price points, 431

price promotions, 21

price range, 255, 315
  assortment plan and, 261–62

price-ticket stub, 283

price war, 432

PriceWaterhouseCoopers, 247

pricing
  problem illustrations for, 426–28
  store policies regarding, 429–31
  See also retail price

primary data, 98–99, 102, 197–98

print advertising
  for online retailers, 16, 17*f*

privacy, invasion of, 16, 146, 303

private brands, 90, 175, 264, 274,
      347, 416–18
  buyer and, 44–45
  buying office and, 112
  data mining analysis and, 143
  exclusivity of, 158, 255, 400, 402
  manufacturer and, 309
  national brands compared,
      255–56, 315, 400, 401–3, 416
  negotiations, 400–404
  profit and, 416, 417, 432
  Talbots, 121

private buying offices, 114

product assortment. *See* assortment

product category, 219

product development, 165

product elimination, 174

product features, 160–61, 460

product information, 450

product-knowledge training, 82

product lifecyles, 169–71, 172*f*, 173,
      174

product line, 155–56
  in assortment planning, 256–58

product-line departmentalization,
      80–81

product placement, 220

product trends, 98, 155–88
  creating product differences,
      174–78
  durability and quality, 160
  fads, 166–68, 172*f*, 184–86
  fashion appeal, 161–63
  licensed products, 175–77
  mass customization, 178, 181–82
  new products, 164–66
  review activities, 179–81
  selection decisions, 155–58
  types purchased, 158–68

professional associations, 199

profit and loss statements, 281

profit margins, 21

profits, 65, 91, 210, 437
  advertising and, 220
  assortment plan and, 225, 258
  calculations for, 472
  estimate, 425
  GMROI measure of, 289–90
  private label and, 416, 417, 432
  standardization and, 75
  turnover and, 423

promotional activities, 112, 445–70
  budget for, 456–57
  cooperative advertising in, 457
  coordination of, 461–63
  developing plan for, 454–61
  evaluating, 460–61
  Lillian Vernon, 466–68
  merchandise selection for, 458–59
  objectives in, 454, 456
  online, 16
  personal selling, 450–51, 462
  private brands and, 401
  publicity, 451–52
  retail, 446, 447–54
  review activities, 464–65

promotional activities *(continued)*
  scheduling, 459
  special events, 451, 452–53
  vendor-supported, 399
  visual merchandising, 401, 448–50
  See also advertising
promotional buying, 404
promotional mix, 447, 456
promotional performance analysis, 143
promotional price analysis, 143
promotion department, 80, 82
psychographic data, 8, 146
psychographic trends, 134
publicity, 451–52
Public Pulse (newsletter), 108
Publix, 417
purchase commitment, 338
purchase order, 291, 373
  followup on, 409
  parts of, 407, 409
  placement of, 406–9
purchase quotas, 309
purchase records, 283
purchasing, 393–418
  private brands and, 400–404, 416–18
  source tagging and, 399, 415–16
  special buying conditions, 400–406
  terms of sale, 394–400
purchasing agent, 65

Q

qualifications, for buyers, 47–51
quality, 25, 176, 314, 467
  checks for, 373, 409
  durability and, 160
  foreign sources and, 337
  generic brands, 256
  irregulars and seconds, 406
  price range and, 255, 431
  private brand and, 401, 402, 403
  sourcing strategies and, 350
  testing, 402f
quantitative performance, 46–47, 319
quantity checks, 409
quantity discounts, 311, 314, 395, 396
Quick Response system, 290–95
  implementing, 293–94, 298–99
  measuring impact of, 294–95
  requirements for, 291–93
quotas, 340, 341–42

R

R. L. Polk (research house), 145
rack jobbers, 311
Ralcorp Holdings Inc., 417
Ralph Lauren, 256, 315
rational buying motives, 137–38
reach, of promotions, 459
recalled products, 356–57, 417
Record-Rama Sound Archives, 84
reductions, planning for, 425–26
  See also discounts; markdowns; shrinkage
refund slip, 285
regional distribution centers, 77
regular orders, 407
relationship marketing. *See* database marketing
reorder period, 237
reorders, 407
  automatic systems, 43–44, 281
reporting services, 108
research, 108
  buying offices and, 112
  marketing, 96–100, 120–22
research houses, 145
reserve, 237
résumé, 57–58, 64
retail formats, 10–20

buying at different, 70–75
customer diversity and, 124–25
direct marketing, 11–12
electronic, 13–17
superstores, 18–20
retailing and retailers
buying office of, 114
careers and jobs in, 55–56*t*, 58, 63–64
classification of, 71
fast-changing environment of, 4
globalization of, 345–48
merchandise planning by, 222–23
off-price, 405–6
online marketplaces and, 374
organizational structure of, 40–41
partnership with vendors, 310
positioning in, 6
Quick Response system and, 293, 294
rack jobbers and, 311
size of, and buyer's responsibilities, 41
top global, 335, 336*t*
top ten in U.S., 71*t*
trends and challenges in, 20–28
vendor-owned, 323–24
See also small independent retailers
Retailing Today, 108
retail life span, 331
retail math formulas, 471–72
Retail Merchandiser, 442
Retail Merchandising Service Automation (RMSA), 245–46
retail method, inventory valuation, 388–89
retail price, 422–35
adjustments to, 433–35
elements of, 423
factors affecting, 428–33
suggested, 443
target market and, 428–29
See also markup; price and pricing
retail strategy, 5–6, 10, 215
retail values, 226

return privileges, 399–400
return records, 284*f,* 285
returns, 316
revolutionary change, 164
RFID (radio frequency identification), 301–3
Robinson-Patman Act of 1936, 395
Roger Starch Worldwide, 136
ROG (receipt of goods) dating terms, 397

S

safety standards, 357
Safeway grocery chain, 75
Saks Fifth Avenue, 107, 317*f*
salaried (fixed-fee) buying office, 113
sales, 294
inventory control and, 279
sales analysis, 229
sales associates, 41, 280
centralized buying and, 78
communication with, 75
customer needs and, 102
experienced and courteous, 139
informal surveys by, 98
product knowledge of, 92
promotions and, 461, 462
training of, 82, 84, 317, 322, 450
want slip system and, 101
sales data, 100–101
sales expertise, 84
sales floor visits, 102
sales forecasts, 193–94, 201
markup and, 424–25
in merchandise plan, 228–29
See also forecasting
sales potential, changes in, 200
sales promotion, 447
See also promotional activities
sales promotion manager, 56*t*
sales records, 100–101, 461

assortment plan and, 252
  forecasting and, 193, 200, 203
  inventory and, 283, 285
sales representatives, 312–13, 367
sales volume per week, 237
samples, from vendors, 112
Sam's Club, 19
scanners, 280, 281f, 300–301
  Quick Response system and, 292
Schwarz Untermehmens Treuhand, 336t
Sears, 22, 40, 72, 77, 336t
  centralized buying at, 76
  Kmart and, 71, 89
  meteorologists at, 217
  private brands of, 403
  store brands of, 175
seasonal basics, 253, 442
seasonal discounts, 396
seasonal market trips, 365
seasonal staple, 172f
secondary data, 98, 99, 197, 198–99
seconds and irregulars, 406
selection factors, 261–64
selective distribution, 315
Selexyz (Netherlands), 302
selling points, 460
seniors. *See* over-55 market
Sensormatic, 416
sequences, in data mining, 142
shipping, 77, 111, 310, 323
  FOB terms and, 398–99
  timing of, 409
  See also delivery
shoe classifications, 259t
shopper profile, 219
shopping products, 160
short-term forecasts, 193
showrooms, online, 374
shrinkage, 279, 281, 426
  source tagging and, 415
Singapore, 344t
six-month merchandise plan, 224–35, 236t
  basic stock planning and, 235, 237

components of, 225–28
  inventory control in, 225
  planned BOM inventory, 226, 230–31
  planned purchases at cost, 226, 234–35
  planned purchases at retail, 226, 233–34
  planned reductions in, 226, 232–33
  planned sales in, 228–30
  preparation of, 228–35
  purposes of, 224–25
size
  changing requirements in, 262–63, 266
  foreign sources and, 338–40, 347
size, assortment plan, 267
S&K, 405
skimming, 430
SKUs (stockkeeping units), 20, 280, 292, 299
small independent retailers, 27, 70, 90–92
  buying in, 41, 83–85
  customer service and, 84–85, 90, 92
  decline in, 22
  inventory control at, 282
  market research and, 98
  market visits and, 365
  merchandise plan and, 228
  sales representatives and, 312–13
  specialty, 74
smart cars, 164, 165, 183–84
SmartCode Research, 303
social and cultural awareness, 343
Society for Human Resource Management, 186
soft lines, 67–68
source tagging, 399, 415–16
sourcing. *See* foreign sources
Southeast Asia, 346
Spain, 344t. See also Zara
special buying situations, 400–406
  private brands and, 400–404

special events, 451, 452–53
specialization, in buyer's job, 41
specialized department stores, 72
specialized superstores, 20
special orders, 407
specialty products, 160, 254
specialty stores, 22, 74
    buyer role in, 40
    profit at, 423
specification buying, 404
sports, licensed products and, 176, 177
Springs Industries, 391–92
Sri Lanka, 347
Standard Classification of Merchandise, 260
Staples, 20
SteveMadden.com, 182
Stew Leonard's supermarket, 84
stock control, 318. *See also* inventory control
stock levels, 285, 287
stockouts, 285
    assortment plan and, 252, 258
stock-to-sales ratios, 207–8, 231, 471
stock turnover rate, 208–11, 310, 471
store brand, 175. *See also* private brand
store image, 165–66, 185, 314, 457
    assortment and, 250
    private brand and, 403
store location and layout, 157
store manager, 56*t*, 101
    See also management
store policies, 255
    pricing decisions, 429–31
store promotions, 317
store records, 100
Strategic Weather Services, 217–18
style, 161–62
style assessment, 104*f*
subclassifications, 258–60, 261, 265
substitutions, 409

supercenters, 18
supermarkets, 74–75, 252
    private brands of, 403, 416
    rack jobbers and, 311
superstore retailing, 18–20, 74
SuperTarget, 18, 71
Survey of Buying Power, 200
The Survey of Buying Power, 199
surveys, of customers, 35, 103, 121
Syms, 405

T

tactics, in negotiation, 380–82
Taiwan, 346
Talbot's, 13
    in Japan, 347–48
    marketing research by, 120–22
Target Corp., 23, 72, 74, 89, 302, 329, 336*t*, 442
    supercenters of, 18, 71
    as upscale Wal-Mart, 21
target market, 9, 26, 157
    characteristics of, 265
    lifestyle changes in, 197
    retail price and, 428–29
target marketing, types of, 9–10
tariffs, 335, 341
teamwork, 42–43, 47
technology, 27
    buyer and, 65, 66
    communication and, 323
    electronic data interchange, 322
    fashion changes and, 162–63
    source tagging, 415–16
    toy industry and, 388
teen market, 170
    computers and, 133*f*, 135
    fads and, 167, 185
    Hispanic, 151–52
    teen boards, 103
television, 163
terms, 316

terms of sale, 394–400
  allowances and, 399
  discounts, 395, 396–98
  price negotiation, 394–95
  return privileges, 399–400
  transportation, 398–99
Tesco, 336*t*
timing and timeliness
  of appointments, 372
  of delivery, 323, 409
  with foreign markets, 340
  for markdowns, 434
  of new products, 174
  for shoppers, 134–35, 198
  in vendor negotiations, 381
T.J. Maxx, 405
Tobe, 110*t*
top-down planning, 223–24
TopUSAJobs.com, 64
toy industry, 364
  fads in, 167, 168*f*
  international fair, 387–88
  recall in, 357
Toys "R" Us, 20, 23, 84, 443
Toys Unlimited, 443
trade associations, 98, 106, 107, 199
trade barriers, 335, 346
trade discounts, 396–97
trade publications, 98, 105
trade shows, 106, 364
  foreign sources and, 343
Tradeweave.com, 374
trading blocs, 348
training programs
  management, 51, 55*t*
  sales associates, 82, 84, 317, 450
transfers, 283
transportation, 398–99
  See also shipping
trends, 39, 338
  demographic, 128–29
  forecasting (*See* forecasting)
  lifestyle, 134–36, 197
  merchandise manager and, 46
trends and challenges, in retailing,
  20–28

changing demographics, 25–26
consolidation and shakeouts,
  21–22
customer service, 23, 25, 28
database marketing and, 26–27
globalization, 23
smaller niche markets, 22–23
technology and, 27
too many stores, 21
  See also product trends
Turkey, 347
turnover, 208–11, 225, 246, 413
TV shopping channels, 13–14

U

ultimatums, 382
undifferentiated target marketing, 9
uniqueness, 337
unit control, 280
unit control analyst, 44
UPC (universal price code), 280,
  292
  See also bar coding
upscale image, 177
upward flow theory, 173
urban market, 216

V

value, 138
  customer service and, 23, 25
  price and, 422
  private brand and, 401
value-added programs, 25
Value Retail News, 331, 444
variable expenses, 423
velocity, of product life cycle,
  169–70
vendor diary, 318–19
vendor-owned stores, 323–24

vendors, 140, 307–31
    analyzing performance of, 318–21, 367
    buyers' expectations of, 322–23
    consolidation of, 323–24
    contacting potential, 311–14
    criteria for selecting, 314–18
    distribution policies of, 315
    future trends, 323
    information from, 106
    as key resources, 313–14
    order cancellation and, 241
    outlet stores and, 330–31
    reputation and reliability of, 316
    review activities, 326–27
    sales representatives and, 312–13
    samples from, 112
    services provided by, 316–18
    terms offered, 316
    types of, 308–11
    visiting, 371–73
    See also negotiation with vendors
vendors, partnerships with, 310, 314, 321, 442
    buyers and, 65–66
    negotiation and, 382, 384
    Quick Response systems and, 291, 293, 299
    substitutions and, 409
Vernon, Lillian, 466–68
VF Brands, 298–99
vice president for merchandising, 56t
Victoria's Secret, 468–70
Vietnam, 344t
Visa, 247
vision, 48
visual merchandising, 401, 448–50, 461
vulnerable customers, 34, 35

Buy American campaign of, 348–50
    customer base of, 6, 8, 89
    customer service at, 25
    data warehousing by, 140
    dollar stores and, 216, 441–42
    in Germany, 346, 355
    global expansion of, 23, 356
    people greeting in, 451
    RFID tags at, 302
    Sam's Choice brand at, 175
    small retailers and, 83, 91
    Target compared, 21, 72, 74
want slip system, 101
warehouse clubs, 18–19
warehouse requisition plan, 77
weather forecasts, 217–18
Web sites, 468, 469
    See also Internet; online sales
weekly sales reports, 44
wholesale prices, 288, 436
wholesalers, 309–10
Williams-Sonoma, 140
Winn-Dixie grocery stores, 123
women shoppers, 33
women's wear
    plus-size, 262–63, 274–75
    product life cycle in, 170
    sizing of, 339t
    Zara and rapid response, 353–54
working under pressure, 48
working women, 131–32

Y

Youth Intelligence, 107

W

Wal-Mart Stores, Inc., 18, 21, 22, 89, 336t

Z

Zara, 353–54

Credits

Chapter 1
1.1: Courtesy of Fairchild Publications, Inc.
1.2: The DMA "Economic Impact-U.S. Direct & Interactive Marketing Today," 2002.
1.3: Courtesy: HSN.
1.4: © Lands' End, Inc. Used with permission.
1.5: Courtesy of Fairchild Publications, Inc.
1.6a and **1.6b**: AP

Chapter 2
2.1 and **2.2**: Courtesy of Fairchild Publications, Inc.
2.3 and **2.4**: Courtesy of Macy's Inc.

Chapter 4
4.1: Alamy
4.2: Courtesy of the Doneger Group.

Chapter 5
5.1: Young Consumers Data Overview, Consumer Technographics North America, © Forrester Research.
5.2 Based on information from *USA Today*, 2001.
5.4: Courtesy of Fairchild Publications, Inc.

Chapter 6
6.1: Courtesy of Fairchild Publications, Inc.
6.3a, **6.3b**: Getty Images

Chapter 7
7.1: Reuters
7.2: © 2000 Jack Ziegler from cartoonbank.com. All Rights Reserved.

Chapter 9
9.2: Courtesy of Fairchild Publications, Inc.

Chapter 10
10.3: Courtesy of J.Crew Group.

Chapter 11
11.1 and **11.2**: Courtesy of Fairchild Publications, Inc.
11.3: Courtesy of AquaMarin Watches.

Chapter 12
12.1: US Department of Commerce, 2007.

Chapter 13
13.1 and **13.4**: Courtesy of Fairchild Publications, Inc.

Chapter 15
15.1 and **15.3**: Courtesy of Fairchild Publications, Inc.

Chapter 16
16.1 and **16.2**: Courtesy of Fairchild Publications, Inc.
16.3: Ithaca® Brand POSjet® 1000 Color Inkjet Printer, courtesy of Trans-Act Technologies, Inc.
16.4: Courtesy of Macy's Inc.